In Pursuit of the People

Also by Jessica Wardhaugh

PARIS AND THE RIGHT IN THE TWENTIETH CENTURY (*editor*)

In Pursuit of the People

Political Culture in France, 1934–39

Jessica Wardhaugh

Junior Research Fellow, Christ Church, University of Oxford

First published 2009 by
PALGRAVE MACMILLAN

Palgrave Macmillan in the UK is an imprint of Macmillan Publishers Limited, registered in England, company number 785998, of Houndmills, Basingstoke, Hampshire RG21 6XS.

Palgrave Macmillan in the US is a division of St Martin's Press LLC, 175 Fifth Avenue, New York, NY 10010.

Palgrave Macmillan is the global academic imprint of the above companies and has companies and representatives throughout the world.

Palgrave® and Macmillan® are registered trademarks in the United States, the United Kingdom, Europe and other countries.

ISBN-13: 978–0–230–20277–1 hardback
ISBN-10: 0–230–20277–2 hardback

This book is printed on paper suitable for recycling and made from fully managed and sustained forest sources. Logging, pulping and manufacturing processes are expected to conform to the environmental regulations of the country of origin.

A catalogue record for this book is available from the British Library.

Library of Congress Cataloging-in-Publication Data
Wardhaugh, Jessica, 1976–
  In pursuit of the people : political culture in France, 1934–9 / Jessica Wardhaugh.
    p. cm.
  Includes bibliographical references and index.
  ISBN 978–0–230–20277–1
  1. France—Politics and government—1914–1940. 2. Political culture—France—History—20th century. I. Title.
  DC396.W37 2008
  306.20944′09043—dc22
                                                         2008030094

10 9 8 7 6 5 4 3 2 1
18 17 16 15 14 13 12 11 10 09

Printed and bound in Great Britain by
CPI Antony Rowe, Chippenham and Eastbourne

In memory of my father, George Michael Irons (1940–2000)

Contents

List of Figures

Acknowledgements

This book has been written in good company, and it is a pleasure to express my gratitude to all whose support, wisdom, and encouragement have sustained me on my journey. Firstly I would like to thank my former supervisor Robert Gildea, whose constructive criticism and encouragement to pursue new lines of thought were a great inspiration during my doctoral research. He also supported my enrolment at the University of Paris-I, where I learned much from my participation in the DEA seminar series on social and cultural history, and from my encounters with Pascal Ory and Danielle Tartakowsky. I am grateful to my D.Phil. examiners Ruth Harris and Simon Kitson, both of whom encouraged me to develop the thesis into a book; and to Martin Conway, who commented valuably on a number of chapters while also providing me with opportunities to present my research before a wider audience. Katya Andreyev, my college adviser at Christ Church, was a ready source of sympathetic encouragement and useful advice throughout my doctoral study. I was first introduced to the Popular Front through the lectures of David Barry, whose continuing interest in my research project has been greatly appreciated.

I am very grateful to the Arts and Humanities Research Board for funding my doctoral research, and to Christ Church, Oxford for electing me to a Junior Research Fellowship in 2004, thus offering me the opportunity to transform the thesis into a book. The college has provided a stimulating and supportive environment for my research, and I am indebted to the colleagues whose lunchtime conversation has provided such a welcome counterbalance to solitary writing.

During my research trips to Paris, I received valuable practical assistance and advice, and I would like to express particular thanks to the staff in the Centre National de la Cinématographie, the Bibliothèque de l'Arsenal, and the Archives de la Préfecture de Police, as well as to Tangui Perron at the Institut d'Histoire Sociale de la CGT in Montreuil. Nathalie Cappelle gave me many interesting insights into lesser-known political movements; Bernadette Lucet, Jean-Louis and Martine Arbey, treated me to warm hospitality and vivid descriptions of the streets that were 'noir de monde' during the demonstrations of the Popular Front period.

I am also grateful to those who have assisted me in the technical preparation of this book. Permission to reproduce the images has kindly been granted by the Bibliothèque Nationale de France, the Archives de la Préfecture de Police de Paris, and by *L'Illustration*, who own the copyright for all photographs reproduced in their publication. I would like to express my particular thanks to Michael Strang and Ruth Ireland at Palgrave Macmillan, and to the anonymous Readers who commented on the manuscript. All errors and shortcomings that remain are, of course, my own.

The companionship and solidarity of my friends and family have been an enormous source of strength throughout my research. Among them I would like to express my special gratitude to Sally Howlett, Courtney Voelker, Astrid Schielke, Alison Carter, Clare and James Welham, Imogen Davies, Olivia Rowland, Anothai Na Pattaloong, Christina and Annika Kuhn, Denise Brocklebank, Ralph Walterspacher, Jan Kulok, and Young-Ju Kim. My mother and brother have been invaluable in helping me to keep both the thesis and the book in perspective, and I am deeply grateful for their unfailing love and support. My father encouraged my interest in research from the beginning, and it is to his memory that this book is dedicated. Lastly I would like to thank my husband Benjamin for his unstinting generosity with his time and technical assistance, and for supporting me throughout the preparation of this book with love, patience, and humour. My gratitude to him is beyond words.

Jessica Wardhaugh
Christ Church, Oxford
May 2008

Abbreviations

Abbreviations in the text

AEAR	Association des Artistes et Écrivains Révolutionnaires
ARAC	Association Républicaine des Anciens Combattants
CFTC	Confédération Française des Travailleurs Chrétiens
CGPF	Confédération Générale du Patronat Français
CGT	Confédération Générale du Travail
CGTU	Confédération Générale du Travail Unitaire
CVIA	Comité de Vigilance des Intellectuels Anti-Fascistes
FNC	Fédération Nationale Catholique
GAR	Groupes d'Action Révolutionnaire
JOC	Jeunesse Ouvrière Chrétienne
PCF	Parti Communiste Français
PDP	Parti Démocrate Populaire
PPF	Parti Populaire Français
PSF	Parti Social Français
SFIO	Section Française de l'Internationale Ouvrière
UNC	Union Nationale des Combattants

Abbreviations in archival references

ACGT	Archives de la CGT
ADS	Archives Départementales de la Seine Saint-Denis
AN	Archives Nationales de France
APP	Archives de la Préfecture de Police de Paris
ASP	Bibliothèque Nationale, Département des Arts du Spectacle
BHVP	Bibliothèque Historique de la Ville de Paris
BN	Bibliothèque Nationale de France
CNC	Centre National de la Cinématographie, Bois d'Arcy
n.d.	No date
n.p.	No place of publication

Introduction: The People on Stage, 1934–39

Like their European counterparts, the stadiums of Paris were used for more than sporting fixtures in the 1930s, and the Parc des Princes was no exception to the rule. Situated on the outskirts of the capital between the nineteenth-century pleasure gardens of the Bois de Boulogne and the ultramodern Renault factory at Boulogne-Billancourt, the Parc was the scene for demonstrations and counter-demonstrations, mass meetings and theatrical performances, conflict and reconciliation. Conflict could be both rhetorical and physical, and on a sultry afternoon in early October 1936 the Parc was the epicentre of a violent encounter between left and right, one of the many street battles to disturb the peace of the French capital in the interwar years. Crowded inside the stadium, 40,000 Communists in red scarves and red berets protested angrily against a proposed mass meeting of the Parti Social Français, a new party of the extreme right. Outside the enclosure, 20,000 members of the new right-wing party infiltrated shops and cafés, equally incensed that the government had authorized the Communist meeting and not their own. Some wore workers' caps to escape detection, for the police guarding the stadium were under strict instructions to allow passage only to the 'visibly left-wing'. When the Communist meeting drew to a close and its participants spilled out into the streets, policemen struggled hard to separate the warring factions, holding back raised fists on one side, raised arms on the other. The air was thick with the exchange of insults, and the street battle soon spread far beyond the direct confrontation of political adversaries: right-wingers tossed soda siphons out of cafés, smashed taxi windows, and energetically resisted arrest, while sympathetic locals shouted support from their apartments and threw tricolour flags into the crowd. Despite the violence, and the arrest of more than a thousand demonstrators, the following day

1

was one of self-congratulation. The Communists prided themselves that their supporters, the people of Paris, had defended the liberty of the capital against the fascists of the Parti Social Français. The Parti Social Français rejoiced that its followers, the people of Paris, had defended liberty against the 'Soviet fascists' of the Communist Party.[1]

Transforming the masses into the 'people' was one of the greatest political challenges of the 1930s, and one in which street politics were to play a vitally important role. The masses were omnipresent: workers in hot, dusty factories and in the grinding labour of the fields, strikers and demonstrators whose shouts, songs, and slogans reverberated around densely packed streets and squares, and the unemployed who clustered outside factory doors and soup kitchens. The problem of representing them was twofold. First, it was a practical challenge, for the masses looked for parties and associations to speak in their name and represent their political and economic interests, and political and economic organizations consequently competed to attract the masses. Secondly, the problem of representation was ideological. Parties and associations, political leaders and journalists, even theatre and film directors claimed to speak not only for the masses but also for the people. Political organizations claimed to derive their legitimacy from the people, whether their sympathies were democratic or not. The problem of representing the masses as the people was not only a question of organization, but also a question of depiction. Who were the people? Were they working-class or middle-class, rural or urban, Catholic or republican, conservative or revolutionary? And how far could images of a single, united people be imposed on the spontaneity, disorder, even violence, of the masses? As economic depression deepened the dissatisfaction of the masses and heightened their political involvement, and as the legitimacy of the parliamentary Republic was increasingly called into question by groups of extreme left and right, the representation of the people came to the centre of political controversy.

This book is a study of the pursuit of the people in France in the tumultuous years 1934–39. Its aim is to investigate how the masses were attracted, organized, and depicted as the people in the streets and on stage, by political groups, parties, and trade unions, and by theatre and film directors. Its focus is the urgent contest to define a political future for France at a time when parliamentary democracies were ceding to authoritarian rule in many European countries. The need to imagine and realize a united popular community, a community that would transcend inherited divisions as well as contemporary social and political tensions, was of primary importance. In France more authoritarian neighbours, political opposition was increasingly suppressed by dictatorial rule. In France, however, left and right continued through the 1930s to develop rival visions of the people in the public sphere. This book explores those rival visions, moving from the riot of 6 February 1934 through the conflict between the left-wing Popular Front movement and governments and its right-wing opponents, to the authoritarian Radical government of Édouard Daladier in 1938–39. Studying the organization and depiction of the crowd, workers, electorate, nation, and symbolic community, it explores tensions and parallels between rival representations of the people.

Political conflict in 1930s France is well documented: examples abound of hostility between left and right, royalists and republicans, Jews and anti-Semites, or Catholics and anti-clericals. Paradoxically, however, the very polarization of the decade has obscured the nature and development of political rivalry. Left and right have often been studied separately, notably in sympathetic (if not uncritical) histories of the Popular Front as the defence of democracy, or in polemical discussions of the relationship between the French right and fascism. The representation of the people, in so far as it has been explored in this period, has generally been associated with the left, especially with the Popular Front's now famous image of a triumphant, pacific people celebrating left-wing victory in 1936. This book, the first comparative study of the question, demonstrates that the representation of the people was at the centre of an ongoing political contest, and that the image of the people was, even on the left, rarely static.

Underneath the very real sociological and ideological differences between right and left, the 1930s were a time of rhetorical fluidity and shifting political identities. The street battle around the Parc des Princes is one such example. The social composition and ideological sympathies of the Communist Party and the PSF were on one level sharply distinct. Police photographs of their encounter depict PSF members predominantly well-dressed and wearing hats, and Communists in caps (hence the decision by some of the right-wingers to appear in working-class disguise). When PSF members confronted their adversaries with the republican hymn *La Marseillaise*, the Communists responded with *L'Internationale*, a song of final proletarian triumph. Yet behind this ritual and rhetorical opposition, the situation was more complex. PSF members may have disguised themselves as workers in 1936 to escape detection, but a breakdown of party membership in 1937 included 20 per cent urban workers and 20 per cent employees. Local sympathizers of the PSF threw tricolours into the crowd, but inside the stadium the Communists waved tricolours as well as red flags, and sang *La Marseillaise* as well as *L'Internationale*. In their pursuit of the people, the left became more explicitly patriotic, moving onto traditionally right-wing territory, while groups and parties of the right endeavoured to dispel their presumed identification with middle-class interests and to reach out to urban and rural workers. Studying the organization of the masses as the people thus provides a vital insight into the evolving relationship between left and right.

In October 1936 the Parc des Princes had been at the centre of conflict: in July 1937 it was the scene for reconciliation. On the evening of 17 July, 80,000 young Catholic workers filled the stadium to participate in a grandiose celebration of the tenth anniversary of the Jeunesse Ouvrière Chrétienne. In the gathering darkness, they created a mass spectacle entitled *The Joy of Work* and *The Meaning of Work*, in which the working people became the builders of the ideal city, reconciled with their work and with each other. The spectacle was a celebration of working-class dignity and of the dignity of labour itself, and a call for workers to be respected for their contribution to human and divine creation. It was a call that echoed the concerns of political leaders, parties, and journalists, as well as the aspirations of religious organizations. Indeed in June 1936, the Catholic royalist deputy Jean Le Cour Grandmaison described this common concern for the working people as one aspect of the 'partial community of thought' that united even those who appeared most divided.[2] As a comparative study of the pursuit of the people, this book explores how far such a community of thought may be said to exist.

The people: A social question

The challenge of representing the people is perennial: its particular significance in 1930s France was the result of a dangerous combination of circumstances. Foremost among these were the growth of the urban working class, the social and economic crisis of the Depression, and the growing disillusionment with liberal parliamentary democracy as an effective form of twentieth-century government. These affected both the sociological composition of the French—and thus the 'people' who could be appealed to and organized by political organizations—and also the meaning and importance of the people as a political concept.

In social terms, the word 'people' could refer either to the entire nation—the 'French people'—or to particular social groups within the population as a whole. In the 1930s, the population of France consisted, broadly, of 14 million peasants, 13 million workers, and 14 million members of the middle classes and bourgeoisie. The devastation of 1.3 million soldiers killed in the First World War, and the millions of children who had not therefore been born, created what the French termed the 'empty generation', and the population did not return to its pre-war size until 1950 (its increase in the interwar years was primarily the consequence of immigration).[3] At the top of the social pyramid were the *grande bourgeoisie* and wealthy aristocratic families. These included the affluent elite who sat on the Council of the Banque de France and comprised its 200 principal shareholders (often referred to in consequence as the '200 families'), and whose influence was felt not only in economic and financial policy but also in a number of newspapers. France's wealthiest businessmen also filled the Confédération Générale de la Production Française, a powerful association of employers created with state support after the First World War. Not only had they benefited from arms sales during the war, they also profited from the post-war reconstruction, with its attendant technical and industrial growth.[4] In fact, the families who could afford the grand bourgeois lifestyle—servants, stables, yachts—numbered rather more than 200. They constituted a high (and largely Parisian) society which maintained the jewellers of the Place Vendôme and the furriers of the Rue La Boétie. Fascinated and appalled, Henri Noguères—a young socialist of the Latin Quarter—recorded their excesses: a magnum of champagne in one of their nightclubs cost as much as a department store worker could earn in a month.[5]

If the idea of the 'people' often excluded these higher echelons of bourgeoisie it nonetheless encompassed a very broad spectrum, patterned by the variety of social groups within the middle classes, which included members of the liberal professions as well as small shopkeepers, employees, and farmers. Differences between the working and middle classes could be striking—from the visible, everyday distinction between the proletarian cap and the middle-class hat to differences in income, housing, education and hopes of social mobility. Middle-class families were more likely to own a radio and a car (by 1930 there were more than 1,100,000 automobiles in France), and they were also more likely to enjoy central heating and a bathroom. Visible difference from and superiority to working-class households was keenly pursued. When the working classes acquired gas cookers, the middle classes bought refrigerators. According to Noguères, one of the most fundamental characteristics of middle-class status was their scrupulous distinction between the dining-room table and kitchen table, the two being identical in working-class dwellings. The middle classes might describe themselves as originating from the 'people', but they were also sensible of their ascent of the social ladder, and of the importance of education as a path to social success within a theoretically meritocratic Republic. Yet their position remained precarious, at the mercy of economic fluctuations and government policy: and the difficulties of the Depression would make the middle classes, especially the lower middle class, the focus of an intense and urgent contest for their political support.

Fundamental to the make-up of the 'people'—and indeed often synonymous with them—were the workers, both rural and urban. French employers had been notoriously wary of technological change in the nineteenth century, but the early twentieth century witnessed rapid and significant development, leading the urban population to outnumber its rural counterpart for the first time in the census of 1931. Between 1906 and 1931 France mechanized more rapidly than either the United States or Britain. Large firms such as Renault introduced rationalization even before the First World War, employing methods pioneered by the American engineer Taylor to monitor physical labour and to eliminate wasted time.[6] This increasing mechanization exercised a profound effect on the nature and structure of the French workforce. Prior to the First World War, it had consisted of qualified workers and manual labourers. Mechanization created a new category: the easily replaceable specialized worker who could learn his job in the workplace in a matter of days. The new category threatened traditional trades: craftsmen who had trained at length to become metal forgers, textile doublers, glass blowers, or boiler men in the steel industry now faced an uncertain future.[7] At the same time, the dangerous and difficult working conditions once associated primarily with the textile industry—dust, noise, and heat—became rapidly widespread. Little attention was paid to the protection of the worker, who might be required to labour at considerable personal risk. In rubber vulcanization, for example, no safeguards protected the workers from the regular inhalation of toxic vapours, nor were the resulting nervous afflictions recognized as genuine 'industrial illnesses'.[8]

Another significant change in the composition of the working people was the participation of women in the workforce, which increased rapidly in the years before the First World War and peaked in 1912 (the same level of participation was not achieved again until the 1960s).[9] Although female employment actually declined after the War, for the decreasing number of female workers in the textile industry was not compensated by rising female employment in heavy industry, the number of middle-class women entering work continued to rise gradually, exercising a disproportionate influence on political and social debate. Women in the workforce were not welcomed by the unions—the CGT, like the government, supported the idea of a male breadwinner—but their growing presence in political and social organizations made them a vital component of the 'working people', and an important political presence in demonstrations and associative life, even though they were not to be enfranchised until after the Second World War.

While industrial productivity increased dramatically in France in the 1920s, the social costs of alienating and repetitive work on the production line were correspondingly high, and became an increasingly important political and intellectual concern. A terrifying gulf seemed to open between material and moral progress, prompting intellectuals such as the Jewish socialist Jean-Richard Bloch, and the 'utopian pessimist' Simone Weil to call for the triumph of man over machine and for the realization of a more humane order in the workplace.[10] As the pacifist Andrée Jouve observed in 1924, deeply concerned by the rapid importation of American rationalization to Europe: 'We are threatened with losing the joy of living and working; threatened with (. . .) the fatal sadness of the mechanized world.'[11] The effects of increasing female participation in the workforce on family life were particularly feared, as France had been suffering from a decline in the birth rate since the nineteenth century. Female employment, although rising mainly for middle-class women after the First World War, was seen as a dangerous move away from the *foyer*, and a threat to the large families necessary to French survival.[12]

Mechanization and post-war reconstruction increased the number and proportion of the working people; they also increased their concentration in expanding cities and suburbs. More than 1000 towns had been destroyed during the First World War and a further 3500 seriously damaged, while a total of 300,000 homes required rebuilding.[13] Reims, for example, lost 7000 homes out of a total of 14,000, and in 1921 more than 12,000 people were still housed in temporary barrack-style accommodation, where many were to remain during the 1930s.[14] At the same time, new suburbs expanded rapidly around major towns and cities. One highly significant development was the expansion in mechanical engineering that led to the growth of large establishments on the outskirts of Paris: Ivry, Saint-Denis, Aubervilliers, and Boulogne-Billancourt. In response to such industrial expansion, an area one and a half times the size of the capital was made available for new building in the 1920s, with few regulations to establish standards of building or hygiene. By the time the Loi Loucheur was passed in 1928 to promote the construction of social housing, hastily constructed and insalubrious dwellings clustered thickly round the city. Many inhabitants were to wait more than 20 years for electricity, running water, and adequate drainage. With no sewers, and roads of beaten earth dissolving into quagmires in rainy weather, it was little wonder that infant mortality remained high, particularly among immigrant families, and that the highest lncidence of tuberculosis in Europe was in France. In 1930s Paris, tuberculosis claimed a victim an hour.[15]

These burgeoning suburbs—especially around the capital—not only concentrated the population but also created a people uprooted from their rural and provincial origins. In 20 years the population of the Seine department increased by over a third; that of the Seine-et-Oise by almost half. In the northern Parisian suburb of Bobigny, the local population increased by 14 per cent per annum between 1921 and 1926: in 1930, over half of its inhabitants originated from the provinces, and only a fifth from the Parisian region.[16] Although France offered a relatively rural image compared with some of its more industrialized neighbours, the French were highly sensitive to the cumulative—and recently accelerated—rural exodus. Nostalgia for the idealized values and traditions of rural life permeated art and architecture, popular culture, and political rhetoric. In the architecture of post-war reconstruction, it was not modernism but regionalism that determined the dominant tone,[17] while regionalism was noticeably more prominent in the 1925 *Arts Décoratifs* Exhibition and the 1937 International Exhibition than it had been in the exhibitions of 1889 and 1900.[18] Guides to the exhibition of 1937 proudly celebrated the diversity of trades, customs, and climates exemplified by the pavilions of the 25 regions of France, 'from the flowery terraces of Nice to the chapels of the *savoyard* Alps, from the industrial regions of the Nord and Lyons to the rural vineyards of Bordeaux, Champagne and Burgundy...'[19] In 1938, three out of the four principal prizes for literature were awarded to novels of bucolic character.[20] Of course, life in the countryside was by no means as inevitably restorative as its literary and cinematic celebrations suggested. Noguères recalled his dismay at the conditions in which day-labourers (especially immigrants) were obliged to work, sleeping in barns not even on straw mattresses but on the straw itself, restricted by a 7 o'clock curfew in summer and winter, and provided with a single outdoor pump for their communal morning ablutions.[21]

The continuing importance of small-scale enterprises and agricultural protectionism gave the French a confident sense of immunity at the first signs of economic depression. In 1929, France's economic and industrial situation seemed remarkably favourable.[22] Production of electricity, automobiles, and steel reached record levels, and in 1930 only 1700 were registered as unemployed. But although the French were late to experience the effects of the Depression, they struggled long and hard to overcome them. Whereas the British economy began to recover in 1932, and the German economy in 1935, France battled to control the effects of economic crisis throughout the 1930s.[23]

The largely ineffective search for economic solutions to the Depression was to have dangerous political repercussions. Not only was the national budget significantly reduced when German reparation payments were curtailed by the Treaty of Lausanne in 1932, but successive governments also found it impossible to agree on economic policy. Governments were generally unwilling to adopt the German solution of isolating the country from the global market to maintain strict state control over the economy; they also tended to reject the British and American solution of devaluation, preferring instead to remain on the Gold Standard. The rare politicians who recommended devaluation—such as Paul Reynaud and Raymond Patenôtre—were highly unpopular. Reynaud was excluded from government until 1938, and during the 1930s received numerous death threats as well as menacing letters from former supporters. In 1936, he was sent a letter by a group of electors in the second *arrondissement* (district) of Paris who described themselves as 'artisans, small shopkeepers, employees and men of modest private incomes', and denounced both his character and policies, withdrawing all support from a man they now associated with reckless speculation.[24] Reynaud and Patenôtre identified the potential benefits of devaluation: cheaper French products on the global market, liberated funds with which the government could boost the national economy. Shopkeepers, artisans, men of private means, and employees saw only its negative implications: the collapse of their savings and the threat to the stabilized 'Poincaré franc' of 1928.[25]

Unwilling to adopt the economic solutions of other countries, French governments responded to the Depression with largely palliative measures. They aimed to keep existing businesses afloat rather than encouraging fundamental reform, and to limit agricultural production while guaranteeing producers a fixed minimum price. Such limitations led to the accumulation of vast stocks of produce (often later destroyed), images of which permeated propaganda films and even popular songs. The most consistent government policy was deflation, adopted by men of the right such as Pierre Laval and André Tardieu in 1931–32, Gaston Doumergue and Pierre-Étienne Flandin in 1934–36, and by men of the left such as Édouard Herriot, Joseph Paul-Boncour, Albert Sarraut, Camille Chautemps, and Édouard Daladier in 1932–34. Deflation included the practice of raising funds by lowering the salaries of civil servants or the pensions of war veterans. Such measures provoked angry outcries and even street protests from these important social groups, igniting their sympathy for extra-parliamentary movements. Street protests were also swelled by the unemployed, likewise victims of the Depression. Between 1931 and 1936 the number of workers in employment was reduced by 1.8 million, 1.4 million of whom belonged to the working classes.[26] In some towns unemployment affected almost a third of the entire population: in the small *savoyard* textile-manufacturing town of Landry, for example, 4000 were registered as unemployed out of a total population of 13,300.[27]

On one hand, the Depression inflamed class tensions and increased the extent and visibility of social problems, especially the sufferings of the workers and unemployed. On the other, the failure of successive governments to produce an effective economic response highlighted the weaknesses in the political system itself. The apparent inability of parliamentary democracy to deal with economic crisis gave ammunition to those who accused current parties and deputies of inadequacy as representatives of the people, and fuelled interest in political alternatives. By the 1930s the difficulties that had destabilized the Third Republic since its creation were rapidly accelerating into a political crisis, in which the representation of the people was of central significance.

The people: A political challenge

The ageing Republic of the interwar years had already been subjected to strident criticism in its youth, notably of its weak executive, the distance between political institutions and social elites, and the lack of representation of professional economic groups. Created by liberal conservative Orleanists, the Third Republic had been defined in the Constitution of 1875 as a delicate equilibrium between the Chamber of Deputies, the Senate, and the President. Deputies were elected to four-year terms from single-member constituencies by universal adult male suffrage; senators were elected to nine-year terms by local officeholders, with a third of the seats renewed every three years. The President (who had little actual power), was elected for a seven-year term by the Senate and Chamber. Since the single-member constituencies were limited to a maximum of 100,000 people, deputies were extremely numerous (there were 612 in 1936) and tended to be highly independent. It was indeed some decades before a party system developed, and parties were particularly slow to develop on the right. Cabinet government was unstable:

the premier handed ministerial positions to faction leaders and hoped—often vainly—for their co-operation. Many cabinets survived for days; the longest only three years. With his limited powers, the President could do little to secure stability and cohesion, while tensions between ambitious and independent deputies soon gave the impression of querulous parliamentary caste. By the 1880s a gulf was already emerging between professional politicians and the republican elites trained at the Paris Bar and the École Libre des Sciences Politiques.[28]

Critics within the system called for proportional representation, the reinforcement of Presidential authority, and the limitation of parliamentary control of financial and economic matters, while critics unsympathetic to the Republic imagined or planned its eventual downfall. On the right, the *provençal* writer and royalist Charles Maurras denounced the regime's decadence and individualism, and outlined a doctrine of 'integral nationalism' to reconcile France with its monarchical past and with its classical and Christian tradition.[29] Maurras led a bohemian existence in Paris, isolated from the sounds of the city by the profound deafness that had afflicted him since childhood, and was to be one of the central figures in the Action Française movement and its eponymous review (later daily newspaper). Despite the rigidity of his doctrine, which remained largely unchanged throughout his life, he and his movement were profoundly influential on their contemporaries.[30] In the early twentieth century there were links between Action Française and anarchist circles (indeed, royalist and anarchist street militants joined in an attack on the apartment of Alfred Dreyfus in February 1909),[31] and left-wing critics were certainly no less forthright in their attacks on the early Third Republic. Monarchists and revolutionary trade-unionists shared a common contempt for an individualistic regime predicated on an abstract idea of the citizen, and searched instead for the representation of communities—family, region, nation, or workplace. The revolutionary syndicalism of the Confédération Général du Travail (CGT) in its early years was strongly marked by an opposition to politics, parties (even socialist parties), and the state, and by a belief in the self-sufficiency of the workers and their economic organizations.[32] Despite the growth in reformism within French trade unionism, this anti-state and anti-parliamentary feeling remained an important undercurrent in the interwar years.

The sacred union (*Union sacrée*) of the First World War united even the Republic's most recalcitrant opponents in the name of national defence, yet the victory of 1918 did not resolve the Republic's political difficulties. Rather, the moral and material devastation of the war deepened the search for reform and renewal, sharpening criticism of pre-war parliamentary leaders. Georges Duhamel—poet, doctor, and essayist—captured this desire for fundamental reform when he described his reaction to the declaration of war in a reflective article of 1924. He had, he recalled, been sitting under a fig tree in Provence, on holiday with his artist friend Henri Doucet. As a doctor, Duhamel was to witness the bloodshed of the war with remorseless immediacy, yet his first thought was not of the slaughter, nor even of the ruins to come. Rather, the most horrifying prospect for him was the post-war challenge to rewrite the rules of society, and to reconstruct an entire moral universe.[33] Equally devastating, in the aftermath of victory, was the realization that such reconstruction was not taking place. Post-war parliament was dominated by the right-wing Bloc National, too involved in the economic and material aspects of reconstruction to pursue institutional and ideological change, and unable to prolong the sacred union into the very different situation of peacetime. Nor were subsequent governments noticeably more preoccupied with fundamental reform. Left-wing victory in the elections of 1924 brought to power the short-lived government of the *Cartel des Gauches*, an attempted revival of the anti-clerical, left-wing bloc of the early twentieth century. Yet the Cartel provoked lively opposition and new formations on the right, and its financial policies split Radicals and socialists while also provoking strident antagonism from the business world. Radicals also participated in the early years of the right-wing coalition government of 1926–32, and scored highly in the 1932 elections, but the Radical leader and premier Édouard Herriot preferred to defend traditional principles of cautious reform and secularism rather than to renew republican institutions or form new political alliances.

Inflexible parties, ministerial instability, and a chronic inability to co-operate in economic and financial matters thus characterized successive governments in the 1920s and 1930s. On the left and centre, the Socialist Party (Section Française de l'Internationale Ouvrière) and the Radical Party (Parti Républicain Radical et Radical-Socialiste) disagreed strongly over the nature and scope of left-wing policy and principles, as well as suffering from internal divisions. The SFIO had been founded in 1905 as a revolutionary Marxist party aiming to overthrow the bourgeois state and inaugurate a classless society. Under the leadership of Jean Jaurès it became more reformist, but remained wary of full participation in the parliamentary republic. After the Congress of Tours in 1920, when the majority of the party voted to join Lenin's Third International and became the SFIC (Section Française de l'Internationale Communiste), the Socialist leader, deputy, and journalist Léon Blum defined the role of the old party with rhetorical dexterity, justifying the 'exercise of power' within a bourgeois political system without rejecting the goal of socialist revolution.[34] Although the SFIO accepted electoral alliances with the Radicals in 1924, 1928, and 1932, it refused to participate in subsequent governments, or to share the Radical predilections for free trade and piecemeal reform. Socialist rebels against this refusal—among them the talented writer, orator, and future collaborationist Marcel Déat—were excluded from the Party in 1933, highlighting the SFIO's doctrinal divisions. The Radical Party, which did not exclude its renovators, was similarly divided. Founded in 1901, the party was (despite its name) neither excessively radical nor particularly socialist, but committed to anticlericalism and to the defence of the Republic. Sociologically, the Party was of pivotal importance, representing what Marx had called the 'dangerous class' of the petty bourgeoisie (lower middle class, liberal professions, and the peasantry), and was in this period highly decentralized.[35] While men such as Édouard Herriot preferred to pursue traditional Radical goals, a number of younger party members (including the *provençal* Édouard Daladier) debated new alliances and state reform. Tensions between the 'two Édouards' were a strong undercurrent in the party. Herriot, Daladier's former teacher and 12 years his senior, was from a wealthy, republican family; Daladier was proud of his artisan origins (his father had been a baker) and of the tolerance between his Catholic mother and republican father.[36] His family name was, as the regionalist poet Frédéric Mistral once pointed out, derived from the *provençal* word 'dalader': the resilient olive tree of his native region.[37]

Political groups and parties on the centre and right were meanwhile searching for new directions. Within the parliamentary republic, the Alliance Démocratique and Fédération Républicaine were not definitively committed to liberal democracy (and were indeed open to the overtures of the extreme right in the later 1930s). Nevertheless, concrete demands for constitutional reform such as those of the centre-right politician André Tardieu did not necessarily meet with their support.[38] Political Catholics, sensitive to the wider intellectual renewal in interwar Catholicism, were divided between right and left. Some supported the Ligue de la Jeune République of the reformist Marc Sangnier, or the small Parti Démocrate Populaire, established in 1924 to unite democratic Catholics sympathetic to the parliamentary Republic and to gradual reform. Other political Catholic groups, such as Général de Castelnau's Fédération Nationale Catholique, were more conservative and nationalist, and despite the Pope's condemnation of Action Française in 1926, the influence of Charles Maurras on Catholic circles remained strong (*Action Française* was often sold outside churches by the Camelots du Roi: the 'hawkers of the king').[39]

With established republican parties shaken by doctrinal division and personal differences, new political formations began to emerge of increasing importance. The extra-parliamentary leagues created in the interwar years were not an unprecedented phenomenon, but their aspirations for political change were often broader and more extreme than those of their predecessors. In the 1880s, the nationalistic Ligue des Patriotes had been founded to promote the reconquest of Alsace-Lorraine (lost to the Germans after the Franco-Prussian War), while the Dreyfus Affair had prompted the creation of the Ligue des Droits de l'Homme on the left and the Ligue de la Patrie Française and the Ligue Antisémite on the right.[40] In the interwar years the formation of new leagues was also traceable to specific grievances, but the leagues began in some cases to develop into broader, mass organizations with an explicit admiration for authoritarian regimes, and implicit aspirations for regime change in France. After the failure of the Bloc National government, and during the left-wing government of 1924–26, a number of new leagues and pressure groups were founded to express dissatisfaction with traditional right-wing parties. General de Castelnau's Fédération Nationale Catholique was formed to oppose the extension of secularizing laws to the newly regained Alsace and Moselle, and the intended suppression of the French ambassador to the Vatican (re-established in 1921). The Jeunesses Patriotes, founded in 1924 by the Bonapartist deputy Pierre Taittinger (born in Paris, but of a Lorraine family), was close in spirit to the earlier Ligue des Patriotes. Veteran soldiers composed its executive committee, and the influence of Italian fascism was visible in the distinctive uniform and blue berets of its street militants. The combat groups of the Faisceau, founded in 1925 by the autodidactic Action Française dissident and former syndicalist Georges Valois, were deliberately modelled on the Italian *squadre* ('faisceau' was the French word for *fasces*). Some of these 1920s groups lost impetus and influence in the following years: the Faisceau was dissolved in 1928 and the Jeunesses Patriotes rallied to the Poincaré government of 1926, while the Fédération Nationale Catholique became less vocal after successfully blocking the secularization laws.

The 1930s witnessed the rapid expansion and increased significance of such extra-parliamentary movements. The highly influential Ligue des Croix de Feu (a veteran soldiers' movement) was established by Maurice d'Hartoy in 1927, and later presided over and transformed into the Parti Social Français by Colonel François de la Rocque de Sévérac. The Francistes were founded in 1933 by Marcel Bucard, a veteran soldier who was in 1917 the youngest and most decorated captain in the French army. Involved in the formation of both the Faisceau and the Croix de Feu, he based his own movement explicitly on Italian fascism, receiving Italian subsidies and attending the only international congress of fascist movements, held at Montreux in Switzerland in 1934. Francisme was created with funding from the wealthy perfume manufacturer François Coty, and in the same year (1933) Coty also funded the establishment of the Solidarité Française, over which he presided with the help of the retired military commander Jean Renaud. If the exact goals of the Solidarité Française were not always clear, its appearance was unashamedly paramilitary. Members wore grey trousers, blue shirts, and a distinctive badge; combat groups were on bicycle or motorbike. The Solidarité Française remained small, but attracted significant numbers of unemployed workers, keen to claim the promised remuneration for participation in demonstrations.[41]

Demonstrations and street fighting were also strongly associated with revolutionary left-wing movements, notably the Communist Party (Parti Communiste Français) that was set to increase so dramatically in influence and membership in the 1930s. Founded by Ludovic-Oscar Frossard and Marcel Cachin in 1920, the party did not initially follow Lenin's conditions to the letter, and was for some time suspected by the USSR of reformist tendencies. In the 1920s the party pursued anti-colonial and anti-military campaigns, endeavouring to attract working-class socialists and to deprive the SFIO of its shock troops ('plucking the socialist chicken', as the Communists described it). Communists also proselytized by creating networks of cells in the workplace. Co-ordinated by the burly Maurice Thorez from 1930 onwards, the PCF practised a rigid 'class against class' tactic from 1927 to 1934 in which socialists were castigated as 'social fascists': a provocation that sharpened the distaste and suspicion of Socialist leaders for their Communist counterparts. Such divisive tactics reduced Communist party membership substantially, but not for long.[42]

The rapid growth of these new leagues and parties was inseparable from the awareness that parliamentary regimes were ceding to dictatorial rule in many European countries. Some of the new movements in France were explicitly inspired—even financially supported—by these authoritarian regimes. Others denounced the corruption or inefficiency of the French parliamentary republic without suggesting concrete measures for its replacement. It was becoming clear, even to convinced republicans, that the liberal democracy inherited from the nineteenth century was not universally accepted either as inevitable, or as the most desirable form of government.

Uncertainty about France's political future was also deepened by the decline in France's international standing, as well as by fears of national decadence and social and moral breakdown. Indeed, the early years of the 1930s were flooded with books whose titles proclaimed the crisis of the West; of civilization; even of mankind itself. On the one hand, they addressed the neglect of human and spiritual needs in the domain of industrial and technical progress; on the other, they expressed concern that man—*l'homme réel*—was similarly alienated by political systems predicated on the abstract citizen. The American template of material progress concentrated their fears: George Duhamel's *Scènes de la vie future* (1930) denounced the American way of life and work as relentlessly utilitarian; Robert Aron and Armand Dandieu's *Le Cancer américain* (1931) criticized the deadening social and moral consequences of rationalism and materialism. Pierre Drieu la Rochelle, seething with disgust at the decadence of post-war world, denounced not only the 'sad, soulless Americans' but also his whole generation. 'I believe', he confessed, 'in the decadence of Europe, of Asia, America, and of the planet.'[43] Around these writers developed a loose group of intellectuals seeking the spiritual in industrial and political life: men such as Henri Daniel-Rops, Jean Jardin, Denis de Rougemont, Emmanuel Mounier, and Pierre-Olivier Lapie.[44] In reviews such as *Europe*, *Esprit*, *Plans*, and *Ordre Nouveau*, they defended the primacy of the person and the regulation of production with due respect for human needs, and explored ideas of a decentralized state in which man might be reintegrated into more natural communities of region and corporation. Linked to these reviews were technocratic reform groups such as X-Crise, in which the dynamic business manager Jean Coutrot planned utopian productive communities.[45] These writers castigated individualism, but they were often equally troubled by the antidote of collectivism that was increasingly promoted by the new political groups of the time.[46]

The pursuit of the people was therefore central to a crisis of social, political, and even spiritual dimensions. Economic depression had deepened the sufferings of the working and middle classes, sharpening the awareness of the people as a social problem of key political importance. Financial instability and unemployment added to the burdens of inadequate living standards and working conditions, in which mechanization took little account of the needs and rhythms of the human person. Instability could both increase social tensions and also, potentially, unite these social groups as a single 'people', similarly desirous of social reform. At the same time, the unwillingness (or inability) of successive governments to resolve the economic crisis with authoritarian measures furthered a growing disillusionment with liberal democracy. Garrulous provincial deputies, factional strife, and quibbles over the ethics of political participation seemed pitiably distant from popular concerns. Equally, the idea of the abstract citizen with individual rights took little account of the needs of communities within the nation. Parliamentary democracy seemed dangerously close to caste rule, wilfully distant from the realities of street politics that pitted popular action and violence against the legal expression of popular sovereignty. Both as discontented workers and middle classes, and also as a political image, the 'people' called out for representation. Their organization and portrayal was at the heart of a contest to define a future for France at a time of crisis in Europe.

The 1930s: A divided legacy

This book is a study of the pursuit of the people and of the political rivalry within which this battle for representation took place. Its originality is twofold: first as an analysis of the changing meaning and action of the 'people' in this period; secondly as a comparative study of right and left. Research on the 1930s in France has generally reflected the political polarization of the time by focusing on left and right in isolation, perpetuating the notion of 'two Frances ready to tear each other apart' (as one contemporary described it in 1936).[47] The reality of these two Frances is undeniable: it was evident in political structures and institutions, as well as in deep-rooted personal antipathies. Nevertheless, it is only one side of the story. Ideas, rhetoric, and practices could be more flexible than established patterns of allegiance and opposition might at first suggest. In the political and ideological instability of the 1930s, the boundaries of left and right seemed to many contemporaries to have become more fluid, as political groups and parties endeavoured to redefine their supporters, identities, and legitimacy. In representing the people—in organizing and claiming workers, electors, demonstrators, or the nation—there was a constant evolution of rhetoric and practice within the dynamic opposition of left and right. By identifying areas of particular contest between these rivals, it is possible to draw forth common themes, hopes, and fears: the latent—if unrealizable—consensus that Le Cour Grandmaison had described as a 'partial community of thought'.

By exploring this 'partial community' through the question of popular representation, this book takes a different path to the more traditional studies of 1930s France as a country torn between democracy and fascism—while recognizing the important concerns that such studies reflect. Buoyed up by a post-1945 confidence in the future of liberal democracy, studies of the French left (especially of the Popular Front) have often been broadly sympathetic; critical of its shortcomings, yet willing to assimilate its hopes and achievements into a narrative of final democratic triumph. The most enduring image of the Popular Front on the left is that of a pacific, fraternal people, united in anti-fascism and benevolent in triumph after their electoral victory in 1936.[48] This is the image immortalized in the photographs of Robert Capa or Willy Ronis: the image of workers on strike, the symbolic aggression of their raised fists tempered by smiles; of a child asleep on his/her father's shoulders amid the ardour and bustle of a demonstration; or of a couple on a tandem enjoying their first paid holidays.[49] It is also the image celebrated in many of the books, essays, and photographs published to commemorate the seventieth anniversary of the Popular Front victory in 2006. Jean-Paul Rioux, for example, prefaced his edited collection of 2006 with an evocation of the 'fleeting beauty' of the popular hopes of 1936: 'Accordions and dances, cinema, rambles, and poppies for all.'[50] Antoine Prost exalted the Popular Front as 'the intrusion, generally pacific yet resolute, of popular forces, mobilized and organized by the trade unions, into our political history',[51] while Daniel Grason, René Mouriaux, and Patrick Pochet insisted on the contemporary relevance of the Popular Front in its battle against 'social regression, racism, and, in its new forms, fascism'.[52]

More explicitly partisan accounts, such as those produced by the SFIO, PCF, or dissident left, have similarly celebrated the legacy of the Popular Front and its image of the people (while, in the case of the dissidents, deploring its shortcomings as a revolutionary movement).[53] In particular, sympathetic accounts have emphasized the clear opposition between the Popular Front government and the Vichy regime, while underlining the linear development of the anti-fascist movement of the left into later Resistance and Liberation.[54] More recently, left-wing accounts have turned their attention to the cultural innovation of the Popular Front as government and mass movement. Danielle Tartakowsky's work on demonstrations portrays the Popular Front as a profound transformation of popular (left-wing) involvement in politics and culture, while Pascal Ory's encyclopaedic study of the new government's cultural policy illuminates the creative interaction between the state, associations, and individuals in bringing culture to the people.[55] Neither devotes much attention to comparable developments on the right. Similarly, Simon Dell's recent study of press photography during the Popular Front focuses principally on the left's perception of the 'people-nation', and on the Socialist and Communist parties at the expense of the more centrist Radicals.[56]

Studies of the right in this period have tended to seek comparisons with the European right rather than with the French left, and have been characterized primarily by the definition of French fascism. René Rémond established the framework for the debate with his classic 1954 study of the right in France from 1815 onwards, postulating that the French right can invariably be reduced to three distinct tendencies: Legitimist, Orleanist, and Bonapartist. The 'new' right of the 1930s could, in his view, be located conveniently within an ongoing (and less threatening) Bonapartist tradition.[57] Subsequent studies—notably by Zeev Sternhell and Robert Soucy—came to very different conclusions, and in their forthright identification of a French fascism contributed to a powerful debate.[58] The classification of the most substantial right-wing league and party, the Croix de Feu/Parti Social Français, has been central to this discussion.[59] Some have described it as a mass party that was also fascist in character;[60] others have contended that the movement was too legalist and conservative to have been fascist.[61] Despite the enduring fascination with France's immunity—or susceptibility—to the 'fascist temptation', more recent work has sought to move away from this framework of discussion, increasingly described as sterile and restrictive. Indeed, the boundaries of fascism seem all too often to lie in the eye of the beholder, and supposedly fascist traits—militaristic political activity, a cult of leadership, appeals to the petty bourgeoisie, and criticisms of the parliamentary regime—were not in fact limited to the political right. In the most recent studies, including Sean Kennedy's 2007 monograph on the Croix de Feu/Parti Social Français, there has been a deliberate concern to eschew categorization in order to focus more broadly on the nature and activity of right-wing movements.[62]

A dominant characteristic of these studies of French fascism and of the Popular Front is a tendency to obscure the dynamics of rivalry between left and right, and particularly their pursuit of the people. Sympathetic studies of the Popular Front assume that political and cultural innovation were the province of the left. Research on the right seeks comparisons with the European right rather than with the French left, and in its preoccupation with definition of fascism, generally neglects the question of street politics and the portrayal of the people.[63] Yet the points of direct conflict between political opponents—the ideas, strategies, geographical or social constituencies that they have been most determined to claim as their own—are powerfully revealing both of their genuine differences and also of their areas of common reflection. Such ambiguity, a 'force which breaks the predictability of polar opposites', is indeed an important subject for 'Anglo-Saxon' historians of French politics.[64] This book builds on an abiding interest in tensions and ambiguities between the 'two Frances',[65] showing in particular that the areas of common reflection that have been identified between Vichy France and the Resistance—such as Joan of Arc, or rural France—were also central to the political rivalry of the 1930s.

Areas of ambiguity between left and right in the 1930s are not, however, the invention of contemporary historians. Rather, they were perceived by men and women of the time. In 1931, for example, Jean-Richard Bloch described a disconcerting distance between existing structures and definitions, and the new ideas and movements that were spiralling rapidly out of their control.

> We live in dangerous times, because old words are used to describe new forms of life, and because the new words that we need have not yet come into circulation. (...) Every time we try to disengage the ideas expressed by the words bourgeoisie, culture, humanities, nation, revolution, war, classes, or class struggle, we realize that these words no longer correspond exactly to the facts. Life has changed around us and we attempt in vain to define it with an outdated vocabulary.[66]

And in June 1936, shortly after the constitution of the new Popular Front government, the right-wing journalist Pierre Villette (pseudonym 'Dorsay') made a similar observation. 'The words "Republic" and "Liberty", the words "right" and "left", the words "reaction" and "revolution" have not the slightest meaning today,' he remarked. 'We are searching for ourselves outside the old vocabulary.'[67]

Focusing on the pursuit of the people, this book is an exploration of political culture: a study of political language, behaviour, and artistic representation.[68] Its sources include newspaper articles and press photography; police reports of strikes, festivals, meetings, and demonstrations; parliamentary records; and trade-union reports. They also encompass political theatre and cinema, including a number of neglected films and plays. Its characters range from the well-known (and in some cases notorious) political leaders of the time to parliamentary deputies, journalists and intellectuals, and street militants.

In view of the rapid political evolution characteristic of the years 1934–39, the structure of this book is both chronological and thematic, allowing the identification of common action and reflection while also charting their development over time. The first chapter focuses on the demonstrations of February 1934 and examines the political and cultural significance of the demonstration, the translation of the crowd in the street into the voice of the people, and the organization of the people in the street by the right-wing leagues as well as by the emerging Popular Front. Moving on to the years 1934–35, and with particular focus on the celebration of 14 July 1935, the second chapter examines the changing forms of representation employed by the Popular Front and its opponents: the developing organization of both working-class and middle-class support, and the use of documentary and propaganda films. Here, the search for a new political order is shown to evolve from an angry rejection of the Republic to the imagination of a renewed parliamentary regime. The parallels that emerged in rival claims to both public and symbolic territory are studied in further detail in the third and fourth chapters. The third chapter examines the importance and fragility of the image of the people as victors at the time of the elections and strikes of spring 1936, as the Popular Front sought to reassure public opinion in the face of increasing disorder, and to counteract the powerful, rival images of the people as victims of Communist demagogy. The fourth chapter explores the challenge offered by the formation of the Parti Social Français and the Parti Populaire Français, both of which sought to undermine the Popular Front while also creating their own images of the people as an ideal of social and national reconciliation. This interrelation between politics and ritual in the staging of symbolic reconciliation is analysed in the fifth chapter in the context of theatre and cinema, where parallels are drawn between a number of performances in 1936–37 that depicted the people in an idealized past or future. The consequent distance between illusion and reality is reinforced in the sixth chapter, which examines the bloody riot at Clichy in March 1937, and the disintegration of the image of a rational, triumphant people, as well as exploring the increased pursuit of the middle classes by left and right. The final chapter discusses the successful appropriation of the theme of national reconciliation by the Radical Party, and considers Édouard Daladier's portrayal of himself as a national, popular leader, and his endeavour to create a relationship with the people that largely bypassed parliament. By studying how the people were pursued—as crowd, workers, electorate, nation, or symbolic community—this book contends that the 'partial community' beneath the two Frances was both real and unrealizable.

1
From the Crowd in the Street to the Voice of the People: February 1934

In February 1934, the monthly trade-union review *La Voix du Peuple* made an earnest appeal for the people to take to the stage.[1] The occasion was a lesson on popular theatre by Marcel Lapierre, designed for the autodidactic worker to deepen his knowledge of literature and to appreciate the artistic contribution of his class. Drawing illustrative examples from the ancient world to the twentieth century, Lapierre described and exalted the role of the people on stage and in the streets, whether in classical drama, medieval mystery plays, the French Revolution, or recent experiments in social and popular theatre. While sympathetic to the efforts of well-meaning intellectuals to nourish the relationship between art and the people, he was convinced that the time had come for the people to take their artistic and political future into their own hands. At the heart of the city, the theatre of the future should be a collective theatre, exalting a collective—and revolutionary—faith.

La Voix du Peuple proved to be a voice of prophecy, for in February 1934 a series of mass demonstrations brought the image of the crowd in the street to the forefront of public and political consciousness. On 6 February, a demonstration by right-wing leagues (and others) against the new Radical government of Édouard Daladier exploded into violence, leaving 15 dead and hundreds injured. On 7 February, the Daladier government collapsed. The following week, Communists, Socialists, and trade unionists took to the streets in their own opposition to the leagues—and in some cases also to the government—and these demonstrations and counter-demonstrations mobilized hundreds of thousands not only in Paris but also in the provinces. The significance of the demonstration of 6 February far surpassed even its immediate political consequences. That a violent demonstration could bring down a government revealed not only the power of the crowd in the street but also the importance of its representation in a climate of fear and anxiety, when the role of the press in creating scandal and instability was of critical importance. The angry demonstrators of 6 February became, through a sympathetic right-wing press, a righteous people protesting against parliamentary scandal and corruption. Meanwhile, the crowds who swelled the counter-demonstrations of the left became a people united in definitive rejection of fascism. Through articles, sketches, and photographs, the cacophonous shouts and slogans of the masses thus became the clarion voice of the people: an 'honest people' united against scandal and corruption, or a 'working people' united against the 'fascist' aspirations of the right-wing leagues. In the context of challenges to parliamentary democracy across Europe, these rival claims to the voice of the people were highly significant. This chapter explores how and why these images of the people were created, and considers whether any signs of a nascent 'community of thought' can be detected in the reactions of left, right, and centre to the crowd in the street.[2]

A crisis of representation?

Recent research has described the unrest of 1934 as symptomatic of a deeper crisis of representation: a dangerous 'slackening of the ties of representation',[3] even a 'crisis of authority for the representative regime' in which the legitimacy of the parliamentary Republic was called into question.[4] Certainly disillusionment with the parliamentary system was rapidly increasing. There was a strong desire for wider political participation that was frustrated by the persistence of pre-war politicians: men such as the socialist turned centrist Aristide Briand (a regular figure of fun at the Parisian cabaret) and the senator Joseph Caillaux, who had long been associated with political scandal (and not least when his wife shot the editor of *Le Figaro* in 1914). Young politicians met with inevitable electoral defeat while pre-war veterans remained, it seemed, unshakeable, which both heightened the tension between generations and also sharpened the suspicion that the parliamentary system was fusty, inefficient, and corrupt. The relationship between the deputies and the electorate was, moreover, often brusquely curtailed by the briefness of their electoral mandates: almost 40 per cent of all interwar deputies held their seat for only one legislature.[5] By the end of 1933, this latent dissatisfaction with the current regime—and with the concept of parliamentary democracy itself—was augmented by serious allegations of corruption. The most notorious scandal of the time was the case of Alexandre Stavisky. An ambitious swindler with friends in high places, Stavisky had been briefly imprisoned before recommencing his career of deception, and his latest scheme of fraudulent bonds had received the support of numerous Radicals, including the Minister of the Colonies. His fraudulent gains of 230 million francs made national news head-lines, as did the revelation that his trial for a former offence had been postponed 19 times by the Paris prosecutor's office since 1927.[6] On 8 January 1934 he was found dead, and there was much speculation that he had been assassinated lest he should unmask his protectors.

For many, the parliamentary system seemed weakened not only by corruption but also by its habitually inconclusive debates. During January and February 1934, the right-wing weekly *Je suis partout* pub-lished a series of cartoons of parliamentary life and corruption, featuring parliament as a boxing match without conclusion, or as a group of doc-tors so involved in their own convoluted arguments that they failed to pay any attention to their ailing patient, French democracy. Doubts about the survival of the current system were also expressed in Parlia-ment: even fervently republican deputies recognized that France stood increasingly alone beside its more dictatorial European neighbours, and wondered whether nineteenth-century ideals were really the most pertinent solution to twentieth-century problems.

The crisis of representation reflected a wider loss of faith in parlia-mentary democracy across Europe, and a profound concern to rethink the representation of the people. The problem was not necessarily the notion of popular sovereignty itself, but rather the effectiveness and legitimacy of its current representatives. If the will of the people con-ferred legitimacy, the exact definition of this 'people' was also contested. As political actors and as a political community—and especially as a body of interchangeable citizens—the people could be frustratingly elusive.[7]

The people in the street: Image and precedent

In portraying the role of the people and in transforming the actions of the crowd into an expression of the popular will, the groups and parties of 1934 were inevitably influenced by historical precedent as well as by ideological predilection. Writers and artists portraying the people in the street were not working on a blank canvas, but rather created pictures that incorporated, or deliberately painted over, some of the outlines already so deeply etched in collective memory. The descent of the people into the street, particularly in Paris, was rich with historical precedents and symbolism, and any description therefore reacted, consciously and unconsciously, to existing narrative traditions. The people had already been cast in many distinct—even contradictory—roles: heroes or villains, victors or martyrs. If the voice of the people in the street as an expression of legitimate popular sovereignty could be traced back to 14 July 1789, then the same date was also central to rival traditions portraying the people as an instinctive and potentially barbaric force, incapable of rational action and guided only by demagogic minorities.

This concept of the people as irrational and barbaric provided a counter-image against which the groups and parties that were to become the Popular Front could construct their own image of the people as rational, triumphant, and optimistic. For the Socialists (as for the non-Communist left more broadly), the image of the sovereign people was associated with 1789, with humanist ideas of fraternity in 1848, and with the concept of a political utopia potentially achievable in republican form. A typical elaboration of this concept can be found in the works of Jean Guéhenno, a socialist intellectual who became closely involved in many Popular Front organizations. Guéhenno was the son of a rural cobbler, keenly conscious of his identity as a 'man of the people', and equally of the education that now separated him from his popular origins. His political ideal was a rational, intellectual, and pacific revolution, spreading through education the principles of 1789 in such a way as to benefit and unite the whole people. He firmly believed that men were 'more similar than different',[8] and his faith in the mystic communion between all humans ('the simple word "man" ', he confessed, 'fills me with awe'[9]) had been nourished by his reading of Jules Michelet, Alphonse de Lamartine, and Victor Hugo.[10] In particular, Michelet's vision of a society in which 'all desired to be brothers'[11] seemed to Guéhenno a necessary antidote to the pessimism of the First World War, in which he himself had suffered great personal losses. It was through the people that new hope could be found, and a new society created. Unlike many intellectuals of the time, Guéhenno eagerly embraced the idea of being one of the masses,[12] yet he was drawn more to the inclusive 'people' than to the exclusive 'proletariat'. His imagined revolution was not a dictatorship of the proletariat but the achievement of an egalitarian society that would benefit all humanity. This was for him 'the revenge of Michelet over Marx',[13] and a mark of his preference for the French Revolution of 1789 over the Russian Revolution of 1917. In many ways Guéhenno's conception of the people was close to that of Léon Blum, to whom Guéhenno was sympathetic, although he never actually joined the Socialist Party (SFIO). Both grounded their socialist philosophy in the ideas of Jaurès, who had sought to temper Marxism with the humanist socialism of 1848.[14] Both likewise conceived of the revolution less in class terms than as the ultimate realization of the aspirations of 1789. Blum, for example, criticized the Russian Revolution for its departure from European socialism, for its equation of revolution with a political coup, and for the Bolsheviks' undemocratic understanding of the role of the party. In their imagination of the people as political actors, Guéhenno and Blum thus represent a particular (and important) trend among French socialists. They were attracted to the idea of a fraternal people as broad as humanity; their sympathies lay with the working people and the proletariat; yet despite their exaltation of the role of the people during the French Revolution they were uneasy at the thought of future violence in the streets, even for a revolutionary cause.[15]

The questions of popular violence and proletarian dictatorship led to sharp divisions within the Socialist Party. General Secretary Paul Faure believed considerably more fervently than Blum in the revolutionary nature of socialism as a doctrine, provided that the proposed revolution took place within a national context. Jean Zyromski, a vocal figure in the Fédération de la Seine and leader of the group known as the Bataille Socialiste, was also more attached than Blum to the rhetoric of class struggle and mass action, and did not believe in compromise with the bourgeoisie. The dynamic and often recalcitrant Marceau Pivert shared this enthusiasm for the revolutionary proletariat.[16] A semblance of unity was thus achieved only through conscious ambiguity on doctrinal problems,[17] while the dilemma of governmental participation in the current Republic was temporarily resolved by Blum's theory of the 'exercise of power'.[18] Such distinctions reflected the awkwardness of a party that had developed within a parliamentary system and yet remained keenly aware of its duty to speak for the masses.

No such inhibitions regarding popular street violence troubled members of the French Communist Party (PCF), often to be found aggressively confronting right-wing activists in the streets of Paris (and in other towns and cities). Their recruitment among the masses was, moreover, becoming increasingly successful. Although the revolutionary 'class against class' tactic prescribed by the Comintern had dramatically reduced Party membership in the 1920s,[19] a network of local and regional organizations was gradually being built through the establishment of individual cells in organizations and factories. These cells—for which there was no equivalent in the Socialist Party—were intended to promote direct contact with the masses, and increased rapidly from 1934 onwards.[20]

The Communists' vision of the people, as developed by their ambitious, Stalinist leader Maurice Thorez and in their daily newspaper *L'Humanité*, was also explored in dramatic form by the Communist-led Fédération du Théâtre Ouvrier de France (FTOF).[21] The importance of theatre in diffusing Communist propaganda and preparing for revolution had been emphasized since the very foundation of the PCF at the Congress of Tours, and throughout the 1920s small amateur groups had been furthering the causes of both art and revolution through their performances at meetings and demonstrations. The FTOF, which had been founded clandestinely in January 1931,[22] organized sketches during strike action and forged close links with other agit-prop groups across Europe and in the USSR.[23] The contrast between the image of the people later presented by the Popular Front and that developed by the Communists through the FTOF was considerable. While the Popular Front was to present a triumphant, pacific people, the FTOF presented a powerful and angry proletariat, wholeheartedly committed to merciless class struggle, violently opposed to the bourgeois Republic, and deeply critical of the 'reformist' Confédération Général du Travail and the compromising Socialist leaders. Its monthly bulletin *La Scène ouvrière* advised working-class directors that 'the bourgeoisie must be characterized as they are seen in reality; their hidden decadence must be revealed'—and illustrations of suitably decadent costumes were provided for this purpose.[24] The bulletin also contended that the people must be represented as a single, powerful body of workers. To this end, the technique of the spoken chorus (increasing in popularity in the 1930s) was used to particular advantage, offering a visible and audible expression of working-class unity, resolution, and solidarity. Indeed, the technique of the spoken chorus was even described as 'a new and aggressive form of the proletarian struggle against capitalism and its "art for art's sake",' the same author asserting that, 'its origin lies in the masses, the collective spirit of the masses is its creator.'[25] Just as new techniques were to serve the cause of class struggle through the theatre, so should the theatre itself be prepared to move out of purpose-built bourgeois buildings and into the streets, the stage of the proletariat. In June 1931, *La Scène ouvrière* featured an article by Nina Gourfinkel on the festivals of the Russian Revolution, which described the development of Bolshevik street theatre 'in the midst of the crowds'. As Gourfinkel was eager to emphasize, the distinction between mass theatre and mass movements could often be blurred.[26]

Divisions between Socialists and Communists over the image of the people and the means of their organization were also reflected in the trade-union movement, dominated in 1934 by the broadly anti-fascist Confédération Générale du Travail (CGT) and by the Communist-dominated Confédération Générale du Travail Unitaire (CGTU). The CGT, already low in membership in 1914, had lost members after the War to the CGTU and to the Confédération Française des Travailleurs Chrétiens, and was, as its Communist detractors noted, largely concerned with reform, both economic and educational.[27] Although the CGT maintained a rhetoric of working-class power, its strong focus on education led to the development of the image of a people who needed to prove themselves worthy of their own emancipation. Indeed, the national congress of 1931 underlined that 'only the enlightened masses, conscious of their rights and of the limits of their strength, can demand and usefully exercise control over the organization of work, and so realize their liberation.'[28] Meanwhile the CGTU followed closely in Communist footsteps by envisaging a revolutionary proletariat with clear political aims, and roundly rejected the compromises of the CGT.[29] It proposed a close co-operation between rural and urban workers, supported by 'intellectual workers' who also identified themselves as part of the people, and who looked forward to the overthrow of the existing system.[30]

The CGTU appealed to the masses with a programme of concrete proposals, and by 1934 was beginning to make use of the street as a means of furthering solidarity and bringing the people to public attention. In December 1933 a hunger march was organized by the national CGTU committee for the unemployed, demanding unemployment benefits and a 40-hour week, while also protesting against war and fascism. Along the journey, solidarity committees were organized to support the demonstrators, offering practical support and (according to the CGTU) bolstering a sense of working-class unity. Such unity was intended to provide the impetus for future action. It was, as one militant insisted, 'an essential condition for the victory of the proletariat over the system that engenders unemployment, fascism, and war.'[31]

If the role of the masses in the street provoked conflicting reactions from Socialists and Communists, and divided members of the CGT and CGTU, it was also an important point of contention between the left and the more centrist Radical Party.[32] The Radicals (themselves divided) recognized that the 'supreme authority is that of the people'[33] and presented themselves as heirs to the people of the French Revolution.

Édouard Daladier, indeed, informed Léon Blum and Maurice Thorez that the Radicals were the modern incarnation of the 'petty bourgeoisie who stormed the Bastille with the proletariat.'[34] The prominent Radical and future Finance Minister Georges Bonnet defined the Radicals as neither conservative nor revolutionary, and as representing 'the modest workers of town and country, one of the most vibrant forces of France.'[35] For the Radicals, therefore, the 'people' were a broad people, both bourgeois and proletarian, defined by their republicanism and their opposition to 'reaction' in its political, social, or religious form. Despite profound differences with the Socialists, notably over questions of individualism,[36] the Radicals were periodically open to non-Communist left-wing unity, especially under the banner of 'social justice and the progress of mankind'.[37] But although they believed in the supremacy of popular sovereignty, they nevertheless preferred its expression to remain within the walls of the Chamber of Deputies. Even if Daladier identified Radical ancestors among the people of 1789, he was not sympathetic to the contemporary crowd as a rival expression of the popular will. Indeed on 6 February, as the angry crowd surged ever closer to Parliament, he referred warily to the dangers of this potential 'fourth power', a hindrance to the efficient functioning of the executive, legislature, and judiciary.[38] Earlier in the Third Republic, a number of extreme Radicals and Socialists, notably Camille Pelletan in 1884 and Édouard Vaillant in 1907, had campaigned for greater freedom to demonstrate. But for the majority of the Radical Party in the 1930s, the legitimate use of the street to represent the popular will remained very much with the state.

On the right, the people were imagined both in reaction to the rational citizen of 1789 and in remembrance of the sacred union of the First World War. Particularly on the extreme right, critical responses to the French Revolution and a late nineteenth-century interest in crowd psychology nourished an image of the people in the street as the epitome of dangerous vitality. Among the most influential exponents of this intellectual trend were the historian and philosopher Hippolyte Taine (1828–93), the sociologist Gustave Le Bon (1841–1931), and the criminologist Cesare Lombroso (1835–1909), each of whom presented the people as the very antithesis of the rational citizen of 1789. They agreed that man was irrational by instinct, and that the dangers of such instincts were most clearly demonstrated in the case of the crowd. In terms of irrationality and animal behaviour, they saw little to choose between the man of the people, the criminal, and the savage.[39] The stark brutality of popular behaviour was vividly depicted in Taine's account of peasant violence at the time of the French Revolution.

> Suddenly one witnesses the emergence of the barbarian, and, worse still, the primitive animal, the grimacing monkey, bloodthirsty and playful, which cackles as its kills, and gambols on the destruction that it has caused.[40]

If a crowd could liberate such primitive and terrifying instincts, then it merited consideration in its own right. According to Gustave Le Bon, a pioneer in the study of crowd psychology, this transient transformation of individual men into a collective entity so defied the deterministic boundaries of heredity and milieu that it called for a new means of analysis.[41] Both Taine and Le Bon recognized the inherent difficulties in controlling a crowd, but considered that collective behaviour might be manipulated through the scientific determination of its characteristic traits. While describing the crowd as a power which 'no-one can control', Taine accepted that a crowd would obey revolutionary leaders even after forsaking more 'natural' ones,[42] and that it was particularly susceptible to the influence of illusory and simplistic solutions. 'Before taking root in their brain, an idea must become a myth, as absurd as it is simple', he observed.[43] For Le Bon, 'impressing the imagination of the crowd is a sure means of governing them.'[44]

Le Bon implied that any individual could be transformed within a collective situation; that any group of individuals could exhibit the destructive traits of the crowd. In practice, however, both he and Taine equated the crowd with the working classes. Both therefore condemned the role of the working class in politics as a destabilizing and uniformly negative force. While conceding that the 'people' might contain various strata, notably a hardworking majority and a more revolutionary minority,[45] they were consistently reluctant to endorse any form of popular action, which would inevitably be divorced from reason and intellect. Le Bon also predicted that the people would dominate the politics of the future: 'The age we are entering' he insisted, 'will be essentially the age of the crowd'.[46] The future, as he saw it, was dark with threats to civilization. If man was primarily irrational and instinctive, and the crowd a context for the liberation of animal instincts, mastered only by illusion and despotic leadership, then the age of the masses would be the assault of the new barbarians on the civilized world.

Supposing, however, that the destructive potential of the crowd was to be channelled towards positive ends, both Taine and Le Bon feared the achievement of the crowd's subconscious desires, yet Le Bon's work in particular suggested that this achievement could be potentially beneficial. Crowds might behave irrationally, subject to myths and illusions, but their actions could be heroic as well as criminal,[47] and a leader who manipulated their irrational beliefs might well succeed in channelling their otherwise unfocused energy towards preconceived goals. If these goals included the destruction of the political regime, then the attraction of such theories was considerable. Such a realization underpinned the development of a number of groups on both left and right. According to Georges Sorel, whose theories on the regenerative power of proletarian action were widely read, the vitality, spontaneity, and even violence of working-class action—especially in the context of the general strike—could catalyze social and political renewal.[48] 'Not only is proletarian violence capable of provoking future revolution,' he wrote, 'but it seems moreover to be the only means by which European nations, brutalized by humanism, can rediscover their former energy.'[49]

The image of the people in the street as an instinctive and potentially violent force was widely influential—so much so that Sorel has been described as laying the foundations for both fascism and bolshevism.[50] For the conservative right, it was a sobering reminder that the people in the street, either uncontrolled or dominated by dangerous minorities, constituted a profound threat to order and civilization. For the extreme right, as indeed for the extreme left, it was an encouraging sign that the people in the street were capable of toppling the government, and even the Republic itself.

The right-wing leagues of the 1930s were strongly influenced by these images of the people, and street militancy was particularly associated with the Camelots du Roi of Action Française.[51] The Camelots, renowned for their enthusiasm and aggression since the early years of the twentieth century,[52] numbered approximately 1000 by 1914. They were reformed after the First World War and were extremely active during the 1920s and 1930s.[53] In the 1930s, the street was frequently a forum for direct confrontation between Action Française and its opponents. At a meeting of 650 Camelots du Roi in November 1932, the sculptor and energetic militant Maxime Réal del Sarte praised the ardent action of the Camelots in the streets of Paris, commenting in particular on 'the brilliant manner in which you began the [academic] year by showing the Socialists and Communists that the streets of Paris do not belong to them.'[54] Léon Daudet, the editor of *Action Française* who described himself as 'so reactionary that I can hardly breathe',[55] was similarly enthusiastic. Indeed, he sent Réal del Sarte a letter of congratulation, praising the Camelots for their response to the 'anti-French' demonstrations of their left-wing opponents and adding that '[the Camelots] have thus confirmed to the people of Paris the existence of patriots determined to preserve the honour of France.'[56]

Action Française opposed the left's appropriation of the street and the people not only in practice, but also in theory. For Charles Maurras, the concept of street violence as a means of revitalizing the nation—and as a potential prelude to the collapse of the Republic—was an attractive one. The energy and enthusiasm of Action Française's young supporters in the early years of the century, and their apparently inexhaustible determination to insult republican officers, buildings, and even statues, led Maurras to conclude that political impetus in the streets had passed from left to right (and he included other contemporary right-wing leagues in his assessment).[57] Maurras frequently deplored the distance between national institutions (*le pays légal*) and the nation itself (*le pays réel*), and for him the patriotic people in the street were capable of personifying the *pays réel*, especially when street militancy achieved a symbolic victory over the forces of republican order.[58] In his eyes, Action Française was developing the theory and practice of street violence in direct competition with Georges Sorel, with one significant difference: the violence of Action Française was 'in the service of reason'.[59] By this he implied that right-wing street violence served the supposedly rational goal of destroying the Third Republic and restoring the monarchy. Victims of the Camelots' zealous defence of reason understandably thought otherwise.

Action Française thus contrasted the republican crowd and revolutionary 'people' with its own image of the people in the street as the incarnation of the *pays réel*. In similar vein, leaders and militants of Action Française opposed Socialist (and later Communist) appeals to the workers or masses. The 'good people' (*bon Peuple*) pursued by the Socialists were certainly not neglected in Maurras' theories. 'Nothing could have been more obvious,' he wrote retrospectively of the early twentieth century, 'than the fact that the working class were at this time deprived and despoiled. The problem of the century was to save and elevate them.' He also claimed that the major social reforms obtained through the lobbying of Socialist deputies had already been outlined 30 years before by benevolent senators, many of them Catholics with a strong social conscience such as Count Albert de Mun (another was the father of Jean Le Cour Grandmaison, deputy in 1936).[60]

Action Française was unusual among right-wing leagues of the 1930s in the extent of its political theorizing, but highly influential for the same reason. Indeed many writers later to join other right-wing movements or parties, such as the future collaborator Robert Brasillach, began their intellectual and political journey in the 'school' of Action Française, whose consequent influence has been likened to that of the Communist Party.[61] Although other leagues offered less theoretical analysis of the meaning of street violence[62] or of the image of the crowd or of workers, they nonetheless shared a number of Action Française's convictions. They believed in a patriotic people defending the honour of France, and in a working people reconciled with the nation. They also believed in the importance of street militancy as a demonstration of patriotism and as a path to renewing the political order.

The concept of a patriotic people defending the nation was fundamental to the association of the Croix de Feu, one of the largest and most influential of the leagues.[63] Founded by Maurice d'Hartoy in November 1927, the association was originally apolitical.[64] Membership was open to those who had been awarded the Légion d'Honneur or the Croix de Guerre, while membership of the associated 'Briscards' was dependent on service in the front line. The intention of the Croix de Feu was to reassemble veteran soldiers in a spirit of camaraderie, to recreate the supposed fraternity of the trenches, to commemorate military victories and sacrifices, and to safeguard the glory of France. The association also expressed its opposition to capitalism in so far as this oppressed 'the labouring classes, which are the purest forces of the nation, and which deserve to be generously rewarded'.[65] In 1929, the association came under the control of the millionaire François Coty, founder and editor of *L'Ami du Peuple*. But it was not until Lieutenant-Colonel François de la Rocque de Sévérac became president of the league in 1931 that it began to expand more rapidly, forming the Association des Fils et Filles des Croix de Feu for the children of existing members, and the Ligue des Volontaires Nationaux for new male recruits. It also began to adopt a more political stance. Colonel de la Rocque was a man whose family background, piety, and military experience convinced him of the need for moral and civic renewal through elite leadership and popular mobilization. His father, General Jean-Pierre Raymond de la Rocque, was a naval artillery officer who had become embittered with republican politicians, turning to politics in his retirement with the design of mobilizing patriotic Catholics against a secular regime. The future leader of the Croix de Feu was thus influenced by both Church and army from his earliest days. Graduating from the military training college of Saint-Cyr as a cavalry officer, La Rocque *fils* went first to North Africa, where he served under (and was greatly influenced by)

Marshal Louis-Hubert Lyautey. He also participated in a retreat organized by the soldier-missionary Charles de Foucauld, and studied the
works of Catholic thinkers such as Frédéric Le Play and René de la
Tour du Pin. La Rocque was subsequently awarded six citations for his
bravery on the Western Front, and served after the war in Poland (1921–
22) and in Morocco (1925–26). Shortly after the death of Jean-Pierre
Raymond in 1926, the younger La Rocque retired from military service
and worked for the Compagnie Générale d'Électricité, while continuing to write articles on military affairs. François de la Rocque's articles
echoed his father's distaste for the factions and compromises of the
Third Republic, and became increasingly focused on the problem of
national renewal, particularly influenced by Lyautey's famous article of
1891 on the social role of the officer. Joining the Croix de Feu in 1929, La
Rocque rose rapidly to leadership, and in 1931 produced a programme
of action that criticized the instability of the parliamentary Republic,
and demanded greater presidential power and economic representation.
Before the 1932 elections La Rocque encouraged his followers to vote
against the Marxists in defence of French and Christian civilization, and
to fulfil the noble aspirations of those who had died for the sake of the
Patrie.[66] It was in the military roots of the movement that he sought the
foundations for his idea of the people, discerning in the experience of
the First World War a fraternity that transcended class divisions, as well
as a spirit of self-sacrifice for the common good. This supposed unity of
a nation in wartime was often evoked by members of the Croix de Feu
in opposition to contemporary political divisions.

Other right-wing leagues also highlighted the contrast between a
people firmly associated with the nation and the restless international
proletariat exalted by the left. The Jeunesses Patriotes (founded shortly
before the Croix de Feu in 1924) addressed their propaganda specifically to the people of Paris, and claimed to understand more deeply
than the contemporary left their desire for work, order, and peace.[67] The
Solidarité Française and the Francistes, more directly inspired by Italian
fascism and the corporatist system, adopted similar strategies. Founded
by François Coty in 1933, the Solidarité Française was taken over by
the retired military commander Jean Renaud in 1934, and it claimed
to further the interests of the people not by directing them towards
politics but by working towards their integration within the nation.[68]
The Francistes, led by the war veteran Marcel Bucard (who attended the
international fascist conference of 1934), were more openly extreme
than the other leagues, and made particular efforts to attract former
Socialist and Communist militants. Claiming to promote 'an economic

and social order based on the nobility of work and the primacy of the worker', they saw themselves as a truly revolutionary movement, aiming to transform society by a revolution 'with the people and for the people'.[69]

The images of the people developed by these political groups and parties were diverse, yet certain common trends can nonetheless be discerned. For the left, the rational citizen people of 1789 were a constant point of reference, and concern for social reform was a potentially unifying factor—even if Radicals, Socialists, and Communists reacted differently to the crowd in the street and to its possible violence against the Republic. On the right, the people in the street were also associated with the possibility of violence. For the conservative, parliamentary right, popular street action could be a cause for concern (although members of such parliamentary groups as the Alliance Démocratique and the Fédération Républicaine were sometimes favourable to the demonstrations of more extreme, non-parliamentary groups). For the extreme right, the crowd was a source of possibilities: a potential weapon against the Republic, and a people that could also be disciplined to present an image of political order, as in the case of the leagues of veterans. The working people were likewise seen as a source of potential support and as an agent of political change: a people to be pursued and organized, and to be integrated theoretically within the framework of the nation. The clearest distinction was between those who feared the crowd unequivocally and those who looked to the people in the street as a potential weapon for change and renewal; between those who embraced street politics, and those who preferred to confine political activity to government and parliamentary debate. In practice, the fact that the behaviour of the crowd was so often unpredictable—and likely to elude the control of even the most strenuous political discipline—was a problem for both.

The night of 6 February 1934, in parliament and the street

These differences over the role of the crowd as a political actor were brought into particular focus on the night of 6 February 1934. The immediate context of the violent riot was an acute crisis of governmental instability. Since the left-wing victory in the elections of May 1932, there had been a number of short-lived governments that had foundered on differences between Socialists and Radicals regarding economic questions. Daladier, who first became premier on 31 January 1933 as Hitler rose to power in Germany, had sought and failed to acquire Socialist support for Radical measures of deflation. His government collapsed in

October 1933, and was followed by a brief government under Albert Sarraut before another Radical, Camille Chautemps, formed a cabinet in late November. Chautemps was a Radical of considerable pedigree— his father Émile had been a deputy and minister as well as president of the Senate; his uncle Alphonse had been a deputy and a senator; and his brother Émile had also been a deputy. Yet not only was Chautemps compromised by his association with the Stavisky affair (as were a number of his ministers), but he also had little patience with street politics. By early 1934, the streets of Paris were regularly overrun by Action Française, the Solidarité Française, and the Jeunesses Patriotes, noisily defaming the premier and his allies ('Camille Chautemps, head of a band of thieves and assassins!' proclaimed *Action Française*'s headline on 10 January). On 28 January, Chautemps resigned: his was the fifth government to fall since December 1932. It seemed to the President of the Republic Albert Lebrun that the country was in need of a coalition government—even a 'government of public safety'—but who was the man who could create a cabinet in such a climate, faced with rising levels of unemployment and widespread disgust at the scandal of Stavisky? Poincaré had succeeded in 1926, but he was ill and dying. Lebrun approached the former President of the Republic Gaston Doumergue, the President of the Senate Jules Jeanneney, and the President of the Chamber Fernand Bouisson, but all three declined. There remained the Radical leader Édouard Daladier. Solid in appearance, forceful in oratory (he was known as the 'bull of Vaucluse'), Daladier was renowned for his organization and capacity for hard work. Enigmatic in character (even to his own family),[70] and increasingly taciturn since the death of his wife Madeleine from tuberculosis in 1932, he nonetheless possessed a reputation for energy and integrity. He accepted Lebrun's offer. In the final days of January, Daladier formed a cabinet that included Radicals, independent socialists, and left-wing republicans (the Socialist Party refused to participate). Yet no sooner was his Cabinet formed than a decision to transfer the Prefect of Police Jean Chiappe to the position of Resident General in Morocco provoked the resignation of a number of centrist ministers, and cries of outrage in the right-wing press—for Chiappe was notoriously sympathetic to the leagues. As Daladier prepared to present the new government to the Chamber on 6 February for the customary vote of approval, so did the right-wing leagues (and a number of left-wing groups) prepare to take to the streets in strident opposition.

The stenographic account of the parliamentary session of 6 February makes dramatic reading.[71] Tempers were increasingly frayed, and the clamour both inside and outside the Chamber was deafening (Figure 1).

Figure 1   The Chamber of Deputies, 6 February 1934, *L'Illustration*, 10 February 1934, © *L'Illustration* (Courtesy of *L'Illustration*).

The presentation of the new government was interrupted by cries of 'Les Soviets!' and by offensive interjections from the Communist leader Maurice Thorez, who responded on being called to order that he was merely speaking in the language of the proletariat. Amid noisy unrest, Daladier endeavoured to present his vision of the proper functioning of republican institutions as a path to political salvation. His call to defend liberty and the Republic won applause from the left and interruptions from the right; his appeal for a vote on the budget in order to respond to the sufferings of the workers, the peasantry, and the anxious middle classes was a desperate appeal to common ground. Above all, he resolutely decried the influence of the street and insisted that the deputies—not the crowd—remained the true representatives of popular sovereignty. 'The people have delegated their sovereignty to you,' he asserted. 'Strong in the authority that your confidence will grant us, we will defend the regime and make the law explicitly respected.' Rigorously condemning the sympathy that right-wing deputies such as the anti-Semitic Xavier Vallat had expressed towards the leagues, he insisted that street agitation must not become the 'fourth power' in the Third Republic.

Daladier's insistence came too late. Outside the Chamber of Deputies, angry demonstrators were crowding the streets of Paris, heaving up paving stones, setting fire to newsstands, and hindering the mounted police by throwing marbles under their horses' hooves. The demonstration, which began at five that afternoon and continued in some areas until two-thirty the following morning, brought together right-wing leagues, veteran soldiers' associations, Communists, and municipal councillors in noisy opposition to the new government. Though their motivations were different and their respective demonstrations initially separate, the epicentre of action and violence was the Place de la Concorde, just across the Seine from the Chamber of Deputies. Communists and PCF sympathizers in the ARAC (Association Républicaine des Anciens Combattants) gathered on the Champs-Élysées in the west of the capital to protest against government attacks on war pensions—and were supposed to remain in this area, suitably distanced from the Chamber, but in practice many of them moved elsewhere. Veteran soldiers in the 900,000-strong Union Nationale des Combattants (theoretically apolitical; in practice right-wing) were likewise supposed to demonstrate independently against the Radicals' pension reforms, converging first at the Place de l'Opéra (Figure 2). Yet many also headed towards the Place de la Concorde. Their leader, the right-wing municipal councillor Georges Lebecq, later claimed that they had been prevented by the police from pursuing their intended path through the capital. La Rocque insisted similarly on the independent action of his Croix de Feu (and according to the right-wing councillor Charles Trochu, he resisted strong pressure from the other leagues for common action).[72] Two groups, one on the Rue de Bourgogne and the other near the Petit Palais, had been instructed to meet outside the Chamber, and observers were posted in public telephones along the route in order to relay the latest developments to La Rocque himself. On 22 January La Rocque had written an open letter to the premier demanding national union around the tricolour, and suggested that his own Croix de Feu were not afraid to employ violence to achieve this end. But as soon as the demonstration of 6 February began to degenerate into violence, La Rocque gave orders for his supporters to disperse. Whatever the designs of individual Croix de Feu members on the Chamber of Deputies were, La Rocque was not prepared to risk such an obviously anti-republican (and possibly undisciplined) course of action. Members of other right-wing leagues had fewer scruples. Action Française, the Solidarité Française, and the Jeunesses Patriotes had called their supporters to demonstrate outside the Chamber, and certainly made no attempt to conceal their antagonism to the

Figure 2 Veteran soldiers in the Place de l'Opéra, 6 February 1934, *L'Illustration*, 10 February 1934, Photograph: J. Clair-Guyot © *L'Illustration* (Courtesy of *L'Illustration*).

Daladier government. The Jeunesses Patriotes processed from the Hôtel de Ville (town hall of Paris) led by right-wing municipal councillors and deputies (including their leader, Pierre Taittinger), and seemed hopeful of overturning the left-wing majority as in 1926, and perhaps of bringing another Poincaré to power.

Some years later in 1944, when La Rocque and Daladier were in the same prison in Itter, La Rocque claimed that Taittinger, Action Française, and their sympathizers had genuinely intended to storm the Chamber, even if their only means of eluding the police had been the sewers of Paris.[73] It was certainly difficult to draw any definite conclusions about the motives of the demonstrators, which contributed in turn to widely varying accounts of the demonstration and its significance. But the immediate consequence of the riot was unambiguous. Daladier received a vote of confidence of 360 to 220, but after writing an appeal to the French people to exhort them to calm, he then resigned on the advice of the Presidents of the Republic, Chamber, and Senate. His confidence was undermined by the resignations of several ministers on whom he had hoped to rely, including his personal friend Guy La Chambre. The police had, moreover, also noted various stockpiles of weapons, and Action Française had threatened to return armed. Daladier's fears of further street violence were not unjustified. The following night there was a further riot, less organized but more violent in places than that of 6 February, and on 9 February the Communists held their own demonstration in the east of Paris, which also led to clashes with the police, resulting in 12 deaths and hundreds of injuries. The most substantial— but most peaceful—demonstration took place on 12 February, when trade unionists, Socialists, and Communists converged on the Cours de Vincennes and processed to the Place de la Nation, prevented by the police from continuing into the centre of Paris. Not intended as a demonstration of left-wing unity (tensions were in fact running high between Communists, Socialists, and Radicals), the demonstration became in retrospect the founding moment of the Popular Front. Communist and Socialist supporters merged columns with cries of 'unity!', and the impeccably dressed Léon Blum railed in his high-pitched voice against the dangers of royalism and fascism, striving to raise his voice above the clamour and applause of the surrounding crowd.

Diffusing the *vox populi*

The demonstrations of February 1934 brought hundreds of thousands into the streets, projecting the image of the crowd—angry, violent, or pacific—into the centre of public consciousness, not only in Paris but also in the provinces. In the context of a widespread preoccupation with the problem of popular representation, it was vital for political groups and parties to translate the inchoate masses into a cohesive 'people'. But how could the clamour of the crowd be transformed into the *vox populi*?

For the right-wing leagues, the angry demonstrators of 6 February were transformed through speeches, sketches, and newspaper articles into a united, honest people demanding a thorough renewal of political life. Demonstrators became 'patriots', 'honest folk', and also 'the people'. Some commentators, such as the municipal councillor Jean Ferrandi, underlined the novelty of seeing the nationalists as masters of the street: the sudden predominance of 'Vive la France!' in contrast to the more familiar and 'unpatriotic' cries of left-wing demonstrators.[74] Yet it was seen as no surprise that the masses—here described as the people—should both support and participate in these displays of patriotic sentiment. The right-wing press, largely sympathetic towards the demonstrators, was keen to emphasize their number so as to present them not merely as representatives of the people, but as the people themselves. *Action Française*, whose role in encouraging the anti-parliamentary sentiments of these people had been considerable, described the vastness of the demonstration with a creator's pride.

> Countless thousands of Frenchmen, on the march to save their pillaged patrimony and the honour of their fatherland, coalesced into vast processions in the icy mist: it was impossible to estimate their strength.
>
> The protests, songs, and shouts that resounded at the close of the day echoed throughout the city like the powerful and furious voice of a noble and indignant people, determined to put an end to the ignoble dictatorship of the band of criminals who have dominated them.[75]

The unbridled energy of these people was also captured in the image of the sea that was to be applied so frequently to the crowds of the Popular Front. 'They move forward like an immense wave' wrote *Action Française*, 'and nothing can stop them.'[76] *Je suis partout* employed similar images, illustrating with a sketch the 'rising sea' of a justifiably angry people (Figure 3). Not only was the crowd described as the people of Paris, but it was also seen to represent the entire people of France, believed to share in the same sentiments of furious indignation at the corruption of the parliamentary system. 'The whole of Paris was against the government,' contended the right-wing historian Pierre Gaxotte, 'and what the capital accomplished with the panache of its official role, twenty provincial towns have also achieved, responding to the desires of the whole of France.'[77]

These accounts rarely mention the social composition of the crowd. The 'rising sea' of people pictured in *Je suis partout* on 10 February was a dense mass of men of all classes (judging from their styles of dress); the actions or appearances of individual demonstrators received correspondingly little attention. Far greater interest was accorded to the symbolic significance of 6 February as the voice of the entire nation against a corrupt parliament. In the eyes of the right, this voice of the people

Figure 3   'The rising sea', *Je suis partout*, 10 February 1934 (Courtesy of the Bibliothèque Nationale de France, Paris).

was the unanimous voice of honesty against corruption. Whereas the demonstrators were described as 'honest folk', the deputies appeared in contrast as 'thieves' or 'assassins', condemned not only for their support of Stavisky but also for having plotted his death. Cowardly and ignoble, the deputies were clearly incapable of regaining their resolution after the explosion of popular anger.

> The cries of the crowd were heard: 'Down with the thieves!' And at this moment the deputies had but one concern: to close the session and flee (. . .) But when they heard the angry cries of the people at the threshold of their cavern, they recoiled and, once again, lay low.[78]

On a wider scale, the revolt of the people symbolized a rejection of the entire political regime. While Charles Maurras drew his customary distinction between the *pays légal* of the parliamentary system and the *pays réel* of the street, Pierre Gaxotte maintained in *Je suis partout* that 'this bloody week reveals—and how!—the complete divorce between the nation and the regime.'[79] If the anger of the demonstrators against the regime seemed fully justified, however, their violence posed a greater challenge. Clearly, no group was prepared to take responsibility for the full extent of the violence witnessed in the streets of Paris—and in this sense, the actual behaviour of the crowd jarred particularly sharply with their depiction in subsequent accounts. Pierre Gaxotte refused to accept that the demonstrators had fired on the police rather than *vice versa*, and *Je suis partout* drew a careful distinction between the patriotic associations demonstrating their legitimate dissatisfaction with the regime and the bands that later roamed the streets, the latter conveniently characterized as 'professional rioters, eager to pillage and steal.'[80] Such disorder was even attributed to Léon Blum, portrayed as in close contact with and thus capable of mobilizing the more sinister elements of the population.[81] Yet not all violence was as resolutely denied. Action Française and the Solidarité Française were prepared to accept at least some of the aggression as evidence of the energy and fervency of the demonstrators. The former celebrated the incandescent anger of the people and particularly praised their attacks on the firemen, drenched with their own hoses.[82] The latter sought to legitimize street violence by encompassing it within the scope of a wider revolutionary movement.

> The parliamentary system, in the form in which it has functioned for almost half a century, expired on 6 February. The system was overthrown in the course of a magnificent revolutionary movement, an expression of an effectively unanimous popular rejection of party politics in France.[83]

Indeed, the apparent collapse of parliament's representative ability was seen to justify all action taken against it. The demonstration of 6 February not only revealed the depth of division between parliament and the people, but its consequences suggested that the people were by far the more powerful of the two forces. Not one cabinet but two fell in rapid succession, seemingly unable to withstand the strength of popular anger and street politics. According to Gaxotte, this was a definitive end to the illusion that the *pays légal* remained capable of governing and representing the people. 'Thus,' he observed with evident satisfaction, 'is sovereign parliament humbled before its master.'[84]

   Right-wing determination to represent the demonstrators of 6 February as the people of Paris, legitimately and consciously opposing Parliament, meant according a very different status to the Communist and Socialist demonstrators of the following days. Since these demonstrators were naturally portrayed as the people of Paris by left-wing supporters and participants, their numerical and symbolic significance had consequently to be undermined. The leagues therefore attempted to represent them as disorderly, misguided, and lacking in conviction. The participation of Communist veteran soldiers, side by side with members of the leagues and in common opposition to the parliamentary regime, was conveniently forgotten. If Communists were present on 6 February, they argued, then it was as elements of disorder, seeking to profit from the revolutionary atmosphere of the demonstration to accomplish their own sinister ends. While honest demonstrators were falling as martyrs on the Place de la Concorde, Communists were allegedly operating without restraint on the adjoining Rue de Rivoli, overturning cars, cutting gas cables, and starting fires. Furthermore, in symbolic gestures of unpatriotic defiance, they were also attempting to wrench the statue of Joan of Arc from its pedestal in the Place Saint-Augustin and to mutilate statues in the Jardin des Tuileries.[85] Numerically, the later Communist and Socialist demonstrations were described as scarcely meriting consideration. Georges Gaudy reported to *Action Française* that the Communist demonstration of 9 February was so poorly attended that he remained doubtful of having correctly located the demonstrators. 'Perhaps they transferred the main body of their supporters to some other point in the capital?' he suggested. 'On the telephone, I hear that they are burning churches, plundering the Rue de Rivoli, and terrifying the Bastille quarter.'[86]

The large-scale strike and demonstration of 12 February posed a more difficult question of representation. *Action Française* did argue that the strike was not as general as had been intended, but its principal criticism of the strike was that, being largely supportive of the corrupt parliamentary regime, it could not therefore reflect the true voice of the people. If it received support from an undeniably large number of workers—who constituted a part, although not the whole, of the people—this could be explained by the domineering trade-union directives, and was not therefore indicative of the workers' political sympathies. It was a disgrace, observed Pierre Gaxotte, to take advantage of trade-union membership in order to muster working-class support for a decadent parliamentary system.[87] Charles Maurras adopted a similarly critical and paternalistic stance. 'If one enumerates the few thousand workers and employees who have been morally obliged to refuse the service they owe to the state and to society,' he wrote, 'one's heart is heavy with pity.'[88]

For members and partisans of the right-wing leagues, the demonstrations of early February 1934 therefore represented a popular rejection of parliamentary corruption, justified in its anger and energy. The demonstrations of the left—despite evident numerical strength—were concomitantly denied any popular roots. The right clearly struggled with the difficulty of imposing such images on a chaotic and violent situation, and was indeed divided in its opinion of the legitimacy of street violence. Within the extreme right, the group that remained most self-consciously aloof from the violence of the street was Colonel de la Rocque's Croix de Feu, also separate from the other demonstrators on 6 February. La Rocque, fearing that his own imprisonment would deprive the movement of its necessary leadership, was anxious to emphasize the self-discipline of his supporters: although admitting that 140 members of his league had been injured, he insisted that they had remained separate from the more violent elements of the crowd. He even claimed that one of his three formations had remained in the Place de la Concorde with the express (though vain) hope of keeping order.[89] This determination to retain complete control over his movement at the expense of broader right-wing unity was to be a characteristic stance in the years ahead.

The challenge for the left, meanwhile, was to underline the 'fascist' intentions of the leagues and to present the mass demonstration of 12 February as the definitive rejection of fascism by the French people. Even the Radicals, largely distanced from and critical of street militancy, were nonetheless conscious of the urgency of this battle for popular representation. Radical newspapers such as *La Lumière* and *L'Ère Nouvelle* differed in their presentation of 6 February, but shared common ground in their portrayal of the 'republican' reaction of the following week. *L'Ère nouvelle* blamed the riot of 6 February on the 'white Communards' of the Hôtel de Ville (Paris's right-wing municipal councillors), and suggested that their fomentation of general dissatisfaction was closely linked to Hitler's intended domination of European capitals.[90] Albert Bayet, one of the modernizers in the Radical Party, was more conciliatory in *La Lumière*, recognizing that many of the demonstrators were 'fine folk, indignant, just as we are, at the Stavisky scandal', and that their reaction could be assimilated into the general and justifiable outrage of the 'honest people'. He also suggested that such reactions had been manipulated by a minority intent on a genuine *coup d'état*.[91] Both *La Lumière* and *L'Ère nouvelle* presented the mass demonstrations of 12 February as evidence that the workers (and the French people more generally) were united in their opposition to fascism and in their defence of republican institutions. *L'Ère nouvelle* contended that the general strike was devoid of the class-based, collectivist aspirations of its pre-war counterparts; *La Lumière* portrayed the movement as a laudable citizen reaction to the fascist menace—although Bayet did recommend that popular grievances be expressed within the republican system, preferably through the ballot box and in public meetings.[92]

The possibilities for left-wing unity at this stage should not be over-played, for the Communists and the CGTU criticized the Socialists and the CGT for their alleged distance from the masses and for their treach-erous support of parliamentary democracy,[93] and the Radicals remained sharply divided in their response to the demonstrations. But Socialists and Communists nonetheless echoed some of the themes expressed in Radical newspapers, notably a castigation of the right-wing leagues as an unrepresentative, fascist minority, and the equation of left-wing occu-pation of the streets with the resounding voice of the people against fascism.

First and foremost, both Communists and Socialists endeavoured to undermine the suggestion of right-wing tendencies among the peo-ple. Forging the myth of the fascist *coup d'état*, *Le Populaire* described the demonstration of 6 February as 'a genuine riot, premeditated, care-fully and methodically organized by the fascist formations. It is an armed conspiracy against the republican regime.'[94] The demonstrators were, for the Socialists, a mobilized and violent minority, spurred on by the nationalist and fascist press, and unrepresentative of popular sentiment. For the Communists, fascism was equally evident in the Daladier government, which they blamed for firing on a crowd in which they themselves had been present.[95] Claims by either the gov-ernment or the leagues to represent the people were taken as an insult to the true people of the French capital. 'Topaze taking to the streets (...) to save Chiappe,' exploded *Le Populaire*: 'is that the people of Paris?'[96] A few days later, Léon Blum described the forthcoming left-wing demonstrations as a resounding rejection of such suggestions. 'We invite the workers to a demonstration of their strength,' he wrote in *Le Populaire* on 11 February, in anticipation of the general strike and mass demonstration. 'We ask them to prove to the whole of France that there is more to Paris than the storm troops of the royalists and fascists.'

Consequently, Communist and Socialist accounts emphasized the numerical importance of their own supporters to legitimize their claim to the people. The crowd of 9 and 12 February was referred to both as 'the masses' and 'the people'; its vastness was one of its most positive attributes. As in the right-wing press, these people were compared to the sea in their strength and grandeur.

When the sound of the *Internationale* arises, proclaimed by tens of thousands of human beings, this really is the sound of the great voice of the people that the poets have compared to that of the sea.[97]

Thus was the street reclaimed from the so-called men of order who imposed their will by means of terror and violence, while the humiliation of a (transitory) 'fascist' domination of Paris was effaced by the reassuring presence of the true people. 'The people of Paris are not the seditious band that surged, howling, across the Place de la Concorde,' insisted *Le Populaire* after the successful demonstration of 12 February.

> The people of Paris—the real people—have rediscovered themselves. They have been masters of the street for the entire afternoon. And they have behaved with a dignity and a majesty that elicited admiration even from their adversaries. No crowd control was visible during this unique demonstration, other than that provided by the workers themselves.[98]

These people were furthermore described as representing a wider working people. *L'Humanité* emphasized the worldwide significance of the French workers' courageous anti-fascism, publishing a letter in praise of 12 February which was signed by the leaders of the international workers' movement.[99] The Communists also emphasized the variety of the demonstrators, who included Algerian workers as well as working-class inhabitants of the east of Paris and the proletarian suburbs. Reactions in the provinces were described as mirroring those in the capital, and *L'Humanité* praised 'the vigorous, ardent, quasi-spontaneous protest of the labouring masses against the fascist bands and firing-squad government.'[100] Both Communists and Socialists were keen to emphasize the fundamental solidarity of urban and rural people against the fascist minority, with the Communists praising the united proletariat and the Socialists lauding the final triumph of democratic and socialist ideas in the provinces after 60 years of the Third Republic.[101] The image of the demonstration as expressing the sentiments of the entire people was further reinforced by descriptions of more general sympathy. In its monthly publication *Le Travailleur Parisien*, the CGT concluded with pride that 'our general strike movement has been welcomed sympathetically by the majority of the population.'[102] Likewise, the procession organized for 17 February to commemorate those who had died in the demonstrations was described as uniting both spectators and participants. 'Sympathizers crowded the pavements along the path of the demonstration, three or four rows deep,' reported *L'Humanité*. 'Today, we can say that everyone wanted to be in the street.'[103] The photographs accompanying these descriptions offer a similar impression: the demonstrators appear as a dense, united mass of supporters, whereas images of the leagues depict isolated incidents rather than suggesting the overall number of people involved.

As would be expected, the people portrayed by the Socialists and Communists in 1934 were more narrowly defined in class terms than the people of the leagues. The PCF and the SFIO shared in the conviction that fascism was a bourgeois phenomenon incapable of attracting the workers, and intent on destroying working-class movements and liberties. And if fascism was perceived to be fundamentally opposed to the workers, then it was the workers who should counter its threat. These workers were also encouraged to act in solidarity with intellectuals and the lower middle classes. Describing the success of 12 February, *L'Humanité* observed that workers, civil servants, and the lower middle classes had shared in 'a united front of action';[104] and that the demonstrations had served as a powerful impetus for solidarity and the recognition of a common enemy. The PCF deputy André Marty also mentioned the supportive presence of intellectuals in the demonstration of 12 February, including the writers André Malraux, Jean Guéhenno, and Jean-Richard Bloch.[105] These workers included old and young, men as well as women; indeed, the participation of women in the demonstration of 12 February was particularly praised. 'Women, workers and housewives,' reported *L'Humanité*, 'are there in their thousands!'[106] The importance of a visibly working-class opposition to fascism was further underlined when those attending the funerals of the 'martyrs' of the demonstrations were encouraged to come in working clothes.[107]

Socialists and Communists may have been divided among themselves, but they were nonetheless determined to portray the people as united, and believed that this unity was best forged in common action in the street. Although there was no description of the famous convergence between Socialists and Communists on the Cours de Vincennes, *L'Humanité* did stress that workers in the demonstration were drawn together without distinction of allegiance. *Le Populaire*, aware of the divisions between the rival factions, also emphasized this grass-roots unity.

Socialists, communists, members of the united workers' party [Parti d'Unité Prolétarienne], Trotskyists, all were fraternally united, arm in arm and with a single song rising from this great wall of chests, an invincible rampart against the enemies of the labouring class. It was *L'Internationale*, the song of a class in complete communion, sharing the same hope and the same desire for battle.[108]

If this was a united people, it was also a disciplined one. *L'Humanité* angrily rejected allegations that the Communists had set fire to shops on 6 February, and insisted that this was far more likely to have been the Jeunesses Patriotes. Reacting against the image of the demonstrators as an unruly mob, both Communist and Socialist leaders depicted their 'people' as orderly and self-disciplined in their actions. Paul Faure, General Secretary of the SFIO, insisted that the people were far too politically conscious to be the dupes of the reactionary press, and that they were able to act rationally and independently. 'The people appreciate the nature and extent of the dangers that threaten them,' he insisted. 'They won't be easily fooled.'[109]

These disciplined, orderly people were not necessarily seen by Communists and Socialists to be fulfilling the same goals. Certainly, both parties shared in the rhetoric of a working-class march to power, but the common rhetoric concealed contrasting interpretations of action to be adopted and enemies to be confronted. The Socialists and the CGT, who believed fascism to be represented primarily by the leagues, argued that it was through defence of the Republic that the people would best defend their liberties. *Le Populaire* called in general terms for 'all power to the workers!'[110] and Paul Faure described how, on 12 February, 'the people in the streets proclaimed their determination to smash the reaction and to ensure the onward march of the socialist proletariat.'[111] But it was not clear how—or whether—these revolutionary aspirations were realizable in the current situation. Republican loyalty remained uppermost: the CGT described the demonstrators as 'the people, nourished by the principles of 1789, attached to democratic liberties',[112] while Léon Blum announced in the Chamber of Deputies that 'the people who created the Republic will know how to defend it.'[113] Communist accounts, while sharing a similar rhetoric, offered greater conviction in the potential of the people as the revolutionary proletariat. For as far as the PCF was concerned, not even democracy and the Republic were free from the corruption of fascism, and the only solution was to fight for a worker and peasant government. Indeed, the front page of *L'Humanité* on 7 February called for action against both parliament and Republic, while Socialists and CGT leaders were described as traitors in the ongoing class struggle, proposing class collaboration rather than the necessary unity of the proletariat.[114] Within this context, the Communist people of 12 February were not fighting in defence of the Republic, but rather against it.

Yesterday was the triumph of the united action of the Parisian proletariat, rising up not to defend the bourgeois Republic as in the time
of the Dreyfus Affair, but to prepare the overthrow of corrupt democracy by the true Republic of the working-class and peasant people, by
the Soviet Republic of France.[115]

Similarly, the speech at the funerals of the February 'martyrs' by the
Communist senator and director of *L'Humanité* Marcel Cachin captured
the evolving significance of the people in the street. On the day of the
funeral, he observed critically that the Republic had never succeeded in
preventing the deaths of innocent workers, and paid homage to the dead
of 6 and 9 February as victims of an ongoing class struggle. He deemed
their burial in the Père-Lachaise cemetery near their fellow victims of
the Commune particularly appropriate, discerning strong echoes of the
Commune in the supposedly revolutionary intentions of the proletariat
of 1934. After the funeral, he went on to describe the worker-victims as
martyrs for the cause of Soviet France, and by 18 February 1934 he was
seeking to convince his readers that the one million demonstrators of
12 February had intended to replace the French Republic with a Soviet
one.[116]

What had become clear from the demonstrations of 6–12 February
1934 was that the crowd, however violent, chaotic, and difficult to
identify with a single image or assimilate within a reassuring narrative,
was nonetheless central to the battle to imagine and claim the people.
This image of the people in the street could be manipulated for diverse
and contradictory purposes, and in the contemporary climate of fear
and opposition, it was undeniably powerful. A series of demonstrations
had thus transformed the nature and structure of political conflict. For
the right, 6 February was a moment of symbolic domination of the public space; for Socialists and Communists it was a further indication that
the battle for the people would take place in the street.

But if this battle would be won in the street, it would not be won
through numerical strength alone. The politics of the street was important, but so too was the politics of representation. Participants in the
demonstrations could and did represent their own motivations, but
they were not the only ones to do so, and once the performance was
over these actors could not necessarily control the critics' responses.
The masses in the street might parade, protest, shout, or fight, but they
spoke with a multitude of often conflicting voices, and it required some
form of representation for the voice of a single 'people' to be heard.
Indeed, participants themselves were keenly aware of the role of the

press in mobilizing demonstrators and in directing public opinion after the event. On 11 February the CGT's building co-operatives sent an open letter to the premier, claiming that the demonstration of 6 February and the subsequent fear and disorder were a conspiracy of the so-called 'national' Parisian press. The press, they claimed, had so terrorized public opinion that it drew an unusual number of Parisians into the streets on the evening of 6 February, and the same press had then transformed this affluence into evidence of a deliberate attempt by the Parisian people to overthrow the parliamentary regime.

The press, although despised by the entire people and ignored at election time, has played its orchestrated part with unusual skill: by drawing fifty thousand spectators to watch a bloody riot, it has convinced observers in France and across the world that the people of Paris have ousted Daladier and Frot, and created the conditions for a fascism unforeseen in Rome or Berlin.[117]

Without the decisive role of the press, they claimed, few would have believed that the people of Paris were seriously attempting to undermine the Republic, and even the violence of the demonstration would have held no lasting significance. This distorting power and influence was equally feared by the right. When commemorating the demonstration of 6 February two years later in 1936, Colonel de la Rocque described it as a noble occasion on which the citizens of the capital had expressed their dissatisfaction with the corruption of the current regime. The fear and apprehension that the events seemed to have unleashed in public opinion were, he claimed, entirely the fault of the press, which had misled the people of Paris and the provinces by portraying the occasion as an attempted fascist coup.[118]

In the climate of latent and overt aggression in 1934, the February demonstrations developed into the founding myths of the years to follow: the myth of a failed fascist coup and that of a frustrated attempt at Soviet revolution. For the future Popular Front, 12 February became in retrospect the founding moment of the new movement, with the inconsistencies and divisions of the time carefully glossed over. Annual commemorations provided an opportunity to bring the people once more into the street and to reflect on the relevance of 12 February 1934 to the current situation. (For the PCF, this meant denying their participation on 6 February and carefully downplaying their vociferous opposition to the Republic in early 1934.) Meanwhile, the leagues and their conservative sympathizers elevated the victims of 6 February

1934 to the rank of 'martyrs' of the right, their sacrifice symbolically associated with the battlefields of the First World War. As the municipal councillor Jean Ferrandi wrote in *L'Ami du Peuple*:

> Paris of 6 February, Paris of our beautiful young generation which, ardent, patriotic, and disinterested, went to its death on the Place de la Concorde as zealously as its elders in the mutilated woods of Verdun, you must remain watchful and vigilant. France will have need of you.[119]

This image of sacrifice heightened the eagerness of those united in patriotic sentiment to continue the battle. Jean Renaud, leader of the Solidarité Française, described 6 February 1934 one year later as the symbolic beginning of the national revolution that the SF was now preparing, supported by 'the healthy mass of the people'. In commemoration of the 'martyrs', he even opened the meeting by calling the names of the dead, and to the name of each victim the executive committee responded with 'fallen on the field of honour.'[120] The voices of those who had sacrificed their lives in patriotic protest against corruption should not, they believed, be allowed to fall silent.

In search of fraternity

The demonstrations of 6–12 February and their subsequent representations as the 'voice of the people' suggested more than a transitory dissatisfaction with the current parliament, or even with the corruption so decried in the press. They suggested a heightened popular desire for political participation, and a consequent need for new organizations outside or above existing parties. They also suggested the importance of the demonstration itself as a form of political renewal. Both Emmanuel Berl and Jean-Richard Bloch, writers and journalists who kept a watchful eye on political developments in these troubled days, remarked on the significance of the demonstration as a mark of the people's return to politics. According to Bloch, the French people had been 'chloroformed' by their victory in the First World War and were only now awakening to the need for political involvement: the crowd of 12 February thus represented 'the "people-king" reclaiming his kingdom.' Since the War, Bloch argued, only the Camelots du Roi and the Communist Party had maintained any sustained presence in the streets, so this mass participation was decidedly novel.[121] Emmanuel Berl, director of the weekly *Marianne*, similarly described the recent demonstrations as the

first time in 15 years that the people had reacted to politics *en masse*.[122]
For both writers, this popular reaction confirmed the divorce between
the nation and the Chamber of Deputies and the need for 'groups and
organisms that are more vigorous, more flexible, capable of modelling
themselves in response to the renewed energy of a country in the throes
of resurrection.'[123]

The form of this popular reaction against parliament was as important
as its content, and indeed the two were seen to be largely inseparable.
Recent research on the demonstration and the festival has emphasized their importance as an alternative form of politics.[124] Jean-Richard
Bloch and Emmanuel Berl thought likewise. For Berl, the irony of these
days of violent unrest was that they represented a profound search for
fraternity.

> let us not be mistaken, beneath the furious shouts of the crowd
> in these days of rioting there was a primary and pressing need for
> mutual affection.
>   To be convinced of this, one needed only to see a few groups of
> demonstrators, to see these young people pressed against each other,
> not really knowing what they wanted, not really knowing why they
> had come together, and yet happy all the same to be together—and
> perhaps, as indignant as they were, happy that their new friend-
> ship was sealed through common sacrifice and common bloodshed,
> because it is the sad law of humanity that fraternity can be sealed
> only with blood.[125]

Bloch, meanwhile, described the sense of common purpose and the
spontaneity of the demonstration as encapsulating the resurgence of the
medieval festival: a response to profound human needs left unfulfilled
by the sterile political liturgy of the Third Republic. The French had
become increasingly urban and secular, no longer accustomed to the
regulation of life by the cycles of the religious or agricultural year, and
largely deprived of the alternation of the existing order with moments of
ritualized subversion. Carnival was dead, said Bloch, and yet the human
need for carnival remained, leading to its rebirth in new and unexpected
forms, as men sought the necessary balance to order and isolation in
collective action.

> When a militant speaks to us of strikes, when the whole of Italy
> awaits a movement of the *ferrovieri*, I experience that 'commotion
> of unanimity'—to borrow a phrase from Jules Romains—which is the

necessary mark of a public festival, and which makes a festival the younger but consanguine sister of Revolution.[126]

Nevertheless, even if the sense of fraternity of a strike or riot fulfilled a need unmet by the parliamentary regime, it was unclear how this transient experience might form the basis of a new political system. Could the common purpose of a march against corruption or fascism be translated into a more concrete desire for reform, or a durable form of political organization? This was to be the challenge faced by political groups both inside and outside Parliament in the wake of the February demonstrations.

In search of reform

With the new premier Gaston Doumergue (a retired politician suitably distanced from recent intrigue and corruption), reform seemed extremely likely. Doumergue's new government was greeted by Parliament with noisy applause,[127] and he presided over the appointment of a Commission for Reform within the Senate. Newspapers and learned journals devoted considerable space to the question of constitutional modification, which was also considered by its most habitually resolute opponents, notably the centre right and the Radicals. In June 1934 the Youth Estates General (États Généraux de la Jeunesse) held under the administrative guidance of the writer Jules Romains—to whose theories of unanimism Bloch had referred—revealed a surprisingly large consensus on the nature of the changes desired. The Estates included representatives from groups, parties, and trade unions across the political spectrum, from syndicalists and members of the Jeune République movement to Jeunesses Patriotes and members of the Croix de Feu. Their 'confused agreement', as François Monnet has termed it, was primarily negative: an opposition to the capitalist regime and to 'false democracy' and a desire for profound rather than moderate reform.[128] But the resulting 'Plan' of 9 July 1934 was more positive, demanding a stronger executive with extended powers to dissolve Parliament, a National Economic Council and a state-directed economy, and a transitional government leading to a Constituent Assembly. (The parliamentary regime was not considered capable of self-improvement.)

Why were these apparently popular reforms not realized? Doumergue, although committed to reform and eager to 'discuss' it with the French people through radio broadcasts that appeared to bypass parliamentary authority, considered his role a stabilizing rather than a revolutionary one. His primary goal was to restore order—in particular to address the national debt—rather than to seek deeper political renewal. There were also difficulties within the Chamber of Deputies. Discussions in the weeks and months following February 1934 were frank (even violent) in character, and revealed insuperable divisions between those committed to preserving the system in its current form and those who believed in a more radical departure—if only temporary—from democratic principles and practices. While the Communists described dictatorship as the only suitable response to the climate of the times, and interpreted the right-wing leagues as staunch defenders of the capitalist system,[129] socialists such as Léon Blum and René Brunet clung tenaciously to the democratic legality of the Third Republic.[130] Brunet in particular argued that voting full powers to the government to determine the budget—thus obviating the need for further debate in the Chamber—would 'deprive the nation of the powers of discussion, amendment and initiative which are the *raison d'être* of Parliament.'[131] It was a moot point whether exceptional measures could be justified by exceptional times.

The demonstrations of February 1934, bringing crowds into the streets and Parliament into disarray, signified a profound crisis of representation. To describe the clamour of the crowd as the voice of the people—a people united either against a corrupt parliamentary regime or against the threat of French fascism—challenged the representative status of the Chamber of Deputies and suggested a widespread search for political renewal. In the crowd, the demonstrators appeared to find a sense of common purpose, however transitory; to experience a sense of solidarity that responded to their desire for political involvement. But how was parliamentary politics to address the fracture between the people and their representatives? Could new formations, broader than existing parties, reach out and draw the people into politics, building on a transient sense of solidarity in the face of crisis? Was this fleeting fraternity an adequate basis for political organization? And how could the various portrayals of the people withstand the fundamental instability of the crowds themselves—diverse, spontaneous, and unpredictable as political actors? These were to be the challenges of 1934–36.

2
A Double Mobilization against the Established Disorder, 1934–36

Writing in exile in July 1935, the Comte de Paris observed with apprehension that the French were increasingly divided into two hostile fronts. The recent municipal elections had confirmed their growing disaffection with the parties of the centre, while the energetic mass meetings and demonstrations of extra-parliamentary movements testified to the growing strength of the Popular Front on the left, and the National Front (and related leagues) on the right. Yet the antagonistic rhetoric of these two fronts seemed to the Comte de Paris to belie a more complex situation. Similar figures could be found on both sides: unemployed workers, intellectuals, farmers, and shopkeepers, all victims of the Depression. And if the political grievances of left and right centred on capitalism and parliamentary corruption respectively, there was nonetheless a common search for a new order. With a certain pride, the Comte de Paris suggested that as a descendant of the conciliatory Henri IV he might be well-placed to pacify the warring factions, and added that the masses (*masses populaires*) were his particular concern. Were he permitted to return to France, he claimed that he would gladly seek employment in an automobile factory so as to deepen his understanding of the labouring people of France.[1]

This employment was a novel suggestion for a royal pretender, but the explicit concern of the Comte de Paris for the 'masses' was extremely astute. In the search for a new order following the crisis of representation of February 1934, the attraction, organization, and symbolic portrayal of the masses had become essential to political success. Political leaders, militants, and journalists observed with enthusiasm—or trepidation—the potential of the transient resolution and solidarity of the crowd to challenge existing institutions and cement new alliances.

Writers and journalists anticipated the formation of new movements that would compete with traditional parties to represent the voice of the people.

How did such new movements develop? This chapter explores the emergence of the two fronts to which the Comte de Paris referred in his interview of July 1935. It describes a double mobilization against the 'established disorder'[2] and examines how, as the importance of the centre declined, the emerging Popular Front and the right-wing leagues battled to define, organize, and depict the masses as a united people. For if February 1934 had revealed the fears of a divided generation, the years 1934–36 began to reveal its hopes. The Popular Front engaged with republican tradition to organize and present an active, rational, citizen people, capable of providing political impetus and direction. The right-wing leagues projected the image of a French people whose class differences were transcended by national fervour, and who sought a new order through the inspired leadership of an individual or group. And as the Comte de Paris had observed from his position of exile, the two sides were not content to develop essentially separate spheres of ideological influence and activity. Instead their attraction, organization, and portrayal of the people entailed a complex crossing of boundaries in terms of social appeal, strategies of organization, and political symbolism. By exploring these parallels, this chapter adds a further dimension to previous research on the years 1934–36, much of which either accords only brief attention to the political developments between February 1934 and the Popular Front's electoral victory,[3] or emphasizes the political and cultural development of the left at the expense of the right.[4] The chapter also builds on recent studies of the stage-management of the masses in contemporary Italy and Germany, where the potential of political ritual and demonstrations to transcend division and provide (transitory) unity was also recognized.[5] The real challenge in all cases was to stabilize these visions of unity: to prevent them from succumbing to the same transience for which they were supposed to compensate.

The masses: Image and association

February 1934 had revealed a heightened desire for popular participation in politics. The years 1934–36 witnessed a burgeoning of grass-roots movements on left and right in response to this desire, resulting in a noticeable shift towards political extremes at the expense of the centre. By May 1936, therefore, the Radicals were lamenting the demise of their influence and the declining strength of moderates in general.

> The current reality is this: as much in its town council as in its regional council and legislative representation, the Parisian region is represented by two large constituents: a reactionary constituent and a revolutionary one. The government of Paris and its suburbs is disputed by reactionaries and nationalists on one hand, Communists and Socialists on the other. Both elements have made progress, the first in 1928 and 1932, the second in 1934 and 1936. There are no longer any moderates, there are very few Socialist Republicans, and there are increasingly few Radicals.[6]

Political impetus appeared to have passed instead to those groups and parties in most active contact with the masses: the Popular Front movement, which by 1936 encompassed political, cultural, and trade-union associations, and the right-wing leagues, notably the rapidly expanding Croix de Feu.

The nature and focus of the rivalry between left and right was strongly determined by the dynamics of the Popular Front. Although the moment of grass-roots unity on 12 February 1934 has been portrayed in retrospect as the birth of the Popular Front, left-wing unity was by no means strong in early 1934, and the development of common action and alliances was a gradual process of the months that followed, not without its frictions and hesitations. In the wake of the February riots, the Communist (and future leader of the Parti Populaire Français) Jacques Doriot had suggested the creation of an anti-fascist committee uniting Communists, Socialists, and members of the CGT, but his suggestion was quashed, and in May 1934 Doriot himself was excluded from the Party. It was not until the PCF conference at Ivry the following month that a new line of action was proposed: the 'class against class' tactic of the 1920s was to be overruled, and Communists were to seek alliances with Socialists and other democrats to form a common front against fascism. Whether this new line was predominantly French or Soviet in inspiration has been much discussed:[7] certainly it was a dramatic volte-face, and there was much mutual suspicion and antipathy to overcome before such putative alliances could be realized. By the end of July 1934, PCF and SFIO leaders had agreed on a limited common strategy according to which they would abstain from mutual criticism and unite to oppose fascism and the decree laws of the Doumergue government. Forging an alliance with the Radicals was a still greater challenge. The PCF had noisily denounced Daladier for his complicity in the suppression of their February demonstrations, and viewed the Radicals as representing the individualistic bourgeoisie whose destruction was its avowed goal. Such explicit threats to the social order did not endear the Communists to the Radicals, who were also deeply suspicious of the PCF's apparent subservience to Stalin. The Radicals were, however, divided—and it was upon these divisions that the Communists were to play in securing the Radicals' eventual support for the formation of a broad-based Popular Front movement. While Édouard Herriot was favourable to participation in right-wing governments, Édouard Daladier was known to be more sympathetic to left-wing unity, and it was with Daladier that members of the PCF and CGTU met in October 1934, while at the same time proposing the idea of a 'Popular Front' in the Communist daily *L'Humanité*. From May 1935 onwards, impressed by left-wing successes in municipal elections and by Stalin's approval of national defence at the time of the Franco-Soviet pact, the Radicals began to participate more actively in the creation of anti-fascist, left-wing unity. On 18 June, Daladier met with Léon Blum and Maurice Thorez to discuss the common concerns of the Popular Front movement. On 19 June, Édouard Herriot agreed that the Radical party should participate in a show of left-wing solidarity for the celebration of 14 July, and on 21 June the Comité de Rassemblement Populaire (the co-ordinating association of the Popular Front) held its first meeting. The situation was full of contradictions: Herriot and his colleagues were ministers in a coalition government while simultaneously supporting a movement of opposition; Radicals, Communists, and Socialists supported a Popular Front while adopting very different interpretations of its purpose. For the Radicals, it was primarily a defence of liberties against fascism; for Socialists and Communists it encapsulated the potential for social change. Nonetheless, the success of the 14 July celebrations and the palpable enthusiasm for left-wing unity soon led to discussions of common programmes, even of common government. And the appeals to the people in rhetoric and association fuelled the continuing adaptation of the extreme right to the demands of mass politics. While the Popular Front reached out to the middle classes, the leagues intensified their appeals to the workers, and both movements focused closely in their rhetoric on the economic instability affecting the working masses. Both movements also sought to develop their structures of organization and their links with writers and intellectuals.

For the Popular Front, the substantiation of their claim to the people in 1934–36 entailed the transformation of an essentially working-class movement of opposition into a broad-based defence of republican values and parliamentary democracy, with the rapid development of new strategies and spaces for popular representation. As it evolved, the Popular Front that had first united Socialists and Communists before also encompassing the Radical Party began to expand its appeal from the proletariat to an anti-fascist working people. While the discourse of class struggle remained prominent, particularly in *L'Humanité* and *Le Populaire*, this was supplemented by a more broadly based image of the united working people. Victims of the Depression, these working people were portrayed as united in their suffering and anxiety, whether employed in Paris or the provinces,[8] in manual or intellectual work, and whether or not they were already involved in political or trade-union organizations. The organization of the masses in the face of the fascist threat was likewise an important goal for the CGT. As the CGT bulletin *Le Travailleur parisien* explained:

> When we talk of the masses, we are thinking not only of the workers grouped in our unions, the unions of the CGTU, and the political parties of working-class orientation. We also have in mind those millions of workers, manual and intellectual, urban and rural, whose sympathy and adhesion is essential for any social transformation.
>
> These masses are not yet organized. Generally lacking in associative life, they are extremely vulnerable, deeply affected by the Depression, and profoundly discontented. They do not seek to explain the impotence of traditional political parties: they merely observe the fact. These masses know what they dislike, but not yet what they desire.
>
> The goal in this famous competition between fascism and ourselves is to make the masses conscious of their desires, and so attract them to our ranks.[9]

This significant change in emphasis from the proletariat to the whole working people (including some of the middle classes) was accompanied by rapidly evolving structures of organization. For if the Popular Front was to claim to represent the entire working people and to aspire to an image of legitimacy and respectability, then it needed to expand and consolidate its support through mass meetings and associations, as well as in the encouragement of wider sympathy for the movement. In this context, particular efforts were made to attract young men and women. The Jeunesses Communistes, characterized in the 1920s by their aggressive revolutionary rhetoric, now diverted their virulence into an equally fervent anti-fascism. An all-female association known as the Jeunes Filles de France offered a forum for women's activity that rejected the androgynous image of the *militante*, characteristic of the Jeunesses Communistes in the 1920s. It encouraged women to share in the preoccupations of their non-Communist sisters by offering cookery and needlework lessons, and founded a magazine, *Jeunes Filles de France*, that was almost indistinguishable from other women's magazines of the day.[10]

At the same time, increasing interaction between writers, intellectuals, and the Popular Front both broadened support and also offered new possibilities for the representation of the people. The PCF was especially concerned to secure the allegiance of writers and intellectuals, whether or not they subscribed fully to Communist doctrine,[11] and a common anti-fascism and concern for the people certainly did much to secure this growing solidarity. As a political alliance, the Popular Front was by 1935 supported by a number of newspapers and periodicals, notably Jean Guéhenno's *Europe*, Henri Barbusse's *Monde*, and the weekly *Vendredi*, which claimed to represent intellectuals from the pro-Communist André Gide to the neo-Thomist Jacques Maritain.[12] The Popular Front movement also included a number of artistic associations founded on the principles—then compatible—of pacifism and anti-fascism. Particularly influential were the Association des Écrivains et Artistes Révolutionnaires (AEAR), the Maisons de Culture, and the Comité de Vigilance des Intellectuels Anti-Fascistes (CVIA). The AEAR had been founded in 1932 in opposition to bourgeois culture, but in 1934 opened its ranks to all anti-fascist writers, among them Jean Giono, André Malraux, Jean Guéhenno, André Chamson, and Julien Benda. From then on the aims of the AEAR reflected the aspirations of the Popular Front, and focused less on the art of revolution than on the encounter between a culturally disenfranchised people and their national heritage, believed to be the most effective means of protecting them against fascism. In 1935, the AEAR established a series of Maisons de Culture to provide the focal points for cultural activity on a local level; the Paris Maison de Culture was directed by the Communist and surrealist Louis Aragon. Aragon believed firmly in the importance of a shared culture in creating a united people: it was necessary, he said, to encourage common action between intellectuals, workers and the petty bourgeoisie, to allow intellectuals to share their knowledge of culture, and workers to share their experience of industrial life.[13] A similar motivation inspired the creation of the CVIA, whose first public declaration was a manifesto to the workers on 5 March 1934.[14] Here too, the desire for interaction between intellectuals and the working people was extremely strong. Within a few weeks, the association had more than 2000 adherents, including university professors, writers, scientists, journalists, and members of political parties, and was declared by its leaders to be 'at the service of workers' organizations'.[15] The association reached out to social groups believed to be targeted by fascist propaganda, publishing brochures such as *Le Fascisme et les paysans* and *La Jeunesse devant le fascisme*.[16] Like the AEAR, the CVIA also played a guiding role in the organization of Popular Front demonstrations. Both associations belonged to the Comité de Rassemblement Populaire, the co-ordinating committee of the Popular Front that brought together more than 100 political and social associations by the end of 1935.[17]

Meanwhile, the Popular Front's concern to represent the people was also evident in the increased use of documentary and propaganda films. Marceau Pivert, the notoriously outspoken leader of the Socialist Federation of the Seine, assembled his own film crew in order to record and publicize Popular Front activity such as the 1 May demonstrations of 1935.[18] Paul Faure, General Secretary of the SFIO, even suggested that a victorious Popular Front in the elections of 1936 should transform the cinema into a state institution: it was too powerful a means of propaganda to remain autonomous. Supporters of the Popular Front also established the Independent Cinema Alliance, and at the end of 1935 the PCF began to organize the shooting of *La Vie est à nous*, a propaganda film intended for its forthcoming election campaign. Jean Renoir was one of the directors, and had already indicated his sympathy for the Popular Front in *Le Crime de M. Lange*, an upbeat tale of the solidarity between workers and intellectuals in the struggle against an unscrupulous capitalist (exuberantly played by Jules Berry).[19] With a script by Jacques Prévert and actors from the October Group, the film satirized Prévert's customary targets of the Police, the Army, and the Church, and was, according to *L'Humanité*, 'a rough and ready tale, yet always cheerful and optimistic.'[20]

While the Popular Front was expanding its networks of popular support and its forms for representing the people, the leagues of the right were undergoing a parallel transformation—and one that has generally received much less attention. February 1934 had demonstrated to the extra-parliamentary right, as to the left, the supreme importance of common action and new strategies in increasing and consolidating popular support. Thus while the Communist, Socialist, and eventually Radical parties were joining forces in the Popular Front, some of the right-wing leagues—the Jeunesses Patriotes, Action Française, and the Solidarité Française—were combining forces within the National Front, formed in

May 1934 for the celebration of the festival of Joan of Arc. This National Front was grounded in fervent patriotism and an equally fervent opposition to the doctrines of class struggle and revolution proposed by the left.[21] Yet in parallel to the Popular Front, it was the more moderate movements that were increasing most rapidly in size and influence. Conspicuously absent from the National Front was La Rocque's Croix de Feu (despite Marshal Lyautey's initial support for the Front, and La Rocque's respect for Lyautey's judgement). Although there was considerable grass-roots enthusiasm for common action—and indeed Croix de Feu members often participated in demonstrations with members of other leagues—La Rocque nonetheless preferred to retain complete control over his movement, for he suspected that his league would be weaker within a broader right-wing formation.[22] And it was the Croix de Feu that was achieving the most notable successes, attracting many new members while some of the other leagues, notably the Solidarité Française, were becoming more marginal.[23] By April 1936 La Rocque was claiming a million supporters, and the Croix de Feu had established a strong base in Paris, as well as in Lille, Lyons, and Marseilles. It was also powerful in northern Catholic strongholds, as well as attracting approximately 14,000 recruits in Algeria by the summer of 1935.

Membership of the leagues was predominantly middle class: an analysis of Croix de Feu members in Nîmes in 1934 reveals, for example, an important majority of bankers, merchants, industrialists, and urban property owners.[24] But in the years 1934–36 they began increasingly to make appeals to the working classes, confronting the emerging Popular Front on its own territory. In November 1935, Jean-Pierre Maxence of the Solidarité Française emphasized, as did the Popular Front, that the proletariat and middle classes were united in their economic vulnerability, and similarly receptive to political propaganda.[25] M. Lauridan, also of the Solidarité Française, particularly underlined the need to attract the lower middle classes, and in so doing echoed Édouard Daladier's recent emphasis on the importance of representing the petty bourgeoisie, the contemporary face of the Third Estate of 1789.[26] Believing the current situation to be as potentially explosive as that of 1789 or 1793, Lauridan urged political leaders to rely on this contemporary Third Estate of shopkeepers and artisans as a 'regulating mass' that would save France from the revolutionary prospects of Popular Front rule.[27] Indeed, both the Popular Front and the leagues needed to obtain the support of workers and petty bourgeoisie alike if they were to provide a convincing claim to represent the entire people. In the case of the Popular Front, particularly the PCF, it was claims to the middle classes that provoked the greatest surprise. In the case of the leagues, claims to the workers were the most controversial. The leagues themselves were determined to challenge their stereotypes. As the Francistes argued in their manifesto:

> It is not true, as one says on the right, that we must oppose the left in its entirety, and protect ourselves from every aspect of its ideol ogy. It is also false, as one says on the left, that nationalists are all reactionaries and enemies of the people.[28]

In similar vein, the leader of the Solidarité Française (Jean Renaud) complained vociferously to the police of the violent Communist attacks on workers professing nationalist allegiances (and membership of his league).[29] Equally violent—although usually only verbal—attacks were made in Parliament, as Communist deputies berated the right for its allegedly outrageous claims to the workers. In July 1934, the Communist deputy André Marty upbraided municipal councillor Jean Ferrandi for the very suggestion that working-class support for right-wing movements might be genuine, and urged his own supporters to disrupt such occasions, especially the meetings of the Croix de Feu.

> Go to their meetings—why? So as to convince any workers who might have strayed into the Croix de Feu that it is nothing but fascist demagogy: to show them that they are in reality the pawns of capital, which aims only to turn them against their own class.[30]

In the light of these controversies, it is not surprising that both the Popular Front and the leagues regularly accused each other of hypocrisy in claiming closeness to the people. While *Le Populaire* ridiculed the popular pretensions of the Croix de Feu by depicting meetings taking place in luxurious chateaux,[31] *Le Flambeau* responded with sketches of Marxist militants in evening dress, keeping their battered caps and red scarves in the boots of their chauffeur-driven cars (Figures 4 and 5).[32]

It was not, of course, sufficient to claim to represent the people: this claim had to be substantiated by the creation and extension of forms of organization. The knowledge of and contact with social realities that this indicated was, according to La Rocque, the characteristic that distinguished the extra-parliamentary groups from their parliamentary counterparts, the latter irrevocably 'isolated from all contact with the people.'[33] His own group was the most successful in this structural transformation. Initially the right-wing leagues had a fairly narrow base, and were often most visible in the activity of small, militant groups. Such

— Pourquoi nous réunissons-nous toujours chez des châtelains !
— Pour bien prouver que nous sommes un mouvement populaire
et démocratique !

Figure 4 'At the Château of the Croix de Feu', *Le Populaire*, 15 July 1935 (Courtesy of the Bibliothèque Nationale, Paris).

groups were employed to put up posters around the capital, distribute tracts, and act as protection and crowd control at private meetings and at larger, public gatherings. This was the role of Action Française's notorious Camelots du Roi,[34] and also of Colonel de la Rocque's reserves (*dispos*), led by the chief propagandist for the movement, Paul Chopine, and his assistant Charles Vallin.[35] Characteristic of the Croix de Feu in the years 1934–35, however, was the rapid creation and expansion of other groups within the movement. As an elitist military association, the Croix de Feu certainly underscored the importance of guidance and leadership for the people. But in order to adapt to the changing political situation, the masses themselves needed also to be enlisted. In 1935, La

Figure 5 'Revolutionaries in dinner jackets', *Le Flambeau*, 2 February 1936 (Courtesy of the Bibliothèque Nationale, Paris).

Rocque lowered the membership fee so as to appeal more effectively to rural and urban workers,[36] and Communists alleged that in a number of Parisian factories, employment was conditional on immediate adhesion to the Croix de Feu (an allegation that even supporters of the league did not deny).[37] In parallel to the Croix de Feu and the Briscards, La Rocque also developed civilian groups involving not only men but also women and children. In particular, while military processions and commemorations tended to remain male-dominated, other processions and propaganda meetings came to involve both sexes. Photographs in *Le Flambeau* show men and women marching together in Joan of Arc processions and at propaganda meetings.[38] In 1934, the Section Féminine of the Croix de Feu was established with the impetus of the tireless Antoinette de Préval, and with the official leaders Marie-Claire de Gérus and Germaine Féraud.[39] (La Rocque's daughter Nadine also contributed devotedly to the social activities of the league before her death from typhus in August 1934 at the age of only 20.) New female members were asked to complete a form detailing their possible contributions to the movement, including bookkeeping, typing, delivery of letters and publicity, supervision of after-school activity, and work in the Croix de

Feu's soup kitchens.[40] These kitchens were central to the Mouvement Social des Croix de Feu[41] (sometimes referred to as the Mouvement Populaire des Croix de Feu).[42] Indeed, they became notorious on the left through the anarchist poet Jacques Prévert, whose satirical spoken chorus *Mange ta soupe et tais-toi*[43] instructed workers to consume the soup provided without swallowing any of the Croix de Feu's demagogic propaganda. Radical newspapers likewise featured cartoons of La Rocque in his soup kitchens, standing stiffly behind a large tureen and with a sword at his side.[44]

The Croix de Feu also encouraged the participation of children, both through the Fils et Filles des Croix de Feu and through the Cercle de moins de 16 ans, whose members were occasionally pictured in *Le Flambeau* performing exercises in disciplined formation.[45] La Rocque addressed meetings of his youthful supporters with speeches on French military and moral grandeur, and assured them that they should represent 'all of France: the old France of Clovis and Joan of Arc, as well as the France of Valmy and Verdun.'[46] The participation of children in the Croix de Feu movement was deliberately contrasted with the indoctrination of the young by the Popular Front. Thus, *Le Flambeau* of 22 February 1936 featured two photographs of children's activities under the headline 'Symbolic attitudes'. The children of the Croix de Feu were shown seated at a long table, obediently facing the camera and watched over by a row of neatly dressed Croix de Feu members, under the heading 'The Croix de Feu movement: reconciliation.' But the children of the Popular Front were pictured in chaos, shouting and raising their fists in a disorderly demonstration. 'The Popular Front: the school of hatred' was the provocative title.

Overall, the express aim of the Croix de Feu's civilian groups was to provide a new idealism for 'the healthy elements of the French people',[47] and by February 1935 La Rocque was claiming a total membership of 220,000, not including those under 16 or the 40,000 who belonged to the North African branch of the movement.[48] Indeed, membership was escalating so rapidly that he was obliged to organize a number of simultaneous mass meetings at different points in the capital,[49] and the front pages of *Le Flambeau* characteristically included a photograph of a vast, seated audience listening with rapt attention to a speech by one of its leaders.

Some studies of right-wing meetings and festivals tend to downplay their camaraderie and conviviality,[50] yet these characteristics were certainly present. Indeed, the argument that the activity of the right was restricted in this period to disciplined processions is belied by an increasing number of local fêtes, galas, and family celebrations. At the Centre National de la Cinématographie at Bois d'Arcy there is, for example, a little-known collection of silent films produced by the Croix de Feu that provides a fascinating glimpse into their activity in 1934–36. Here, the playful attitude of Croix de Feu members and supporters towards the camera is reminiscent of the spontaneity and humour often associated with participants in the fêtes and strikes of the Popular Front.[51] *Les Dispos de la dix-huitième arrondissement à Reims, le 14 avril 1935* features a group of young men in the leagues' characteristic berets and long coats: some deliberately hiding; one peering at the cameraman through binoculars. *Les Croix de Feu commémorent l'armistice, 1935* follows images of the military procession with those of the subsequent family picnic; young children of Croix de Feu members are seen chasing each other through a wood while a whole ox roasts in the background. These people are visibly not from the same social background as those who would attend the annual *Fête de l'Humanité* organized by the PCF at Garches, but this is not to deny that they came from the 'masses' to which both the Popular Front and the leagues were seeking to appeal.

The use of film to record the new spheres of activity of the Croix de Feu reveals a growing sense of the need to create and project an image of the people. Although very little is known about the Groupe Photo-Ciné des Croix de Feu, there is a small number of documents in the Police archives that describe the making or showing of the films now at the Centre National de la Cinématographie at Bois d'Arcy. Clearly these films were integrated into the social life of the movement. Although costly to produce (and there was no soundtrack for reasons of economy), they could be rented for a modest sum from the Propaganda Section to enliven local meetings.[52] In December 1935, a fund-raising fête at the Palais de la Mutualité featured dancing, conjuring, and the projection of a short film on the Croix de Feu.[53] But while these films appear to present a characteristic sample of Croix de Feu activities, they should not be taken entirely at face value, for some elaborate stage-management was also involved. One report of February 1936 describes, for example, how a group of Volontaires Nationaux assembled at the house of a wealthy patron, and were required, for the purposes of the film, to form a procession, sing *La Marseillaise*, and cry 'Vive la Rocque!' They then mimed their attendance at a meeting for the attendant film crew, who planned to show the short film of supposedly characteristic Croix de Feu activity at forthcoming events.[54]

More broadly, articles in *Le Flambeau* often addressed the question of French cinema—although they were often pessimistic, since the legacy of 'Papa Lumière' seemed to have passed to the Americans.[55] Jean Renaud of the Solidarité Française also recognized the importance of cinema as propaganda,[56] as did Action Française, whose meetings began to include the projection of films, as well as the more customary songs and revues of the Camelots du Roi.[57] On 3 April 1935, a meeting organized at the Mutualité (a sizeable meeting hall in the fifth *arrondissement* of Paris) featured *Le Sentiment populaire en monarchie*, a film which dealt explicitly with the role of the people in a monarchical regime, and also, more generally, with the relationship between the people and their leaders. Among the scenes of popular fervour was the image of a crowd of 60,000 workers acclaiming Hitler (greeted unfavourably by the Action Française spectators), the funeral of King Alexander of Yugoslavia, the coronation of Leopold III, and the marriage of the Duke of Kent. Naturally, the French monarchy was also included in this pageant of popular enthusiasm. The same evening included a documentary film, *La Croisère du Campana*, in which the Comte de Paris welcomed the Action Française leader Maurice Pujo on board his ship, and was depicted treating all his people with scrupulous courtesy.

> The prince was represented in different aspects of modern life: playing ping-pong, swimming with great proficiency, interested in the life of the sailors of the *Campana*; and finally receiving all passengers on board deck, making no distinction of class or opinion. This visit was followed by short speech by Maurice Pujo, then the prince expressed his appreciation, and shook the hands of those who, for him, represented the French people, 'his people'.
> M. Lucien Lacour explained that the passengers on board the *Campana* included people from all social classes: engineers, doctors, teachers, craftsmen, manual labourers, and employees.[58]

Artistic and fund-raising evenings organized by the leagues also included theatrical performances, whether by sympathetic actors from the Comédie-Française[59] or by their own members. One member of the Toulouse branch of the Croix de Feu performed songs and short plays about the First World War for members of the league in 1931,[60] while Parisian members of the Croix de Feu were offered reduced-price seats for the performances of *L'Heure H*, a comedy in three acts at the Théâtre de l'Humour.[61] Plays were likewise popular at the children's holiday camps which the Croix de Feu regularly organized.

A number of the leagues also endeavoured to create partisan and popular songs. Among the *Chants Francistes* was a *Chant des Travailleurs* dedicated to Marcel Bucard and encouraging the 'men of the factory and the countryside' to fight against Parliament and foreigners with equal determination, under the robust guidance of their leader

> Perjured tribunes and poor guides
> One day at last you'll understand
> That you have but to disappear
> In a regenerated land!
> With the people who now work
> If we must reach even to you
> The leader will direct the fight
> We'll follow him until it's through![62]

There is no indication of its relative success, although other nationalistic songs—such as the *Chant des Croix de Feu et des Volontaires Nationaux*—were reported by the police to be among the least popular in the 'Palace Chansons' on the Boulevard de Strasbourg. Unfortunately for the Croix de Feu, said the reporter, the clientele of the establishment were more enthusiastic about the latest popular successes, and thus 'the *Chant des Croix de Feu et Volontaires Nationaux* is not much in demand...'[63] (Figures 6a and 6b).

Participating in the creation of these images of the people were intellectuals, journalists, composers, and lyricists, as well as film and theatre directors. Narratives of the Popular Front sometimes assume its quasi-monopoly on intellectual support, and tend to play down or ignore rivalry with the right.[64] But the importance of intellectual support for the leagues and for the press of the extreme right should not be underestimated. La Rocque may have been less concerned to exalt intellectuals than to praise men of action such as Jean Mermoz (the popular hero and aviator who broke the world record for crossing the Atlantic in 1930), yet in 1934–36 *Le Flambeau* attracted a number of respected writers, and began to feature an increasing number of articles on film and theatre. Gabriel Boissy, editor of the theatrical review *Comœdia*, wrote regularly for *Le Flambeau* on the complex relations between politics and theatre, as well as writing the lyrics for the less than successful *Chant des Croix de Feu et des Volontaires Nationaux*. A collection of little-known pamphlets at the Bibliothèque Nationale also reveals that Colonel de la Rocque inspired lyric poetry, notably by George Henry (a keen Bonapartist, to judge from his other poetic works), and Gérard Jaussaud.[65] Inspired by

February 1934, Henry dedicated a lengthy poem to La Rocque in which he praised 'the Leader who, enfolded in the tricolour, will bring about a new and splendid dawn', while Jaussaud prefaced a series of his poems with quotations from La Rocque or *Le Flambeau*. Describing the disciplined 'people of Paris' who had attended the Croix de Feu's Joan of Arc

(a)

Figure 6 (a) and (b)   Chant des Croix de Feu et des Volontaires Nationaux (Courtesy of the Archives de la Préfecture de Police, Paris).

(b)

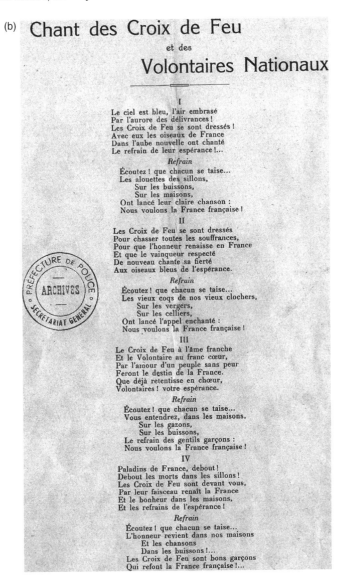

Chant des Croix de Feu

et des

Volontaires Nationaux

I

Le ciel est bleu, l'air embrasé
Par l'aurore des délivrances !
Les Croix de Feu se sont dressés !
Avec eux les oiseaux de France
Dans l'aube nouvelle ont chanté
Le refrain de leur espérance !...

Refrain

Écoutez ! que chacun se taise...
Les alouettes des sillons,
   Sur les buissons,
   Sur les maisons,
Ont lancé leur claire chanson :
Nous voulons la France française !

II

Les Croix de Feu se sont dressés
Pour chasser toutes les souffrances,
Pour que l'honneur renaisse en France
Et que le vainqueur respecté
De nouveau chante sa fierté
Aux oiseaux bleus de l'espérance.

Refrain

Écoutez ! que chacun se taise...
Les vieux coqs de nos vieux clochers,
   Sur les vergers,
   Sur les celliers,
Ont lancé l'appel enchanté :
Nous voulons la France française !

III

Le Croix de Feu à l'âme franche
Et le Volontaire au franc cœur,
Par l'amour d'un peuple sans peur
Feront le destin de la France.
Que déjà retentisse en chœur,
Volontaires ! votre espérance.

Refrain

Écoutez ! que chacun se taise...
Vous entendrez, dans les maisons,
   Sur les gazons,
   Sur les buissons,
Le refrain des gentils garçons :
Nous voulons la France française !

IV

Paladins de France, debout !
Debout les morts dans les sillons !
Les Croix de Feu sont devant vous,
Par leur faisceau renaît la France
Et le bonheur dans les maisons,
Et les refrains de l'espérance !

Refrain

Écoutez ! que chacun se taise...
L'honneur revient dans nos maisons
   Et les chansons
   Dans les buissons !...
Les Croix de Feu sont bons garçons
Qui refont la France française !...

Figure 6   (Continued).

procession, Jaussaud condemned the Communists' drunken reactions, and implied that they were unlikely to attract the true people of France. One of his longer poems described a Croix de Feu holiday camp and the conversion of a Communist worker by his son (the latter a beneficiary of the Croix de Feu's work of 'social reconciliation').[66] Other writers who contributed to *Le Flambeau* included members (or future members) of the Académie Française such as Henry Bordeaux, Jacques de Lacretelle, and Claude Farrère, as well as the popular novelist and historian André Maurois, the feminist writer Marcelle Tinayre, and the popular novelist Colette Yver.[67]

Charles Maurras—later to be admitted to the Académie Française—achieved a still wider intellectual radiance, and *Action Française* formed a generation of young right-wing writers.[68] Many of these—such as Robert Brasillach and his brother-in-law Maurice Bardèche—became journalists for the acerbic weekly newspaper *Je suis partout*, writing not only on political developments but also on film and theatre (on which they also published more widely).[69] *Je suis partout* likewise featured regular articles on film by Pierre Villette under the pseudonym 'Dorsay', as well as political reflections by the historian Pierre Gaxotte. It was the skill of these writers that rendered the virulence of the extreme-right press so potent, and so damaging to its victims—and these newspapers were moreover widely read. Indeed, it was in direct opposition to such publications as *Candide, Gringoire*, and *Je suis partout* that *Vendredi* was founded, aiming to offer an alternative, Popular Front perspective on politics and culture. Newspapers and periodicals of the opposing groups were often interdependent, with a high level of symbolic ripostes. In October 1935, for example, a manifesto published in *Gringoire* in favour of Mussolini's campaign in Ethiopia was met the following day by a counter-manifesto in *L'Œuvre*, for which Jules Romains enlisted the support of many intellectuals in the anti-fascist movement.[70]

The development of the Popular Front and the extra-parliamentary right in the years 1934–36 must be seen in the light of the dynamics between them. Both sought to appeal to the masses, transforming their organization as well as their forms of cultural representation in response to the changing political situation. While the balance of power was shifting to the left, partly on account of the greater cohesion and more effective mobilization of the nascent Popular Front, this should not obscure the uncertainty experienced by members of all groups and parties, and the evolving nature of ideological self-definition. Two parallel coalitions were emerging, each recognizing the need for the stage-management of the masses. And the rivalry between the opponents was to be found not only in their organization of private meetings and local sections, but also in a more direct confrontation over public and symbolic space.

The public space: Parades and demonstrations

The potential dangers of street politics were, as has been demonstrated, widely recognized. Successive coalition governments in 1934–36 endeavoured for this reason to restrict the role of the demonstration, and the decree law of 23 October 1935 confirmed that the law of 1880 concerning the illegality of street meetings was still in effect. Demonstrations, processions, and other gatherings remained conditional on the approval of the mayor (or Prefect, in the case of Paris), and applications for such approval needed to be made several working days in advance. Controversial demonstrations, and particularly those leading to counter-demonstrations, were likely to be refused permission.

Notwithstanding these restrictions, there were between February 1934 and May 1936 an estimated 936 demonstrations in the streets of Paris, approximately one-third of which were organized by the right.[71] In many cases, the demonstrations were carefully restricted to the traditional territories of left and right, and followed the paths of well-established commemorations and festivals. The spaces occupied by each group in its staging of the masses were in such cases very distinct.[72] In general, demonstrations of the right focused on the west of Paris and often led to the Arc de Triomphe, whereas those of the left were usually in the east.[73] The military leagues displayed their respect for sacrifice and the *Patrie* by assembling in the Place des Pyramides by the statue of Joan of Arc, or processing along the Champs-Élysées to pay homage to the Unknown Soldier. The Socialist and Communist parties showed their respect for sacrifice and the final goal of revolution by commemorating the *Communards* at the Mur des Fédérés in the Père-Lachaise cemetery, and remembered the assassination of Jaurès with a minute's silence outside the Panthéon.[74] The rivalry between the leagues and the Popular Front was thus frequently played out in the street, particularly in Paris, and both were proud to claim that they could take command of the street at a moment's notice. When on 8 July 1934 the Croix de Feu proposed to rekindle the commemorative torch at the Arc de Triomphe, the response of the Socialist and Communist Parties was immediately to organize a rival demonstration of their strength on the same day. 'Next Sunday, the Croix de Feu propose to take to the streets again,' declared the PCF deputy André Marty in Parliament. 'They will find themselves confronted by the workers!'[75] Similarly, the Croix de Feu militant M. Laffon declared in January 1935 that, following instructions from La Rocque, '200,000 Croix de Feu members can be in the street whenever required, either to combat the Popular Front, or if necessary even to seize power.'[76] The participation of greater numbers in these demonstrations and commemorations transformed the significance of the occasions themselves, described as offering images of the people rather than of partisan groups. Furthermore, the rivalry between the Popular Front and the leagues made itself felt both in the organization of separate demonstrations and also in a common concern to create an image of popular participation in national commemorations, such as those of 14 July and 11 November.

Two particular moments of rivalry can be used to illustrate these tendencies: 11 November 1934 and 19 May 1935. On both occasions the organization of separate demonstrations by the leagues and the Popular Front revealed important points of conflict between their respective ideologies, while also suggesting their broadening aspirations as representatives of the people of France.

The commemoration on 11 November of victory and sacrifice in the First World War had for a number of years been one of the most important annual rallying points for the military and nationalist leagues, though not for the internationalist and pacifist left. Indeed in the 1920s and early 1930s such occasions of national fervour had been ridiculed by the PCF, which targeted those attending with pacifist and internationalist tracts.[77] On 11 November 1934, however, while the Croix de Feu made its traditional march to the Arc de Triomphe, 28 organizations of veteran soldiers—brought together by the pacifist Comité de Lutte contre la Guerre et le Fascisme—made their own procession from the Place de la Bastille to the Place de la Nation, acclaimed by the supporters of the Popular Front. On the same day there were therefore two processions to commemorate the sacrifices of the First World War, and both the leagues and the Popular Front claimed their own procession to be the one supported by the people of Paris. The Croix de Feu exalted the sacrifice of the victims and veterans of war, and called for the final realization of their aspirations; the Popular Front deplored the tragedy of bloodshed and claimed the veterans as the most ardent defenders of peace. The Communists also associated their demonstration with overt opposition to the current coalition government, which they held responsible for workers' deaths in the February demonstrations.

The organization of these rival events was highly significant. It marked the changing allegiance of many veteran soldiers, formerly associated more firmly with the demonstrations of the right, and also made clear that the Popular Front was contesting the Croix de Feu's claim to legitimate representation of this important social group. As *L'Humanité* proclaimed on 11 November:

> From the Place de la Bastille to the Place de la Nation, acclaim the veteran soldiers! Defend their rights! Defend our liberties! The real soldiers of the front, who desire neither war not fascism, will march through the streets to the cheers of the people of Paris.

By November 1935 (by which point the Radicals had also joined the Popular Front) such claims to the veterans were still more significant. Before the Popular Front, La Rocque and his supporters had treated the Champs-Élysées almost as their personal territory: a place of triumph and commemoration. Now this area of Paris, so deeply patriotic in its connotations, had been visibly reconquered by the left, no longer relegated on 14 July and 11 November to separate demonstrations in the east of the city. As the Radical newspaper *La Lumière* observed:

> The People of Paris (...) came to take possession of the Champs-Élysées, and their tranquil force demonstrated their superiority over the Hitlerite-fascist bullies, who did not even recover their spirit or their voices until the following day.
>
> The veteran soldiers elude the fascists; the republicans have once again mastered the streets of Paris. These two points are essential, and the anger of the reaction is a good measure of their importance.[78]

The development of two rival 'peoples' on left and right, each associated with a particular vision of France, was also clearly evident in the demonstrations of May 1935. In this year the annual festival of Joan of Arc was postponed by the government in order not to coincide with the second round of the municipal elections, and took place on 19 May, when the Socialists and Communists were also holding their annual commemoration of the Commune. Provincial delegations increased the size of both demonstrations in what became not merely a battle of numbers but also a battle for legitimacy.

The coincidence of the two celebrations was employed by the Popular Front and the leagues as a reminder of the potential danger of their adversaries. For the Croix de Feu this was the occasion for a documentary film in which images of La Rocque's procession and of the tricolour were carefully interspersed with headlines from opposing newspapers.[79] 'More than 100,000 Parisians have paid their respects to the Heroine [Joan of Arc]' was the headline of one nationalist newspaper, while from *l'Humanité*: '200,000 at the Mur des Fédérés: never before has such a crowd commemorated the Commune'. Emphasizing the legitimacy of the Croix de Feu as representative of France and its people, the film juxtaposed references to the Commune with images of the statue of Joan of Arc, and contrasted the Communist headline 'Long live Stalin, leader of worldwide Revolution!' with the patriotic image of the tricolour. But while rival newspaper cuttings were depicted, there was no comparable juxtaposition of crowds of left- and right-wing supporters, possibly because the Croix de Feu were reluctant to suggest the numerical strength of their adversaries. The rest of the film was therefore devoted to the Joan of Arc procession, focusing first on the feet of the marching soldiers to capture their perfect timing and discipline, and subsequently on the vast crowd of men, women and children singing *La Marseillaise* and listening attentively to their leader. 'The Croix de Feu disperse, having given a magnificent lesson in order and disciplined force' was the closing caption. Thus while the people were portrayed as ordered and unified, it was the Croix de Feu movement that emerged as the leading example of order and discipline.

The Communists were keen to present their commemoration of the Commune as a triumphant accompaniment to Popular Front successes in the recent municipal elections. Their numerical force was particularly emphasized: 'the strength of anti-fascist defence depends primarily on the strength of the masses,' observed *l'Humanité* on 20 May, drawing a flattering comparison between their own procession and the '35,000 fascists seen this morning'. This was a decisive victory, visible proof that 'national Joan of Arc day belonged ultimately to the people of Paris and the Commune.'[80] The impressive number of supporters also justified the Popular Front's claims to represent the true people of Paris: not simply the working people, but also the intellectuals whose presence added a forceful sense of legitimacy to the movement as a whole. For the presence of veteran soldiers, civil servants, writers, and students all belied right-wing assertions that the 'people' of the left were nothing but the dregs of society.

> The 'mob', the 'criminal underworld' has descended on the Père-Lachaise cemetery, writes the fascist press in horror. The underworld? Men like Langevin, Rivet, Prenant, pioneers of science? This right-wing rage is really something!
>
> The underworld? Those thousands of veteran soldiers and war invalids; all who bear in their flesh the imprints of the last butchery, and wear crosses and medals so dearly purchased?

What about those war widows, those thousands of students from the Law faculty, Sorbonne, École Technique, and other schools! And those medical students? Those students from the École Normale at Vincennes? Are they supposed to be the 'underworld' who paraded past the Mur des Fédérés on Sunday?

Ardent youth!

In truth, it is the real people of Paris who were at the Mur des Fédérés and who paraded under the trees of the old cemetery: 200,000 fighters for liberty.[81]

As for the Croix de Feu procession, it was—according to *Le Populaire*— nothing but an excuse to commemorate 6 February, and as such a 'veritable army of civil war'. The participants were as stiff as automata and the crowd of minimal importance, except around Saint-Augustin, the church of La Madeleine, and the Place des Pyramides.[82] The real people were, it seemed, only to be found at the Mur des Fédérés—for it was almost impossible to concede that the people might be divided, with some attending one of the celebrations, and some attending the other.

The demonstrations of February 1934–July 1935 reveal an important transition in the representation of the people by the Popular Front and its adversaries. As both reinforced their claims to represent the people, broadening their support through the development of new networks of organizations and developing cultural activities for their members, the images of the people presented were themselves transformed. The image of the angry, exclusive people of February 1934 was replaced with that of the masses, drawn together in solidarity through their common experience of economic uncertainty. While the groups of the right continued to emphasize their traditional values of patriotism, order, and discipline, the Popular Front was developing a complex, dual identity, inspired by both proletarian solidarity and republican defence. It sought increasingly to claim traditional supporters of the right—such as the veteran soldiers—as its own, and to undermine the legitimacy of the extra-parliamentary right by playing on fears of disorder and illegality. Through speeches, films, photography, and in particular through demonstrations and their representation, the Popular Front and the leagues endeavoured to describe the social and geographical boundaries of their respective 'peoples' while also defining the people's symbolic qualities. In the organization of the masses as the people there were close parallels in the strategies employed, even if membership of the two movements was not identical in social terms. And in the creation of a symbolic people there were both deep-rooted contradictions, and also important crossings of established left–right boundaries.

The symbolic people of 14 July 1935

Rival celebrations and portrayals of 14 July 1935 provide a significant insight into the construction of the symbolic 'peoples' of left and right, each conceived as a response to crisis and as a promise of new order. For the Popular Front, the construction of an ordered, republican people relied on the equation of the leagues with disorder and fascism, on the minutely detailed organization of their own supporters, and on the selective use of republican and national traditions. For the leagues, the construction of a national people in search of a leader relied on the equation of the Popular Front with revolution and chaos, the presentation of the leagues themselves as representatives of order and leadership, and on a myth of national unity transcending political and class divisions. The most fundamental distinction between the two images was clear: the Popular Front's people were to realize a new order through their own rational thought and action, whereas the right-wing people were to realize their full potential under worthy leadership.

The construction of these images took place in a highly charged atmosphere in which politicians, journalists, and the police were similarly fearful of anarchy and civil war, and in which volatile street politics often threatened to undermine the concomitant images of a new order. As the neo-socialist deputy Marcel Déat observed on 9 July:

> The least reassuring aspect of the beginning of this month of July 1935 is that as economic fears retreat, political passions—and thus ideology—come to the fore. Now every civil war is essentially a war of religion. People go on strike for a better salary, and they rebel for more grain. But they do not kill easily, or risk death willingly, except for gods. And the gods are beginning to emerge above the crowds.

In Parliament itself, those who had previously feared 1 May demonstrations as a potential uprising (*grand soir*) now attributed the same revolutionary aspirations to rival formations on right and left.[83] The Minister of the Interior not only warned prefects of the vastness of the proposed demonstrations but also asked to be supplied with all possible information on the anti-fascist groups and on the 'troops' of the Croix de Feu.[84] Shortly afterwards he gave strict instructions for any foreigner found participating in the demonstrations to be placed under an immediate order of expulsion.[85] The principal concern seems to have been the danger of disorder (even revolution) that the masses foreshadowed as they filled the streets. Members of parliament feared the violence of direct confrontation between opposing groups, but also the possibility that leaders might be overwhelmed by the sheer volume of their supporters.[86] Even if the leaders appealed for calm, troublesome elements might easily transform disorder into chaos. 'The real danger', warned the police, 'is the extent of a popular movement that surpasses all the calculations of leaders and parties.'[87]

The potential of the masses to undermine the carefully constructed image of an ordered people was a strong influence on the symbolism of the Popular Front in July 1935. Anxious to channel popular fervour to their own advantage, Popular Front leaders and militants played upon fears of fascism and on the general restlessness for political renewal in the weeks leading up to the national festival. Henri Barbusse published a special edition of the anti-fascist review *Front mondial* in which he referred to La Rocque's preparation of 'the most shameful and bloody of fascist putsches.'[88] The Communist municipality of Drancy was more inventive still, producing posters with detailed procedures to be adopted in the event of a fascist coup, when public transport would be ready and waiting at a moment's notice to serve the population.[89] Against this background, the Popular Front's celebration of 14 July was presented as a 'vast gathering for the people, for peace, and for liberty'[90]—a united and disciplined front against fascism that offered a reassuring response to the wish for change.

For this image to be effective, it was essential to employ careful measures to control the masses. *Le Populaire* clarified shortly before the demonstrations that red flags were forbidden, and reminded its readers that foreigners were officially excluded from participation, although they were fully thanked for their support and solidarity.[91] Preparations for the processions and celebrations of the fourteenth were made in Paris, the provinces, and Algeria,[92] and in many areas these were the largest processions since the victory parades of 1918.[93] Organizers drawn from the Comité National de Rassemblement Populaire called for the formation of local committees of anti-fascist action in every district of Paris,[94] and old feuds were temporarily buried: the CGT and CGTU joined forces for common action, as did the two tendencies within the Radical party. *Front mondial* featured a list of the 47 organizations that now formed part of the Popular Front: political and trade-union groups, movements for pacifism and social reform.[95] It was, as the trade-union militant Georges Lefranc later commented, the first time since the War that the left had presented a united front and a common programme.[96]

The people imagined within this framework were an independent, rational, republican people, emblematic of national unity. Indeed, as Simon Dell's recent work on the photomontages of 14 July 1935 suggests, this particular month epitomized the resurgence of a 'Republican imaginary'.[97] In constructing such an image the Popular Front was seeking to reconcile the legacies of 14 July 1789 and 14 July 1790: the politically active, powerful masses on one hand, and the united Third Estate—a nation in themselves, as Abbé Sieyès had argued[98]—on the other. As was to become characteristic of the Popular Front, commemorations of the Revolution emphasized fervour and idealism at the expense of violence, seeking to encourage the 'commotion of unanimity' that Jean-Richard Bloch had described as the younger sibling of Revolution.[99]

These symbolic people had a will of their own, echoing that of their revolutionary ancestors: a determination to tear down contemporary Bastilles and to claim for themselves the physical and symbolic territory wrongfully occupied by the 'reaction'. This was clear in descriptions of specifically Popular Front celebrations, such as the commemoration of the planting of 'liberty trees' during the Revolution, a commemoration that took place in Montreuil on 13 July 1935. The commemoration began with an account of 1792: a description of how the 'labouring masses', fearful of opposition to the Revolution, crowned the king with a Phrygian bonnet and swore loyalty to the nation. Then followed a theatrical entertainment by the Fédération du Théâtre Ouvrier de France, and a speech in which the Socialist Gaston Allemane, deputy for Champigny and general secretary of the Socialist Federation of the Seine, exalted the Popular Front as the true heir to the French Revolution. What was clear, he said, was that the re-appropriation of 14 July signified an intention to fulfil the legacy of 1789.[100] The united people who had once declared their sovereign will to the monarch in 1792 were now declaring to the government—with equal resolution—their determination to oppose fascism in every form.

The determination of this symbolic people was supposed to be matched by its deliberate calm and political maturity, a recurrent theme in Popular Front symbolism and one that was often difficult to reconcile with spontaneous popular action. This tension underpins descriptions of the Festival of Revolutionary Song that took place on the evening of 13 July in the Salle Bullier. The room was decorated with a large banner proclaiming that 'the young want to live by their labour, in peace and liberty',[101] and the festival began and concluded with speeches by the socialist music critic Georges Pioch, who emphasized the devotion of the French people to democratic liberties and their antipathy to capitalism. The Revolution, commemorated through the solo and thereafter mass performances of *La Carmagnole, Ça ira,* and *La Marseillaise,* was appropriated somewhat selectively. 'Do not say: Revolution or death,' Pioch admonished the assembled crowd of 3000 people, 'but cry from the depths of your heart: Revolution, independence, liberty, life!'[102] There was, however, an evident conflict between the harmony so desired by Popular Front leaders and the less than harmonious sentiments of the crowd towards their 'fascist' adversaries—a conflict evocatively captured in the account by the socialist journalist and dramatic critic Magdaleine Paz. Paz evoked the fusion of the crowd into a single entity in glowing terms, comparing their force and grandeur to those the sea, and estimating their number optimistically to be in the region of 10,000: 'maybe more; it's impossible to tell, no-one can tell: their many bodies are as one.'[103] Yet her idealized image of a fraternal people contrasts strikingly with their contemporary variations on *La Marseillaise* ('And if we don't hang them, we'll break their jaws!'), and with their habitual invectives against La Rocque and Chiappe, which far outlasted the music. The 'commotion of unanimity' and the violence of revolution were not always as clearly distinct as partisans of the Popular Front would have wished.

Nonetheless, the Popular Front celebrations of 14 July endeavoured to reinforce the image of the people as a united national community as well as underscoring their strength as independent political actors. On the morning of 14 July, the so-called Assises de la Paix et de la Liberté were held in the Buffalo Stadium, deliberately modelled on the Fête de la Fédération and bringing together delegations from all areas of France.[104] The event was open to members of every association linked to the Comité de Rassemblement Populaire,[105] and those leading the meeting symbolized the wide-ranging solidarity of the Popular Front, representing the Radical, Socialist, and Communist Parties, the CGT and CGTU, the Confédération de Paysans, and also the army. The occasion included an oath to remain united—consciously echoing the Tennis Court Oath of 1789—and a number of speeches celebrating symbols previously associated with the 'reaction'. Victor Basch, *Dreyfusard* President of the Ligue des Droits de l'Homme and of the Comité de Rassemblement Populaire,[106] opened the meeting with a eulogy for the people of Paris. Their defence of liberty was exemplary, he insisted, their fervour an inspiration:

To see the movement of the great crowd of people in this immense enclosure, and to feel this sea of human hearts beating, fills me with deep and momentous joy. Just as the people of Paris demolished the royal dungeon on 14 July 1789, so are they resolved on 14 July 1935 to make an assault on the Bastilles that still survive: the Bastille of fascism, the Bastille of criminal laws, the Bastille of poverty, the Bastille of economic and financial assemblies, and the Bastille of war.[107]

Jean Perrin, Nobel Prize winner for Physics in 1926, then celebrated the readoption of the symbolic space that he considered proper to the Popular Front. Even Joan of Arc, celebrated heroine of the right, was now ardently reclaimed as a daughter of the people.

Take this handful of modern-day feudal lords, a few hundred of them, who claim they can seize power. They have usurped Joan of Arc, daughter of the people, abandoned by her king and burned at the stake by the priests. They have attempted to usurp the flag of 1789, the noble tricolour that symbolizes republican victories. This tricolour, once again adorning the Phrygian bonnet of 1792, will also wave at the head of our groups next to the red flag, now the flag of the Soviet Republic and a symbol of hope for the downtrodden. You will not let [the reaction] triumph—this day must symbolize the dawn of an era of peace and fraternity.[108]

Jacques Duclos (PCF Secretary) then reaffirmed the new identity of the Communist Party as the true inheritor of the Revolution,[109] and recalled the use of the red flag by the people of the Revolution, the martyrs of the Commune, and the workers of the USSR. It was, he underlined, only too appropriate that the tricolour symbolizing past struggles should now be associated with this red flag, the symbol of future victory. 'We Communists are the heirs to the glorious revolutionary tradition of our country,' he concluded. 'Onward, people of France: fascism will not pass.'[110]

The final celebration organized by the Popular Front employed the image of the people to consolidate contemporary left-wing unity as well as to suggest unity with the republican past. On the afternoon of 14 July, supporters marched in procession from the Place de la Bastille— where the July column was decorated with a large rosette displaying the dates 1789 and 1935—to the Place de la Nation (Figure 7). The vast procession (an estimated 80,000 according to the police) was headed by two cars: Communists Maurice Thorez and Jacques Duclos and Socialist Paul Faure in the car flying the red flag, Professor Paul Langevin and

Figure 7   The Popular Front demonstration, 14 July 1935, *L'Illustration*, 20 July 1935, Credited: Wide World, © *L'Illustration* (Courtesy of *L'Illustration*).

Radical deputy Pierre Cot in the car bearing the tricolour.[111] Also heading the procession were two bands, which played *L'Internationale, La Carmagnole, La Jeune Garde*, and occasionally *La Marseillaise*. Red flags outnumbered tricolours by 610 to 202, despite *Le Populaire*'s warning that they were not authorized. Not surprisingly, given this predominance, police reporters recognized many from the extreme left in the procession, but they also commented on the number of women and children participating, an estimated 5000.[112] The procession concluded peacefully with a speech by Maurice Thorez in the Place de la Bastille, in which the PCF leader appealed for the unity of all democratic parties in opposition to fascism.

The celebrations and demonstration of the Popular Front thus furthered its transformation of the image of the people, as well as developing its relationship with the people to the street. The use of parallel symbols—the tricolour and the red flag, *La Marseillaise* and *L'Internationale*—testified to the multi-faceted identity of the movement, endeavouring to incorporate all those who favoured a broad, anti-fascist unity, from Communists to Radicals, working to middle class. The singing of *La Marseillaise* was described as a popular triumph over the reaction,[113] while La Rocque's pretensions to represent the people in his own 14 July processions were roundly ridiculed. *Le Peuple*, for example, featured a caricature of the Colonel and his military cronies in the streets of Paris. 'Those ruffians at the Place de la Bastille?' remarks La Rocque sardonically. 'Don't make me laugh! *We* are the real people of Paris!'[114] Even the Radicals, more sceptical of the crowd's political potential, nonetheless described the crowd as a confident, mature, and trustworthy people. 'These people on the march,' observed *La Lumière*, 'so self-confident and so self-disciplined, represented a force that is decidedly invincible.' The demonstrations of 14 July were also interpreted as a popular call for left-wing government, to which 'the nation's elect' should not hesitate to respond.[115] With such explicit support on the part of the Radicals, the Popular Front could integrate itself more firmly within the republican tradition, seeking its points of reference in the Fête de la Fédération of 1790 as well as in the fervour and idealism of the revolutionary masses. It could reach out to encompass the army—'sons of the people'—as well as Joan of Arc—'daughter of the people'—wresting these symbols from the right. With the people increasingly portrayed as supporters of the Republic, their occupation of the street became less of a challenge and more of a celebration, with order a high priority. Indeed, the people were presented as the guiding force in the search for a new order, themselves guided by both instinct and reason.

By its large-scale occupation of the cultural and symbolic space of the right, the Popular Front forced its opponents into a position of defence and reaction. Although the framework of the National Front drew some of the leagues together they were by no means well co-ordinated, partly on account of La Rocque's continuing resolution to maintain a separate sphere of action for the Croix de Feu.[116] Nevertheless, the leagues were concerned both to devalue the claims of the Popular Front and also to propose their own rival images of the people and of the search for a new order.

Despite their divisions, the leagues were united in their determination to describe the Popular Front as an unworthy representative of the nation and Republic, and they portrayed it as misleading for the true people and attracting those who did not qualify as the people at all. The Socialist and Communist adoption of the tricolour, *La Marseillaise*, and the language of the nation was seen as offensive and deeply suspect. Members of the National Front were indeed scandalized to learn that the tricolour would be flown in parallel with the red flag, and greeted by the singing of *L'Internationale* and *La Carmagnole*.[117] Jean Renaud, leader of the Solidarité Française, voiced his disapproval in no uncertain terms in *L'Ami du Peuple*, declaring that he was 'determined to refuse the Soviet rag a place next to the tricolour, the emblem of our traditions, our sufferings, and our glory.'[118] On 10 July he outlined the alleged Communist plan for a ruthless *coup d'état*: a programme of nightly arrests in preparation for a complete monopoly over the capital, the communications system, and finally the entire country.[119] Thus the Communist and Socialist adoption of *La Marseillaise* should not be taken as a genuine conversion to patriotism.[120] In similar vein, other right-wing newspapers objected not merely to the Popular Front's appropriation of the nation, but also to its self-styled role as defender of liberty and the Republic.

> The newspapers of the radical-socialist-communist coalition even deny patriotic republicans the right to celebrate the anniversary of the storming of the Bastille, the anniversary of what is considered to be the dawn of an era of liberty. They dare to say 'We are the Republic' or 'We are Liberty'.[121]

Meanwhile, the task of undermining the Popular Front's image of the people took place on several levels. *Action Française*, while claiming to remain aloof from the democratic game of numbers, nonetheless sought to challenge the Popular Front's supposed monopoly of the masses by describing its figures as grossly overestimated.[122] At the same time it sought to ridicule the presentation of such crowds as the 'people'.[123] The participants might be numerous, but for *Action Française* they consisted overwhelmingly of foreigners and undesirable elements, even though the organizers of the Popular Front demonstrations had been at pains to limit the participation of foreigners, and even though the Minister of the Interior had threatened such participants with immediate expulsion. Pierre Gaxotte wrote in lurid terms of the supposed origins of many in the Popular Front crowds, describing the 'Red Front' as composed almost entirely of 'Soviet personnel, Stavisky supporters, foreigners, anarchists vomited forth by Italy, deputies released on bail, and the filth of the ghettoes, swept away by Germany.'[124] In short, the Popular Front was described as almost incapable of attracting the real French people, and so the only elements of the people present were to be pitied rather than condemned for being led astray by their revolutionary leaders.[125]

The leagues varied in their degree of opposition to the existing, parliamentary representation of the people, with opposition greatest in such newspapers as *Action Française* and *Je suis partout*. Yet they all visualized a people in search of new order and new leadership, and this dominated their celebration and portrayal of 14 July. In the crisis experienced by the honest, hardworking French people, existing political structures were considered to be woefully inadequate. 'The divorce between the French people and its false leaders deepens from day to day, from hour to hour,' wrote Colonel de la Rocque on 11 May 1935. 'How right we are to oppose the parliamentary parties! They no longer represent anything vibrant.'[126] As a veteran of the First World War, and having seen what he described as a new, more fraternal order prefigured in the common suffering of the trenches, he deplored the continued dominance of pre-war elites who seemed oblivious to the social and technological transformations of the twentieth century. Only those who had come of age through their engagement with and suffering in the modern world could be deemed worthy of leadership. The leagues did not always approve explicitly of imposing leaders on the people, a solution seen as totalitarian, but instead anticipated that the people would search for the leaders they deserved. Even Action Française, whose extreme remedy to the situation of crisis was the restoration of the monarchy, sought to portray the restoration in these terms. 'France needs a leader: she must therefore choose between the proletarian regime and the monarchy,' asserted the militant Léon Mirman at a meeting of 4300 on 20 June 1935. 'Only the monarchy will restore France to its former place in the world. It is not a question of handing France over to the Duc de Guise, but of restoring to France her rightful king.'[127]

It was in explicit response to this alleged call for leadership that the leagues sought to present themselves as harbingers of the new order and as defenders of the nation. Unlike 6 February 1934, the celebrations of 14 July were not a call for the people to take to the street in angry opposition to the existing regime, but rather an opportunity for leagues and people to unite in common respect for national tradition and military sacrifice. For these reasons, the Parisian demonstrations of the right were on a smaller scale than those of their adversaries, and were also less numerous in the provinces.[128] In any case, while practical difficulties prevented the Solidarité Française from holding the vast demonstration that it had planned for the Parisian suburbs,[129] too many of the Jeunesses Patriotes were absent from Paris to warrant a separate demonstration, and Action Française, overtly critical of 14 July, preferred to leave the Communists to discredit themselves with their own excesses rather than to organize a specific demonstration against them.[130] Rumours that La Rocque was planning to dominate the Paris skyline with his own aeroplanes also proved unfounded, although the police kept all aerodromes under close supervision.[131] The celebrations of the right were thus restricted to a small-scale ceremony by the

Figure 8   The Croix de Feu procession, 14 July 1935, *L'Illustration*, 20 July 1935,
Credited: Keystone, © *L'Illustration* (Courtesy of *L'Illustration*).

Solidarité Française, a joint commemoration of the Unknown Soldier by
the Solidarité Française and the Croix de Feu, and to the more customary
participation in processions to the Arc de Triomphe (Figure 8).

The ceremony of the Solidarité Française was significant in that it took
place in the Place de la République in the east of Paris: a crossing of
boundaries into the recognized territory of the left and a challenge the
Popular Front's republican fervour. Firstly, Jean Renaud laid a wreath of
flowers at the foot of the Statue of the Republic—a 'symbolic gesture
from a nationalist movement, countering the questionable activities
that will take place tomorrow in this same place.'[132] He then made a
brief speech affirming his antipathy to dictatorship (despite the Solidarité Française's overt sympathy for Italian corporatism), and emphasizing
his own faith in the Republic. The symbolic value of the short ceremony was appreciated by only a small crowd of supporters, for despite
previous announcements that the event would take place in the afternoon, it was actually held at 10 o'clock in the morning, when the Place
de la République was almost entirely deserted. Nevertheless, this claim
by the extreme right to the Republic was not without its effect, for
members of the Solidarité Française who arrived in the afternoon to
lay a second wreath at the foot of the statue were angrily intercepted
by a group of Popular Front supporters. Cries of 'down with fascism!'

resounded around the increasingly busy square, and as the members of the Solidarité Française struck up *La Marseillaise*, so did the Popular Front respond with *L'Internationale*. [133] Symbolic opposition later degenerated into direct conflict, and the confrontation concluded with a violent exchange in a café and with several arrests—evidence of the constant tension between political antipathy and the promised visions of order.

Not all of the leagues were equally enthusiastic in their defence of the Republic, but they were nevertheless united in celebrating popular acclamation of the army as a foretaste of the communion between people and nation. This, for the leagues, was a foreshadowing of the new order: an order founded on the common memory and sacrifice of the First World War, and rising above the partisan political sentiments of the Popular Front. Indeed the transient unity and solidarity experienced during the War was broadly equivalent to the 'commotion of unanimity' exalted by the left. As well as describing their own separate commemorations of the Unknown Soldier on 13 July, the Croix de Feu and the Solidarité Française thus devoted considerable attention to the military parades of the fourteenth, in which army, veteran soldiers, and the vast crowd of men, women, and children were seen as united in memory of national sacrifice. In the weekly Croix de Feu newspaper *Le Flambeau*, the occasion was pictured in a full-page photograph, and described as a moment of spiritual unity: 'The only true grandeur in the heart of a people is when its spiritual clarity is complete, its conscience perfect.'[134] The procession itself was portrayed in disciplined, symmetrical ranks, bordered on each side by the orderly crowd and by the trees of the Champs-Élysées. Occupying two-thirds of the photograph, against a background of trees and sky, the procession appeared impressive rather than oppressive. The people—here presented as spectators rather than as actors—were central to the significance of the occasion. Through their presence, their profound respect for the veteran soldiers and their wider commemoration of the dead, they appeared to offer a visible reminder that the sacrifices of the First World War had established an indelible unity and solidarity among the French. It was certainly not 14 July 1789 or even 14 July 1790 that were the object of commemoration, but rather the sacrifices of army and people, and their communion within the nation. 'The people do not want us to pander to them,' contended La Rocque. 'They want us all to be incorporated within the united nation.'[135] And if the French people's determination to defend their country and liberty could certainly be traced back to the Revolution, it was August 1914 that was evoked as the more binding memory. 'Every time (…) that the masses have believed the fatherland to be in danger, they have formed a front against the invader,' wrote Pierre Bermond of the Solidarité Française. And he added pointedly: 'The second of August 1914 is still in everyone's memory.'[136]

Order and disorder

The battle to transform transient popular solidarity into more permanent political structures was fundamental to the organization of the masses in 1934–36. Both the leagues and the emerging Popular Front movement sought to counter the 'established disorder' of corrupt parliamentary politics with mass political organizations that also responded to their members' cultural needs. For the Popular Front, now explicitly supported by the Radicals, there was a genuine prospect of creating a new order within the existing parliamentary system through electoral victory and a Popular Front government. Meanwhile, the less effective organization of the leagues and their equivocal attitude to parliamentary politics made this course appear—for the moment—an unlikely choice of action for them. As these political opponents battled to organize and present their respective visions of a new order, one of the fundamental problems was the establishment of order itself, for in the unpredictability of the demonstration the distinction between fervour and violence was all too easily blurred.

One of the most notorious moments in the battle to represent order— and one that established the superior respectability and legitimacy of the Popular Front—came with 13 February 1936, when Léon Blum was brutally attacked on the Boulevard Saint-Germain by a gang of Action Française dissidents. The incident occurred when the car carrying Léon Blum, Georges Monnet, and his wife encountered the funeral procession of the right-wing author and former *Action Française* journalist Jacques Bainville. Objecting forcefully to what they viewed as a provocative 'intrusion', a band of right-wing militants smashed the windows of the vehicle, injuring both Blum and Monnet, and were restrained from further violence only through the timely intervention of some local workers. The attack at midday caused an immediate uproar, not least in the parliamentary session of that afternoon where there were urgent cries to apply the new law of 10 January 1936 to dissolve the leagues.[137] Shortly afterwards the government dissolved Action Française, its student section, and the Camelots du Roi, while the Popular Front organized a mass demonstration for the following Sunday, 16 February. Although permission for the demonstration was requested without the legally required period of notice, it was granted immediately.

The violence of this shocking and unprovoked attack played straight into the hands of the Popular Front, which was thus given a powerful opportunity to present a peaceful, ordered display of its own supporters. Men, women, and children took part in its procession from the Panthéon (in the heart of the territory normally associated with the Camelots du Roi) to the Place de la Nation. Despite a concern for order, however, the demonstration was punctuated by ritual hostility, and described by the Communist senator Marcel Cachin as an opportunity for the people of Paris to affirm their hatred of 'the fascists, concealed behind the net curtains of the very bourgeois houses of the faubourg Saint-Germain.'[138] Indeed, as the procession moved through the Latin Quarter, a man leaning out of a window on the top storey was seen to make the fascist salute, and was greeted with angry shouts from the demonstrators, and a young boy making the same gesture provoked such hostility that some of the demonstrators attempted to force entry into the building. Student groups around the Théâtre de Cluny shouted 'France for the French!' and sang *La Marseillaise*, to which the Popular Front supporters responded with *L'Internationale*.[139] Violence was also proposed by the Trotskyist groups of revolutionary action, which threw tracts into the crowd as it passed through the Faubourg Saint-Antoine. These tracts criticized the Popular Front for its increasingly conservative stance and called for 'revolutionary workers' to create popular militias to oppose fascist with proletarian violence.[140] It is perhaps unsurprising that, given this undercurrent of hostility, the government sent instructions to all prefects in France and Algeria that no films of this event were to be shown.[141]

In contrast to the violence revealed by police reports, Popular Front accounts of the demonstration endeavoured to create a reassuring image of a peaceful, family occasion, posing no threat to republican order. They stressed that *L'Internationale* was accompanied by *La Marseillaise*, the red flag by the tricolour, and that the procession itself included not only Socialist and Communist leaders, but also the Radical leader Daladier. *Le Populaire* commented with satisfaction on the presence of the so-called 'enemies of the family' with their wives and children, on the adoption of the tricolour by the 'enemies of the nation',[142] and claimed that the people were concerned merely to defend democratic liberties and to oblige the 'fascist formations' to obey republican law. The numerical strength of the demonstration reinforced the image of a triumphant people on the path to power; and for those who participated, the sense of being part of such a people was evidently overwhelming. SFIO deputy Amédée Dunois described his 'intense, raw pleasure' at being able to 'lose myself in [the people], feel with them, join my cry to theirs, my song to their song, to respond with my raised fist to their raised fists.'[143] Even Radical newspapers described the demonstration as a 'spectacle of sovereign majesty.'[144]

The right might cavil at these images of left-wing order and discipline—La Rocque denied that cries of 'Soviets everywhere' could be taken as the voice of the people[145]—but circumstances were certainly more favourable to the Popular Front than to the leagues. Parliamentary debates in the weeks that followed revealed an evident preference on the part of the Radical premier Albert Sarraut for the Popular Front, to the extent that critics spoke of a 'partisan government, a Popular Front government' long before the elections of April 1936.[146] Sarraut defended his decision to authorize the demonstration of 16 February—despite an insufficient period of notice—on the grounds that the 'great and awakened republican conscience' of the Parisians required an outlet, and that opposition would have sparked further violence and illegal street gatherings.[147] Right-wing deputies protested that Communist violence, and in particular an attack on a right-wing meeting on the evening of 13 February 1936, received little publicity or condemnation from the government. And as feelings ran high, deputies even came to blows in the corridors of the Chamber of deputies.[148] But the Popular Front seemed to be in the ascendant.

The years 1934–36 thus witnessed the increasing success of the Popular Front in organizing and portraying the working masses, although this is not to deny either the importance of its opponents or the potential fragility of its image of the people. After the anger and fear of February 1934, the following years witnessed the urgent search for a response to this crisis of representation, in which existing political institutions seemed no longer capable of responding to the social, economic, and international instability of the 1930s. While the successful expansion of the Popular Front in this period certainly owed much to the persuasive power of its anti-fascist rhetoric, the Popular Front as a wider movement was much more than a reaction to fascism. Rather, it was symptomatic of a deeper concern to counter the experience of instability with the reassuring image of a new order encompassing the entire people. In its political and cultural transformation, the Popular Front therefore came into close rivalry with the leagues of the right that had been born into the same period of crisis. Both sought to play on the fears of economic instability and international tension experienced by the masses in order to expand their structures of organization, incorporating men, women, and children into political and cultural associations, developing their programmes of meetings and demonstrations, and portraying these in words and images as moments of popular unity rather than as partisan gatherings. Equally, while the symbolic 'peoples' of the leagues and the Popular Front were in clear opposition—the Popular Front proposed a rational, independent, republican people, while the leagues described a people in search of a leader and united in memory of wartime sacrifice—nevertheless there were emerging overlaps in symbolism as well. Both formations sought increasingly to rise above the class struggle in their imagination of the people, even if their sociological composition remained different. They also tended to define this people as exclusively French. By July 1935, the Popular Front was noticeably more successful in its conquest of the masses, but the battle was far from resolved. In particular, the Popular Front's image of the people in the street as a disciplined, independent force preparing a new order rested on a dangerous assumption about the rationality of the crowd. As long as the people conformed to the image of a peaceful and majestic force, then the Popular Front could appear to embody their voice and their political will. But if in their restless spontaneity the people transgressed the boundaries of their designated role, then the very nature of the Popular Front would be open to question.

3
'His Majesty the People'? Elections, Strikes, and the Perils of Victory in 1936

> Today, society hears its greatest creditor knocking at the door: His Majesty the People.[1]

On 10 May 1936, *Le Populaire* printed an illustrated reflection on the events of the past week by its regular caricaturist, Robert Fuzier. Most of the figures represented were stock characters in the unfolding political drama. Charles Maurras, leaning on a fleur-de-lys-topped walking cane, expounded on the complex relationship between the *pays réel* and the *pays légal*;[2] the President of the Municipal Council of Paris Jean Chiappe defended himself with a heavily armed guard;[3] and Colonel de la Rocque claimed that the ignominious retreat of the Croix de Feu was merely the desired result of his military strategy. But the hero was a very new one, and was making his first and (for many) long-expected appearance as victor rather than victim on the political stage. A robust, stocky character, he wore working clothes and a worker's cap, and around his belt were the words 'Popular Front'. Toppling Colonel de la Rocque and delivering a well-aimed kick to a dandified Louis Marin (President of the Fédération Républicaine), he appeared in the last sketch towering proudly over a diminutive capitalist, the latter clad in his characteristic top hat and bow tie. 'Come now, my good man,' said the triumphant hero, confident of his superior strength and revelling in his electoral victory, 'You would do better to accept it, and try not to provoke my anger!'[4] (Figure 9).

This hero, a composite image of the Popular Front, the electoral people, and the workers, powerfully reflected contemporary hopes for the unity of all three. In May, the will of the electoral people brought the Popular Front to power, winning 380 of the 612 seats in the Chamber of Deputies for the anti-fascist coalition. While the overall gain for the left since its previous victory in 1932 was not dramatic, there was a

Figure 9   Robert Fuzier, 'This week's comedy', *Le Populaire*, 10 May 1936 (Courtesy of the Bibliothèque Nationale, Paris).

substantial shift in the balance between parties: the number of Radicals in the Chamber dropped from 158 to 106, whereas the Communists increased their parliamentary presence from 21 to 72. The largest single party in the Chamber was now the SFIO with 147 deputies (97 in 1932), and Léon Blum duly became the country's first Socialist premier. Although the new government did not take power immediately (republican law stipulated the elapse of one month), the triumph of the Popular Front brought the people into the streets in celebration, their hopeful faces captured in the iconic photographs of Willy Ronis and Robert Capa.[5] The wave of strikes that followed brought further images of a victorious people—this time the workers, who claimed their place in popular memory with their dances and self-discipline, and faced the camera in disciplined ranks, their clenched fists raised in unison. Under the direction of the new government, the Matignon Agreement of 8 June 1936 promised higher wages, collective contracts, a 40-hour week, and paid holidays, crowning the strike movement too with an aura of victory. An indelible connection was forged between the new Popular Front government and mass leisure, with paid holidays soon symbolized by the image of a couple on a tandem. It was an image that Léon Blum described as 'a little beauty, a ray of light'[6] against the dark backdrop of fascism and civil war in neighbouring countries. Strengthened by such victories, the will of the people—crowd, workers, or electorate—seemed indivisible and unshakeable. The fraternity of the strikers and their justified desire for a more human order in the workplace reflected the 'commotion of unanimity' so essential to the creation of political community. Meanwhile, Popular Front supporters conflated the opposition of the disgruntled factory owners and an embittered right-wing press into 'the assault of the vanquished':[7] the jealous reaction of those disappointed by the electoral results, and whose irrational hatred of the people was surely as virulent as their hatred of the Popular Front itself.

This was—and, to a large extent, remains—one of the most power-ful and widely held images of the Popular Front: a victorious working people triumphing with poignant brevity over an inhuman workplace and over the generally sombre character of 1930s politics. Not for noth-ing has the utopian intellectual Simone Weil's description of the 'pure, unadulterated joy' of the strikers become the most frequently cited description of this time of social upheaval.[8] Accounts of the strikes and electoral victory in recent research are often marked by the same themes that underlie Weil's description: community, dignity, working-class pride, and a sense of popular sovereignty and optimism.[9] The period is described as the 'dawn of a new era for the workers' and as the natural expression of a new humanism, 'a generous conception lead-ing to the liberation of man.'[10] Critical depictions of the Popular Front's images of victory, such as Simon Dell's recent portrayal of them as a misleading denial of class discord, are noticeably rare.[11]

The powerful effect of the image of 'His Majesty the People' is easily understandable. Given the duration and extent of the strike movement, the near-absence of violence was remarkable: by 7 July there had been 1382 police interventions in the Paris, yet of 196 dossiers drawn up, only 10 resulted in convictions.[12] There is an obvious appeal in the optimistic images of the celebratory crowds and the ordered, hopeful workers; a poignancy in the capacity for innocent enjoyment that pro-claimed (as the Popular Front was anxious to make clear) a desire for improved salaries and working conditions rather than a thirst for revo-lution. Despite the duration of the movement, it was sufficiently brief that these utopian images of fraternity and solidarity remained untar-nished. Moreover, if these victorious people have been viewed through the ardent prose of Simone Weil, they have also been viewed through Léon Blum's famous speech of 1942, in which he evoked the 'ray of light' that the Popular Front had brought into the lives of ordinary working people. On trial in Riom for the defeat of France in 1940, and accused of a leniency towards the strikes that had poisoned social relations and undermined levels of production from 1936 onwards, Blum defended his actions and beliefs so skilfully that the trial had in the end to be suspended. His response to his accusers, which immediately assumed mythic status among sympathizers in both France and England,[13] was to stress his fidelity to republican legality and to the will of the peo-ple throughout the Popular Front regime, and especially in reaction to the strikes.[14] If he had failed, he said, it was only through an excess of idealism and confidence in the working people, in which he him-self saw nothing dishonourable.[15] With the vindication of Léon Blum at the Liberation came the vindication of his image of the people, and of the correlation between the people and the Popular Front. Challenging the Popular Front myth can thus appear as an attack on republican tradition and as an apology either for the dissident left or for a 'reaction' composed of the factory owners, the leagues, and the press of the extreme right.

Yet the relationship between the Popular Front and 'His Majesty the People' was considerably less straightforward than its proponents suggest. Placing the events of April–June 1936 within the battle to represent the people, it is possible to reveal a number of important dimensions that have hitherto been obscured. First, the reforms now almost synonymous with the Popular Front were not explicitly proposed by its manifesto, although they were to some extent implied by its rubric of 'bread, peace, and liberty.' But the 40-hour week and paid holidays were in fact proposed by other electoral manifestos, and the concern to establish a more humane order in the workplace was rooted in important assumptions shared across the political spectrum.

Secondly, while the images of the sovereign people and the victorious workers are rightly considered as images of strength, they were nonetheless emphasized to counteract a very real fragility in the Popular Front's position. The Popular Front had successfully mobilized an image of a mature, self-disciplined political people, engaged to respect the republican order. The fact that after electing their representatives, the people (in the form of the striking workers) should then proceed to take their representation into their own hands was a considerable problem. Not least, it revealed a lack of trust in the new government's ability to address popular concerns through existing legal structures. Where now was the voice of the people? With the new Popular Front government, elected but unable to assume power for a further month? Or with the striking workers, who might—or might not—conform to the reassuring image that the Popular Front had created to contain them? It was all very well to create an image of a mature, independent, and politically aware people: but were not such people revolutionary, especially if they appeared reluctant to relinquish their political role after having elected a government?

Thirdly, previous research on the strikes mentions the reactions of the right only in so far as these reflected fears of revolution and a Communist plot.[16] Yet disapproval of the strikes did not inevitably signify a dislike of the workers, and in fact the groups and parties of the right continued to develop their own images of the working people, as they had done in the preceding years. It is these three points—generally obscured in existing accounts—that this chapter seeks to illuminate, tracing the evolving pursuit of the people from the crowd and the masses to the workers and electorate. This is not a denial of the enthusiasm or idealism that accompanied the Popular Front victory, nor a denigration of the brilliance and persuasiveness of Léon Blum's wartime speech. It is rather an endeavour to add depth to these powerful images by situating the portrayal of 'His Majesty the People' in its rightful context, and to explain why, however powerful, it does not tell the full story.

In pursuit of the electorate

May 1936 has entered French history as a great electoral victory for the left. Yet the right remained strong (the left gained 5,420,000 votes; the right 4,230,000), and the winning electoral promises were by no means unique to the programmes of the Popular Front. It was not of course surprising that certain themes and slogans—especially the successful Popular Front slogan of 'bread, peace, and liberty'— should have become prominent in the campaigns of many different parties. What was surprising was that a superficial similarity of electoral slogans was deepened by the closely comparable manner with which such themes were addressed, reflecting the evolution of the Popular Front in general, and the Communist Party in particular, towards an ideological territory more usually associated with the right. A comparison of the electoral programmes of 1936 (some produced by parties presenting their own candidates, others by groups or associations recommending candidates to their supporters) reveals the particular importance of patriotic defence, the regeneration of the French race, the defence of the family, and the advancement of social reform.[17]

The propaganda of the Communist Party attracted particular comment for its uncharacteristic conservatism, and its electoral film *La Vie est à nous* (produced by Jean Renoir) provides a sharp insight into the conflict between its old and new rhetorical postures.[18] The opening sequence juxtaposed images of France's agricultural abundance with the poverty of its working people, cut off from their rightful inheritance by the selfishness of the 'two hundred families'. The film, which included both documentary footage and fictional sequences, inevitably presented the PCF as the necessary force to redress the balance of an unjust order—but it did so in two languages. Maurice Thorez was portrayed as demanding complete working-class unity, acknowledging the traditional tactics of class warfare. But he was also shown calling for a broader 'union of the people of France (...) the reconciliation of the French nation against the two hundred families.' And while the principal focus of *La Vie est à nous* was the working class, united in solidarity against French 'fascists' such as the Croix de Feu and the Volontaires Nationaux, images of the processions on 14 July 1935 gave a clear indication of social diversity, thus reflecting the evolution of the Party in 1934–36. This reassuring image of a people united within the nation was also evident in the PCF's calls for defence and regeneration of the race and family. In its electoral manifesto, the party deplored the dangers of 'infant mortality, physical degeneration, the declining birth rate and the disintegration of the family.'[19] Such a tone was in line with the transformation of the official Communist attitude towards women, increasingly appealed to as wives and mothers rather than militants.[20] It was also echoed in the notorious policy of the 'outstretched hand' (*main tendue*): an appeal made by Maurice Thorez on 17 April 1936 to Catholics and even to former members of the Croix de Feu, calling for their co-operation with the Communists in the interests of the working people.

This ambiguous relationship between divergent discourses was matched by an ambiguity in street politics. Local reunions, especially in the Communist municipalities of the Parisian suburbs, often maintained the combative, revolutionary culture of earlier years—evident, for example, in commemorations of the Commune at Issy-les-Moulineaux in May 1936. Here, the unveiling of a plaque in commemoration of the Communards was attended by the Communist mayors of Malakoff and Issy, and the assembled crowd were addressed by a former Communard, Repiquet, who urged them to support the Popular Front as a means of overthrowing the capitalist regime. There was certainly nothing conciliatory about his image of the militant, working-class people, nor about the fervent singing of *L'Internationale*.[21] Yet police records also show that specific instructions had been given to Communist militants not to voice any revolutionary sentiments at the time of the elections. In particular, they had been enjoined to refrain from singing *L'Internationale* and shouting 'Soviets everywhere!', and were requested not to demonstrate overt hostility towards *La Marseillaise*.[22]

It was natural that the Communist Party should seek strategies to attract the maximum number of voters. What was striking was the implicit recognition that its own programme did not have a majority appeal, and the consequent crossing of boundaries onto the habitual territory of its opponents. Certainly its adversaries did not miss the

opportunity to comment on this volte-face. As Charles Maurras wrote
on 23 April:

> The most interesting aspect of the electoral campaign witnessed by
> the French people is, on the one hand, the fervour and intensity
> of Communist propaganda, and, on the other, the absence of any
> pattern of Communist thought.
>   Furthermore—and this is even more remarkable—the Communists
> are making themselves anticommunist. They deny, forget, erase the
> principle of an international fatherland, and the French fatherland
> appears to them, as once the Roman fatherland appeared to Virgil
> and to Rutilius Numantianus, as the most beautiful thing, *rerum
> pulcherrimum Roma*.
>   Property? They salute it, and consider it the most important of pos-
> sessions. Order? They'll be responsible for its protection (...) There is
> not a single principle of capitalist society that they do not emblazon
> on their manifesto.[23]

The Popular Front was competing for electoral support both with the
parliamentary right, which presented its own candidates, and with the
extra-parliamentary right, which could recommend sympathetic candidates to its voting members. The rivalry between the Popular Front and
the parliamentary right (such as the Alliance Démocratique) focused
on national reconciliation, 'respect for democratic principles and liberties', and social concerns such as new housing for workers, a tougher
fight against unemployment, and the encouragement of popular sport.[24]
With extra-parliamentary leagues that engaged actively with the electoral process (such as the Croix de Feu), the social question was similarly
important as a focus for electoral rivalry. The Croix de Feu not only
suggested nationalist candidates for whom its members could vote,
but also produced a manifesto entitled *Pour le Peuple, par le peuple*,
the front cover of which depicted the symbolic union between a factory employee, standing on a map of industrial France, and a farmer,
standing on a map of rural France (Figure 10). There were a number
of close parallels with the Popular Front manifesto, including a call for
deputies not to hold other positions concurrently. But the greatest parallel was the shared determination to tackle social problems, which *Pour
le Peuple* described as 'the essential question of our troubled times,' provoked principally by the irreconcilable demands of technical and social
progress.[25] In his manifesto La Rocque called for measures to be taken
against unemployment, as well as for paid holidays and the organization

ÉLECTIONS LÉGISLATIVES DE 1936

MANIFESTE CROIX DE FEU

POUR LE PEUPLE

PAR LE PEUPLE

Figure 10   The Croix de Feu's electoral manifesto: *Pour le peuple, par le peuple*. Photograph: the author. Private collection.

of leisure (he focused particularly on 'horticultural leisure' as a means of strengthening the bond between the French people and their land). Ambitiously, he described the Croix de Feu movement as 'borne along by the people themselves' and as 'a great corporation symbolizing sincerity, fraternity, and honour.'[26] He also emphasized his adherence to republican legality, and implied a desire to rebuild France within the framework of the existing regime. Explicitly favouring corporatism, the leader of the Croix de Feu differed significantly from the Popular Front in the detailed solutions that he proposed. Yet both the Croix de Feu and the Popular Front suggested that their ultimate aim was to achieve the reconciliation of the French people: rural and urban, bourgeois and working class. La Rocque's slogan was 'Work, Family, and Fatherland' (*Travail, Famille, Patrie*), later to be adopted—much to La Rocque's satisfaction—by Marshal Pétain. Yet which electoral manifesto of 1936 would not have been accurately described by these words?

A broader consideration of the social concerns of electoral programmes reveals that the reforms later carried through by the new
Popular Front government reflected what was almost a latent consensus on the working-class condition. This is reinforced by a consideration
of political Catholics, particularly in their responses to the 'outstretched
hand' of the Communist Party. The offer by Maurice Thorez threw down
a challenge that was difficult for Catholics to ignore, whether or not they
were politically engaged, for his suggested collaboration was in the name
of the sufferings of the working people, whether on the right or the left,
Christian or non-Christian. Catholics unsympathetic to Communism
were nonetheless challenged by this appeal to their social conscience,
and indeed the plight of the workers received much attention in
Catholic circles, and had been underlined in Pius XI's recent encyclical of 1931, *Quadragesimo Anno*. The willingness of some Catholics
to vote for the Popular Front—and thus to accept the 'outstretched
hand'—has often been described as indicating an increasing diversity
of Catholic political opinion. Research has emphasized Catholic sympathy for Emmanuel Mounier's *Esprit*, and the emergence of the radical
Christian-Marxist movement Terre Nouvelle, a possible foreshadowing
of the post-war dialogue between Christians and Marxists.[27] Yet the
Catholics who voted for the Popular Front were not the only ones with a
social conscience. Even while condemning Communism and the influence of the left on Catholic circles,[28] Catholics of the right recognized
the strength of the 'outstretched hand' and the need to provide a rea-
soned response to the PCF's proposal. For some years the right-wing
Fédération Nationale Catholique had been fighting against the assumption, widespread in republican propaganda, that Catholics were the
'enemies of the people' and thus intrinsically opposed to social reform[29]
(Figures 11a and 11b). Jean Le Cour Grandmaison, vice president of the
Fédération Nationale Catholique, freely admitted the existence of parallels between Catholic and Communist responses to the suffering people,
even while emphasizing the incompatibility of their solutions.

> We are, Maurice Thorez says to the Catholics, burdened by the same
> worries. This is to a large extent undeniable. The economic and
> financial crisis, with its consequences of unemployment, high cost
> of living, and general instability; the so-called 'social' curses such as
> slums and tuberculosis; the threats of war, whether civil or foreign; all
> of these evils weigh as heavily on the electorate of M. Maurice Thorez
> as on the electorate of Canon Desgranges.
>   But there is something more. Communism and Catholicism offer
> very similar judgements on today's society.[30]

Figure 11 (a) and (b) Postcards of the Fédération Nationale Catholique (Courtesy of the Archives de la Préfecture de Police, Paris).

Le Cour Grandmaison then cited two such judgements on the sufferings of the workers at the hands of a rich minority, one from the Pope and the other from Maurice Thorez. He also explained that in building a more human social order, the Communist suggestion of practical collaboration for apparently common ends seemed, on the surface, genuinely appealing. His decision to dissuade Catholics from accepting the invitation was not prompted purely by suspicion of Communist duplicity (contemporary Catholic publications were heavy with tales of the martyrdom of Spanish Catholics under the Spanish Popular Front government).[31] Rather, it sprang from his conviction that the new order required an agreement on moral as well as material questions, and he considered Communist and Catholic visions of man to be irreconcilable. Preliminary co-operation—even for worthy ends—was thus ultimately sterile, and would even be dangerous if it facilitated the realization of specifically Communist designs.

It was against this background, and with these thoughts in his mind, that Le Cour Grandmaison delivered his lengthy speech in the Chamber of Deputies on the 'partial community of thought' uniting the French people. As the new government of Léon Blum waited for the customary vote of approval, Le Cour Grandmaison insisted on the striking similarity of electoral proposals from right to left, Catholic to Communist. He could not say whether such coincidence was the result of cynical opportunism. But he could say that the appearance of such strong common themes revealed the preoccupations shared by the French people, since the powerful slogans of Popular Front propaganda were also echoed in the words and thoughts of other groups and associations, cumulatively drawing together millions of French people, from veteran associations to the Croix de Feu movement or the Fédération Nationale Catholique.

> In order to attract the people of France, one does not need to propose class struggle, the dictatorship of the proletariat, collectivization, a Soviet regime, or a disregard for the law. One needs to appeal to those values so deeply rooted in our land and in our hearts: liberty, fatherland, family, professional interests.[32]

According to Le Cour Grandmaison, even Thorez openly acknowledged that many Communist voters had not been voting for revolution. And the reason for this 'partial community of thought' among the French people was to be found in their common reactions to a social order turned over by the excesses of economic liberalism: in a common opposition to capitalism, and a common search for a more humane order in which the working people would be justly remunerated and more fully integrated into the social and political system.

> A multitude of French people, reflecting every nuance of the political horizon from the extreme right to the extreme left, following all manner of philosophical or religious doctrines from Communism to Catholicism, converge in their judgement on the contemporary social order (which provokes the same criticisms) and in their desire to replace it with an order based—as your electoral programmes

testify—on respect for the human person and for liberty, on respect for the family and the fatherland, and also on the restriction of the destructive power of capital.[33]

Could this 'partial community' be transformed into common action? The social reforms of the Popular Front were soon to receive almost unanimous parliamentary approval—lending strength to Le Cour Grandmaison's hypothesis—but this near-unanimity was the consequence not only of shared concerns but also of the unexpected action of the workers themselves: the largest wave of strikes that France had ever seen.

His Majesty the People?

The Popular Front's electoral victory might have appeared as the consummation of its relationship with the people. But as the CGT leader René Belin observed on 5 May, the electoral victory was merely the curtain closing on the first act.[34] Rather than securing the position of the Popular Front, the electoral victory laid it open to a series of new challenges. As a movement and political alliance, the Popular Front had established its legitimacy in the image of a mature, ordered, self-disciplined people whose desires it claimed to represent. As a government, the Popular Front's relationship with the people—especially the crowd and the workers—was more complex. Any disorder, implying disharmony between the people and the new government, threatened the claims of the Popular Front to represent the popular will. Disorder also threatened the status of the government as the guarantor of peace and stability.

Elected in early May, the new government respected republican legality and tradition by not assuming power until the following month. During the month of May, the elected but effectively impotent new government needed to sustain a relationship with the people that would both justify the hopes of its supporters and calm the fears of its adversaries. In this it faced two major challenges: the volatility of street politics, and the disorder of the strike movement. The image of the triumphant, majestic people proposed by the Popular Front was not only a reflection of genuine optimism and jubilation, but also a necessary counterbalance to the fragility of the Popular Front's position.

This fragility was evident even in the celebrations following electoral victory, including those surrounding the annual commemoration of the

Commune. Unlike in 1935, this did not fall on the same day as the right's Joan of Arc procession: in 1936, the two events took place on 24 and 10 May respectively. And there was another important difference. In 1935, the Popular Front was still a movement of opposition, gradually securing wider support and respectability but nonetheless distanced from government. Its association with a partisan, left-wing celebration of insurrection did not represent a serious threat to its status. But by May 1936 the Popular Front was both a movement and also an elected national government that included the Radicals. The apparently official support for a divisive and partisan occasion was therefore highly problematic.

On one level, the procession to the Mur des Fédérés offered the first major opportunity following the elections to picture the newly victorious people. The occasion, celebrated by the united forces of the PCF, SFIO, and the trade unions, was depicted not only in the customary newspaper articles and photographs but also in a 10-minute documentary film created by the PCF at a cost of 3070 francs, and later shown to Popular Front supporters in film evenings organized by *Ciné-Liberté*.[35] As in 1935, the commemoration was presented in deliberate opposition to the recent Joan of Arc celebrations of the right-wing leagues,[36] and Popular Front accounts highlighted its own numerical strength (which conferred legitimacy) as well as emphasizing the diversity of the crowd. Thus *Le Populaire* and *Le Peuple* mentioned the common action of manual and intellectual workers,[37] and the juxtaposition of the red flag and the tricolour that again recalled the solidarity of the working classes with a wider republican people.[38] *Le Peuple* celebrated the participation of women's organizations, and the presence of children, soldiers, theatre groups, and Jewish associations.[39]

Characterizing all of these accounts was a sense of celebration and confidence in the future of the Popular Front. This demonstration marked with particular intensity the transformation of the people from victims to victors, from the martyrs of the Paris Commune to the masters of their own destiny. Marcel Cachin, who praised the success of the demonstration in *L'Humanité*, suggested this metamorphosis in his description of the people.

> The entire people were there, proclaiming their hope and also, in sudden outbursts, their anger against their enemies.
> They were the sons and heirs of the innumerable victims of the Commune and of the revolutions of the past. But this time they had not come to the Wall [Mur des Fédérés] to lament their fallen heroes.

Standing in front of the communal grave where their martyrs rest, they showed how close they are to their definitive rise to power, and how conscious they are of the fact.

These people were victorious, disciplined, and confident in their own future: a people who constituted a new force in French politics. But was this force compatible with the success of the Popular Front? Although *Le Populaire* and *L'Humanité* lauded the development of common action, and although the PCF had proposed the demonstration to the Comité National de Rassemblement Populaire as 'a Popular Front demonstration, that is to say not only Communist and Socialist, but also Radical',[40] the Radicals did not themselves support the occasion. They were indeed loath to be associated with a celebration of the Commune, although they hastened to add that they did not object to Popular Front demonstrations in general. The accounts provided in Radical newspapers of the occasion were brief, factual, and non-committal.[41] Furthermore, although the demonstration was seen as successful, it did raise the question of whether the newly elected government was really capable of satisfying the demands of the people. At a Communist meeting on 25 May, PCF leaders remarked on the frequency of demands for 'energetic acts' from Léon Blum, and concluded that popular support would need to be consolidated by rapid reforms.[42] Blum's position as the new premier was certainly difficult. A principled intellectual whose aesthetic demeanour made him an unlikely leader of a working-class party, he was committed to socialist revolution yet resisted demands from left-wing Socialists to pursue radical change in defiance of republican legality. Critics on the left found him cautious and effete; critics on the right despised him as a Communist pawn and as a Jew. Even before taking office, Blum had been warned by the President of the Republic Albert Lebrun that his premiership might lead to strikes; his Jewish friends simultaneously voiced their concerns about the possible rise in anti-Semitic sentiment.[43] On 5 June Blum confided to his doctor that he, too, feared for the future of his new government.[44]

The opponents of the Popular Front were only too swift to underline these difficulties: the claims to national status made for a partisan celebration, and the potentially explosive relationship between the newly elected government and its demanding supporters. Charles Maurras, despite his scepticism of numerical strength as an indicator of legitimacy, argued that the alleged 600,000 at the Mur des Fédérés were by his calculation only 72,000.[45] Since many of them were not French, their claim to be a representative sample of the people was fairly tenuous. They could be dismissed without too much concern as 'the mob' or 'the red hordes', and their lack of respect for the graves of the Père-Lachaise cemetery was seen as further proof of their lack of civilization.[46] Those on the right who accepted this crowd as representative of the people placed their emphasis on the dysfunctional relationship between these people and their supposed leaders. *Le Temps* noted that the Popular Front leaders, disconcerted by the unprecedented vastness of the crowd, were visibly losing control as the afternoon progressed, and that the crowd was so overwhelmed by its own importance at centre stage that the arrival of Léon Blum passed almost unnoticed.[47] Pierre Cousteau of *Je suis partout* described the crowds as 'sympathetic, even in their stupidity', and argued that the real danger lay in their susceptibility to demagogic manipulation, and their increasing inability to make rational decisions.

> The crowd, which has just acclaimed an army lieutenant and which cries: 'The police are with us!' is ready to shout 'The priests are with us!' or indeed anything, anyhow, anywhere. They are ready to see M. Blum review the military parade on horseback, or M. Stalin make his first communion. They no longer know how to react. They are entirely gullible. They are bewitched.

The concept of the corruptible crowd emerges very strongly from such accounts, and indeed it was in this context that the images of the crowd presented by the Popular Front and its right-wing opponents were at their most irreconcilable. Whereas the Socialists and Communists portrayed the crowd at the Père-Lachaise cemetery as an independent, politically mature, and inherently disciplined people, the opponents of the Popular Front could not accept the notion of the crowd as rational political agents, let alone leaders. It was for this reason that, as in 1935, the right deliberately directed the celebration of Joan of Arc on 10 May against the celebrations organized by the Popular Front.[48] As Colonel de la Rocque commented in *Le Flambeau*:

> It is by the people, through the people, and for the people that our future must be found. Joan came from the people, guided them, and wanted only to return to them. And thus, by her sacrifice, she rescued the fatherland.[49]

The conflicting rhetoric and images accompanying commemorations of Joan of Arc and the martyrs of the Commune were an established ritual of opposition: the crowds processing towards the Père-Lachaise cemetery and the Place des Pyramides were treading on familiar territory. In dramatic contrast, the strikes that broke out in late May and that continued throughout the establishment of the new government were as unexpected as they were unprecedented. With 12,142 strikes and 1,830,938 strikers in June alone,[50] this was by far the most extensive strike movement that the Third Republic had ever known. The strikes had begun at Le Havre in early May; by the last week in May they had reached the Parisian region, where over 70,000 workers were now on strike, many of them occupying their factories and workshops. The strikes affected all types of industrial and commercial enterprises, from small locksmiths' workshops to the large Renault plant at Boulogne-Billancourt. Strikers included highly unionized workers such as coalminers and dockers, but also the relatively unorganized, such as employees in department stores. Almost every region of France was affected. The new Socialist-led government and the signing of the Matignon Agreement seemed to have little effect on the movement, and the number of strikers reached its peak on 11 June. Although the strikes declined relatively sharply in the second half of the month, they continued in some areas until July or even August. Through this unprecedented movement, the working people seemed to be taking their new majesty at face value, occupying factories with an apparent disregard for property rights, and organizing the maintenance of buildings and machinery.

The Popular Front leaders might subscribe in theory to the independent action of the people, but it was quite a different question when the people translated this theory into practice. The image of the people portrayed by the Popular Front during the strikes of summer 1936 must be seen against the deep concern privately expressed by those responsible for its creation: as a deliberate response to the fears of the Popular Front leaders themselves, and as a symbolic riposte to its adversaries. Police reports for the month of June reveal high levels of anxiety among Communist, Socialist, and trade-union leaders about the scale of the strikes and their inability to control the strikers. By 4 June Communist leaders were already overwhelmed by demands for extra militants to advise the strikers, while Blum was asking his Socialist colleagues whether the new government was adequately prepared to rule.[51] Owners of department stores deplored the effects of the strikes on visitors to Paris—many of whom had already purchased tickets to travel to London[52]—while trade-union leaders endeavoured anxiously to ensure that food supplies to the capital remained undisrupted.[53] By 13 June Communist and trade-union leaders were clearly troubled by the failure of their militants to influence the workers, and complained that further strikes continued to break out even after the Matignon Agreement, some allegedly started by militants of the extreme right.[54] Although the Radicals asserted their sympathy for the strikers' economic demands,[55] they nonetheless condemned the illegality of the strikes and the apparent lack of trust in the new government's ability to secure the well-being of the workers. Strikes foreshadowed anarchy, and the collapse of a Republic which was, for them, most effectively preserved by 'the normal functioning of institutions.'[56] As *L'Ère nouvelle* insisted: 'Authority is not in the streets. We need to hear this reaffirmed.'[57]

The very volatility of the situation played a vital role in determining the depiction of the workers on strike, leading to an emphasis on the primacy of economic rather than political motivation, on the self-discipline of the strikers and on their talent for festival rather than revolution. The strikers were described as reacting principally to the hardship of the Depression, and as receiving in consequence widespread approval. Referred to as the people, the workers, or the proletariat, the strikers were presented in *L'Humanité*, *Le Populaire*, and *Le Peuple* as sufficiently abreast of political realities to limit their demands to precise economic and social reforms. 'Our proletariat is well aware that the government has not been voted the task of destroying the capitalist regime' wrote Jean-Baptiste Séverac, Deputy General Secretary of the SFIO:

> The clear and precise mandate that it has received is to preserve and restore, within the context of the existing regime, all the dignity and well-being of the working class, which together with the entire country suffers greatly from the Depression.[58]

He hastened to reassure his readers that work would be resumed immediately upon the government's elaboration of the necessary social and economic measures, and highlighted the concurrent failure of the right to address the needs of the people. Popular initiative was thus firmly restrained within a reassuring framework of legal reform. CGT leader René Belin made a similar point in *Le Peuple* on 12 June, criticizing the leaders of the country for having failed to respond earlier to this desperate plea for better conditions, and describing the strikes as provoked by a wilful blindness to human suffering. 'Today' he wrote, 'the people tremble, move, awaken.'[59] For the CGT, these legitimate economic and social demands united the entire working people, both working and middle class—and the different strata within the working people were increasingly pictured in co-operation, as in the special edition of *Le Peuple* for 1 May 1936.[60] Even *La Vie Ouvrière*, which expressed the more aggressive stance of the former CGTU, contended that the strikers were acting not merely for themselves but rather for the wider people:

> They are not working for themselves alone. Their victory will also be that of veteran soldiers, minor civil servants, railwaymen, and employees in public services, whose grievances the future government will resolve.
>
> Their victory will be the victory of labouring France, and the small shopkeepers, artists, and peasants will benefit from their increased purchasing power.
>
> This is why the current strikes, clearly justified, are taking place in an orderly manner and in a climate of popular sympathy.[61]

Because the strikes were portrayed as aiming for specific reforms rather than to overthrow the system, special attention was devoted to the agreements reached with employers, while the outbreak of further strikes was judiciously downplayed. *Le Populaire* began to talk of 'victory' as early as 31 May, although the strikes were to continue for the whole of the following month, and in some cases until August. *L'Humanité* likewise insisted that 'the workers organizing factory strikes have no intention of turning out their employers.'[62] In order to calm rising fears and confront the allegations of the right, the workers were described as showing exemplary composure and self-discipline, which was indeed a broadly accurate representation. Respect for factory property was frequently mentioned as evidence that these strikers, although perfectly capable of running the factories on their own, had no intention of doing so on a permanent basis. As well as maintaining the machinery in suitable working order, they were reported as minimizing their employers' electricity costs by their parsimonious use of candles, and respecting the demands of decency and morality by organizing separate dormitories for women in the occupied factories, or allowing them to return home at night.[63]

The image of the strikes that emerged from Popular Front accounts was of a temporary disruption by a mature and disciplined people, striking in the name of legitimate economic reform rather than out of disappointment with their new government. The temporary nature of disorder was also reflected in the images of carnival that have received such enthusiastic attention, described in recent research as the resurgence of pre-industrial forms and rituals in a generalized reaction against the anonymity of the factory system.[64] The idea of carnival, translating the occupation of the factories into the realm of theatre, captures the creativity of the workers but also the illusory nature of their control, a temporary escape from monotony rather than a systematic attempt at revolution. In descriptions of carnivalesque activities, the choice of images made by the Popular Front press and cinema was also significant. *Grèves d'occupation* (a 6-minute film produced by the CGT) offers a rare and lively picture of these festivities, celebrating the imagination and resourcefulness of the strikers.[65] There are images of both ritual and spontaneity: the workers organize games of billiards, dances, and music hall entertainment, as well as taking part in processions, and the marriage of two young strikers is also depicted. There are images of carnival: the symbolic burning of a figure representing the 40-hour week, and the execution of another representing Capital. Reactionary fears of the Communist as 'the man with a knife between his teeth' are satirized as the camera homes in on several men in masks, with false moustaches and knives ostentatiously displayed. 'The kitchen knives gleaming between their teeth leave no doubt as to the ferocity of these executioners' is the narrator's ironic observation. Despite images of theatrical violence, his tone remains reassuring and light-hearted, and the character of the film is reminiscent of contemporary newsreels, with little attempt to create a new, proletarian style. As a CGT production, the film was a celebration of the recent victory of the organized working class in the Matignon Agreement, and of the rapid increase in trade-union membership. Action by the workers is explicitly identified with the Popular Front: reference is made to the support of the new Ministry of Culture for workers' entertainment, and to the role of the government in the Matignon Agreement.

Similar images can be found in the Popular Front press, which accorded greater attention to processions and entertainment than to symbolic violence against the system. *Le Peuple* continued its photographic series entitled 'Images of work' throughout the strike period, providing reassuring pictures of diligent workers at work (or in disciplined formation when on strike) alongside commentaries on the strikes themselves. A photograph in *Le Populaire* of the strikers in the Citroën factory depicted rows of workers with raised fists, seated in orderly rows and symmetrically situated against the iron and glass structure behind them: a reassuring image of the 'exemplary discipline' referred to in the accompanying article.[66] Images of carnival were considerably less frequent, although on 8 June there was a photograph symbolizing opposition between the workers and La Rocque.

The workers on strike in a metalwork factory in the Parisian suburbs have produced the following for their amusement: two hand-made models at the entrance of their workplace, one of which represents a proletarian worker embracing a mast from which the red flag is flying, while the other represents Colonel de la Rocque hanging from a gibbet.[67]

In general, however, the focus was on the reassuringly close relationship between the people and the Popular Front, and if the red flags in the factories and the singing of *L'Internationale* were mentioned, reporters also insisted on the presence of the tricolour and *La Marseillaise*.

The workers: Victors or victims?

References to right-wing depictions of the strikes often mention their fears of a revolutionary Communist conspiracy:[68] these fears were both real and widespread. Police reports noted that, in addition to more general concerns about escalating disorder and the disruption of public services, there was also serious anxiety in industrial organizations about the economic consequences of the strike movement, and the possibility of bankruptcy in factories where no agreement had yet been reached. Commercial and industrial representatives considered that the militants directing the strikes were unlikely to respond to appeals for calm issued by the Socialist government, and that in any case Léon Blum and his colleagues were incapable of imposing order on chaos.[69] And such suspicions were to play a significant role in the attitudes of employers to the Popular Front as a government.[70]

The press of the extreme right expressed similar fears. On 12 June, *L'Ami du Peuple* included a cartoon in which a fearful Léon Blum was shown driving a car with a CGT flag at an alarming speed. 'Do you know how to stop it?' he asks the CGT leader Léon Jouhaux, who is seated beside him. 'No,' replies the latter, 'like you, I only know how to start it up' (Figure 12). It was not surprising that in these circumstances the press of the right should attempt to alarm its readers with tales of

— *Tu sais comment ça s'arrête ?*
— *Non, je suis comme toi; je ne connais que la mise en marche.*

Figure 12   *L'Ami du Peuple*, 12 June 1936 (Courtesy of the Bibliothèque Nationale, Paris).

imminent revolution. As a tactic for increasing newspaper sales, it was indisputably effective. As the police noted on 8 June:

> At around midnight, some newspaper salesmen who were not professional hawkers began shouting the titles of their papers at the tops of their voices: *Paris-Soir*, *Action Française*, *Gringoire*, and so on, (...) giving details on the forthcoming revolution. This manner of presenting the situation tempted a number of buyers, who did not hesitate to pay the prices demanded, from 0.50 francs to 2 francs an issue.[71]

Reactions to the workers on strike from the right-wing leagues were not, however, confined to sombre warnings of imminent revolution. Movements such as the Croix de Feu and the Parti National Populaire (created by Pierre Taittinger, leader of the Jeunesses Patriotes) were still intent on developing their existing organizations for the working people, and had no wish to present themselves as fundamentally opposed to the workers. Police reports at the time of the strikes noted that Taittinger was endeavouring to proselytize among the workers by forming a Union Corporative des Travailleurs as an alternative to trade unionism, as well as a special Commission Ouvrière to address working-class concerns. Similarly, the Solidarité Française was beginning to organize a series of Comités de Défense des Jeunesses Françaises Ouvrières et Paysannes, with the aim of creating popular restaurants, employment agencies, libraries, and universities.[72] And although some workers had decided to leave the Croix de Feu after the elections for fear of reprisals by Popular Front supporters, such defections were nevertheless fairly rare.[73]

In depicting the strikes, the leagues of the right were keen to acknowledge the legitimacy of the workers' economic demands while condemning the strikes themselves as of foreign inspiration. They were careful to distinguish between those who had actually organized the strikes and those whose involvement was neither premeditated nor—they claimed—particularly enthusiastic. To a certain degree, these attitudes were also shared by the right-wing press in general, where condemnation of the strikes did not signify condemnation of the people. The Matignon Agreement was a case in point. Since it had been introduced by the Popular Front government, it could not be approved wholeheartedly by the Popular Front's adversaries, and yet many of the reforms it promised had also been demanded by the right-wing leagues. Many Catholics likewise welcomed the reforms, claiming them to be in the spirit of social Catholicism symbolized by the work of Count Albert de Mun and René de La Tour du Pin.[74] Colonel de la Rocque—who had already accused the Popular Front of appropriating his manifesto as its own—now criticized the government for taking sole credit for these reforms. In a reduced edition of *Le Flambeau* (production having been affected by the strikes), he claimed that 'the demands presented by the CGTU unions (minimum wage, paid holidays, collective contracts, and so on) respond to concerns that the Croix de Feu have been developing for some time.'[75] His criticism was that the Popular Front reforms neglected the family, and that they had been drawn up in a situation of disorder. Pierre Gaxotte, writing in *Je suis partout*, was similarly convinced of the necessity for reform, but accused the Popular Front of committing the unforgivable crime of making impossible promises to the people. No one could deny the right of every worker to paid holidays and to a 40-hour week, he observed, but why raise such high hopes when the government was incapable of fulfilling them?[76]

Although right-wing leagues were known to receive both moral and financial support from industrialists (the Croix de Feu league, for example, was supported by a large electricity company), police noted that these movements were increasingly critical of factory owners at the time of the strikes. M. Junger, a member of the Union Corporative des Travailleurs et Producteurs de France, explained at a meeting of the Parti National Populaire (former Jeunesses Patriotes) that the factory owners were largely to blame for the current situation, having remained obdurate to the workers' legitimate pleas for better salaries and conditions.[77] Police reports noted with some surprise that forthright criticism of the factory owners was by no means restricted to the left, and surmised that the uncompromising factory owners had prompted many in the lower middle classes to approve of the strikes, in solidarity with their more proletarian counterparts.

> What is striking is the lack of sympathy that the employers generally receive. 'If they succumbed so easily and so quickly to the demands of their personnel, it must be because the demands were legitimate'— this is the most common reaction. In their eyes, the employers 'exaggerate', and wait until their personnel, driven to the end of their patience, make complaints, threats, or go on strike, before they accede to their legitimate demands.[78]

At the same time, the Croix de Feu in particular were emphasizing the practical benefits of their own unions, the very existence of which was the subject of angry articles in *Le Peuple*. René Belin, for example, ridiculed the entire venture, criticizing La Rocque for failing to propose higher salaries and reduced working hours, and concluding that 'the Colonel is wasting his time: he insults the country with his insubstantial theories and errors of syntax, and he insults the working class by imagining them idiotic enough to swallow his ridiculous suggestions.'[79] On the same day, La Rocque himself was asserting to a large audience at Magic-City that the Popular Front had stolen his reforms, and that his own corporatist unions would ensure greater working-class benefit from industrial progress.[80]

La Rocque and other critics of the Popular Front were thus prepared to approve of its social reforms (at least in principle) without condoning the strikes themselves. Not only were these deemed to be illegal, and in particular a violation of the laws of property, but they also represented the tyranny of a revolutionary minority over the French people as a whole, especially over the middle classes and rural workers for whom the strikes were of little benefit. Although both the Popular Front and its adversaries were now claiming the middle classes as part of the people, the strikes led to an important difference in emphasis. While the Popular Front hastened to identify itself with the workers on strike, its opponents sought to capitalize on middle-class fears, even if they continued to express their sympathy for the legitimate demands of the workers. The strikes should not, they claimed, become the opportunity for a minority to triumph over the collective and national interest. 'Where is France? Where are the French people?' demanded Pierre Gaxotte on 13 June, just as La Rocque was calling for the middle classes to awaken from their stupor in order to avert a calamity.[81] Indeed it seemed to Gaxotte that the electoral people (whose will had some nominal legitimacy) were now being overtaken by a people who threatened the very existence of democracy.

> Democracy ceases to exist when universal suffrage, victorious in political terms, sees itself overwhelmed—and how!—in the social arena. Where does the threat come from? From all those foreigners who do not vote, but who are admitted to the unions. From the under-20s, who do not vote either, but who are admitted to the unions. From women who do not vote—which is absurd—but who dominate the unions.[82]

It was in this context that the question of revolution was posed, as the French people appeared liable to become the victims of a domineering minority. Blaming the revolutionary character of the strikes on a minority, especially a foreign one, was also a means of exculpating the people as a whole. The more terrifying the tyrants, the less the people themselves could be held responsible for organizing the strikes or for promoting disorder and division. In order to save the people, Gaxotte believed, it was futile to have confidence in such Jewish leaders as Léon Blum, Jules Moch, or Jean Zay, 'those individuals [who] carry with them the germs of decomposition'.[83] Those organizing or deliberately failing to repress the strikes could not have the interests of the people at heart, and *Action Française*, with its inveterate suspicion of foreigners in such situations, added that the Soviet leaders were quite probably aided in their designs by German exiles and members of the Gestapo.[84] It was, of course, Moscow that was invariably identified as the real culprit, and *Le Flambeau* even traced the organization of the strikes to the Congress of the Comintern in 1935.[85] Meanwhile the majority of French workers, the genuine 'people of France', were seen as unwilling and vulnerable victims in a situation beyond their control. *Action Française* cited an example of the punishment of strike leaders by ordinary workers in the Maine-et-Loire region, and argued that:

> These reactions prove that the communist agitators are meeting with serious resistance from the French people. If the majority of workers intend to defend their rights and fight for their professional demands, they do not want to be manipulated by politicians, and they remain defiant of Communist tyranny.[86]

Despite the right's inflammatory allegations of revolution, the Popular Front and its right-wing adversaries were both, ironically, seeking to present the people as a largely pacific force. The Popular Front hoped thereby to reassure the public that further disorder was unlikely, and to imply that the people shared with their new government not only the same goals but also a sense of co-operation in achieving them. The right suggested that the real aims of the Popular Front and the people were widely divergent, and endeavoured, by making the Communist and Socialist leaders the scapegoats, to exculpate the people from any deep-rooted responsibility for the strikes. The only groups that consistently emphasized the revolutionary character of the people were those that remained faithful to the anti-republican, proletarian rhetoric of 1934: the opposition groups of the extreme left.

The very existence of these groups reveals how far the Popular Front's image of the people had evolved over the previous two years, and how public opinion appeared to have evolved with it. The idea of an 'elusive revolution' (*révolution manquée*) was developed both in 1936 and subsequently by those who had participated in these movements of opposition and by their sympathizers.[87] Daniel Guérin, whose *Front populaire, révolution manquée* clearly exemplifies this tendency,[88] was himself a participant in the strikes of June 1936, and, as a member of the Gauche Révolutionnaire, claimed in his autobiographical account to be speaking on behalf of his late colleague, Marceau Pivert. Jacques Danos and Marcel Gibelin, whose account of *June '36: Class Struggle and the Popular Front in France* described how 'the revolutionary spirit of the class collided with their leaders' determined passivity'[89] had also belonged to this movement. The characteristics of this vision were closely inspired by the Popular Front's apparent desertion of left-wing principles. Left-wing dissidents endeavoured to undermine the relationship between the people and the Popular Front by arguing that the interests of the two had became increasingly irreconcilable in the period 1934–36. In particular they criticized the image of a non-threatening, all-embracing people as a dramatic betrayal of faith in the revolutionary proletariat. The collaboration of the Socialist and Communist Parties with the Radicals— and thus with the hated bourgeoisie—was roundly condemned, as was their support of national unity, a sacrifice of working-class interests on the altar of bourgeois patriotism. With reference to the strikes of 1936, those on the extreme left envisaged the revolutionary masses as ready for direct action, but betrayed by the Communist leaders' cynical desertion of their former beliefs.

In 1936 these views were characteristic of a number of minority groups. Among them was the Gauche Révolutionnaire, organized within the SFIO in October 1935 under the leadership of Marceau Pivert, and which called for a 'militant Popular Front' and the replacement of the bourgeois state with democratic mass organizations.[90] 'In peace as in war' insisted Marceau Pivert, 'ONLY the proletariat, rising up against the bourgeoisie in violent struggle, can obtain a progressive result.'[91] A similar attitude was adopted by Jean Zyromski, who condemned the class-inclusive strategy of the Popular Front and exalted the idea of a proletarian dictatorship 'invigorated by the working masses, the fire of revolution'.[92] Meanwhile the Jeunesses Socialistes Révolutionnaires similarly attacked the Popular Front's idea of the people, denying any commonality of interest across class boundaries or within a national framework.

> Yes, there is a 'fraternity', but this fraternity has nothing in common either with the nation or with the French people. It is a class-based fraternity, a fraternity that unites the exploited just as it has united the exploiters.[93]

Also active at this time were the Groupes d'Action Révolutionnaire (GAR), created on the initiative of three members of the SFIO but excluded from the party in February 1936 during the purge of its more extreme tendencies. They expounded their views on revolutionary proletarian action through their own newspaper, La Commune de Paris, and attracted considerable support from Trotskyites, even though Trotsky himself denied any allegiance to their movement in December 1935.[94] Together with the Jeunesses Socialistes Révolutionnaires and the Bolshevik–Leninist group, the GAR founded the Parti Communiste Internationaliste, a section of the Fourth International.[95]

During the strikes, *La Commune de Paris* urged the workers to take direct control of the factories and criticized the attitudes of Communist, CGT, and ex-CGTU leaders. The rhetoric of the GAR was so aggressive that by 5 June the groups were threatened with legal sanctions for provocation to murder and violence.[96]

What was striking about these groups, however, was not simply their uniform exaltation of a revolutionary proletariat in opposition to the pacific Popular Front people, but also their failure to achieve widespread resonance either in public opinion or among the supposedly revolutionary masses. The GAR recruited in both Paris and the provinces, but had only 500–600 members by May 1936. Appeals to rural workers were particularly unsuccessful.[97] Meanwhile the activity of Marceau Pivert's Gauche Révolutionnaire was temporarily curtailed when Pivert himself was given a post in the government under Jules Moch, implementing government policy for the press, radio, and cinema.[98] But the fundamental problem seemed to be the reluctance of the people on strike to show the expected signs of revolutionary initiative or ambition. With unconscious irony, Marceau Pivert—who believed that the masses should achieve revolutionary goals through their own initiative—blamed the absence of revolution on the dearth of suitable leaders.

> The anxious masses have an obscure awareness of all the possibilities of the moment; they are ready for every sacrifice, as events in Brest and Toulon have shown. (...) But where are the managers, the strategists, and the strategies to lead them to success?[99]

Between April and June 1936 the conflict over the image of the people reached particular intensity, as the Popular Front sought to claim not only the victorious electorate, but also the celebratory people in the streets and the working people on strike. Its image of the people as pacific victors should not be taken at face value, but rather situated in the context of the Popular Front's strategy to consolidate its own position. Its relationship with these various 'peoples' was constantly challenged by a mordant right-wing press, by the self-styled national-popular organizations such as the Croix de Feu and the Parti National Populaire, as well as by political Catholics. All of these groups attempted to present comparable solutions to the social question, even to the extent of calling for paid holidays and a 40-hour week, and of accusing the Popular Front of appropriating their own social programmes. The right's response to the potential subversion of the people in the street and on strike was not merely to emphasize the danger of revolution, but also to vindicate the French people by blaming foreign and revolutionary leaders. At the same time, the far left challenged the very idea of a class-inclusive, national people, and lamented the failure of the revolutionary proletariat to live up to its expectations. However strongly Popular Front accounts might claim it was the sole representative of the people, it was, as its strategy suggested, still part of a continuing contest, and its image of a peaceful, rational people rested on very fragile foundations. The electoral victory might have changed the character and boundaries of the conflict, but old rivalries were set to continue in new forms.

4
The Challenge from the Right: The Parti Social Français and the Parti Populaire Français

At 11.15 on the morning of 19 June 1936, police in the twelfth *arrondissement* of Paris made a startling discovery. As they patrolled the streets for subversive flags or placards at the windows of private apartments, they noticed a large kitchen knife, carefully suspended from the balcony of 2, Rue de Charolais.[1] Cross-examining the residents to discover the meaning of the gesture and ordering the knife's immediate removal, they discovered that it had been attached to the balcony by Mademoiselle Pélissier, a fervent admirer of the dissolved Action Française and of Charles Maurras' encouragement to take direct action against one's political enemies.[2] Three days later, a tricolour accompanied by two offensive slogans was sighted at the window of a house on the Rue des Ursulines in the Latin Quarter: one banner proclaimed 'death to the Jews' while the other denounced the 'Comrades' Republic'. Several white flags were also on prominent display: potentially royalist symbols, although the owner of one such flag claimed that his primary concern was peace at a time of civil war.[3] These self-consciously symbolic gestures encapsulated a particularly visceral, violent opposition to the Popular Front and its leaders, but they also reflected a wider phenomenon. On 18 June the remaining right-wing leagues had been dissolved, and the Popular Front government seemed in a particularly strong position to dominate the public space and to undermine its adversaries. Yet as Mademoiselle Pélissier's reaction suggested, the dissolution of the leagues did not diminish the resolution of their supporters. Pélissier's statement of opposition was unambiguous, violent, and illegal, like many other expressions of opposition noted by the police in June and July 1936. But the summer also witnessed the resurgence of the right in legal form, as a series of new parties were created within the parliamentary Republic, notably Colonel de la Rocque's Parti Social Français and Jacques Doriot's Parti Populaire Français. Doriot's supporters were to reach 100,000; La Rocque's new party rapidly became the largest political party in France.

This chapter investigates how the new government and its restructured opposition continued the pursuit of the people that had been developing in 1934–36. The Popular Front was now transformed from a partisan, left-wing movement into the government of the French Republic, with the means to develop its image of the victorious people in the public space through mass communication and popular culture. For this reason the festivities marking 14 July 1936 have often been considered its moment of apotheosis, portrayed by sympathetic historians as a 'dress rehearsal for the popular festival and the paid holiday' that was held in 'an atmosphere of joy, of tranquil revolution'.[4] The swiftness with which the Popular Front's social reforms were elaborated and voted on was symptomatic of the government's initial rush of legislative activity. In its first 12 weeks, Blum's government passed a series of new laws to dissolve the right-wing leagues, nationalize the arms industries and semi-nationalize the Bank of France, establish a Wheat Marketing Board, and institute a programme of public works. Blum's cabinet included dynamic young men: the Socialist Léo Lagrange for the new position of Undersecretary of State for the Organization of Sport and Leisure, and the Radical Jean Zay as Minister of National Education. These two men in particular were to shape the new government's cultural policy. It also included three women, a considerable novelty at a time when female suffrage was yet to be introduced. The Radical Cécile Brunschvicg was chosen as Undersecretary of State for Technical Education, the Socialist Irène Joliot-Curie as Undersecretary of State for Scientific Research, and Suzanne Lacore as Undersecretary of State for the Protection of Children.[5] These early days appeared even more hopeful in retrospect, for no sooner had the Popular Front celebrated its victory with the festival of 14 July than Franco's military coup against the Spanish Popular Front government provoked the outbreak of the Spanish Civil War. On 20 July Blum received a direct appeal for planes and arms from his Spanish counterpart José Giral—but despite strong sympathy for a fellow Popular Front government, Blum decided after three weeks of agonizing debate to pursue an official policy of non-intervention. Given the considerable support for Franco on the French right, and the danger that foreign aid to both sides might escalate into a second World War, it seemed impossible to choose otherwise. Nevertheless, the policy of non-intervention was to prove fatally divisive for the

Popular Front. The Communists in particular continued to lobby the government in the name of the Spanish republicans, and to encourage the strikes in August that were similarly supportive of the Spanish left. Yet Blum remained adamant, and provoked further opposition when the flight of capital following industrial unrest prompted the government to devalue the Franc on 25 September. During the Radical Party Conference in Biarritz in October, pro-Popular Front speakers were shouted down by other members, and the final vote of support for the Popular Front stipulated the immediate cessation of the strikes, an end to Communist agitation for the Spanish republicans, and explicit government respect for middle-class demands.

In the light of the Popular Front's rapidly changing fortunes in the summer of 1936, references to its relationship with the people in this period have focused either on the image of popular triumph in the festivities of 14 July or on the more combative image of the people associated with the republicans (and the International Brigades) in the Spanish Civil War.[6] Yet the formation of new right-wing parties at the very moment of Popular Front triumph, explicitly challenging its representation of the people within the framework of the Republic, continued rather than diminished the rivalry that had been developing in 1934–36. Since the riots of February 1934, the focus of this rivalry had shifted from the representation of the crowd in the street to the organization of the masses in associative life. By 1936, the representation of the people not only as political actors but also as a political community was centred on a search for national reconciliation, reflecting a 'partial community of thought' around questions of social reform and an imagined community above geographical and class boundaries. Studying the rivalry between the Popular Front and the new right-wing parties (the latter more normally analysed within the debate on French fascism)[7] reveals a twofold evolution. In rhetoric, the determination to imagine national reconciliation continued to intensify; in street politics, the deep-rooted antipathies between left and right developed likewise.

The Popular Front government and popular festival

When the Popular Front government came to power, its supporters were by no means agreed on the image of the people to emerge from the demonstrations and festivities of the coming weeks. In particular, there was a sharp distinction between the combative political role envisaged for the people by more extreme Socialists and Communists, and the reassuring image of popular fraternity that had become the official Popular Front image of the strikes. During the SFIO Congress of 30 May–2 June there was a noticeable friction between Marceau Pivert, who advocated the creation of a 'popular guard' to smooth the path to working-class rule, and Léon Blum, who reminded the congress that the Popular Front government had not been elected to realize the goals of socialist revolution.[8] While Pivert was planning a 'popular guard' the Communists were discussing the creation of 'Popular Front committees'—similar, so the police feared, to militant working-class associations in Russia in 1917.[9] At a local level, these committees would assemble delegates from Popular Front organizations; in a wider context, they would bring together urban and rural workers, soldiers, and the middle classes to participate in popular councils. Closely supervised by the Communist Party, such committees could be used to 'take the temperature of the masses', exerting pressure on the government to fulfil the popular will and defending the Popular Front against its adversaries. The police were alarmed by the prospect of what appeared to prefigure a 'veritable illegal government' alongside the elected government of the Popular Front, and kept the committees under careful observation (although their fears proved in this instance to be unfounded). Meanwhile, the concept of a politically conscious and combative people also influenced Communist plans for 14 June demonstrations. These had been suggested by the Communists in celebration of the Popular Front victory, but were viewed with circumspection by the Radical and Socialist Parties, which preferred to devote full attention to the resolution of the strike movement and to the victory celebrations that were to be incorporated within the traditional festivities of 14 July. The celebrations of 14 June were therefore organized on Communist initiative alone, and were presented as a powerful demonstration of strength to their 'fascist' opponents. The character of the occasion was twofold: a synthesis of aggressive Communist rhetoric and the all-inclusive discourse of the Popular Front. 40,000 supporters were crowded into the Buffalo Stadium, where the Communist deputy Marcel Gitton described the juxtaposition of red flags and tricolours during the strikes symbolizing the united cause of workers and middle classes, and Paul Vaillant-Couturier promised 'to fight for the greatness of the people of our country and for the defence of the international proletariat.'[10] Speeches were followed by gymnastic displays, and processions in which the most combative workers in the recent strikes were accorded pride of place.[11] Introducing the processions, Jacques Duclos observed with strategic ambiguity that the Communists had been closely involved in the strikes without, however, directing them. The meeting concluded with a rousing rendition of *La Marseillaise*, during which a large painting was revealed of the Republic marching towards liberty, her fist raised in triumphant defiance of her enemies—and in suitable reflection of the crowd below.[12]

The Popular Front celebrations of 14 July should be seen against this background: a lavish popular festival that endowed the image of the united, national people with official approval, while masking underlying tensions. If the people appeared spontaneous in their celebrations—and *Le Populaire* claimed that it was this spontaneity and enthusiasm that distinguished these festivals from those organized by dictatorial regimes[13]—the celebrations were nevertheless the result of scrupulous preparation. Leaflets provided details of the meeting points and trajectory of each participating group,[14] and ministerial notes from the end of June onwards reveal a keen determination to increase mass participation in these events through an extensive mobilization of transport and communications. Léo Lagrange placed particular emphasis on government co-operation with the Comité National de Rassemblement Populaire: 'I must insist', he wrote, 'on the exceptional importance of this demonstration, with which it is appropriate to associate—for the first time—the masses of our country.'[15] As well as funding the habitual decoration of public buildings, the government also subsidized rail tickets for those travelling from the provinces, and provided platforms for the speakers. On 10 July, Jules Moch (head of the General Secretariat in Blum's government) wrote to the Minister of Post, Telephones, and Telegraphs to complain of the absence of sufficient equipment, 'which risks depriving the demonstration of 14 July of a means of propaganda and expression to which I attach great importance'[16]—and he specifically requested large numbers of loudspeakers for the afternoon procession. His appeal appears to have been heard, for descriptions of the procession made particular mention of the effective strategies of communication. One participant described in *L'Œuvre* how Léon Blum's speech in the Place de la Nation was broadcast to the dense crowd of supporters in the Boulevard Diderot.

> We could hear the cheers that greeted him at the invisible Place de la Nation. And the crowd joined its spontaneous applause to the applause coming from the loudspeakers, to which we looked with friendship and confidence.[17]

These speeches were also broadcast on national radio and sold as records,[18] furthering the communion between a visible people in the street and the people of France. It was a communion that the partisan press sought to promote as it emphasized the diversity of those participating. Unity across class boundaries had already been suggested by the programmes issued to participants: the cover featured a sketch of two workers holding a hammer and sickle respectively, and singing from the same book as a white-collar worker in a suit and tie.[19] *La Vie ouvrière*, while devoting special attention to the miners and provincial delegations that took part, likewise described 'the desire of the people of France to unite against the factious [leagues] and the two hundred families.'[20] The participation of these miners in their working clothes reflected the exaltation of the proletariat within the wider working people—and the miners were not the only workers to come attired in the clothes of their profession, for one of the other CGT delegations included 'washerwomen, cleaners, and cleaning ladies [who] laughed as they brandished their brooms and feather dusters, which made a delightful impression.'[21] Indeed, sympathetic reports on the processions often emphasized the participation of women and children, notably within the Femmes Socialistes de la Seine, the Comité Mondial des Femmes contre la Guerre et le Fascisme, and the Fédération de l'Enfance. The women of the Faubourg Saint-Antoine were particularly praised.

> Dear, magnificent street; dear, magnificent faubourg! This is where we can see at the windows, majestically attired in ample, scarlet dresses, the descendants of the citizens who stormed the Bastille and went to Versailles to demand bread. There can be no popular festival without these powerful goddesses[22] (Figure 13).

Figure 13 *L'Œuvre*, 15 July 1936 (Courtesy of the Archives de la Préfecture de Police, Paris).

The people of Paris, explicitly identified with their revolutionary ancestors, were also represented as the people of France. Delegations from the suburbs, the provinces and the French Empire attended, and *Le Populaire* was at pains to emphasize the national character of the festival—'national because Paris has reflected, with all its republican and revolutionary spirit, the vibrant faith of the French provinces.'[23] The image of people in the street thus mirrored that of the national community. And this popular celebration was portrayed not so much as a homage to the revolutionary past or to the Republic, but as the writing of a new page in French history. Completely identified with the Popular Front, these were a people whose calm demonstrated their deep resolution and maturity. 'This year's 14 July has been a triumphant one,' concluded *Le Populaire*.

> Not the 14 July of a people drunk with victory. But that of a nation content to be restored to health, respectful of tradition, and determined to direct its own destiny calmly and methodically.[24]

Now that the Popular Front was in power the demonstration was one of several means by which it endeavoured to organize the people and identify its interests with theirs. One facet of the new government's cultural policy was an increased control of communications, explicitly intended to undermine right-wing influence. In part this was a response to the Rassemblement Populaire, which had demanded liberty of the press and the declaration of its financial resources, as well as the organization of state radio broadcasts. Such broadcasts were supposed to ensure 'the precision of news reports and the equality of political and social organizations at the microphone'[25] (although it was clear that some of these organizations were to be more equal than others).[26] With Marceau Pivert in the department of state radio, programmes remained highly sympathetic to the Popular Front movement, if not always to the government's official line. Not only did Pivert ensure regular broadcasts on the Spanish Civil War, despite the government's official policy of non-intervention, but he also replaced broadcasts on colonial policy with CGT broadcasts, notably by the Socialist Georges Lefranc and his wife Émilie, both closely involved in the running of the Centre Confédéral d'Éducation Ouvrière (an educational body established by the CGT in 1932).[27]

The Popular Front also employed its official powers in more direct neutralization of its adversaries. As well as anticipating closer government control of the radio and the press, the Rassemblement Populaire had demanded the dissolution of the right-wing leagues, and it was not long before this was approved by Parliament. Unofficially, Popular Front groups had reinforced public suspicion of the leagues for some time, and the dissolution of these leagues was frequently voted at the end of private meetings. In May 1936 the police recorded that the economic reform movement JEUNES (Jeunes Équipes Unies pour une Nouvelle Économie Sociale) was secretly fabricating counterfeit Croix de Feu posters, each including the Croix de Feu symbol and the slogan 'All power to La Rocque' or 'Long live fascist France'.[28] These were displayed in prominent places, intended to reinforce the public's identification of La Rocque with fascism (an identification that La Rocque himself never explicitly accepted). Further campaigns had been conducted in the press—especially *L'Humanité*—to challenge the leagues and their respective journalists with allegations that they were stockpiling weapons or receiving funds from shady financial dealers. Some preparation had thus already been made for the governmental decision of 18 June to dissolve the Croix de Feu, the Parti National Populaire (former Jeunesses Patriotes), the Parti National Républicain (former Solidarité Française), and the Parti Franciste.

The PSF and the PPF: Social patriotism and national communism

Following its assumption of power and dissolution of the leagues, the Popular Front government held a powerful position in the rivalry to represent the people, seemingly justified in presenting its images of the masses as the reconciled French people, and the festival of 14 July as the new 'Fête de la Fédération' of a united, anti-fascist France. But although the dissolution of the 'factious' leagues provoked allegations of hypocrisy (militant Socialist and Communist groups were seen by the right as equally 'factious'), the dissolution was not the severe blow to right-wing forces that the Popular Front had intended. Indeed, as the right-wing deputy Xavier Vallat argued in Parliament, the dissolution was likely to be beneficial for nationalist action as a whole. In particular, he hoped that whereas the leagues had failed to act in unity, their dissolution might prompt the formation of a single body of nationalists.[29] The question of a right-wing 'National Front' or 'National Popular Front' had already been much discussed. In February 1936, the leader of the Parti National Populaire in Garenne-Colombes had called for all right-wing associations (including the Croix de Feu and Action Française) to rally to what he described as the 'National Popular Front'.[30] And on 14 July 1936 the Prefecture de Police received the demands of a Rassemblement Populaire—not the Rassemblement Populaire of the Popular Front, but a rival association formed by the dissolved Solidarité Française and Parti National Corporatif that merely happened to have the same name.[31]

Once the leagues and some of the right-wing parties had been dissolved, there was nothing that in theory prevented the formation of national popular parties within a republican framework. Since the new parties would be in opposition, they could benefit from public dissatisfaction with the Popular Front. They could propose comparable solutions to social problems, and offer strong leadership in contrast to the weak Socialists and dangerous Communists they described as currently betraying the people of France. It was in this context that La Rocque's Croix de Feu movement, already broadening to include associations for women and young people, was reborn as the Parti Social Français, combining an explicit republicanism with an equally explicit social concern. Similarly, Jacques Doriot's Parti Populaire Français was created to encompass many members of the dissolved leagues who wished to continue their political activity—and within a wider framework than had been possible with the leagues themselves. Both parties sought to counter the Popular Front on its own territory, whether in structural organization, portrayal of the people as political actors, or the imagination of the national community.

For Colonel de la Rocque and his PSF, the people to be attracted and represented by the new party were the French people whose unity had been sealed in their wartime suffering and generosity: a people who were patriotic, heroic, and self-sacrificing. Deeply rooted in the ideology of the Croix de Feu, the people of the PSF were also imagined in direct reaction to the Popular Front's victory of 1936. First, and in deliberate opposition to the narrow equation of people with proletariat that La Rocque believed to be characteristic of the new government, his image of the people was marked by fraternity above class barriers. This fraternity had often been mentioned in the propaganda of the Croix de Feu, which emphasized the solidarity in the trenches of the Great War and in the common experience of personal loss,[32] and denounced the Popular Front's lack of respect for the military (Figure 14). Within the body of the wounded, national people, class tensions were insignificant in comparison to the binding pain of common suffering. The unity of the entire people in a time of national danger provided the essence of the 'mystique'—a word frequently employed by La Rocque—that was central to his ideology. Building on these foundations, and in a deliberate reflection of the Popular Front's language of reconciliation, La Rocque

14 *Juillet 1936... Le nouveau salut au drapeau.*

Figure 14   Le Flambeau, 18 July 1936 (Courtesy of the Archives de la Préfecture de Police, Paris).

proclaimed the primary objective of his new party to be 'the reconciliation and fraternal collaboration of the French, regardless of the class to which they provisionally belong, and with the aim of ensuring the greatness and prosperity of the fatherland'[33] (Figure 15).

Secondly, the patriotism of the PSF people was emphasized to highlight the 'foreignness' of the current Popular Front leaders: Léon Blum was viewed as a hapless pawn of the Communists, and the PCF depicted as unswervingly obedient to Stalin. At the founding meeting of the PSF in the Salle Wagram in Paris on 10 July 1936, the Basque deputy Jean Ybarnegaray accused Blum's government of preparing imminent revolution 'on Moscow's orders',[34] and presented the Popular Front as the prelude to both civil unrest and international conflict. According to the leaders of the new PSF, the people of France deserved better than to be dragged into fratricidal war by foreign revolutionaries. Capable of great courage and valour in the tradition of the First World War veterans (*poilus*), these people demanded worthier leaders who would direct their energies towards the service of state and nation.

Patriotic, united, and heroic, the people imagined by the PSF were not, however, inherently self-disciplined. La Rocque's adversaries attributed his wariness of spontaneous popular action to a profound fear of the

Figure 15   Poster of the Parti Social Français (Courtesy of the Bibliothèque Nationale, Paris).

people inherited from his aristocratic ancestors, seen as traitors to the nation during the French Revolution. Paul Chopine (a disillusioned ex-member of the Croix de Feu) even described this fear as pivotal to La Rocque's fascination with the word 'people':

> Companions who have also attended one of La Rocque's meetings can vouch for this: he simply cannot pronounce the word 'people' in a straightforward manner. He puts a certain emphasis on the word; one feels that he can talk of nothing else, and that he fears the sovereign people instinctively.[35]

But if La Rocque had few illusions about independent popular action, he retained confidence in the potential of the people when under suitable guidance. Not only did he condemn the leadership of the Popular Front as foreign; he also described it as ineffective, prompting popular action to degenerate into anarchy. With deliberate evocation of the military bravado that had been a prerequisite for Croix de Feu membership,[36] he belittled the leadership of Léon Blum by observing that 'his strategies as a commander were not learned in the trenches of the front line.'[37] Similarly, the vice-president of the PSF and popular aviator Jean Mermoz compared the leadership of the PSF with the leadership of a flight crew, emphasizing the necessity for absolute obedience, and the unity and fraternity forged through common sacrifice in time of danger.

> Silence your petty individualism. Beware of those who do nothing but chatter: maintain your interior discipline, and think only of the common task. Do not criticize your leader: follow him. What a joke to say that the masses give orders and the leaders obey! The leaders command and the masses obey. When the masses are not obedient, it is because they no longer have a leader. We have one.[38]

While the PSF deliberately opposed the parties of the Popular Front in its image of the people as political actors, it imitated its adversaries in its structure and support base. At the founding meeting on 10 July, La Rocque made clear that if the government had authorized the creation of a party on the lines of the conservative Fédération Républicaine, he himself had other ideas in mind. 'I don't want a party of conservatives or moderates,' he insisted, 'interested only in chatter and not action, who play into the hands of the ruling powers and the demagogic authorities. We will organize ourselves like the SFIO by creating local committees, regional and departmental federations focused on Paris.'[39] And indeed the statutes of the SFIO served as a model for the new party's administrative structure, established in many departments within weeks of the new party's foundation.[40]

After the dissolution of the league, internal divisions and rivalries led to the departure of Joseph Pozzo di Borgo (a wealthy aristocrat who hoped to be La Rocque's successor) and with him some of the more upper-class members,[41] and so the PSF sought to appeal, as the Mouvement Social des Croix de Feu had done, to a broad-based working people. Local headquarters were established in residential areas, and targeted the lower middle classes by appealing to their powerful anti-Communist sentiment. In Paris, regular meetings were organized for the PSF members of particular factories and trades, where professional matters could be discussed at a safe distance from the pressures of trade unions (and indeed the CGT banned its members from attending such meetings).[42] Since men, women, and children could all be registered as members of the new party, membership figures rose rapidly, and the PSF deputy Charles Vallin noted with satisfaction that the party was well represented in parliament, as well as in municipal and departmental committees.[43]

The PSF faced the obvious disadvantage that the Popular Front government restricted its use of public space for demonstrations and celebrations, yet it contrived nonetheless to organize and depict private meetings as evidence of popular support. Continuing in the tradition of the 'motorized meetings' of the Croix de Feu, the PSF held a number of open-air assemblies, where loudspeakers were installed to project La Rocque's speeches to his supporters, and charabancs hired to transport them to and from the chosen site.[44] The constitutive meeting of the PSF, which according to *Le Flambeau* assembled 15,000 new members,[45] was also an aptly timed opportunity to oppose prevalent images of the Popular Front's 14 July celebrations with photographs of the PSF's own numerous and disciplined supporters. Silhouettes of La Rocque and the other PSF leaders appeared in *Le Flambeau* on 18 July, accompanied by two large photographs of the seated crowd, intently focused on their speeches.[46]

While Colonel de la Rocque modelled his new party on the structure of the SFIO, the ex-Communist Jacques Doriot created his Parti Populaire Français in explicit opposition to the PCF. Born in 1898 to a peasant family in the Oise department, Doriot had evolved from one of the PCF's rising stars into its most uncompromising critic. Thick-set in appearance and pugnacious by temperament, he had worked in his youth in a factory in Saint-Denis, joining the Jeunesses Socialistes and becoming renowned for his skill in street combat. After fighting in the First World War he joined the PCF in 1920, training in its Moscow leadership school between 1921 and 1923. In 1924 he was elected deputy, then mayor of Saint-Denis, and in 1927 was briefly General Secretary of the PCF. Stalin, who met him in 1926, was impressed by his drive and commitment. Yet Doriot and Maurice Thorez were bitter rivals, and when Doriot proposed a common front against fascism before it became official party policy, he was brusquely exiled from the party. In 1936 he founded the Parti Populaire Français: a dramatic turning point in the evolution from communism to fascism that has formed the overarching theme of his biographies.[47] While the imagination of the people is not a particular focus in these studies, they do emphasize the synthesis of nationalism and communism from which Doriot's concept of the people as political actors was to develop. They also emphasize his ideological eclecticism—Doriot was a man of action rather than a man of thought—and the consequent importance of some of the intellectual converts to the Party, notably the Jewish journalist Bertrand de Jouvenel,[48] the anti-Semitic Paul Marion (a former member of the Croix de Feu), and the novelist Pierre Drieu la Rochelle, whose *Socialisme fasciste* of 1934 had already indicated the direction of his sympathies.[49]

Doriot proclaimed his new party to be 'of the people', and duly named it the Parti Populaire Français. 'We know the people far better than some of those who claim to speak in their name', he announced, 'because we come from the people ourselves.'[50] Simon Sabiani, the Corsican leader of the PPF in Marseilles, likewise proclaimed himself to be a 'man of the people, son of the people, friend of the people',[51] and Bertrand de Jouvenel claimed that, while not himself of popular origin, he had come to know and understand the people through his involvement with the PPF in Saint-Denis.[52] How then did Doriot and his allies imagine the people—and did those attracted to his party correspond to the ideal-type? While La Rocque's image of the people was rooted in a supposedly collective memory of the First World War—a remembrance of unity, sacrifice, and self-discipline—Doriot's image of the people was marked by his conception of the revolutionary proletariat, transposed from a communist to a nationalist framework. The 'people' described and appealed to by Doriot were instinctively patriotic, like those of La Rocque, but they were also reckless and hot-tempered, like Doriot himself. One of his favourite role models was the revolutionary hero Danton, whose words Doriot was proud to borrow when he proclaimed to the people of the sixth *arrondissement* 'What do we need to conquer the enemies of the fatherland? Audacity, more audacity! Always audacity!'[53]

Audacity was certainly one of the most salient characteristics of Doriot's image of the people. For Doriot, as for his ideologues, the people combined revolutionary potential with a submission to the higher authorities of leader and nation that the current circumstances were seen to demand. Condemning Soviet (PCF) interference in French affairs, Doriot described the French people as requiring no such external inspiration: 'These people are intelligent, combative; they do not need lessons from anyone in the art of revolution.'[54] He expressed his confidence in the ability of the people to translate their own desires into political and social reality, even if this necessitated the overturning of democratic institutions.[55] Sabiani, too, made threatening predictions of the destructive majesty of popular anger when he described the inevitable revolt against existing political structures: 'I predict an immense national upheaval. It is inevitable. For one day the great anger of the people will turn against those who have unleashed it, against the Moscow Communists and their servile allies.'[56] However it was not only among the proletariat that such energy and anger could be found. 'At the present time, the workers are not the only dynamic force,' insisted Doriot. 'There are also the peasants, the middle classes, the young generation; all of these represent the progressive forces in the country.'[57]

Since the Communists lacked the audacity to engage with this popular will for change,[58] the leaders of the PPF considered it their task to compensate for the deficiency. 'Fight under my command—and take the risk of falling!' was Sabiani's cavalier attitude, while Doriot evoked a fusion of people and leader in what he referred to as the 'supreme battle'. 'I know', he claimed, 'that the people of this country are brave enough to follow me—and win.'[59] Drieu la Rochelle, following obediently in this perspective, went as far as to describe the *Patrie* as the mother of the people and Doriot as the father: 'all his life he has been ardent, daring, generous, combative.'[60] As in the case of the PSF, it was difficult for the PPF to represent these relationships in the public space, yet Doriot ensured that *L'Émancipation nationale* featured regular images of mass meetings, whether in vast halls in Paris or in the open air, and that he himself featured prominently as leader of the people. One such mass meeting in Marseilles at the end of July 1936 was pictured in *L'Émancipation nationale* in the form of a collage, with photographs of PPF members arranged around a disproportionately large photograph of Doriot brandishing a flag. Four other large photographs of Doriot were placed around the central collage, depicting his theatrical gestures and seeking to reinforce his image as the man of the people (he was attired in a shirt and trousers; La Rocque habitually wore a suit).[61] Underneath the collage was a long photograph of the stage, with Doriot raising his arm in salute,[62] imitated by all present. Such common rituals and experience were presented by Doriot as contributing to the triumph of the collective body—the nation—over the individual.

> The collective psychosis necessary for the accomplishment of great transformations is not created by quibbling over academic details. It is created by repeating the same ideas, the same formulae that must be stated and restated; the same truths that must be told and retold a hundred times before they become an idea common to the entire country.[63]

The controversial nature of this PPF claim was clear from the reactions of the Popular Front. Both *L'Humanité* and *Le Populaire* responded immediately to the creation of the PPF, focusing their anger on the scandalous claim of the new party to attract the people, especially the workers. *Le Populaire* reassured its readers that betrayal by those who had 'crossed the barricade' was an unfortunate but not serious phenomenon in the course of the people's march to power, and characterized the new PPF as nationalist, anti-Marxist, and fervently against the people.[64] *L'Humanité*, still more directly challenged by the renegade Doriot, denied with fervour that his party possessed any ability to attract the workers.

> If a worker happened to stray into a [PPF] meeting, what a revelation the presence of such henchmen as [Marcel] Bucard and [Pierre] Laval would be! A consortium of scheming and prying traitors, embittered and mediocre, and soliciting employment from big business—this is M. Doriot's party.[65]

The Communists refused to accept that his venture could be successful in Saint-Denis, and proclaimed their own conviction that the French people would know better than to support Doriot once they had realized his fascist sympathies. For just as Doriot accused his former colleagues of betraying the nation through their actions as Stalin's obedient servants, so likewise did the Communists accuse Doriot of betraying the nation as an agent of Hitler.[66] Were they mistaken, or wilfully blind to the actual composition of Doriot's party? Jean-Paul Brunet, in his study of the implantation and development of the Parti Populaire Français, suggests that the PPF was genuinely working class in its membership. He admits that exact statistical indications of PPF membership are difficult to obtain: most statistics originate from the PPF and must be treated with circumspection. But he estimates that working-class membership of Doriot's new party was probably as high as 50 per cent, and noted that the proportions of working-class delegates at the conferences of November 1936 and March 1938 were 49 per cent and 37 per cent, respectively.[67] Doriot's party thus represented a considerable challenge to the general strength of the Popular Front in the Parisian suburbs.

Imagined communities of people and nation

Claims to the 'people' by the Parti Social Français and Parti Populaire Français deliberately challenged the image and constitution of the Popular Front. Both the PSF and the PPF sought to reveal flaws in the Popular

Front's image of a triumphant, rational, and pacific people by reducing the Popular Front victory to that of a proletarian minority, lacking in self-discipline and suitable leadership. In contrast, the new parties pictured a people who were heroic or audacious, characterized by the willing sacrifice of personal or partisan interests for the sake of national grandeur and defence. The intended membership of the new parties was popular in the broadest sense, and in the case of the PPF it seems that members came from similar social backgrounds to those of the Popular Front. The rivalry between the Popular Front and the new parties of the right thus continued the appeal to the masses (and the sharply distinct presentations of these masses as political actors) that had characterized the pursuit of the people in 1934–36. This rivalry also continued in the imagination of national unity, particularly in the representation of the nation as territory and community.

When describing the nation in territorial terms, the Popular Front and the new right-wing parties remained clearly distinct: for the Popular Front, the nation was associated primarily with ideas and ideals rather than with the military sacrifice of the First World War (even if the army were increasingly celebrated as the 'sons of the people') and for the right, the military sacrifice remained paramount. Thus when the socialist writer Jean Guéhenno described the recent resurgence of patriotic sentiment on the left in his 1936 work *Jeunesse de la France*, he hastened to explain that the French nation was defined more by the principles of the French Revolution than by specific national territory.

> Devotion to the fatherland now signifies only a devotion to these ideas. We owe nothing to interests. We can do nothing for territory. We owe everything to—and can do everything for—these ideas. The only legitimate imperialism is the imperialism of reason.[68]

In his understanding, the French nation was not defined by the patriotism for which so many lives had been sacrificed in the First World War. France was, he believed, a young nation, but its youth derived from its origins in the Revolution rather than from the ardent young generation of 1914. Words as much as actions shaped its growth, and in *Jeunesse de la France* he traced the emergence of the French national identity primarily through the works of writers and intellectuals. Only those whose ideas won his approval were deemed to have been influential: whereas Rabelais and Montaigne might legitimately qualify as having shaped the French nation, the counter-revolutionary ideologue Joseph de Maistre most certainly did not. Guéhenno continued his logic into the contemporary period, describing Henri Barbusse, André Gide, and Romain Rolland as representing France, but excluding from this privilege both Charles Maurras and Jacques Bainville.[69] This association of national identity with ideas traceable back to the Revolution was also characteristic of the PCF manifesto of January 1936. Here Maurice Thorez explained that 'the French nation means the admirable people of our country, with generous hearts, proud independence, and indomitable courage', and in his subsequent analysis of the French people and nation, his first theme was the intellectuals whose work prefigured the emergence of Communist ideology. He then described the nation as the proletariat whose ancestors had fought in 1793, 1830, 1848, and 1871 (not mentioning 1914); as the peasantry whose ancestors had attacked the property of their noblemen; and as the young people who would write the future history of France.[70]

For the dissolved leagues and the new parties of the right, the territory of the French nation was more tangible. Incensed by the Popular Front's ban on nationalist processions to the tomb of the Unknown Soldier, the right sought solace in emphasizing the government's failure to understand the true meaning of the nation, which they saw as linked to a tradition of military sacrifice and to a Barresian cult of the earth.[71] The leagues and parties conceived of the nation as the 'complete reconciliation of the people of France (...) reconciliation beneath the folds of the tricolour flag, the emblem of French traditions and French glory.'[72] The nation was not only the reconciliation of the French people around a certain idea of France, it was also their communion with those who had sacrificed their lives for the fatherland in a past still very much within living memory. The particular devotion of the peasantry, sacrificing themselves for French soil in both life and death, was frequently mentioned.[73] It was for this reason that the Popular Front's juxtaposition of the red flag and the tricolour, *La Marseillaise* and *L'Internationale*, was seen as a wounding insult to the heroism of French military sacrifice, and as a clear threat of Soviet domination. Thus Henri Brunesseaux, municipal councillor for the first *arrondissement* and member of the Parti National Populaire, described his horror at seeing 'the rag of that red Pope, Léon Blum' displayed next to the tricolour that symbolized the patriotism of all the 'true' French.[74] Léon Bailby, sympathetic to the Parti Social Français, likewise described this debate over matters of ritual as concerning the very future of France, 'not merely because it touches the deepest feelings of our people, but because it touches the very position of the French state.'[75]

Beneath these violent disagreements over the nation as territory, however, were overlapping conceptions of the nation as community: a community reconciling not only social classes but also Paris and the provinces, metropolitan France and its Empire. The Popular Front had, after all, described the nation as a symbolic focus around which the people of France could unite, regardless of class. 14 July 1936 was depicted by *L'Humanité* as the renewal of the oath of unity between the working and middle classes, 'the rediscovered fraternity of all the genuine workers of the nation'[76]—and the nation was described more generally as the reconciliation of all who opposed the 'two hundred families', and as uniting Communists and Socialists with Catholics and even with ex-members of the Croix de Feu. The idea of the nation as a community also provided a means of imagining the reconciliation between urban and rural people—and indeed the latter were assuming increasing importance in Popular Front propaganda and for government reform. *La Vie est à nous*, the PCF film produced for the elections of 1936, included the story of a rural Communist in Saint Aubin-Le-Monial whose protection of his non-Communist family from economic hardship and exploitation earned him the respect of the entire population.[77] After the electoral victory, as the new Minister for Agriculture Georges Monnet prepared for the creation of the Wheat Marketing Board, both Socialist and Communist parties intensified their appeals to the rural population. Aware of their predominant association with the urban masses, they produced regular articles and pamphlets to assert their equal concern for the rural workers, anxious to undermine rural sympathy for the opposition.[78] By the end of May, leaders of both the SFIO and the PCF were even formulating plans for an 'Estates General of the Peasantry', while CGT militants were encouraging the joint participation of rural and urban workers in demonstrations, emphasizing the solidarity of the working people as well as the variety of their needs.[79]

It was striking that the Popular Front should employ the idea of the French nation not only to suggest the unity of the rural and urban people but also to celebrate the diverse traditions of the French provinces. In the early 1930s images of traditional rural France produced by the SFIO and PCF had often been critical, identifying the provinces as a bastion of conservatism and clericalism. The point was made visually in films such as *Colonies de vacances*, a PCF production of 1932 that contrasted the sombre interiors of rural homes with the outdoor activities and entertainment of a Communist holiday camp.[80] Yet in the demonstrations and propaganda of the Popular Front, the diversity of the provinces within the French nation was increasingly presented in glowing colours.

In May 1936 the former surrealist and AEAR militant Louis Aragon organized a Festival of French Folklore for the Comité National Féminin de Lutte contre la Guerre et le Fascisme. This event included regional singers and dancers from Alsace, Brittany, Provence, the Île de France, the Basque region, and the Auvergne,[81] and offered a medley of traditional melodies for its Parisian audience, many of whom would have grown up in the countryside. The provinces were also firmly integrated within the electoral victory celebrations:[82] delegates from across France took part in the Communist meeting in the Buffalo Stadium on 14 June dressed in regional costume, and the Rassemblement Populaire encouraged provincial delegates taking part in the 14 July festivities to dress likewise. *Le Populaire* commented admiringly on the distinctive appearance of these delegations, whether from the provinces or from North Africa,[83] and a considerable number of colonial workers also took part, proclaiming the slogans of the Popular Front in their respective languages.[84] While demonstrators in Paris were seen to represent the people of the provinces, there were also simultaneous demonstrations in the provinces as well as in the colonies, the larger of which were given special coverage in the Popular Front press. The reconciliation of races within the nation was given careful prominence, not least in reaction to Xavier Vallat's infamous insult to Léon Blum in the Chamber of Deputies, when Blum was presenting his new government for approval. Resisting Édouard Herriot's attempts to silence him, Vallat had observed that France was about to have its Disraeli, and accused Blum of being unable, as a Jew, to represent the old 'Gallo-Roman' nation of France. The nation would be better governed by anyone with peasant roots, Vallat had argued, than by this 'subtle Talmudist'.[85] *Le Peuple* recorded this parliamentary debate in detail, emphasizing Édouard Herriot's much-applauded response that there were in the Chamber 'neither Jews, nor Protestants, nor Catholics—but only Frenchmen.' It also recorded Léon Blum's spirited defence of his new government, and commented supportively that 'coming from the very depths of the nation, [the government] knows that the people intend to conserve what they have conquered by more than a century of sacrifices.'[86]

The parties of the right were similarly adamant in their vision of the nation as a reconciled social and geographical community—even if in practice, such reconciliation was dependent on exclusion. Addressing his audience at the first meeting of the PPF at Saint Denis on 28 June, Jacques Doriot argued that 'the struggle of the popular masses must take place within the framework of the nation',[87] and Drieu la Rochelle emphasized the PPF's synthesis of national and social concerns, a synthesis previously seen by many as unrealizable. In the PPF, he argued, 'We do not need to sacrifice our love of France to our love of the people, our social requirements to our national requirements. We have discovered that France is the people and that the people are France.'[88] Appeals to the peasantry in the language of wartime sacrifice were reinforced by images of the nation as the reconciliation of rural and urban people, especially as this became a point of contest with the Popular Front. The Croix de Feu had always exalted the peasantry as having suffered most deeply from the losses of war and, in a pamphlet issued before the elections, had stressed the urgency of revitalizing French agriculture.

> The Croix de Feu, the Volontaires Nationaux and their friends have continued the pure tradition of the Fallen, who died on the very soil that they had enriched by their efforts. The primary objective of the Croix de Feu movement is to honour this sacred soil.[89]

Now the largely urban character of the Popular Front's support—and the controversy surrounding its Wheat Marketing Board and introduction of agricultural social insurance—seemed to play into the hands of the Parti Social Français. Since the Matignon Agreement was explicitly directed at resolving urban conflict, the Parti Social Français and the Parti Populaire Français were in a strong position to proclaim to the rural people that their needs were not being met by the new government. One of the most fundamental tasks of the new PSF, according to La Rocque, was therefore the restoration of the peasantry to their primary importance within the nation and its economy. The Popular Front was dividing France in two, 'those of the fields and those of the towns', and explicitly favouring urban workers instead of honouring the peasantry for their sustenance of the French people and their defence of French territory. 'As our ancestors proclaimed the rights of man and of the citizen', asserted La Rocque, 'so the PSF will assert the unrecognized rights of the peasantry.'[90] And he suggested that the gulf between these two Frances might be narrowed by better education, by holiday camps that would bring urban children to the countryside, and by the honouring of rural cinema and literature. Jacques Doriot played on a similar concern for the disadvantaged peasantry when he proposed equal status for both rural and urban workers:

> Contrary to the Soviet dictator, we do not want to turn the peasant into a second-class citizen. We want him to be equal to the urban worker. The peasantry represent the greatest virtues of our people.[91]

He also identified provincial loyalty and ardent nationalism as closely compatible, describing a common allegiance to the nation and the *petite patrie*: 'One can love France only by remembering one's village and celebrating one's region.'[92] Like the PSF, the PPF demanded due honour for the peasantry's contribution to the national economy: rural France should be respected for its provision of both food and soldiers for the sustenance and defence of national life.[93]

In parallel to the Popular Front, the PSF and PPF likewise conceived of this united French people and nation as encompassing not only the provinces but also the Empire. *L'Humanité* exalted the participation of the Algerian population in the demonstrations of the Popular Front:[94] the Parti Social Français established a network of support in Algeria, building on the sections that had been created by the Croix de Feu and pictured in *Le Flambeau* in vast, ordered formations.[95] Networks were also developed in Tunisia and Morocco, and sections established in Cameroon, the Ivory Coast, French Indochina, and the Île de la Réunion. Even the most remote sections were supposed to receive a weekly information bulletin on the activity of the PSF as a whole.[96] Similarly the Parti Populaire Français, which was to build increasingly on the idea of the Empire as fundamental to the strength and unity of France, referred explicitly to France's imperial grandeur in its original manifesto.[97]

Unity across ethnic and religious boundaries was a more sensitive point. Theoretically the PSF was open to all faiths, but in practice it defended the interests of the Christian European settlers in Algeria and was to oppose the Blum–Violette reform (a suggested extension of the vote to 20,000 members of the Algerian elite which did not require them to reject Islamic law).[98] Anti-Semitism was an established characteristic of the press of the extreme right, and was increasingly evident in the PPF, as well as among some members of the PSF. Yet the national community was nonetheless seen by some as offering the potential to realize a higher unity. On 14 June 1936 La Rocque provoked considerable anger on the left by attending a commemoration of Jewish victims of the First World War, a ceremony held at the Synagogue on the Rue de la Victoire. Indeed of the 1200 people who attended, 700 were members of the Croix de Feu and the Volontaires Nationaux. Their presence was significant—demonstrating, as the presiding Rabbi Kaplan explained, that belonging to the French nation was in no way dependent on religious affiliation, and that Jewish soldiers had been firmly united with their fellow soldiers in a spirit of sacrifice. 'The war is an immense cauldron', he observed, 'in which all souls are melted into one.'[99]

The increasing closeness between the idea of the people and that of the national community was also reflected in the depiction of the 'enemies of the people'—who were, for both the Popular Front and its opponents, generally portrayed as foreigners and capitalists. A vocal opposition to the involvement of foreigners in public affairs was, indeed, a growing tendency on both left and right in the 1930s.[100] While the Communists had always presented the enemies of the people as unscrupulous capitalists, they were now increasingly emphatic about the foreign sympathies (and funding) of these particular adversaries, as well as describing them as closely united.

> The enemies of the people intend to enslave the whole country: men like La Rocque, Maurras, Taittinger, and Jean Renaud, who make cynical appeals for violence against the French population, and follow the commands of the two hundred families.
>   Their design, in the same spirit as the orders of their foreign patrons, is to deprive the people of France of their liberty and so lead them more easily into war, for fascism equals war.[101]

The same dangerous unity was described in vivid terms in the propaganda film *La Vie est à nous*, where a short sequence showing 'French followers of Hitler'—a Croix de Feu procession—was immediately followed by Hitler's speech to an assembled crowd, with the sound of a dog barking offered in mocking substitute for his actual words. The same film included an album of the infamous 'two hundred families' designed by the artist Jean Effel, and a scene in which aristocrats were shown taking target practice at a cardboard cut-out of a worker, identified by a tell-tale cap. 'A real ruffian's cap!' as one of the 'enemies of the people' is heard to exclaim. The appearance of Jacques Doriot as leader of the Parti Populaire Français was instantly identified within this same framework: 'As for Doriot, Hitler's phonograph, he's now on the side of La Rocque and Taittinger, in his true place as enemy of the people.'[102] These enemies of the people were not only united in international collaboration, they were also situated within a continuing tradition of aristocratic betrayal of both nation and people. La Rocque in particular was frequently condemned as being *Coblenzard* or counter-revolutionary.

> Isn't treason a tradition among the wealthy and the privileged? How could Count Colonel de la Rocque fail to follow the lead of his illustrious forebear, a colonel in the army of the Prince of Condé and the King of Prussia, fighting against the soldiers of the First Republic?[103]

Like the right-wing leagues that preceded them, the PSF and PPF adopted many of the caricatures also employed by the Popular Front. The Croix de Feu and Parti National Populaire had already voiced criticism of the factory owners during the strikes of May and June 1936, and at a meeting on 17 June a Croix de Feu militant remarked that although many factory owners had hoped to find in their movement both sympathy and support, they had been swiftly disappointed.[104] Later Doriot adopted a similar stance, commenting that it was the selfishness of the capitalists that had unleashed the 'social explosion'.[105] The real international capitalists and enemies of the people were instead the Communists, ruthlessly enslaving the unsuspecting French in preparation for Moscow's ultimate triumph. 'Integral communism and international capitalism are exactly the same thing', declared La Rocque on 18 July. 'Which great capitalist has not dreamed of being sovereign in the image of the master of the Kremlin?'[106] The article was aptly illustrated with a sketch of Marianne imprisoned in a cage with a Russian bear, while the same issue also featured a caricature of the PCF secretary Jacques Duclos crying 'Long live the Popular Front!' with a heavy Russian accent. Capitalism and betrayal of the nation were thus seen as the principal characteristics of the enemies of the people, and allegations of foreign identities or sympathies were consequently used as insults, particularly of the Communists.

Rivalry in the streets

By the end of summer 1936, the conflict over the people between the victorious Popular Front and the supposedly vanquished right had been reborn in new forms and with equal fervour. The battle lines were drawn between two mass movements: on one side the Popular Front, and on the other the PSF and PPF, supported to some degree by the press of the extreme right, including newspapers explicitly linked to dissolved leagues and parties. With the new republican parties of the right effectively exiled from legitimate occupation of the street by the government, the conflict between the two sides took place initially on the disputed symbolic territory of people and nation, with each side presenting its own images of disciplined crowds at mass meetings (usually held at a safe distance from one another). It was not until October 1936 that an unexpected public confrontation arose, revealing both the influence of symbolism on street politics and the increasing challenges to the already fragile relationship between the people and the Popular Front.

By October, the illusion of a victorious and euphoric people was becoming difficult for the Popular Front to sustain. Inflation over the summer months had eroded much of the salary increases promised by the Matignon Agreement, and the strikes that broke out in September to defend the Agreement against the opposition of the factory owners were more militant and bitter than those of May and June. In response to the inflation the Senate voted to devalue the franc, and discussions began in parliament about the possibility of legal action against La Rocque for reconstituting a dissolved league as the Parti Social Français. Meanwhile, Blum's decision for non-intervention in the Spanish Civil War was continuing to splinter the Popular Front alliance, provoking increasingly forthright criticism from Communists in Parliament.[107] No longer, it seemed, were anti-fascism and pacifism to be compatible, and as the left anxiously debated the relationship between the French and the Spanish people, left-wing dissidents questioned whether the Popular Front represented the voice of the people at all. Meanwhile, in response to accounts of violence against priests and religious in Spain, demands were made in French convents for plain clothes and passports, so that nuns could escape to England or Italy in the event of an emergency.[108] Bishops recorded similar demands from priests in certain dioceses.[109]

It was in this context of heightened emotion and public concern that La Rocque applied to the local authorities for permission to hold a mass meeting in the Vélodrome d'Hiver on 2 October. The Socialists and Communists, incensed by his proposed intrusion into one of the working-class areas of Paris, declared the political situation too fraught with potential danger to allow such a 'provocation', and promptly organized a counter-demonstration.[110] The government then chose to ban La Rocque's meeting, yet granted permission for a Communist meeting in the Parc des Princes (to the south-west of Paris) on 4 October. La Rocque was incensed in his turn by this evident partiality, and organized a counter-demonstration to be held in the vicinity of the Parc.[111] Rumours abounded that Doriot was to lend the support of 10,000 PPF members to La Rocque's cause, and on 3 October the two leaders were seen examining the Parc des Princes from all sides for possible points of assembly and attack.[112] Other right-wing groups were less supportive, with members of Pierre Taittinger's Parti Républicain National et Social choosing to abstain, and supporters of the dissolved Action Française dismissing La Rocque's meeting as unworthy of their involvement.[113]

On 4 October there was, therefore, a public confrontation between two counter-demonstrations: two rival orchestrations of the people in the same area of Paris on the same day. The symmetry between the opponents was both rhetorical and theatrical. On 30 September Jacques Duclos published an open letter to Léon Blum, speaking on behalf of the people of France and calling for the defence of republican liberties in the face of renewed provocation. He described the danger of the fascist leagues, well supplied with weapons, and threatened that if suitable measures were not taken, then the enemies of the people would provoke civil war in France. He concluded with a wish for governmental success in the maintenance of public order. A few days later, following the withdrawal of official permission for the PSF meeting, La Rocque also wrote a letter to Léon Blum, reproduced in *Le Flambeau* on 10 October next to Duclos' missive (Figure 16). Here, in almost identical terms, La Rocque spoke on behalf of the French people and republican liberties, accused the Popular Front of harbouring weapons and provoking violence, and asked that suitable action be taken against the enemies of the people

UN APPEL DU COMITÉ REGIONAL DE COORDINATION

Travailleurs de la région parisienne !

Le colonel de La Rocque et ses Croix de feu, camouflés en Parti social français, font connaître leur prétention de se rassembler dans l'un des quartiers les plus prolétariens de notre grand Paris (au Vel' d'Hiv').

L'heure est trop grave pour tolérer une telle provocation.

Tous debout pour une puissante contre-manifestation.

Toutes instructions seront données par les responsables à partir de 15 heures, dans les permanences suivantes :
18, rue Cambronne;
26, rue Frémicourt ;
70, rue Lecourbe ;
57 rue Linois;
78, rue Mademoiselle;
117, rue Saint-Charles;
13, rue Duruy ;
72, avenue Félix-Faure.

Discipline ! Unité d'action !
A bas le fascisme !

LE COMITE REGIONAL DE COORDINATION
(Parti socialiste, Parti communiste).

Un Appel du Parti Social Français

Travailleurs sociaux et patriotes de la région parisienne,

Marcel CACHIN, Jacques DUCLOS et Maurice THOREZ, fascistes des Soviets russes, font connaître leur prétention de se rassembler dans l'un des quartiers les plus paisibles de notre grand Paris (Parc des Princes).

L'heure est trop grave pour tolérer une telle provocation.

Tous debout pour une puissante contre-manifestation.

Toutes instructions seront données par les responsables à partir du samedi 3 octobre, à 15 heures, dans nos permanences.

Discipline !
Unité d'action !
A bas le fascisme !
Vive la Liberté! Vive la France!

Le Comité Exécutif
du Parti Social Français.

Figure 16 *Le Flambeau*, 10 October 1936 (Courtesy of the Archives de la Préfecture de Police, Paris).

who were provoking civil war. His concluding paragraph, calling for the maintenance of public order, was copied verbatim from Duclos' letter. This disconcerting symmetry was also evident in rival posters around Paris, each calling for support, each addressed to the working people, and each proclaiming 'Discipline! Unity of action! Down with fascism!'

The rhetorical parallels were to continue in the rival gatherings of the masses on 4 October itself. The Communist meeting in the Parc des Princes, attended by approximately 40,000–50,000 supporters, was presented as a united response to the renewed fascist threat (represented by Franco in Spain and by Doriot and La Rocque in France).[114] Indeed La Rocque's 'provocation' provided an ideal opportunity to revive the militancy of a movement that was in danger of splintering into a seemingly over-cautious government and a mass of discontented supporters. As Marcel Cachin emphasized in his speech at the PCF demonstration, La Rocque and his partisans must not be allowed legitimate occupation of the streets of Paris, for there was a real danger of a new 6 February. André Marty, recently returned from Spain, explained that the only solution was to reinforce solidarity between the French and Spanish peoples, and Maurice Thorez spoke on behalf of the French people to call for active measures against the reconstituted league of the Croix de Feu, and for a forceful and immediate application of the Popular Front programme.[115] In a show of determination to conceal the growing divisions within the Popular Front, the stadium was decorated with red flags featuring a tricolour emblem and the letters RF ('République française'), and *L'Internationale* was resolutely paired with *La Marseillaise*.

While the Communists were calling for the unity of the French people against its warmongering opponents, singing *La Marseillaise* and celebrating the French nation, the members of the PSF were busily gathering outside the Parc des Princes. Having failed to implement their original plan of occupying the stadium and cutting the cables of the loudspeakers, an estimated 20,000 assembled around the Parc, and others infiltrated nearby cafés, many of them dressed as workers so as to escape suspicion.[116] Orders were given not to cause unnecessary provocation, but to respond to *L'Internationale* with *La Marseillaise*, to impress their adversaries with a show of order and discipline, and to protect the people of Paris by preventing the Communist demonstrators from occupying the streets after their meeting. In police photographs the demonstrators appear as generally well-dressed men, processing through the streets and brandishing tricolour flags. The call to order was not always respected. One photograph, for example, shows an attack on a taxi, and police reports mention that there were 1249 arrests in the course of the day, and 30 policemen injured.[117]

As the Communists poured out into the street after the conclusion of their meeting, police endeavoured to keep the rival factions at a safe distance. The result was a theatrical display of opposition in words, songs and gestures.

> A few hundred members of the Parti Social Français actually managed to assemble at the Porte de Saint-Cloud, and here again they sang *La Marseillaise*. There was whistling, barricades, and the police held back raised fists on one side, raised hands on the other. On both sides, of course, there were torrents of abuse, and a vigorous alternation between cries of 'Long live La Rocque!' and 'Death to La Rocque!'[118]

After the confrontation, each side indulged in a self-congratulatory eulogy of the successful defence of republican liberty and the people of Paris, acclaiming the discipline and unity of their respective demonstrators. The Communists congratulated themselves on having prevented La Rocque's proposed meeting, and called for the dissolution of the PSF as a threat to public order; La Rocque and his followers congratulated themselves for having reduced the misguided Communist supporters to a frightened crowd, and called for the dissolution of the PCF.[119] Roger Salengro, the ill-fated Minister of the Interior who was blamed for the government's partiality, responded that proposed demonstrations in Paris would henceforth be banned if they were likely to lead to such adverse reactions.[120]

The confrontation of 4 October 1936 was the first major conflict in the streets of Paris between the Popular Front and the Parti Social Français, its most powerful new rival. The occasion was striking in revealing an explicit symmetry between the two sides, even to the point of quasi-identical letters to Léon Blum and quasi-identical posters for the people of Paris. The direct opposition of raised fists and raised arms contrasted with the common adoption of *La Marseillaise* and the tricolour; the divergent solutions proposed by the political enemies contrasted with their common association of the people with nation and republic. Although 4 October was exceptional in being a public conflict between enemies now separated by the Popular Front's official control of the public space, it played out in the theatre of the streets of Paris a rivalry already evident since the formation of new right-wing parties. This rivalry had been mapped out in the period 1934–36 as the leagues and the Popular Front movement sought with increasing resolution to situate the people within the public and symbolic space most appealing to the electorate. Far from resolving the conflict, the Popular Front victory merely transformed it, and the new parties continued to develop their representations of the people in close parallel. But the demonstrations of 4 October revealed more than an ongoing rivalry: they also revealed the increasing tensions between official organizations and parties and the people in the street who claimed to be Popular Front supporters. Such tensions had been latent since the electoral victory, for the creation of an image of the people as victors—rational, self-disciplined, and fully synonymous with the Popular Front—meant that the legitimacy of the movement and government was in turn dependent on the action and ordered behaviour of the people. In the carefully controlled spheres of popular culture and the 14 July festivities, it was possible for the Popular Front to give a convincing production, a close identification of the visible and symbolic people. Now that the new government was responsible for public order, however, any unofficial or illegitimate occupation of the street (whether by Popular Front supporters or by members of the new right-wing parties) was liable to present new challenges to the representation of the people.

5
Building the Ideal City in Popular Culture, 1936–37

Built for bicycle races and a mass audience, the Vélodrome d'Hiver was the setting for both tragedy and utopia in its short existence. Its association with tragedy is the better known, for in July 1942 the stadium served as a temporary shelter for arrested Jews following the operation now deeply etched into collective memory as the 'roundup of the Vél d'Hiv'. But in October 1937—less than five years previously—the stadium had hosted a utopian mass spectacle by the Jewish playwright Jean-Richard Bloch entitled *Naissance d'une cité*. This play, begun in 1934 and completed in 1937, recounted the journey of a group of workers from the relentless demands of the production line to the building of an ideal city on an island in the Atlantic. To the accompaniment of music by Arthur Honegger and Darius Milhaud, a familiar universe of urban labour was exchanged for a utopian community on virgin territory, where men and women could rebuild social relations on a convenient *tabula rasa* and be reconciled with their natural and material environment. *Naissance d'une cité* was certainly an ambitious project: an attempt to create theatre by the masses and for the masses, to imagine an ideal society in which the worker would be fully integrated into society and politics, and to present this ideal as theoretically achievable. It was Bloch's desire that the spectacle should offer the image and experience of fraternity on a human scale in the age of the masses.

Critics of the new spectacle were impressed by the boldness of the concept and design, but unconvinced by the vision of utopia. The composer and conductor René Leibowitz, attracted by the promise of music by Honegger and Milhaud, praised Bloch's encouragement of mass theatre, and his engagement with the problem of man's tendency to become victim rather than master of industrial and technological progress. But he doubted Bloch's assumption that the audience would

151

respond only to a disordered medley of sound, light, and movement: that a mass audience would identify only with collective music and collective action.[1] The playwright Jacques Copeau, in correspondence with Bloch while reading his manuscript the previous summer, was still more forthright. Such an ambitious project could be realized, he considered, only by a director such as Vsevolod Meyerhold,[2] and was unsuited to the French context. 'I would add,' he concluded, 'that your ending or denouement does not convince me. It does not provide an answer to the formidable question.'[3]

The 'formidable question' to which Copeau referred was the problem of transforming the masses into a community, and *Naissance d'une cité* was remarkable not for its failure to resolve the problem, but for its determination to address it in the first place. Jean-Richard Bloch's own introduction to the play, his correspondence with Jacques Copeau, and the eventual criticisms of the performance held one characteristic in common: a belief that it was right and necessary for theatre to address the 'problem of the masses'. Theatre, they believed, should engage with the masses in both subject matter and performance strategy. Bloch's motive was not to pander to a desire for escapism, but rather to connect with the lives of those around him. 'The drama that will unfold before your eyes is something neither joyful nor sorrowful,' he explained in his introduction. 'Rather, it is intended as an honest and realistic depiction of our work and our daily lives, of our thoughts and our destinies: a true image of ourselves.'[4]

Popular culture and the creation of community

Transforming the masses into a community required more than electoral promises and structures of organization: it also demanded imaginative representation. The search for community led political groups to represent the masses as a united people in the context of street politics, and to celebrate such occasions through live radio broadcasts as well as in recordings, documentary films, photographs, and the press. Meanwhile, the theatricality of politics was echoed in the politicization of the theatre: in a comparable engagement with mass audiences and an endeavour to depict the 'people' on a public stage. The stadiums used for diverse political meetings during the Popular Front period were also the settings for a number of ambitious theatrical productions, Bloch's *Naissance d'une cité* among them. If culture was thus to play a role in the representation of the masses as the people, then the nature of this role demanded reflection and definition.

The cultural initiatives of the Popular Front have generally been portrayed—and with justification—as an enthusiastic attempt to bring culture to the people. Pascal Ory's *La Belle Illusion: culture et politique sous le signe du Front populaire* provides the most detailed study to date of the government's democratization of high culture;[5] Julian Jackson and Danielle Tartakowsky have similarly celebrated the Popular Front's cultural achievement as a 'breaking down of barriers' between the people and culture, encouraged by the generous support of government ministers for individual and group initiatives.[6] In Tartakowsky's view, this could even be described as a 'cultural revolution'.[7] Yet the Popular Front's action and reflection on culture and the people were not an isolated phenomenon, and indeed Ory mentions briefly that parallel criticisms of contemporary culture were made by political writers of both left and right.[8]

This chapter is not a catalogue of the cultural achievements of the Popular Front government: these achievements are described in Pascal Ory's comprehensive account, which focuses explicitly on policy rather than on the content of cultural productions. Here, in contrast, the focus is on the ideological problems at the heart of the discussion and elaboration of popular culture, and on the broader context in which the Popular Front government was operating. One of the central concerns in this book is the political endeavour to create and control the 'commotion of unanimity' that, fleetingly experienced in the strike, demonstration, or mass meeting, seemed to suggest the possibility of constructing a more durable consensus and community. The Popular Front sought unanimity in demonstrations and celebrations, where, as the Socialist journalist Magdaleine Paz believed, 'every one of several thousand faces seemed like a member of the family'.[9] The leagues and parties of the right pursued this unity in their associations, in memories of wartime sacrifice, and in the relationship of the masses to their leader. For Colonel de la Rocque, the 'French social mystique' transformed the masses into 'an immense family, whose members share a common soul.'[10] Jacques Doriot similarly described the aim of the PPF as that of 'forging the collective soul.'[11] References to the soul in this context were not coincidental: if these parties aimed to fulfil the political, social, and cultural demands of their members, they often aimed to fulfil their spiritual needs as well. Even for right-wing groups and parties that did not explicitly denigrate loyalty to established religion, the religion of the fatherland often came first.

It was not always easy to create a framework within which the 'collective soul' or 'commotion of unanimity' could be experienced. Use of the streets for demonstrations was strictly monitored by the authorities, and in any case the 'people' in such demonstrations had the disconcerting habit of defying the boundaries of their designated role. Nor was the experience of reconciliation or solidarity inevitable on such occasions. In contrast, both theatre and cinema offered attractive opportunities for the potential achievement of this political ideal. Here, the image of a reconciled community of 'people' could be shown to a mass audience, and the audience could, through shared experience and emotion, also become a single 'people'. Such experiments were also repeatable, even though a comparable effect could not be guaranteed. There were, naturally, many other reasons for the development of theatre and cinema for the people to be considered desirable by political groups and parties, but the contribution of such culture to the creation of community was a question of primary importance. Moreover, it was in this context that the deepest concerns regarding the importance of the 'people' were often expressed.

This focus on the creation of community was central to reflections on contemporary culture by political journalists on both left and right. Foremost among their concerns was the individualist and escapist nature of culture in general—an apparent evasion of the challenges of the modern world. In contrast, political journalists called for cultural activity to become resolutely social, closely relevant to the problems of the masses. Contemporary theatre was, for example, roundly condemned for its sterile obsession with bourgeois decadence, and a brief glance at the titles in the *Catalogue de la Société des Auteurs et Compositeurs Dramatiques*[12] provides considerable justification for such criticism. The vast majority of performances in these years were, as *Le Peuple*'s cultural correspondent Georges Altman observed in January 1936, variations on a rather tired theme:

> The boulevard theatres continue to offer scenes of adultery; state-funded theatre provides a few stock plays, sincerely and traditionally staged, but rather staid and lifeless; while the casinos and music halls present their lavish expanses of flesh for foreign tourists.[13]

Other critics believed that the French, too, were succumbing to these particular pleasures, and the Catholic playwright Léon Chancerel, whose interest lay in the revival of medieval mystery plays and in the promotion of open-air and scout theatre, called for a dramatic renaissance in order to 'detoxify the theatre'.[14] Even plays of less doubtful taste were roundly condemned by Georges Altman and others for their repetitive obsession with individualistic pleasures, while the cinema was described as focusing disproportionately on the cult of celebrities rather than on collective effort and experience:

> Theatre and cinema that are almost entirely fixated on celebrities—as is the case with French plays and films—can lead only an impoverished life. Plays and films are above all collective enterprises involving collective work and aiming for a group impression, as certain producers here and elsewhere have already understood.[15]

Equally, although the popular press regularly recounted lurid tales of domestic violence and betrayal among the working classes, the depiction of similarly naturalistic tableaux in theatre or film was forcefully criticized. In March 1934, the monthly CGT review *La Voix du Peuple* published a long indictment of contemporary cinema as a predominantly capitalist venture that encouraged unhealthy interests in the morbid and melodramatic.[16] In similar disapproval (although from a very different political perspective) one of the film critics of *Je suis partout* condemned the naturalistic zeal of Julien Duvivier's *La Belle Équipe*, seeing in it an unjustified assumption that violence was essential to a film's popular appeal:

> [The director] calculated, then, that the working-class public must be jealous, malevolent, and crude, and interested only in serials that are full of corpses and generously spattered with blood.[17]

How did these critics imagine an ideal popular culture? If contemporary culture was to be condemned for decadence, individualism, and escapism, then the popular culture that these critics were seeking was to be moral and social. First and foremost, culture was to be accessible in content to the entire people. As Léon Lemonnier, an apologist for the new literary genre of populism, argued in 1931:

> Art is not essentially aristocratic. The artist should not produce works that are capable of interesting only an elite, or rather a clique of snobbish and world-weary individuals, the educated and so-called refined. The artist should maintain contact with everyone: with society, the crowd, and the people.[18]

Theatre and cinema should offer reflections on relevant contemporary problems, rather than endeavouring to diffuse political propaganda or to demonstrate some abstract truth. Works that were obscure or dryly academic should be abandoned, wrote Robert Brasillach, condemning Romain Rolland's popular theatre in the name of popular theatre itself, and claiming that it would interest only the professors of the Sorbonne. The people demanded 'a play that speaks of their own sufferings, their own greatness, their own hopes'—and according to Brasillach they would be unable to identify with the narrowly focused propaganda of Romain Rolland's *Le Quatorze Juillet* (a 1902 play describing the fall of the Bastille).[19] In a similar tone, *L'Émancipation nationale*'s cultural correspondent Lucien Romans argued that truly popular theatre would be sufficiently engaged with human problems to be relevant to everyone. 'There exists a deeply human theatre that is accessible to all,' he explained to his readers. 'This is the theatre we want. It is not dead—it is too essential to the French soul to disappear.'[20] Throughout the summer of 1936 Romans exalted the merits of this 'deeply human' theatre in his weekly column, insisting that it should be 'at the service of man, increasing his self-awareness so that he may live and not kill, understand and not hate.'[21] Comparable concerns were expressed by Georges Altman in *La Voix du peuple* with regard to the cinema. 'Like the theatre,' he wrote, 'the cinema should encourage reflection on the moral problems of society, rather than demonstrating some abstract truth.'[22] It was vital that both media should break out of the adulterous triangle typifying an outmoded and decadent culture, and that they should offer instead a profoundly human interpretation of the problems of the modern world.

To develop the relationship between the people and culture, these critics believed it necessary to transform not only content but also accessibility: to create spaces in which popular audiences could experience the sense of community which they praised so highly. The development of popular theatre was a particular focus for discussion. Lucien Romans called for cheaper seats and lighter taxes on state theatres, for increasing decentralization and for the re-opening of provincial theatres. Gabriel Boissy, who wrote for both *Le Flambeau* and *Comœdia*, went further still, and described his vision of the ideal theatre as a return to the amphitheatres of the past, where theatre was at the heart of the city. (Boissy had indeed been advocating a return to open-air theatre since the early twentieth century, and was an influential participant in the debate over the restoration of the Roman theatre at Orange.)[23]

I firmly believe that in the reconciled, reorganized, glorified France of tomorrow, those shabby, sensual, frivolous little theatres, as well as the kind of fashionable theatres that have suited the taste of 'society' for over a century, will be replaced by large amphitheatres, as welcoming as beautiful cinemas. There, in a broader and more fraternal society, on enormous stages demanding a concomitant depth of inspiration and a powerful muse, poets will offer to our fellow-citizens a theatre and drama currently lacking in France, and which will increase their love of life.[24]

Meanwhile, Jean-Richard Bloch observed that both Nazi Germany and the USSR were developing a synthesis of politics and theatre in their response to the masses, and contended that France should do likewise. Like Boissy, he was convinced that the theatre of the future would echo the theatre of the past in its use of open spaces accessible to the whole people.

Drama will increase from a few thousand spectators to a few million, from a national public to a universal public. Speeches will move beyond the vast enclosure of the theatre, and develop in the open air.[25]

In these often idealistic reflections, popular culture was defined as culture for the people as a whole: as a meeting between a broadly defined people and art, literature, theatre, and film. The culture in question was to be neither exclusively proletarian nor narrowly propagandistic, nor yet was it to be a mass culture that would debase rather than inspire. It could be a democratization of existing culture, or it could be the preservation and promotion of a culture with specifically popular origins, as in the case of the Musée des Arts et Traditions Populaires, established under the Popular Front government to document and preserve regional customs, festivals, costumes, and artefacts. It could be the creation or revival of works produced specifically for the people, such as Romain Rolland's *Le Quatorze Juillet* or Jean Renoir's *La Marseillaise*, although such works were not necessarily accepted as 'popular' by the Popular Front's adversaries. The essential characteristic of ideal popular culture was to be its social quality: an ability not merely to expand individual horizons but also to transcend class tensions and differences. Accessible to all and taking place in large public spaces, it was supposed to unite different social groups in a common and intense experience. As well as being individually beneficial—especially to the culturally disenfranchised—the projected relationship between culture and the people would also be socially useful, encouraging a sense of belonging to a wider community.

Similar themes emerged in the definition and promotion of popular leisure. Shortly after the introduction of the 40-hour week, Pierre Barlatier of *Comœdia* expressed his conviction that popular leisure should be organized politically, forming the basis for a shared social experience, and he looked forward to 'a comprehensive project of organized leisure, a genuine renaissance of dramatic art and popular festival.'[26] Even the CGT, an enthusiastic proponent of working-class self-improvement (especially through its Centre Confédéral d'Éducation Ouvrière), welcomed state intervention. Responding to the critics of the five-day week who feared a related increase in working-class alcoholism, *Le Peuple* demanded an official separation of 'good' and 'bad' leisure.

> The role of the state, as of any large collective body, should be simply to facilitate working-class access to what I would call good leisure, while rendering bad leisure inaccessible.

'Bad' leisure was deemed harmful not only to the individual, but also to 'the family, the social group, and the whole of society.'[27] And the Popular Front was not alone in calling for the development of worthy popular leisure: *Le Flambeau*, *Le Petit Journal*, and *L'Émancipation nationale* made similar appeals. After the formation of the Parti Social Français *Le Flambeau* aspired to an ever-wider readership, and in addition to the sections on the workers, agriculture, and the Empire, there were regular discussions of sport and leisure. *Le Petit Journal*—also directed by La Rocque from 1937 onwards—described and illustrated the development of his young people's sporting association, the Société de Préparation et d'Éducation Sportive. In these newspapers, popular leisure was praised as a means of regenerating the French race and nation, and as an effective means of integrating the individual within the community. Speaking of physical education, La Rocque observed:

> The object of education is thus to consider the human person as a whole and to develop all his energies, those of the body, the soul, and the spirit, enabling his devotion to the service of the community.[28]

The 'cultural revolution' of the Popular Front

Placing recreation at the service of the community was central to many cultural initiatives of the Popular Front period, and not least to those of the government itself. One of Léon Blum's two new ministerial portfolios was the Undersecretary of State for the Organization of Sport and Leisure, assigned to the Socialist Léo Lagrange, while Jean Zay, the Radical Minister for Education, was also keenly involved in cultural policy. This cultural policy was determined not only by political objectives but also by a wider concern with the social and human benefit of culture, aspiring towards an ideal city in which the people would be reconciled with their natural and material environment and with each other. Key features of this policy were thus the popularization of culture, the promotion of images of reconciliation, and the imagination of the masses as a popular community.

The popularization of culture required both the democratization of high culture and also the diffusion of regional culture to a wider audience. Within this context there were pioneering initiatives to bring the people into contact with artistic tradition, not least through the popularization of museums and galleries. In May 1936 the nocturnal opening of the Louvre that had been envisaged at the beginning of the twentieth century with a view to encouraging working-class visitors was finally accomplished, although its success was limited.[29] As well as these attempts to popularize existing art, a number of initiatives were undertaken to increase popular participation in artistic production. The Socialist Party had pursued this objective in the 1920s, and the 1930s witnessed a concerted effort on the part of the Communist Party to encourage artistic development through the network of Maisons de Culture organized by the AEAR. Not all of the suggested initiatives were realized: an ambitious plan conceived in September 1936 to create colleges for applied art, and indeed to develop art education at every level, remained only a proposal.[30] But there were some substantial innovations, for instance a Popular Academy of painting in Paris in 1937–39 provided a focus for amateur photographers and offered free art lessons for workers, given by professional artists.[31] A number of unprecedented (though transient) 'artistic circles' were also created at the Renault and Citroën factories, although none survived later than 1939. Meanwhile, many avant-garde groups found it increasingly difficult to reconcile their objectives with those of the Popular Front. Abstraction Création, an avant-garde artistic association founded in 1935 and initially in favour of the Popular Front as a means of transforming existing society and politics, remained decidedly on the sidelines and disappeared definitively in 1936. A group of artists who described themselves as 'Les Indélicats', and gave an exhibition in 1936 of their 'art of revolution and social protest', likewise found themselves shunned by the very groups that they had been soliciting as potential supporters.[32]

The radio was concurrently developed to offer greater educational and cultural opportunities, and with an estimated five million radio sets in France by 1938,[33] this was an invaluable channel of communication with the masses. During the Popular Front, Georges and Émilie Lefranc broadcast as representatives of the Centre Confédéral d'Éducation Ouvrière, and the director of the Théâtre du Peuple, Henri Lesieur, adapted plays to broadcast to a popular audience.[34] The radio also lent itself to the musical education of the people, and critics in the Communist-led review *Radio-Liberté* favoured composers whose works were strongly influenced by folk melodies. Writing in February 1937, Paul Gsell recommended the music of Mussorgsky, Borodin, and Rimsky-Korsakov for this reason.[35] That these composers were all Russian was not of course, coincidental—but French folk music was also encouraged. Pierre Alberty devoted a series of articles in *Radio-Liberté* to 'the secrets of the popular soul', lamenting the disappearance of folk tunes associated with particular French professions, and suggesting that the radio should restore these melodies to the consciousness and repertoire of the modern worker.[36] *Radio-Liberté* also recommended that such programmes should be scheduled for evening broadcast, to respect the rhythm of the working day.[37]

Under the Popular Front government, there were also new movements aimed at increasing popular participation and representation in cinema, and a number of organizations within the film industry offered their explicit support to the new government. In December 1936 a group of unionized workers in the film industry published an open letter to Léon Blum, proclaiming their wish to reorganize the cinema with government support and thus 'place it at the service of the people of France'.[38] 1936 also witnessed the foundation of an association of Popular Front film directors, which aimed to promote social progress through the cinema and to establish an association of cinemagoers to link the people with the producers. This was assured of government support by a sympathetic Marceau Pivert.[39] Meanwhile, and following in the tradition of the earlier Cinéma du Peuple of 1913,[40] a PCF-led co-operative of technicians, workers, and artists known as Ciné-Liberté produced a number of Popular Front films, projected during popular festivals or in the workplace. The co-operative was directed by Jean-Paul Dreyfus and Jean Epstein and produced a wide range of films: documentaries such as *SOS Espagne* and *Grèves d'occupation*; films devoted to particular professions; Communist propaganda such as *La Vie est à nous*; and full-length films including Jean Renoir's *La Marseillaise.*[41] A special supplement to *Le Peuple* on 1 May 1938 praised these productions as both accomplished and didactic, and added that they fulfilled in innovative and mobile form the aspirations of the early trade unionist Fernand Pelloutier for working-class recreation.[42] Nor was Ciné-Liberté the only organization that sought to bring cinema to the people. Since the early thirties, there had been signs of a wider interest in social cinema in the works of directors like Jean Vigo and René Clair, even if the vast majority of films produced continued to devote little attention to the representation of the workers.[43]

The Popular Front government was also unusual in according direct patronage to popular theatre,[44] and several of the large-scale popular productions of the time emerged from the fruitful combination of state funding and private or trade-union initiative. In November 1935 the Union des Artistes organized an 'Estates General' in order to discuss projects for renewing the theatre, and this Union was affiliated to the CGT and played an important part in the initiatives of the Popular Front period. Meanwhile the Comédie Française provided cheap seats for the young and free evenings for members of the CGT; the Théâtre National de l'Odéon organized economically priced 'popular matinées', and the Russian theatre manager Georges Pitoëff offered reduced price tickets to members of working-class organizations attending performances at the Théâtre des Mathurins.[45] Considerable reductions were made available to trade-union members for specifically Popular Front productions such as *Liberté* and *Naissance d'une cité.*[46]

Opening up the theatre to the people also took place in new spaces. In 1937, the International Exhibition acted as the stage for various theatrical innovations, many of them acclaimed (though not uncritically) by Léon Chancerel. Chancerel recorded that a number of the foreign pavilions were offering displays on their own national theatre, and that there were also a number of other areas specifically devoted to exhibitions and performances. Gustave Cohen (President of the Société des Historiens du Théâtre) had overseen the creation of an exhibition on French drama in the middle ages. Another area of the Exhibition was devoted to a display of scenery and costumes, and another reserved for subsidized productions by the Théâtres du Cartel and for puppet theatre performances.[47] An avant-garde Théâtre d'Essai was unfinished at the time of the Exhibition's inauguration, but later staged some performances by the militant group Art et Action. In July 1936 there were also some open-air performances on the Trocadéro—an idea subsequently revived by Max Hymans, the government minister responsible for the

Exhibition, in 1937. While extremely critical of the plays that tied themselves too closely to the propaganda of the Popular Front, particularly those performed by the Socialist group Mai 36, Léon Chancerel nevertheless admired the fervour of both actors and directors, and praised their attempt to move beyond the boundaries of traditional theatre in search of the people.[48]

The cultural reforms of the Popular Front thus reflected the main themes in critical discourse on both left and right when the new government came to power. Inspired by the ideal of accessible popular culture, and committed to the democratization of high culture and the celebration of regional folk culture for a mass audience, the Popular Front sought to transform art, radio, cinema, and theatre 'in the service of the people'. When their choice of works was condemned by their opponents—as when Robert Brasillach criticized *Le Quatorze Juillet* or when Léon Chancerel criticized the productions of Mai 36—these criticisms were often made in the name of popular culture itself.

Theatrical and cinematic productions associated with and funded by the Popular Front provide a valuable insight into the development of these themes in practice. Jean Renoir's *La Marseillaise* is one such example. This 1937 film, which told the story of the French Revolution from the perspective of the federal army, aimed not only to maximize popular participation but also to draw contemporary parallels with the revolutionary people of 1789. The very production of the film was to be expressly 'popular', as one guide to the International Exhibition proudly described it:

> This film, directed by Jean Renoir on the initiative of the Rassemblement Populaire and with the support of the government and the CGT, will be popular not only in subject matter but also in its entire production, being created in collaboration with the French people as a whole. Even the funding will be assured by the masses.[49]

The proposal was for each contributor to pay an initial two francs, later to be subtracted from the cost of a ticket. It was not a successful method (a failure carefully overlooked by Jean Renoir in his memoirs),[50] but it was nonetheless an innovative attempt to increase popular involvement in the film's production. Furthermore, and in response to a request from the President of the Union des Artistes, the cast of the film included a number of formerly unemployed workers,[51] and 'the People' featured prominently on the list of *Dramatis Personae*. The people were indeed to be the hero of the film. Jean Renoir had even undertaken research in the archives of Marseilles to reassure himself of the unimpeachable character of his revolutionaries, and his explicit aim in the film was to show the people of 1789 in a favourable light as the antithesis of the dangerous hordes depicted by their detractors.[52] Renoir's people were honest and unthreatening, unjustifiably persecuted by the aristocrats who appeared as the eighteenth-century incarnation of the infamous 'two hundred families'. The leading characters in his film—a group of volunteers for the federal army of the French Revolution—are models of national fervour and fraternity. Firmly attached to their native Marseilles, they are also keenly conscious of how the developing Revolution binds their lives to the destiny of a new and wider community— that of the nation. As one of the people of Marseilles informs a sceptical royalist general, 'the nation is the fraternal assembly of all the French. It's you. It's me.' The people of *La Marseillaise* also adumbrate the allegiances proposed by the Popular Front in general and by the Communists in particular. One of the leading volunteers is an eighteenth-century 'intellectual', adept at expressing the ideas of his comrades to the association of the Amis de la Constitution in Marseilles. And one of the earliest supporters of the revolutionary army is a local priest, prefiguring an 'outstretched hand' policy by making common cause with the revolutionaries against the Ancien Regime. When the volunteers finally reach Paris, the explicit solidarity of the Garde Nationale with their cause is warmly depicted, echoing Communist cries of 'the Army is with us!' during the 14 July celebrations of the Popular Front.

The portrayal of the enemies of the people had equally contemporary overtones. Louis XVI—played by Jean Renoir's brother Pierre—is shown as the victim of a foreign conspiracy fomented by Marie-Antoinette and her relations. In line with *L'Humanité*, which regularly condemned La Rocque and his followers as treacherous *Coblenzards*, Jean Renoir depicted the nobles taking refuge in Coblenz as traitors plotting against the French people, planning to march on Paris and to 'exterminate' all revolutionary elements that they might find there. This serves to reinforce the explicit description of the volunteers from Marseilles as 'the will of the nation', spontaneously supported by the people of the different provinces they pass through on their march to Paris, and representing the reconciliation of the provinces within the nation which was also promoted by the Popular Front.

La Marseillaise was the most ambitious cinematic project of the period, but other films produced under the Popular Front and with its specific support also reflected some of these dominant themes, most notably the integration of the working people into the French nation and its history.

Jean Epstein's *Les Bâtisseurs* described French cathedrals as some of the earliest 'houses of the people', and began with a visual celebration of the cathedral of Chartres to the strains of *Kyrie eleison*. *Breiz Nevez*, a CGT film made in Brittany, featured images of local churches and sculpted scenes of Calvary as integral to the popular culture of the region.[53] Meanwhile, Boris Peskine's *Sur les Routes d'acier*—a celebration of the technical merits of the railway produced by the Fédération Nationale des Travailleurs des Chemins de Fer—sought to exalt regional life while simultaneously integrating the provinces within the nation as a whole. The film praised the growing rail network as 'so many veins and arteries bringing life to every part of the country' and likewise celebrated its usefulness in supplying fresh regional produce to urban areas: 'fruits and flowers, an antidote to modern life'.[54] Danielle Tartakowsky has argued that the predominance of such themes indicates the growing politicization of both the trade unions and their cinema.[55] Looking at the interaction between culture and politics from a different angle, it could also be argued that these films were, consciously or unconsciously, reflecting the concern with creating community that stretched beyond both culture and politics.

It is this concern that also helps to explain the resurgence of interest in popular theatre that characterized the Popular Front period: an interest in the theatre of the ancient world and the middle ages, and also in the more recent initiatives of the late nineteenth and early twentieth centuries. Two key figures in this most recent flourishing were Maurice Pottecher and Romain Rolland. Pottecher, the son of a wealthy industrialist and local mayor, established an open-air theatre at Bussang (in the Vosges Mountains) in 1895.[56] Here he directed two plays a year, one free to the public, the second free the following season. The plays were conceived with the local population in mind, but they also toured the Jura mountains, Brittany, the Vendée, and the south of France, and attracted the attention of a number of other playwrights with similar interests, including Romain Rolland, Louis Jouvet, and Firmin Gémier. Pottecher's popular theatre revolved around a trio of convictions. First, the 'people' meant the entire people and not merely the working classes. Secondly, any popular theatre worthy of the name should inspire common emotion; and thirdly, it should thus should contribute to the moral goal of collective communion—a communion between man and nature, artist and audience, and between the social categories constituting the audience itself. 'It creates a connection between spectators whom everything would appear to separate,' Pottecher wrote of popular theatre in 1899; 'it realizes a sort of moral communion and artistic fraternity within the masses.'[57] Romain Rolland's popular theatre was less focused on immediate social harmony, but was nonetheless intended to shape the society of the future. Certainly he recognized the inherent difficulties in the concept of popular theatre, not least the difference between those who wished to bring high culture to the people and those who believed that culture must be created by the people themselves. 'On one side, they believe in theatre,' he observed, 'and on the other, they trust in the people. They have nothing in common.'[58] On both sides, however, were well-meaning intellectuals imposing their ideas of popular culture on the people. Rolland himself saw popular theatre as a weapon against existing society—'a new art for a new world'[59]—and believed that this new art form would encourage the people to realize the image of unity depicted on stage. 'The object of art is not reverie but life,' he wrote in his introduction to the 1901 edition of *Le Quatorze Juillet*: 'action must arise from the spectacle of action.'[60] This conviction that theatre could play an active role in regenerating and uniting the people continued to characterize reflection on popular theatre throughout the early years of the century, with the playwrights Henri Ghéon and Jean-Richard Bloch reinforcing the need for such theatre to recreate moral unity, while questioning exactly how far this might be possible within an increasingly fragmentary society.[61]

In 1936, the young theatre and film critic Jacques Chabannes suggested to Jean Zay that Rolland's *Le Quatorze Juillet* could be staged to celebrate the Popular Front's electoral victory. His suggestion was accepted, and the subsequent production received the government's full support. Intended as a model of Popular Front co-operation, the production was also designed as a means of symbolically blurring the boundaries between the people and their representatives, and was funded in part by a government loan. The production likewise met with the full approval of Rolland himself, who left his self-imposed exile in Switzerland to attend one of the performances. Support was requested from the Communist Maison de Culture, which enlisted 150 amateur actors from the Union des Théâtres Indépendants de France, while the Comédie Française supplied the lead roles. Pablo Picasso designed the backdrop, and a number of renowned musicians, including Darius Milhaud, collaborated to provide the score. Finally, the play was to be made as 'popular' as possible by reducing the price of the tickets to two francs and by organizing a number of free performances. The première, held on the evening of 14 July, was broadcast on Radio-Paris.[62]

First performed in 1902 with the intention of transforming society, *Le Quatorze Juillet* was nonetheless pertinent to the Popular Front in its representation of the people as political actors, and its concern to see in the people a metaphor for nation and community. The prominent role of the crowd had disconcerted critics in 1902, who expected drama to focus on individual will and character,[63] but such a role was closely suited to the climate of 1936. The recommendation of Louis-Lazare Hoche (future general in the French revolutionary army) that 'now is the time to live in the street, in the open air,'[64] could have been taken from any contemporary account of the season of demonstrations, while his optimistic faith in popular potential seemed to prefigure Marceau Pivert's famous announcement that 'everything is possible': 'My poor Hulin,' he says to his soldier-friend (one of the leaders of the Parisian people in the storming of the Bastille), 'do you really know how much is possible?'[65] An unnamed Parisian in the play praises the co-operation between writers and the people, reflecting not only Rolland's faith in the Popular Universities of 1902, but also the idealism of those joining Popular Front associations: 'Each to his own task! They think for us. We must act for them.'[66] Even the rapturous encounter between the people and the Gardes Françaises seems to prefigure the Popular Front's depiction of the army as 'sons of the people', for as Rolland's stage directions ran: 'The people and the soldiers, succumbing to an excess of love and fraternal enthusiasm, weep, embrace, laugh and shout.'[67]

It was significant, too, that the fraternity of the people in *Le Quatorze Juillet* was emphasized at the expense of their violence. In Rolland's script the fall of the Bastille is accompanied by acts of brutality—yet he makes clear in a footnote that this violence is not to be represented on stage. Indeed, he introduces a fictional child to urge the people to liberate the prisoners of the Bastille, implying a certain purity of motive beneath their overt aggression. The focus on fraternity also discredits the view of the people as animalistic—a view expressed in the play by Vintimille, a two-dimensional character who commands the forces within the Bastille without demonstrating any profound understanding of (or allegiance to) the regime that he is defending. His cold cynicism and effete disdain for the powerful instincts of the crowd classify him unequivocally as an enemy of the people. The play also suggests a certain self-identification of the people with the nation, and however anachronistic it might appear for the crowd to possess a clear sense of national rights and duties, they are nevertheless depicted in enthusiastic agreement with Robespierre when he emphasizes the duty of the nation to resist oppression.[68] Indeed, upon hearing of the king's dismissal of Necker (his popular Finance Minister), their immediate wish is to demonstrate the 'sacred terror of the nation'.[69]

Rolland had not intended this sense of fraternity to remain as an image on stage: rather, it was intended to cross boundaries between past and present, actor and audience. Like other apologists for popular theatre, he believed this communion to be possible only through some latent unity of opinion or belief—hence his choice of the Revolution, the source of the republican faith that could potentially unite actors and audience.[70] The conclusion of the play was a 'popular festival on the ruins of the Bastille' that was intended to be a unifying experience, encouraging the public 'to contribute not only its thoughts but also its voices to the action: the People themselves becoming actors in the festival of the People.'[71] In the 1936 performance, Jacques Chabannes concluded the festivities with *La Marseillaise*, which was followed at the end of the première by a spontaneous rendition of *L'Internationale*.[72]

'How utopian to think of interesting a modern crowd with the storming of the Bastille!' wrote Jean-Richard Bloch in 1910.[73] Yet whatever the reservations of the critics of 1936, they freely admitted that the play's impact had been profound, and visibly so. Gabriel Boissy identified in Rolland's work aspirations common also to Maurice Pottecher and to Firmin Gémier, founder of the Théâtre National Populaire. He recognized that in this theatre the people and the nation were to be inseparable: 'For the term "people" is merely false and divisive unless it designates the entire nation, elites and masses together, because every national virtue has at some stage emerged from the anonymity of the people.'[74] He recognized, too, that this concept of people and nation was situated at an ideological crossroads between right and left: 'This is the meeting point of desires and tendencies,' he insisted, 'whether from left or right.' Whether such communion was fully attainable in the context of a play concerning the Revolution was open to question, but the heightened emotion of the audience was certainly remarkable, receiving attention in both favourable and critical reviews. 'A new Iliad for the People of France' wrote Denise Lavie in *La République*:

> A gigantic fresco where individual details are obscured to emphasize the great harmonious traits of the whole; a consecration of the unanimity dear to Jules Romains; an effacement of the individual for the sake of the masses, from which greater vitality and conscious strength are derived.[75]

One critic, drawing an explicit parallel between this performance of *Le Quatorze Juillet* and recent performances of *Le Vray Mistère de la Passion* outside the Cathedral of Notre Dame, observed that the spectacle was as much in the audience as it was on stage, and that somehow both performances were accompanied by a comparable sense of the mystical.[76] Others, drawing similar parallels, were more concerned by the dangerous potential of this collective emotion. Pierre Lièvre of *Le Jour* contended that the Revolution was an inappropriate subject, while Émile Mas praised the impressive fresco of the French people but was concerned that the revolutionary sentiments of the play might be applied literally by members of the audience to the contemporary political situation.[77] François Porché of *La Revue de Paris* was puzzled by a play that eschewed traditional aesthetic standards, and remarked in equal surprise on the emotional reactions of his friends, whose own aesthetic appreciation he had expected to be more subtle. They seemed, he said, to have succumbed to the collective emotion of the occasion, surrendering their individual personalities to the common fervour of the crowd.

> Undoubtedly such ecstasy is dangerous. Undoubtedly it leads to fanaticism, and to excessive fanaticism as well. But no-one can deny that there is a certain force of attraction here, a contagion, and a powerful mystery.[78]

This concern with the collective marks almost all reviews of *Le Quatorze Juillet*. It suggests that Chabannes' 1936 production, coinciding with the heightened hopes and emotion of the summer of 1936, at least partially fulfilled Rolland's original intentions. It was certainly the most successful production of the Popular Front period, probably because it was held at the brief moment of apotheosis of the new regime, and in the midst of the electoral victory celebrations. Rolland's emphasis on revolutionary fervour and fraternity rather than on specific targets for popular anger suited the lyricism of 1936 and the all-embracing nature of the Popular Front's image of the people.

Rolland's play was not the only Popular Front production that endeavoured to represent the people on stage. The *Catalogue de la Société des Auteurs et Compositeurs Dramatiques* records the titles of a number of spectacles in 1936–37 that clearly echoed the concerns and ideals of the Popular Front, although some productions have left little trace. Among these were Paul Colline's *CGT Roi*, Roger Ray's *Le Peuple est Roi*, Henri Dallenne's *Rive gauche laborieuse, Rive gauche joyeuse* and two plays by the actress Muse Dalbray: *Allons au-devant de la vie*, performed in the Galeries Lafayette during the strikes and revived during 1937, and *Le Peuple souverain*, also performed in 1937. Furthermore, the Popular Front government also gave financial support to two other large-scale productions: *Liberté*, which was collectively written and produced, and *Naissance d'une cité*, the mass spectacle created by Jean-Richard Bloch.

Liberté was a series of one-act plays tracing the development of the organization and strength of the Third Estate from the middle ages to the Rassemblement Populaire: its aim was to explore the victory of the Popular Front as prefigured in French history. Commissioned by Léon Blum in October 1936 for the International Exhibition of 1937, the production was also designed as a self-consciously Socialist response to *Le Quatorze Juillet*, which had been closely associated with the Communist Maisons de Culture, although the Socialists had also played an important role in its organization.[79] *Liberté* was collective in both conception and realization, with 13 authors and 12 composers working in collaboration with the SFIO group Mai 36 and a number of other actors, all of whom remained anonymous in the surrounding publicity.[80] Henri-René Lenormand's depiction of the commune of Laon in 1112 provided the opening scene, which was followed by the presentation of various national heroes and heroines including Joan of Arc, Rabelais, Descartes, Pascal, and Molière. Subsequent scenes portrayed the return of La Fayette from America after the creation of its Constitution; the Revolution of 1789; the barricades of 1830, 1848, and the Commune; the foundation of the CGT; and finally the swearing of the oath of unity on 14 July 1935. The project was over-ambitious, and its realization fraught with difficulties on account of the increasing fragmentation of the Popular Front. Designed to celebrate the first anniversary of the electoral victory, it reflected instead the deepening divisions within the movement shortly after Blum's resignation as premier. Even the tricolour backdrop for the final 'popular ball' provoked considerable tension, epitomized by the angry delegation from the SFIO who interrupted Chabannes' work on the set. 'You're not going to leave that tricolour decoration for the final scene!' they exclaimed indignantly. 'Tricolour, that's communist!'[81] Unable to devise a suitable rejoinder, Chabannes reluctantly acknowledged their authority, and when the colour red was deemed offensive to the Radicals, the backdrop was finally designed in an innocuous shade of brown. The impact of the production was correspondingly weak, and even its organizers subsequently referred to its short run at the Théâtre des Champs-Élysées with mingled regret and apology. As Chabannes himself recalled: '*Liberté* was performed a dozen or so times at the Théâtre des Champs-Élysées during the painful inauguration of the Exhibition, with the disorderly strikes on the one side, and disgruntled businessmen on the other.'[82]

While *Liberté* and *Le Quatorze Juillet* endeavoured to encourage popular unity through their depiction of French history, *Naissance d'une cité* was a bold attempt to imagine a community of the future: the building of the ideal city with the French people as an icon of reconciliation. The spectacle has been briefly mentioned by Pascal Ory, mainly with reference to its strategies of production rather than its ideological content.[83] Yet the two must be studied in parallel if the full significance of *Naissance d'une cité* is to emerge as an attempted—if problematic—solution to the 'formidable question' of the masses. Only in this light does it appear as a response to criticisms of contemporary theatre and to the widespread search for lost wholeness in the community of the people.

Jean-Richard Bloch created *Naissance d'une cité* as a spectacle that could be performed by the masses and for the masses. Conceived as a 'veritable opera that would be popular, sportive, social, industrial, gymnastic, and legendary',[84] the production was held in the Vélodrome d'Hiver in order to accommodate a concluding display of athletic and gymnastic feats along the 400-metre cycle track, and included more than a thousand actors and stagehands on stage.[85] There were few individual roles: a chorus voiced the reactions of the masses, and a number of invisible speakers played the roles of narrators—a technique that Bloch hoped would feel familiar to the audience through its suggestion of the radio. Music composed for the occasion by Darius Milhaud, Arthur Honegger, and Roger Desormières (who had also conducted the choir at the end of *Le Quatorze Juillet*) played an integral part in the plot. It was only unfortunate that Bloch's ambitions surpassed the capabilities of the technical equipment available: the poor acoustics of the Vélodrome d'Hiver rendered the choruses and orchestral music almost inaudible, to the disappointment of many in the audience.

The aim of *Naissance d'une cité* was also to propose a solution to what Bloch had previously described as the 'duality of the modern world': the fatal divergence between man's industrial and technical achievements and man himself; between technical advance and human happiness.[86] Progress and technical development were not in Bloch's view synonymous—'Progress is technical advancement converted into dignity'[87]—and such progress required a reassessment of the role and status of the machine. 'The choice is clear,' he wrote. 'Either one must consecrate the machine, or else allow oneself to be consecrated to it and reduced to a grotesque servility.'[88] Bloch believed it possible for man to master progress and so achieve a community on a human scale, rather than falling victim to the relentless rhythms of markets, machines, and military rivalry. *Naissance d'une cité* attempts to translate this duality into unity, and the play therefore falls into two very different halves: first the representation of the industrialized masses in an urban setting, and secondly the construction of an ideal city on an unnamed island in the Atlantic Ocean. The opening scenes portray the sufferings of the working people in their everyday lives: the journey to work in the collective isolation of a crowded metro, and the soul-destroying conditions of factory labour. The male workers assemble a car on a production line; the female workers dress a giant model to take her place inside it—but both creations are then dramatically and noisily destroyed to signify the Depression and the subsequent lack of demand. The inability of these workers either to understand or change the world around them is suggested by an incomprehensible medley of news headlines, and by the sudden and unexplained entry of an army, dividing the assembled people into defensive, national groups.

These early scenes, written in 1934, echo the contemporary Communist image of the suffering proletariat; and it was also in this year that Jean-Richard Bloch attended the first congress of Soviet Writers in Moscow (he joined the PCF in 1938). Reconciling these scenes with the utopian second act, written in 1937, is as difficult as it is to reconcile official Communist discourses on the nature of the people before and after the formation of the Popular Front. In *Naissance d'une cité*, the search for utopia begins when one of the workers encourages his comrades to leave their employment for the chance of building a new community on an island in the Atlantic. Among those who accept is a former lieutenant and engineer, whose participation is conditional on his being accepted by the workers as their equal. The following scenes then trace the construction of the ideal city, starting with the 'communal house'. Yet this is not so much a collectivist utopia as a curious hybrid of an idealized rural society and a miniature French Republic. The foreign workers seen in defensive national groups in the early scenes now zealously sing *La Marseillaise* in celebration of the foundation of the new *cité*, referred to as a little Republic.[89] Meanwhile the engineer adopts a role of moral leadership, marrying a young couple whose union signifies the fruitfulness of the new community, and presiding over the celebration of an engagement and a golden wedding anniversary.[90] This happy ending, written to suit the context of the International Exhibition, was accompanied in the 1937 production by a gala of music, gymnastics, and dance.

Bloch's resolute engagement with the demands of mass theatre was challenged by the technical limitations of the Vélodrome d'Hiver, and his imagination of the people in the ideal city was problematic, not least because it required a *tabula rasa*, here in the form of a virgin island in the Atlantic. Yet if his attempt to solve the 'formidable question' was unsuccessful, his efforts are revealing in themselves. Bloch had previously observed that popular theatre would be unsuccessful without a latent unity of belief between actors and audience: 'a unity of religious belief, of social or national myths.'[91] He himself had doubted whether such unity was possible in the antagonistic climate of the 1930s, and when idealizing the place of the theatre at the heart of the city he had turned to the middle ages, when theatre had been organized by the monarchy, the Church, and local confraternities, and when performances had been endowed with the majesty of court and religious ceremony.[92] Indeed, despite his own fervent allegiance to socialism as 'a sort of spiritual hope in messianic form',[93] he was nonetheless keen to dispel the popular perception of the middle ages as the 'dark ages', and observed that the men and women of the 1930s seemed to aspire in vain towards the universality that the medieval period had apparently possessed. 'Under the banner of catholicity,' he observed, 'triumphed and flourished an idea of universality for which we now suffer and strive once again.'[94] He believed that his contemporaries sought in the representation of the people—and in their own integration within this people—an experience of unity that was not simply political or social, but also spiritual: the sense of belonging to a single body. Could it be that theatre provided the most effective means of achieving this sense of communion, the 'commotion of unanimity' so desperately sought in the political sphere?

Communion and utopia: The people as a mystical body

Jean-Richard Bloch's nostalgic reflections on the middle ages were echoed in the concurrent resurgence of interest in the medieval doctrine of the Mystical Body, not only among Catholic philosophers but also among playwrights and in associations such as the Jeunesse Ouvrière Chrétienne. For the philosopher Emmanuel Mounier, best known for his development of the doctrine of Personalism, the concept of the Mystical Body of Christ suggested a spiritual solution to the problem of mass society. 'The revelation of collectivism must be purified, not blindly opposed,' he observed to his former teacher, Jacques Chevalier, in 1932, 'and the doctrine of the Mystical Body is there to sustain us.'[95] Similarly, in 1936 the Jesuit theologian Émile Mersch published a study of the doctrine entitled *Le Corps Mystique du Christ*, outlining its Biblical foundations in the Old Testament, the Gospels, and the letters of Saint Paul, and then tracing its development through the writings of various early saints, including St Athanasius, St John Chrysostom, and St Cyril of Alexandria. He placed particular emphasis on Paul's concept of man as a social and collective being, and on the importance of the Mystical Body in transforming the disparate, lonely crowd into a living body.[96] As part of the Mystical Body, he wrote, all humans could be in communion, united with each other and with their Creator.[97] J. Lebreton, in a preface to the work, suggested the particular relevance of this concept to the 1930s as well as emphasizing its universal and eternal appeal.

> There is a single life that spreads through the whole body, sustaining, developing, and animating every member. One cannot contemplate this mystery without feeling its attraction, for is not the reality that it proposes the ideal that every human society pursues?[98]

Père Fillère, a lecturer at the Institut Catholique and a regular speaker at large-scale Catholic meetings in Paris, emphasized the particular importance of reaching out to the masses with these doctrines of unity, not least because political associations were adopting quasi-spiritual language so as to appeal to the same needs: 'Because they adopt a mystique, they rally those who, ignorant of the one true mystique, nonetheless yearn for it nostalgically.'[99] In 1937, the philosopher Marie-Dominique Chénu developed a similar theme in *Dimension nouvelle de la chrétienté*, a study of Christian responses to the challenges of mass society. Chénu examined how, in this age of the masses, political and social organizations were making increasing demands on individuals in the name of the common good, seeking in this way to recreate some of the lost wholeness of a society divided by competing and irreconcilable interests. 'These visions of the state,' he observed, 'whether on the right or the left, find in this the grain of truth which renders them attractive and dangerous.'[100] The submission of the self to the common interest could certainly appear a powerful antidote to the dehumanizing effects of industrialization and capitalism, but its very power increased its dangerous potential: could any leader or party hold sufficient authority to determine the common good? Anti-individualism could lead all too easily to disregard for the individual as a person. It was doubly important, Mersch contended, to reveal to the masses the only framework within which such self-abnegation and communion could be truly beneficial: the integration of the human person within the people of God, themselves forming part of the Mystical Body.[101]

Chénu's writings were influential in philosophical circles, but the idea of the Mystical Body was also being discussed more widely—chosen, for example as a topic for debate at a week-long conference in Clermont in 1937, structured around the theme of 'the human person in danger.' 'In the life of this Mystical Body,' explained Eugène Duthoit, one of the speakers at the conference, 'it would be inadequate even to say that we are in solidarity with one another, because we are in communion.'[102] Similar ideas were developed by the Jesuit Henri de Lubac, whose *Catholicisme: les aspects sociaux du dogme* (1938) especially praised the influence of Mounier's 'communitarian personalism' and emphasized the social dimension of the sacraments.[103]

This emphasis on communion and community was also explored in Catholic theatre, which thus presented a significant parallel to the theatre of the Popular Front. Two disciples of Jacques Copeau, Henri Ghéon and Léon Chancerel, both saw their performances as a means to encourage communion within a popular or mass framework. Ghéon, a convert to Catholicism during the First World War, produced a number of medieval plays adapted for modern audiences, and was deeply influenced by Copeau's belief that an acting troupe should see itself as a spiritual brotherhood. His own Compagnons de Notre Dame alternated between major and minor roles, and often celebrated Mass together before performances.[104] The Neo-Thomist philosopher Jacques Maritain described Ghéon's drama as 'Catholic—that is to say, universal, where all human beings may be reconciled',[105] and Ghéon himself justified his production of popular spectacles primarily for a Catholic audience because in this case, 'the notion of community, of communion is not completely absent.'[106] In 1935 Ghéon organized an outdoor performance of a drama inspired by Pentecost—*Le Mystère du feu vivant sur les apôtres*—in the recently excavated Arènes de Lutèce in Paris, and at Pentecost in 1936 he held a large-scale performance of *Le Mystère de la Messe* in the Parc des Princes. This event was attended by 40,000 spectators, who became protagonists in turn through their scripted dialogue with the actors on stage.[107]

Léon Chancerel, a disciple of Copeau who had been deeply influenced by his early training at the Vieux-Colombier theatre, developed his own drama around similar principles, aiming to create a sense of communion among the actors themselves, and also between the actors and the audience. Director of the Centre Dramatique Scout d'Île de France, as well as of the travelling Comédiens Routiers and the Chœur Dramatique des Cheftaines, Chancerel aspired for 'the juxtaposition of a certain concept of the theatre with a certain concept of life, at the heart of a specific community.'[108] Chancerel's ambition was not only to revive the popular theatre of the middle ages, but also to create new plays on the same principles. Although he translated a number of medieval texts, he also composed new variations on medieval themes, and his aim was always to ensure that the new productions were as close to the contemporary French people as the originals had been to the people of their time. There were, for example, performances in rural areas, in the suburbs, and even in factories.[109] His touring theatre troupe, the Comédiens Routiers, were inspired by the idea of bringing theatre of provincial inspiration back to its roots, in open-air performances marked by 'that fresh scent of their origins: earth, wood, flowers and—inevitably—youth.'[110] His doctrine was that the theatre should prove a healthy physical, intellectual, and spiritual training for all concerned.

> A precious instrument for perfecting physical, intellectual and moral qualities, developing physical skill and resistance, combating individualism, drawing the players into a close unity, and freeing them from themselves in order to draw them into a single being filled with love, abnegation, modesty, and Christian charity.[111]

The actors would, he hoped, find a sense of close communion through their work, reinforced by their voluntary anonymity and their willing obedience to the leader of the troupe. Thus subsumed within the 'collective personality' of the troupe, they would relate more closely to the collective desires of their popular audience.

In 1936 Chancerel published a collection of *Récitations chorales*: spoken choruses that were sometimes based on medieval texts, sometimes the collective creations of Chancerel and his actors. The technique of the spoken chorus (which was, as Chancerel well knew, also popular with agit-prop theatre groups), seemed to him an excellent means of ensuring 'an intimate communication between the chorists, and a mastery of mind and body for goals that are not personal but communitarian', as well as having a profound effect upon the audience.[112] *Chant de la route* (1936), written by Chancerel while living in the Parisian suburb of Belleville, would have made an apt song of the Popular Front: a spoken chorus for six actors, which celebrated youthful solidarity and the discovery of the countryside. October 1936 witnessed the première of Chancerel's new variation on La Fontaine's tale *Le Laboureur et ses enfants* (a play also revived by Maurice Pottecher): *Un Trésor est caché dedans*. The play exemplified Chancerel's style: popular theatre pared down to its essential symbolism. It required minimal scenery or stage properties, and the characters were two-dimensional, their actions serving the didactic purpose of the plot rather than revealing their psychological development. In contrast to La Fontaine's original story, Chancerel's version is set on an island, where a dying father reveals to his children that treasure is hidden in the earth that he has worked throughout his life. Tempted first by the pleasures of urban society and then by the money to be made from selling the island, the children are eventually moved by the hope of material gain to follow his advice, finally coming to recognize that his words are purely symbolic. The exaltation of rural labour and of fidelity to the land of one's ancestors was unambiguous. The play toured France, from Nancy to Bordeaux, and was intended to be 'accessible to all classes of society, a contribution to their reconciliation and unity.'[113]

Léon Chancerel sought to develop popular theatre through small-scale productions, often of provincial inspiration, touring the provinces of France. But Catholic popular theatre was also being developed on a mass scale by the Jeunesse Ouvrière Chrétienne (JOC), which celebrated its tenth anniversary in July 1937 with a large-scale performance in the Parc des Princes. Chancerel himself was highly impressed by the spectacle. 'The Jocistes' impressive endeavour should be noted, reflected upon, studied and rigorously pursued,' he wrote. 'It should serve as a model to all who aspire to the organization of popular celebrations.'[114]

The JOC, reflecting contemporary theology, was born of a concern to Christianize the masses by integrating them within a mystic community. Established in Belgium by Joseph Cardijn, a priest of popular origin, the movement spread to France in the late 1920s, and in 1926 began to take shape under the direction of Abbé Guérin, a parish priest in Clichy who was already deeply committed to the interests of young workers. Moving away from the more middle-class Action Catholique de la Jeunesse Française, the JOC rapidly entrusted leadership to young workers themselves, and became closely and actively involved with the problems of the workplace, seeking to realize Pope Pius XI's desire that workers should evangelize one another. During the Popular Front, Jociste workers were sometimes wary of participating in the strikes, but were invariably keen to press for social reforms, and were occasionally chosen as factory delegates. In its first ten years the JOC expanded more rapidly than any other youth organization, and included an estimated 90,000 members by 1938.[115] At the heart of the movement was an emphasis on the sanctity of work and the dignity of the worker, with particular attention to Christ's elevation of manual labour through his own work as an artisan, and on his consequent fraternity with all workers. This was often expressed in visual form in the movement's various publications. For many years, the newspaper *Jeunesse Ouvrière* was headed by a woodcut-style image of Christ as a carpenter; while the bulletin for female militants, *L'Équipe Ouvrière Féminine*, often included sketches of Christ as a 'travelling companion'—seated, for example, in the bus next to those travelling to work.[116] The JOC aimed to raise awareness not only of the value of work but also of the special dignity of the working classes, called to become pure, joyful, and all-conquering (Figure 17). Indeed, Jociste publications were marked by a distinctive pride in the workers, their glorious future and their role in the divine plan of salvation: an image of the people as victors which offered a striking parallel to that proposed by the Popular Front. 'Our cause is a most sacred one,' proclaimed the pamphlet *L'Appel de la JOC* in 1938.

> We carry within us the future of the working class, that great untapped reservoir of hidden virtues, deep energies, patience, determination, courage, defiance of suffering, frugal honesty, and fraternal solidarity.[117]

Like those who sought to bring culture to the people or to represent them in cultural form, the Jocistes conceived of the 'people' as comprising first and foremost the working classes, and as being in a wider sense

Figure 17 'Proud, pure, joyous, and victorious', *La Jeunesse Ouvrière*, June 1932 (Courtesy of the Bibliothèque Nationale, Paris).

open to all those whose activity could be seen as contributing to the greater work of salvation.

The most dramatic visual representation of the people by the JOC was the spectacle that Léon Chancerel had described with such evident admiration, and that took place within the tenth anniversary celebrations in Paris in July 1937: *La Joie du travail* and *Le Sens du travail* (Figure 18). The spectacle was a triptych of two linked plays in the Parc des Princes followed by a mass in French the following morning. The performance of the two plays has received little subsequent attention, and the one detailed study by the former Jociste chaplain Jean-Pierre Coco analyses the triptych with sensitivity but does not explore the idea of the people, nor situate the performance within the context of contemporary Popular Front theatre. One of the most striking aspects of the spectacle, however, was its closeness in language and symbolism to other contemporary attempts to represent the people and the ideal city.[118]

Figure 18   Advertisement for the JOC congress, *La Jeunesse Ouvrière*, April 1937 (Courtesy of the Bibliothèque Nationale, Paris).

The aim of *La Joie du travail* and *Le Sens du travail* was indeed to address the same question that *Naissance d'une cité* had addressed: the transformation of an alienated working class into a united, popular community. *La Joie du Travail* opened with the faint crackle of a popular song on a gramophone record, almost inaudible in the immense space of the Parc des Princes, and presented as a pale escapism pitifully inadequate for the social needs of the masses. In contrast, the Jociste spectacle constituted a great *Symphonie du Travail*: a synthesis of movement and music in which the workers—playing themselves—moved around the arena, dancing traditional dances in regional costume while encircling the machines on stage. The weavers, passing their spinning machines, broke away from the procession to dance around them, thus symbolically incorporating them into their lives, and suggesting a new harmony between man and machinery, similar to the utopian vision of *Naissance d'une cité*. Although there was no representation of factory work in *La Joie du travail*, large-scale models of the workers' creations were nonetheless used in this comparable form of mass theatre: the printers carried a large book, and the masons bore aloft a model château. Meanwhile the sound of the machines in action was echoed and developed by the orchestra. The wearing of provincial costumes and the visual association of particular professions with particular regions—florists from Nice, perfume workers from Grasse, and silk workers from the Rhone Valley[119]—also sought to identify work as an integral and important part of the worker's identity, rather than as joyless, isolating labour. This celebration of the provinces also evoked a reconciliation of man and nature, and a communion between rural and urban France that was, as has been shown, more widely characteristic of contemporary ideology.

While *La Joie du travail* represented work as integral to a worker's identity, *Le Sens du travail* sought to explore its deeper, spiritual significance, and to represent the people as a mystic community engaged in the building of the *cité nouvelle* (Figure 19).

Just as these various processions, bearing the fruits of their labours, journey to the same destination, so each of our working years, each one of our lives, is a journey towards a single goal: the building of the city.[120]

The symmetry of the dances and the movement of the workers suggested an underlying order, with the speaker, echoed by a chorus, describing the city as a living body, for whose good all must work in harmony. In visual reflection, the workers began to join hands, with the

"...C'est toute la cité ouvrière à rebâtir ! "

Figure 19   La Jeunesse Ouvrière, February 1934 (Courtesy of the Bibliothèque Nationale, Paris).

affirmative cheers of the entire audience suggesting their participation in this mystic community. The speaker insisted that the construction of the city was a task to which all could contribute, through activity in the workplace, at home, or even by offering their suffering—and, as he spoke, more than one hundred invalids were carried in on stretchers to join the procession. *Le Sens du travail* concluded with a celebration of the fusion between human and divine creation in the life of the city, describing Christ as both an architect and a fellow labourer. At the same moment, it became clear that each of the objects created by workers and machines in *La Joie du travail* was to have its place in the celebration of Mass in the Parc des Princes the following day: the carpenters had produced the altar, the weavers the altar cloth, the book binders had bound the missal, and the invalids had offered the cross, 13 metre in height. The next morning, the Mass was offered for fellow workers in Germany and the USSR, and was celebrated by a young worker-priest.

The spectacle, which Popular Front newspapers generally downplayed, was acclaimed by sympathetic critics for its theatrical innovation and powerful symbolism. René Schwob, theatre critic for *Les Études*, described the occasion as touching the sublime.

> This procession reached the sublime—and I do not exaggerate. Here was an effortless magnificence, arising from the thrill of pride and joy, freedom and fraternity, in this young generation restored to dignity. Before my eyes, like a dream finally realized, was an image of the people in which I had ceased to believe. The arguments, hatred, jealousy, and vulgarity that I had seen force-fed to the poor people for so many years, and that had finally repulsed them—all this had disappeared in an instant. Before my eyes was their restored portrait, their true image.[121]

Meanwhile, the Catholic playwright Henri Ghéon sought to claim some part in the spectacle, which he believed was in many ways the fruit of developments in popular theatre during the preceding years. 'We have been preparing the faithful people for this for more than fifteen years,' he claimed. 'That is to say, both those who are accorded the heavy and brutal name of the "masses" and also the elite of the Christian world.'[122] This was, in his view, an example of popular theatre that fulfilled its highest goals by uniting actors and audience in symbolic communion. But it also went far beyond theatre, in that the workers on stage were in fact playing themselves, and thus it became an act of faith.

> Theatre thus conceived and thus realized contributes to the greatness of a country, of a religion, of the working-class world, and quite simply to the world itself: it is the image of our hopes; it sustains and nourishes them, and helps to draw us towards them. It rejoins its eternal tradition.[123]

Henri Ghéon had only one reservation about the spectacle: the first three quarters of the performance held no explicit reference to the eschatological significance of the workers or their creation, and a materialist, even a Communist, could have identified fully with the people as they were presented on stage. But this, so the producer replied, was exactly what was intended.

In 1936–37, it was not only in politics that an answer was sought to the 'formidable question' of transforming the masses into the people. Parallel to political reflection (and inseparable from it) was a current of opposition to the narrow individualism of existing culture: a call for culture to relate more closely to the people in both content and accessibility, and to fulfil the social purpose of creating community. The Popular Front government responded not simply to the demands of its followers but also to these wider concerns as it favoured the encounter of the people with cinema, radio, and theatre, and its adversaries criticized the partisan content of such policies and productions, but not the notion of popular culture *per se*. The 'people' imagined in policy and production were threefold: on one level, the working classes, those previously excluded from culture or exposed only to its more debased forms; on a second level, people from all classes, united as a nation sharing a common culture. And on a third level, they were a mystic community imagined as much in political representations as in purely cultural ones: a community in which the individual could be subsumed into a single but collective body. The urgency and fervour with which both political and cultural representations focused on the people as a reconciled community, and the close parallels in the language and imagery employed in politics and theology, suggest a deeper, more fundamental concern to address the spiritual relationship between the individual and the collective. The working people, the nation, the faithful: these 'peoples' seemed to offer the possibility of recreating a lost wholeness of structure and belief, compensating for collective individualism. 'One cannot make the people act without revealing the current state of human conscience,' wrote Henri Lesieur, director of the Théâtre du Peuple, 'without revealing that this conscience is awake. To talk of the people is to talk of metaphysics.'[124] Reactions to the utopian mass spectacles of the 1930s suggest that the idealized vision of the people on stage was by no means guaranteed to achieve the intended effects of unity and community. Yet visions of popular communion were more easily realizable on stage than in the streets.

6
In Search of the Middle Classes: The Tragedy at Clichy and its Consequences

Travelling to Tunisia on board the *Général-Lépine* in April 1937, the philosopher Emmanuel Mounier was struck by the noisy contempt of his bourgeois fellow-passengers for the Popular Front government and its supporters. One lady, an inhabitant of the Parisian suburb of Clichy, was complaining vociferously about the Popular Front demonstration the previous month: a protest against a local meeting of the PSF that had escalated into a violent confrontation with the police. 'You simply had to see it,' she announced portentously to her attentive listeners. 'Red ribbons in their hair. And *this* is what governs us!' Another passenger blamed the continuing disorder on the misguided principles of the Popular Front government. 'It's quite simple', he explained. 'Imagine a budget that begins like this. Item one: a good rest for everyone. I'm sending all my family on holiday.' The unconscious irony of such moralistic reflections—condemning paid holidays for the workers while on a luxurious Mediterranean cruise—provoked bitter reflections from Mounier, who had become disillusioned with the bourgeoisie and was proud to observe that all his grandparents were of peasant origin. Indeed he found it surprising that when speaking of matters unrelated to their class interests, his fellow-passengers could become quite human.[1]

Mounier's barbed anecdote captured three of the challenges facing the Popular Front under Blum's first government that were to transform the pursuit of the people in 1936–37: the problematic relationship between the Popular Front and its supporters, the renewed association of the crowd with violence, and the increasing dissatisfaction of the middle classes with left-wing government. Although the bourgeois passengers on board the *Général-Lépine* complained about government economic policy, they were still able to afford their Mediterranean cruise. Others were not so fortunate. The middle classes, especially the shopkeepers, employees, civil servants, and farmers who were already at the heart of the rivalry between left and right, were to suffer increasingly from the effects of the new policies during the Popular Front's exercise of power.

By the time Mounier was writing in April 1937, the position of the Popular Front government had deteriorated in the eyes of opponents and supporters alike. The official policy of non-intervention in the Spanish Civil War left the Foreign Minister Yvon Delbos with the unenviable task of responding to constant criticism; Communists supported obstructive strikes, while Radicals made their continued support for the Popular Front contingent on the strikes' cessation. Economically, the policies of the Popular Front government were fiercely contested. Blum had hoped to tackle unemployment and boost the national economy with early policies such as the 40-hour week (with unchanged wages), the Wheat Marketing Board, and the programme of public works. But results by September were not encouraging, and seemed instead to signal an end to the recovery from economic depression that had begun in 1935. Levels of industrial production had fallen by 7 per cent (compared with a rise of 4 per cent the previous year), while the number of registered unemployed had increased since the previous September by 34,000. Wholesale prices had risen by 12 per cent; retail prices by as much as 55 per cent.[2] After the devaluation of the franc in September there was a slight improvement: a rise in exports stimulated by their comparatively low prices, a rise in industrial production, and a decline in the number of unemployed workers. But by the spring of 1937 these positive trends were reversed, and the cost of living continued to rise. It was in this context that Blum announced a 'pause' in February 1937 in the implementation of Popular Front reforms, introducing a cut in public spending and appointing a committee of financial experts to chart the progress of the franc since devaluation. But by June the financial crisis had deepened further, the committee had resigned, and Blum was led to demand emergency decree powers to resolve the situation, which he was granted by the Chamber of Deputies but refused by the Senate. He resigned after 380 days in office, to be replaced as Premier by the Radical Camille Chautemps.

While the government's economic and foreign policies provoked criticism and alarm, its relationship with its supporters in the street was little better. Strikes continued into the autumn and winter of 1936—despite Blum's proposals to improve industrial relations through compulsory arbitration—and the violence of the strikes suggested a growing distance between angry working-class protest and the Popular Front's image of a rational, fraternal working people. The bloody riot at Clichy was to be still more devastating to this image, seeming rather to provide evidence for right-wing theories of crowd behaviour. Political alternatives to the Popular Front were concurrently increasing in influence: the PSF was becoming the largest political party in France; the smaller and more extreme PPF was attracting members of parliamentary parties such as the Fédération Républicaine and the Parti Démocrate Populaire to its 'Liberty Front' of 1937. Disillusioned members of the middle classes (including many former supporters of the Popular Front) were badly affected by the Popular Front's social and economic reforms, and were anxious to find associations to represent their interests. In consequence, the definition and organization of the 'people' by political groups and parties took a new turn. The emphasis shifted from popular spontaneity to firm leadership, and from working to middle classes. Images of reconciliation remained powerful, but the achievement of reconciliation through popular efforts alone seemed open to question.[3]

Crowds and workers: From unity to discord

Given the emphasis in the secondary literature on the generally pacific factory occupations of spring–summer 1936, it is important to remember that the majority of strikes during the Popular Front period were not characterized by calm, triumphant workers, but rather by bitterness and dissatisfaction on both sides. By autumn 1936 the strikes were different in character from the previous spring, and were the cause of considerable political tension. The devaluation of the franc had diminished the value of the salary increases offered by the Matignon Agreement, while employers feared that the application of the 40-hour week would require a reduction in personnel, leading to further discontent.[4] CGT leader Léon Jouhaux pressed for government intervention to resolve the conflicts, but the Senate refused to accord such powers unless absolutely necessary.[5] In the continuing unrest, not only were the striking workers criticized by employers and the right-wing press as violent and undisciplined, but the Popular Front itself provoked increasing disaffection by failing to control its alleged supporters.

Striking workers in the factories or in the streets thus began to undermine both the image of the people and also the Popular Front. The difficulty in representing the strikers as the people was particularly acute in that the strikes of autumn–winter 1936 were far more openly hostile than their predecessors. First, there was a sharp increase in social tensions and protests following the development of right-wing unions. In the Paris market of Les Halles, for example, disorder broke out when a butcher's union, affiliated to the PSF, condemned left-wing workers' demands for a two-day weekend as disruptive and impractical.[6] Secondly, there was a growing hostility towards members of the CFTC (Confédération Française des Travailleurs Chrétiens) and non-unionized workers. On 2 December 1936, strikers in electricity companies overturned a lorry and were responsible for a number of individual attacks on workers without union affiliation: two electricians at work on the Church at Saint-Mandé were set upon by eight strikers, and two others were knocked from a ladder and confined in an injured condition to the trade-union centre on the Rue de la Grange aux Belles.[7] Workers who had been attacked or had their equipment confiscated by strike committees sometimes lodged complaints with their employers, who then complained to the government. On 18 December, one factory owner wrote to the Minister of the Interior of 'a significant number of groups foreign to our establishment' who had threatened to devastate the factory and to attack objecting workers unless a strike were immediately organized. The employer's instinctive suspicion of 'foreign' workers was clear, even though in many cases it was immigrant workers who were among the most assiduous in working long hours. 'You must also understand', he concluded, 'that it is regrettable to see these disruptive elements, foreign to our establishment and even to the nation, obstructing freedom of work—and with such effrontery.'[8]

At the very end of December, while Léon Blum was attempting to elaborate a law on compulsory arbitration, a number of strikes in the public sector created further associations between the crowd, the workers, and disorder. One particularly notorious event was the large strikers' demonstration outside the Paris Hôtel de Ville, where municipal councillors were debating salaries and conditions of employment, on 29 December. According to some reports the strikers attempted to force entry into the building, and the police refused to disperse the demonstrators because the government had not authorized strong action against them. Despite the size and fervour of the demonstration, the President of the Municipal Council, M. Raymond-Laurent, refused to deliberate while under pressure from the street—for which he was widely praised in the press. Conversely, the demonstrators created a much less positive impression. While *Le Populaire* described the demonstration as 'peaceful and powerful'[9] and *L'Humanité* emphasized its remarkable discipline,[10] most accounts noted the crowd's anger and violence, and refused to equate its actions with the voice of the people. The fact that these workers persisted in their strike action after the elaboration of extensive social reforms, and despite Léon Blum's continuing efforts to resolve tensions by legal means, undermined the presentation of their grievances as a rational expression of the popular will. Instead the crowd and the strikers appeared as partisan and divisive, dominated by CGT militants and associated with the violent coercion of non-unionized workers. As in the summer of 1936, workers and crowds were a challenge to the Popular Front government: their rival demands and displays of power suggested dissatisfaction with their elected leaders, as well as the concurrent inability of the government to preserve public order and assert its legitimate authority over the 'ministry of the masses'.

The increased incidence of violent street activity in late 1936 was certainly not restricted to the left, and the new right-wing parties soon revealed their shortcomings as self-styled agents of national reconciliation (although without abandoning this particular rhetoric). Allegations in the Popular Front press that the right-wing parties were armed reconstitutions of militaristic leagues were proved, for example, to have serious foundations. In early October 1936 a search of La Rocque's house in Versailles unearthed several truncheons, as well as a knife marked with a swastika in the bedroom of one of his sons.[11] Later the same month a meeting of approximately 1000 PSF members at the Splendid Cinema in Choisy-le-Roi was followed by a police raid (at the request of the local Communists), and a number of firearms were discovered in the garage where PSF members had parked their cars.[12] Indeed, members of the PSF and PPF were certainly not afraid to use their weapons when challenged. On the evening of 16 December 1936, a skirmish broke out at the close of a PPF meeting in Clermont-Ferrand and resulted in a number of serious injuries, some of them among the police. Five PPF members were arrested for carrying prohibited weapons, including truncheons, revolvers, and a bag of pepper.[13] In January, a PSF meeting in Martigues was held in contravention of an official ban, and two PSF members greeted a Communist counter-demonstration with defiant shots from their revolvers.[14] In 1937 there were also a number of political murders, including an SFIO member shot by his PSF neighbour during a political discussion, and a PPF flag-bearer killed by the militant trade unionist Joseph Cesari. In many cases the local authorities attempted to avoid open confrontation by refusing authorization for public (and even private) political meetings. But meetings and counter-demonstrations often contravened these restrictions, and heated political discussions between next-door neighbours were difficult for any government to forestall.

Leadership and the crowd

In the months between the celebrations of summer 1936 and the violent riot at Clichy in March 1937, one characteristic of the organization and representation of street politics was an increase in violence and confrontation, and a consequent reluctance or inability to describe the crowd in the street as the 'people'. A second characteristic—less dominant, but nonetheless important—was a compensatory trend in Popular Front demonstrations to emphasize the relationship between the crowd and its leaders.

One example was the demonstrations of November 1936 in response to the suicide of Roger Salengro, the Popular Front Minister of the Interior who had been subjected to a vicious campaign of right-wing defamation for his alleged desertion during the First World War. Following the official commemoration of his life, the Popular Front press was filled with images of the people in the street: a people in mourning rather than in celebration, but also in calm and disciplined mass meetings rather than unruly strikes. It was an opportunity for the Popular Front to revive the potentially unitive sentiment of anti-fascism by underlining the continuing danger of the French right, and to portray a people who respected their leaders rather than undermining the government's ability to keep order. *Le Populaire* published a manifesto on 21 November signed by many left-wing intellectuals, and the Communists organized large-scale meetings and drew parallels between the activities of Franco in Spain and the right-wing press in France. 'It's the same hand that struck down Salengro that also kills in Spain,' insisted Paul Vaillant-Couturier, calling in response for the unity of the French people.[15] A few days later, Édouard Herriot commemorated Salengro in a speech to the Chamber of Deputies—where the benches of the centre and right were unusually empty—and argued that Salengro's death should inspire the French people to prove the superiority of democracy over dictatorship.[16] What was noticeable in Herriot's speech, as in the article by Vaillant-Couturier, was that although the funeral and commemoration of Roger Salengro offered an opportunity to call upon the people and to represent them, both verbally and visually, in their occupation of the street, they were nonetheless presented in relation to their leaders rather than as an independent and guiding force.

A similar impression was given by the Socialist demonstrations that took place at Nantes and Saint-Nazaire in February 1937, shortly after Léon Blum's announcement of a necessary 'pause' in the application of the Popular Front programme. Blum, who had come to Brittany to lay the foundation stone for a maternity hospital, gave a speech in which he urged the local working class to remember the importance of their collaboration with the government, and with the entire working people of France. *Le Populaire*'s description of the occasion on 22 February 1937 stressed the people's 'unshakeable, fierce will', yet gave no indication of how many were present, and portrayed those attending in a purely passive role, obediently acclaiming their leaders rather than expressing their own supposedly sovereign will. Photographs depicted a crowd of men in caps, neither raising their fists nor obviously vocal; turned instead towards their leaders. Justifying the 'pause' to his listeners, Blum explained that although the relationship between the people and the Popular Front remained paramount, the people should be a source of strength and inspiration rather than a guide. He referred, moreover, to an abstract people, rather than addressing his listeners as such.

> We are the sons of the people of this country. We have been chosen by the popular will. And we rediscover our full strength—should this be diminished in battle—whenever we renew contact with the people. Separation from the people would lead to our defeat.[17]

This image of the relationship between the people and their leaders is rarely associated with the Popular Front. Danielle Tartakowsky's study of the processions and demonstrations in the period neglects this particular form; Suzanne Lachaumette's comparison of right- and left-wing press photographs associates an anonymous, obedient crowd only with the right, while emphasizing a left-wing focus on individual members of the crowd in publications such as the Communist magazine *Regards*.[18] The fact that *L'Humanité* frequently pictured the people as anonymous masses—and that *Le Populaire* portrayed the people as obediently acclaiming their leaders—suggests a more complex story as well as an evolving one. This may have been a minority trend among demonstrations in this period, but it was nonetheless persistent.

The riot at Clichy

Against a background of heightened political tension and governmental determination to preserve order in the streets, the violent riot at Clichy was to have grave repercussions for the pursuit of the people as crowd, workers, and reconciled community. Ironically, it was the government's attempted impartiality that set the scene for this particular tragedy.[19] Honouring the principle of freedom of association, the Minister of the Interior Marx Dormoy granted permission for a PSF film evening in the working-class suburb of Clichy on 16 March 1937. No prominent members of the PSF were to be present, and the evening was to consist principally of the projection of *La Bataille*, a film based on the book of the same name by Claude Farrère. Two days beforehand, however, posters appeared in the neighbourhood to complain of the 'provocation' that the alleged presence of Colonel de la Rocque would offer in such a proletarian district, and to call for a counter-demonstration by the Popular Front. The posters bore the signatures of the local Popular Front committee: the Mayor Charles Auffray, the town councillor Maurice Naile, and the PCF deputy Maurice Honel. This committee addressed itself firstly to 'the labouring population of the factories, building sites, and offices', but then extended its appeal to 'veteran soldiers, small shopkeepers, craftsmen, all republicans, and all democrats'.[20] Concerned by the proposed counter-demonstration, members of the PSF occupied the cinema on the night of 15 March, and Marx Dormoy arranged for a total of 1800 policemen to guard the cinema and (he hoped) deflect the anger of the demonstrators.[21] But this considerable police presence merely inflamed the rising passions of the crowd, and by 9 o'clock an estimated 9000 demonstrators had assembled outside the cinema, compared with a mere 400 PSF members inside. When the demonstrators discovered that the cinema had been successfully evacuated by the police, and that their enemies had thus eluded them, their fury reached boiling point. Honel and Naile appealed for calm from the windows of the Town Hall, and eventually persuaded approximately 2000 of the demonstrators to attend a hastily organized meeting, but the vast majority attempted to break down the barriers that separated the remaining demonstrators from the cinema. Shots were fired, both by the police and also—it was alleged[22]—by the demonstrators, and as the municipal sirens began to sound, drawing further angry demonstrators from the surrounding neighbourhoods, the violence degenerated into anarchy, with heavy casualties on both sides of the makeshift barricades (Figure 20). Policemen were pelted with stones, and the fighting continued late into the night, with shops owned by local PSF members looted and vandalized, including a butcher's shop and a newsagent. When Marx Dormoy and Blum's secretary André Blumel appeared on the scene, they were greeted with contemptuous cries of 'Dormoy, resign!'—and the unfortunate Blumel, caught in the crossfire, received

M. THOREZ (×), DÉPUTÉ D'IVRY, ARRIVE SUR LES LIEUX DE LA BAGARRE   UN AGENT BLESSÉ EST EMMENÉ VERS L'AMBULANCE

Figure 20 The riot at Clichy, *Paris-Soir*, 19 March 1937 (Courtesy of the Archives de la Préfecture de Police, Paris).

two gunshot wounds and was taken to hospital. Léon Blum arrived somewhat later, travelling directly from a concert conducted by Sir Thomas Beecham at the Paris Opera, and his elegant white tie and tails contrasted unflatteringly with the bloodstained appearance of the demonstrators: a contrast of which he himself was only too keenly aware.[23] By the end of the evening, 5 of the demonstrators had already died in hospital and a further 222 were suffering from minor to severe injuries. Police casualties numbered over 250.[24]

The Clichy riot ended with the eventual dispersal of the looters from the damaged shops of the locality, but popular action continued with spontaneous outbreaks of strikes the following day and with a general strike on the morning of 18 March. Ironically, the general strike was organized with the explicit intention of limiting the danger of the workers' reactions, and reflected the growing desperation of Popular Front and trade-union leaders to control their supporters. On 17 March, the building site of the forthcoming International Exhibition was crowded with strikers, restrained from vandalizing the German pavilion only by the swift intervention of trade-union delegates and the police.[25] Léon Blum considered resigning, but was urged to remain at his post by the CGT leader Léon Jouhaux, who feared a fascist coup and assured Blum that a general strike would not be directed against the government. Yet Jouhaux himself was later dismayed to discover that a decision to call a half-day strike had been taken without his advice, and he too threatened to resign if work were not resumed on the afternoon of 18 March. Having almost provoked the resignation of two Popular Front leaders, the strike was in the end a relatively peaceful affair: there were an estimated

610,000 strikers in the Paris area, but their protests were limited to the waving of red flags and the singing of *L'Internationale* on Parisian boulevards.[26] An attempt to process through the Faubourg Saint-Antoine to the Place de la Nation was dispersed by the police, who reported at the end of the day that there had been no major incidents.[27]

The riot at Clichy struck a fatal blow to the Popular Front's image of the people in the street, underlining the dangers of the crowd and the difficulty of its representation as the rational voice of the people. Where was the voice of the people on the night of 16 March? The Popular Front government, striving for impartiality by allowing the PSF meeting, and yet also permitting a counter-demonstration likely to turn violent? The local Popular Front committee, calling upon working and middle-class residents to swell the demonstration, yet incapable of channelling popular aggression? Was the voice of the people represented by Blum and Blumel, hastening to the scene and greeted with angry abuse and gunfire? Or was it the clamour of the masses themselves, driven to frenzy by the (unfounded) suggestion of La Rocque's provocative presence?

Reactions in the press to these tragic events dwelt on the dangers of the crowd and the difficulty of representing the crowd as the people. *Le Populaire*'s description of the incident carefully refrained from its customary equation of the (left-wing) crowd with the 'people': instead, the 'pacifist' demonstrators were referred to as either 'the crowd' or 'the workers'. Violence was blamed on professional agitators: for Socialist observers had apparently noticed 200–300 troublemakers 'of no party allegiance' in the area (although it was unclear how their lack of affiliation could have been discerned in the dark). To provide a positive gloss on an otherwise tragic event, *Le Populaire* praised the local workers of Clichy for their 'victory' over fascist provocation, implying an intended right-wing 'occupation' of this working-class district.[28] Meanwhile, *L'Humanité* blamed the violence on professional agitators, who were clearly identified with the PSF and PPF.[29] 'Fascist' elements within the police were criticized for firing indiscriminately on a 'pacific counter-demonstration', while the general strike, held on the sixty-sixth anniversary of the Commune, was seen as disciplined, popular action against continuing right-wing provocation.[30] Radical newspapers were similarly circumspect in their choice of subject. *La Lumière* chose to ignore the attacks on the government representatives Dormoy and Blumel, and urged 'the people' to remain faithful to the government and wary of fascist provocation. In particular, the left-wing Radical Albert Bayet criticized the 'secrecy' of PSF meetings, as if their secrecy justified their suppression.[31]

For the right, Clichy provided further evidence of the fragility of the government's hold over the masses, and of the fallibility of its image of the people. Action Française leader Léon Daudet described Marx Dormoy as 'a distraught man, torn between the necessity of deploring the violence of the "masses" against the police, and a keen desire not to alienate these same "masses"'.[32] *Le Temps* observed that although the government had acted correctly, it had clearly lost its legitimate power over the people: 'The legal and responsible government allows the emergence of a substitute: the illegal, irresponsible, confused "government of the masses"'.[33] Likewise, the Confédération Générale du Patronat Français (the employers' equivalent of the CGT) criticized the political character of the strike and contended that, 'since the "pause", the troops of the Popular Front no longer obey their leaders.'[34]

The demonstration at Clichy thus appeared to the opponents of the Popular Front to vindicate the argument that they had advanced from the very beginning: namely that the Popular Front had sealed its own fate by remaining faithful to an impossible ideal of mass rationality. The people were not incurably violent or criminal; but they were, in their very humanity, inherently corruptible, and the potential for violence and criminality was thus always present. Where the people were gathered together as a crowd, the danger of corruption was particularly acute. However trustworthy and rational the members of the crowd might be as individuals, the transforming influence of the crowd was overwhelming, necessitating the guidance of a benevolent leader. This interpretation owed much to the theories of Gustave Le Bon, a debt that was sometimes explicit. An account of the riot by *L'Émancipation nationale* described an encounter with a shadowy figure who suddenly detached himself from the demonstration. 'Crowd psychology, my friend,' observed the mysterious individual, directly echoing the title of Le Bon's famous work, and then disappeared abruptly into the night.[35] Descriptions of the spectacular and almost hypnotic transformation of individuals within the crowd were also reminiscent of Le Bon's imagery and characterization. *Le Flambeau* used theatrical metaphors—'the terrible drama for which Clichy has been the theatre'—while the journalist of *L'Émancipation nationale* described his sense of being caught up in 'a horror film' in which peaceable workers were transformed into unrecognizable furies, the victims of violent contagion. A 14-year-old child beside him in the crowd cried 'Put them to death!'; a man probably incapable of killing a fly voiced bitter invective and threats of violence; and a woman, perhaps a mother with young children, shrieked with disfiguring rage and hatred. Most terrifying of all, reflected the journalist, was the thought that these were ordinary people.

> Did I see any particularly shady characters? No. That is what is so terrible. The demonstrators around me, these men and women ready to kill, are normally peaceful folk, calm workers. They are not even Communists. For months they have been stirred up to the point of frenzy. For months they have been told: Fascism is murderous! They've fallen for it. This is the tragic story of all riots prepared by professional agitators.[36]

The role of agitators was a central characteristic of these accounts. 'As soon are there are "masses", there are professional agitators,' observed Léon Daudet, expanding on the enduring fascination of Action Française with the crowd as the preferred hiding place of Jews, foreigners, freemasons, criminals, and other undesirable elements of the population.[37] *L'Émancipation nationale* supplied descriptions of these very agents, noting that one of the most assiduous shouters of the slogan 'Dormoy, resign!' was a calm, calculating individual—'He's a branch secretary', as someone nearby was heard to remark. Even the shouts of the crowd appeared more organized than spontaneous: 'All this is chanted, orchestrated,' insisted the PPF journalist. 'Among the clamouring crowd, slogans are being circulated.'[38] The danger was not that such hardened, manipulative agents outnumbered the men of goodwill within the Popular Front, as Colonel de la Rocque argued; it was that they dominated the mass of more cautious and trusting supporters.[39] When rumours began to circulate that La Rocque might be imprisoned for his supposedly 'provocative' role (and for his reconstitution of a militaristic league), he issued a statement to the press that confirmed his own wariness of a people deprived of enlightened leadership—even when these people were the two million members of the PSF. 'It is now possible that I may be arrested and imprisoned,' he stated. 'At that point the contact with my men will be broken, and I will no longer be responsible for their actions.'[40] La Rocque closely resembled other right-wing leaders in considering the people in the street as both hapless and destructive. 'Poor *populo*', wrote Léon Daudet:

> Poor French people, who provoke such fear after having been excited, irritated, unbalanced, and turned into wild beasts! The wretched creatures who live off the people fail to understand that their furious cries and convulsions call for benevolent authority, guiding reason, and restorative order.[41]

In Parliament, the recognition that crowd psychology was governed by discernible laws—fatal to contravene—dominated discussion. Jean Ybarnegaray (a Basque deputy representing the PSF) contended that the tragedy of Clichy could easily have been foreseen, for no government or group could hope to control a crowd whose anger and resentment was so incandescent. Similarly, the independent republican Laurent Bonnevay refrained from blaming the crowd for its delirium, and insisted that its judgement could not be trusted. 'Crowd psychology has its laws,' he observed, adding that while the PSF might be guilty of acting as a reconstituted league, 'the judge is not the street.' Léon Blum's Popular Front government (Blum himself referred to his 'National Front government' during this debate, before hastily correcting his slip of the tongue) was widely considered to have been seriously undermined by the violence of the crowd. The street was too closely associated with memories of violence to be seen objectively: the left could not forget 6 February 1934, while the right feared Communist aggression or even revolution, as well as the coercion of the workforce by the CGT.[42] To represent the people in an orderly manner, the role of the street had either to be effaced or transformed.

In search of the middle classes

If the pursuit of the people was affected by the changing perception of the crowd and by the renewed association of street politics with violence, it was also affected by the application of the Popular Front's social reforms. These reforms had been the subject of an almost unanimous agreement when voted on by Parliament, yet their intended relief of popular suffering effectively furthered the division of the people into working and middle classes. Notably, discontent was provoked by the election of particularly aggressive militants as factory delegates,[43] and by the reluctance of the CGPF to negotiate with the CGT. The reforms themselves—especially the 40-hour week—proved divisive in a manner that the legislators had not anticipated. Small shopkeepers found the imposition of a two-day weekend highly detrimental to business, especially as the devaluation of the franc diminished the purchasing power of their customers. Meanwhile, and despite the Popular Front's attempts to stabilize fluctuations in wheat prices with an official Wheat Marketing Board, the peasantry suffered from the increased price of manufactured products, and wage-earning rural labourers were resentful of the salary increases of their urban counterparts. Social reforms relevant to urban workers (particularly the 40-hour week and the paid holiday) were difficult to apply to agricultural work, and even the

Popular Front's introduction of a rural social insurance programme, already envisaged by legislators in 1932, met with resistance for its inability to accommodate rural concerns.[44]

The cumulative effect of these difficulties was a challenge to the Popular Front's status as genuinely representative of the people. Defied by militant workers and unbeneficial to the middle classes, the government seemed to many to respond only to the demands of a vocal urban pressure group unrepresentative of the people of France. 'It's the despotism of a minority,' wrote the conservative politician André Tardieu in a pamphlet of 1936, adding that since 72 per cent of the French population were unable to vote, the current system was democratic only in name (and even the enfranchised exercised little influence on government).[45] Other pamphlets advanced similar arguments. *L'Expérience Blum*, an anonymous tract of 1937 not wholly unsympathetic to the Blum government, contended that the real majority were not the working classes.

> Today, with the benefit of hindsight, we must acknowledge that the factory occupations caused discontent among the majority of the French people, for the majority in France is constituted by the middle classes and the peasantry.[46]

This new emphasis in the debate on popular representation led to a change in how the people were pursued. Communists and Socialists had referred to La Rocque's alleged intention to visit Clichy as an intolerable 'provocation' because it appeared to be a bourgeois occupation of a proletarian area. But the real provocation of the PSF's presence in Clichy was perhaps elsewhere. When members of the local Popular Front committee appealed to the residents of Clichy to swell the counter-demonstration, they addressed themselves to 'the labouring population of factories, building sites, and offices', and also to 'veteran soldiers, small shopkeepers, craftsmen, all republicans, and all democrats'. Their target audience therefore included both working and middle classes. But the PSF sought similar supporters. Moreover, it not only appealed to the lower middle classes in Clichy but evidently succeeded in attracting them to its ranks, as shown by the subsequent vandalism and looting of local shops belonging to PSF members. Prior to the PSF reunion, the Popular Front committee had sought to present this meeting as a foreign 'occupation' of a working-class district, attended by the controversial La Rocque. In fact the meeting was a local, family event at which La Rocque had not intended to be present: an example of the cultural and associational life at grass-roots level that parties of both left and right were seeking to develop.

Of course, the Popular Front and the right-wing leagues and parties had been competing for middle-class support for some years already, but it was not until 1937 that the focus in the battle for representation shifted strongly from working to middle class.[47] As La Rocque reflected in the aftermath of the Clichy riot, 'There is a current discovery of the "middle classes". We have long known and esteemed them here.'[48] The recent disturbances provided an incentive to re-emphasize the importance of middle-class work at the expense of working-class strikes; middle-class stability at the expense of working-class militancy and aggression. And the middle classes themselves were at an important turning point. In the words of one pamphlet, 'the bourgeoisie let themselves fall for the honeyed promises of the Popular Front'[49]—but they were now experiencing the costs of its legislation, and their disillusionment made them increasingly important targets for propaganda. As *Le Flambeau* noted hopefully, the revolutionary connotations of the Popular Front were no longer likely to appeal to this section of the population.

> The middle classes (intellectuals, liberal professions, craftsmen, peasantry, small businessmen, tradesmen, shopkeepers, *in close solidarity with one another*) are harshly affected. The Depression requires their integration into the revolutionary army. The trusts threaten them with ruin. The Popular Front is in the service of revolutionary Marxism.[50]

Similarly, in early 1937 *L'Émancipation nationale* featured a series of interviews with shopkeepers and other tradesmen suffering from the rigid enforcement of the 40-hour week and two-day weekend, and emphasized the growing militancy of this newly disadvantaged class.[51]

> The middle classes are tired of being sacrificed to demagogy. They are not against the social laws *per se*, but against their hasty and inconsiderate application. They demand their place in the nation and refuse to be insulted by a minority.[52]

Continuing its persistent rhetorical opposition to social conservatism, the PPF argued that the industrious middle classes were unable to benefit from Popular Front reforms, and also suffered from the selfishness of the 'upper echelons of the bourgeoisie, including the real or self-styled nobility, big business, and the liberal and intellectual elites.'[53] This explicit opposition did not, however, prevent Doriot himself from courting the supporters of associations of the extreme right, whatever their class, or from receiving substantial financial support from large automobile firms, the textile industries in the Department of the Nord, the steelworks of the East, and a number of Parisian banks.[54]

The renewed emphasis on the middle classes did not cause the PSF and the PPF to abandon their claims to the working people. These parties wished to become mass organizations, not defensive class groupings. Thus when La Rocque was accused of reconstituting the Croix de Feu under the guise of the PSF, he responded in a press announcement that, unlike his previous association of veterans, the PSF was a truly mass party: 'Like the Communist and Socialist parties but far more effectively, the PSF leads the masses.'[55] It was true that such mass adherence was not always spontaneous (police reports suggest that in a number of cases the employment of workers was dependent on their nominal membership of the PSF),[56] but La Rocque's words offer an important glimpse of the desired image of his party. In a statistical analysis of party membership so optimistic that the total was greater than 100 per cent, he described the PSF as comprising 23 per cent rural workers, 20 per cent shopkeepers, 20 per cent employees, 20 per cent workers, and 25 per cent other categories. Seventy-two per cent of these were receiving some kind of social benefit—'Which is not really very heartening,' he said, 'but proves that the lowly come to our party.'[57] Similarly, Jacques Doriot continued to boast of his success in winning over a number of 'Communist fortresses'[58] (even Maurice Thorez recognized that some PPF members were former supporters of the PCF),[59] although Doriot's overriding concern was that class origin should become subordinate to party allegiance. From the earliest days of his party, he claimed not to see his followers as former Communists or Socialists, as members of either the working or middle classes: 'I want to know only soldiers of the PPF,' he insisted, 'inspired by a desire to save their country.'[60] Jean-Paul Brunet suggests that the principal motivation for Doriot's decision not to become more explicitly anti-parliamentary and anti-republican at this point was that he recognized the inherent suspicion among many of his prospective supporters of an overtly 'fascist' appeal for imminent and radical transformation.[61] In 1937, Doriot's image of the people was marked by a growing emphasis on the middle classes because this was politically astute, but it retained its all-encompassing rhetoric for the same reasons.

Such political opportunism was also evident in Doriot's foundation of the Liberty Front, a coalition of right-wing groups and parties designed to concentrate their power and prepare the way for an electoral alliance. The Front was allegedly to defend republican liberties (notably freedom of speech and association) and republican institutions, although Doriot pointedly ignored La Rocque's suggestion that it should therefore be entitled 'the *Republican* Liberty Front'.[62] La Rocque himself refused to join the alliance: while acknowledging its electoral usefulness, he preferred to retain maximum control over his own supporters. Approximately 5000 PSF members consequently transferred their allegiance to the PPF,[63] and the Liberty Front was also supported by a number of other parties, including Louis Marin's Fédération Républicaine, Auguste Champetier de Ribes' Parti Democrate Populaire, and Pierre Taittinger's Parti Républicain National et Social. The founding meeting of the new Front took place in the Vélodrome d'Hiver on 7 May 1937, shortly before Doriot was dismissed as Mayor of Saint-Denis on charges of fraudulent administration, and was attended by approximately 17,000 supporters, although 250,000 invitations had been issued. The assembly opened with the fascist salute and the PPF hymn, and included a number of speeches on freedom of work and association, the first of which focused particularly on the consequences of the 40-hour week for small shopkeepers. This was certainly not the realization of Doriot's grandiose dream; but the support of established parliamentary parties such as the Fédération Républicaine and the Parti Démocrate Populaire for an alliance organized by a notorious extremist was nonetheless significant.

Jacques Doriot had also anticipated considerable Radical support for his new Liberty Front. After all, the defence of republican liberties and institutions, the middle classes and the peasantry, was firmly established on the Radical agenda. But for this very reason the Radicals, like La Rocque, preferred to fight their battle alone. As Albert Bayet explained, the Radicals might hear the 'siren call' of the extreme right, but they also remembered the right's reaction to Radical governments in earlier years, not least in February 1934.[64] Thus the Radical newspaper *La Lumière* made its own appeals to the middle classes, especially those adversely affected by the new social legislation, and, while generally sympathetic to the government, nonetheless warned that such legislation should not be dictated by 'misleading illusions'.[65] An influential article by the Radical Albert Milhaud shortly before the riot at Clichy discerned a 'changing wind' in political thought and action, as the disorder of the street made the image of middle-class stability, caution, and industriousness increasingly attractive.[66] This article was inspired at least in part by Daladier's recent speech to the executive committee of the Radical Party on the necessity of saving the middle classes. That Daladier could give such a speech as a minister in the Popular Front government was significant in itself, for his speech was an uncompromising defence of France as a middle-class country with an economy driven by middle-class industry. In 1935, Daladier had claimed a role for the contemporary 'Third Estate' in the Popular Front by arguing that it comprised the direct descendants of the modest, industrious Parisians who had joined their more proletarian counterparts in storming the Bastille.[67] Now no such justification was required. As Daladier insisted to his party, 'France is essentially the country of the middle classes', and it was therefore right and necessary for these classes to organize themselves in the manner of their working-class counterparts. Small enterprises were fundamental to the health of the French economy— and Daladier observed that the oft-despised 'bosses' ('patronat') mainly represented medium-sized or small businesses, and that five million workers were employed in small businesses with less than ten employees. Middle-class employers and employees were also, in Daladier's view, characterized by a strongly developed sense of the common good and the national interest, and could be trusted to support republican stability and gradual social reform. The protection of the middle classes was therefore 'a national duty'.[68] Shortly after Daladier's speech, the Confédération Générale des Classes Moyennes held an assembly in the Vélodrome d'Hiver, and, although critical of the Radical Party at previous meetings in 1933, now seemed to present the very image of middle-class organization that Daladier was anticipating.

This concern to attract and defend the middle classes was accompanied by a determination to represent the peasantry, who were themselves increasingly politicized in this period. Internationally, the Bureau International d'Agriculture in Rome was the peasant counterpart to the Bureau International du Travail in Geneva, and by 1930 had received the adherence of peasant parties in Germany, Austria, Bulgaria, Finland, France, Greece, Lithuania, Poland, Switzerland, and Czechoslovakia, among other countries.[69] In France, the militant Henri d'Halluin (known as 'Dorgères') organized the 'National Peasant Front' (also linked to the Confédération Général du Patronat Français), and in 1928 the Parti Agraire et Paysan Français was founded to provide a more democratic and republican alternative. By the early 1930s this too, had become strongly nationalist, which led to the formation in February 1933 of a splinter party, the Parti Républicain Social Agraire, which had important ties to the Radical Party, and sought to steer a careful path between fascism and collectivism.[70] By 1937, the Parti Agraire et Paysan Français was also losing members in significant numbers to the Parti Social Français,[71] although it forged links with the PPF. Overall, the year 1937 witnessed an important growth in peasant support for the Radicals and for the new right-wing parties, strengthening their position against the Popular Front while also changing the focus in their image of the people.

'It is in idealizing the people that we lose them',[72] wrote Emmanuel Mounier in April 1937—and although he was referring specifically to democracies overtaken by fascism, his comment held particular relevance for the development of the Popular Front during its exercise of power. The violent counter-demonstration at Clichy in March 1937 appeared to many to mark a definitive rift between the Popular Front and the people, who now seemed to offer little resemblance to the myths of summer 1936. Public spaces had become dangerous spaces, with the irruption of the people into the street more likely to undermine the authority of the Popular Front than to provide reassuring evidence of continuing popular support. While the new right-wing parties were strongly associated with street violence, this violence was two-sided. Meanwhile, the reconciled community of working and middle classes that remained so central to political propaganda was rapidly coming to seem unrealizable, not least because the social reforms intended to alleviate popular suffering were alienating these classes from one another. Despite his best efforts, Léon Blum was unsuccessful in securing a lasting agreement between the CGT and the CGPF, and this attempt to resolve the problems of the urban working class appeared to the middle classes and to the rural population as further evidence of their own isolation. This in turn influenced the understanding of the people by the Parti Social Français and the Parti Populaire Français, keen to benefit from the dissatisfaction of the middle classes and peasantry without abandoning their images of a broader working people. The battle to represent the people and to emphasize the importance of the middle classes and peasantry was increasingly dominated by the Radical Party, long established as the protector of these social groups. Now that the image of the people was difficult to identify with spontaneous street activity or with the striking workers, and that the Popular Front government seemed increasingly unrepresentative of the people, new territory had to be found for the realization of a reconciled community.

7
The Call of the Nation, 1937–39

The Parisian fiscal law professor Gaston Jèze was a controversial figure in the 1930s, making his own unintended contribution to the street politics of the French capital even while deploring the dangers of the crowd. In 1935 he acted as legal adviser to the Ethiopian government after the unprovoked attack on the country by Mussolini's Italy: a humanitarian gesture that led to considerable difficulties in the exercise of his Parisian functions. Not only were his lectures at the Law Faculty persistently hissed by student followers of *Action Française* (which called for his resignation), but his left-wing student supporters were no less ardent in his defence than the royalists in their opposition, provoking frequent and often violent encounters in the Latin Quarter. Such was the disorder and disruption that he was eventually obliged to lecture in alternative locations, to which prospective listeners would be directed under police escort.[1]

In the light of his own experiences, it was not surprising that Jèze should have little sympathy for street politics in general, or for militants and strikers who claimed to represent the voice of the people in particular. By February 1938 his cynicism regarding the representation of the people had deepened still further. 'What is the popular will?' he asked in *L'Ère nouvelle*, challenging the legitimacy of those who had claimed to know and represent this will in recent months and years. Where could the will of the people be found, he demanded, when it was claimed by every group of militants, many of whom proposed measures contrary to the national interest? And even if the will of the people was equated with that of the crowd or the electorate, should government be dictated to by a will so easily manipulated and so fickle? In the resolution of problems, whether economic, social, or political, it seemed to Jèze that the will of the people was in fact of little significance. Lasting solutions were those developed through individual reason, observation, and patience. National interest and individual leadership must therefore, he insisted, take precedence over the shifting desires of the crowd, especially if economic prosperity and social harmony were to be secured.[2]

Whatever the controversy of Jèze's earlier actions, his observations of February 1938 reflected a shift in political rhetoric from people to nation that was indubitably widespread: a change in emphasis from the people as the crowd, workers, or electorate to the national community— the French people as whole—under individual leadership. Jèze was no supporter of dictatorship, and his sceptical appraisal of democratic practice echoed the doubts of other committed democrats regarding the regime's ability to confront national and international crisis. His article was moreover acutely relevant to the crisis of government in France in early 1938, as the successive governments of Chautemps, Blum, and Daladier weighed the importance of representing of the people through parliamentary democracy against the importance of national defence.

Camille Chautemps, a veteran politician as renowned for compromise as Blum was notorious for his adherence to principle, assumed the premiership for the third time after Blum's resignation in June 1937. Although he chose Blum as his vice-premier, his cabinet differed sharply in character from its predecessor, with a number of key positions (including Minister of Finances) transferred to well-known Radical critics of the Popular Front. Tensions between Radicals and Communists were unavoidable, not least over the neglect of Popular Front social reforms, and it was after debate on this question that, in January 1938, Chautemps offered the Communists their freedom to leave the Popular Front coalition. The Socialist Ministers then resigned, and the government collapsed. In the ministerial crisis that followed, the former Finance Minister Georges Bonnet attempted to form a government of the centre and right, and in early February Blum suggested various governments of national unity from the Communists on the left to Paul Reynaud on the right—but without success. A second Chautemps government was eventually formed with Socialist participation, but solved neither the problem of leadership nor the continuing social unrest (it was during this government that Jèze's article was written). On 9 March, two days before Hitler's armies marched into Austria, Chautemps resigned. Blum renewed his endeavours to create a government of national unity: resistance from the Radicals led instead to the formation of a second Popular Front government, and a demand for emergency decree powers until July in order to further national rearmament. Blum also proposed an extension of the 40-hour week and a tax on higher incomes—which the Senator Joseph Caillaux deplored as the potential ruin of small farmers. The Senate refused Blum's demand, Blum resigned, and Édouard Daladier then presented a government which was approved by the Chamber of Deputies with an overwhelming vote of confidence of 576 to 5.[3] Daladier, whose previous vote of confidence had been accorded on the fateful night of 6 February 1934, proposed a government of public safety as the most effective protection of liberty, peace, and the fatherland. He also described his own modest origins as a guarantee that the social needs of the people would continue to be met. In fact his regime was to evolve into an authoritarian one ruling by decree law, and became associated with the suppression of the social gains of 1936 and with the consequent strikes and protests. At the end of August he announced the extension of the 40-hour week, by November he was governing by decree, and on 30 November his government responded to a one-day strike of protest with harsh repression. Whatever the weaknesses and uncertainties behind his glowering, bullish exterior, Daladier seemed determined to solve Jèze's problem of the popular will by overriding its alternative expressions (crowd, workers, and electorate), and by representing both people and nation himself. But how had the pursuit of the people led to the acclamation of Daladier?

The Daladier regime is sometimes described as the close of a 'social parenthesis',[4] representing the defeat of Popular Front promises that were to be renewed with the Liberation,[5] and foreshadowing post-war politics rather than continuing the rivalries of the 1930s.[6] Yet it was not a sudden break with the past—and not least in terms of the representation of the people. Under Daladier, the representation of the people as the crowd, workers, and electorate was subordinated to the needs of the national community, requiring the submission of individual or partisan interests to the interests (and notably defence) of the nation as a whole.[7] This shift in emphasis was, however, already in progress, influenced by the increasing association of the crowd with division and violence, and by the tensions between working and middle classes that the implementation of Popular Front reforms had provoked. Even for the left, the ideal of a mature, rational people in the street had become impossible to sustain, especially after the bloody riot at Clichy in March 1937. At the same time, the apparent impossibility of resolving economic problems through parliamentary government led to increasingly frequent demands for full powers and rule by decree law. The use of the word 'people' therefore began to decline, less frequently employed to describe crowds or workers than in previous years, while political legitimacy was increasingly sought through emphasis on the national community, the French people as a whole. Strong precedents can be found for Daladier's development of the ideas of national union and leadership in the rhetoric of previous leaders, and the close identification of people and nation was also characteristic of a new 'community of thought' in which uncertainty and division were concealed behind a rhetoric of national grandeur and defence.

National union and national leadership

Daladier's focus on national union, defence, and leadership built strongly on the (less successful) legacies of Blum and Chautemps. Blum had always insisted that his first Popular Front government was 'a government for the common good',[8] and had even referred to his 'National Front government' in a revealing slip of the tongue.[9] He was moreover highly sensitive to France's image abroad, especially in the aftermath of Clichy. The primacy of national interest was also emphasized by Camille Chautemps, who tempered his respect for the 'popular fervour' that had determined the composition of the Chamber of Deputies in 1936 with a resolution to subdue such fervour when the needs of the nation so required. In the midst of a recrudescence of strikes in the public sector in January 1938, he balanced explicit concern for the social demands of the workers with an emphatic refusal to tolerate a 'revolt (...) against the national interest', and his resolution won him applause from left, right, and centre.[10] It was, moreover, when the Communist Arthur Ramette forcibly identified the popular will with the specific demands of the Popular Front programme and the needs of the working classes that Chautemps granted the Communists permission to leave the Popular Front coalition.

Daladier's emphasis on national union was also prefigured in the parliamentary and journalistic debates following Chautemps' second resignation in March 1938, when the unity and protection of the nation became essential criteria for the judgement of parties and leaders. *L'Ère nouvelle* remarked on the sudden resurgence of 'national reconciliation' as a subject of particular controversy between parties at this time,[11] as they competed in their claims to be the most loyal servants of the national interest. Thus when Blum proposed a government of national union, the SFIO secretary Paul Faure described his party as 'in the service of the nation',[12] while the Minister for Work Albert Serol insisted that Blum's government would respond to 'the instinctive orientation of the French people towards the union of all republican forces.'[13] Even Léon

Blum's subsequent endeavour to form a 'republican coalition govern-ment around the Popular Front' revealed a widespread consensus on the need for coalition—as well as the impossibility of its realization under a Socialist leader. Few quarrelled with the concept of national union, but the PSF could not imagine its realization without the exclusion of 'foreign' elements, which for both the PSF and the PPF included the Communist Party.[14] And for the extreme right in general, Blum as a Socialist and a Jew was incapable of representing national interests.[15] Blum's dilemma was that although the need for national union was widely recognized, partisan differences and personal antipathies ren-dered it impossible for him to achieve it. As he acknowledged before the Senate, almost any other leader might make identical demands for emergency decree powers and be successful (in this he was quite correct).[16]

The primacy of national leadership over parliamentary debate and class interests was also recognized before Daladier's accession to the pre-miership. During Blum's second Popular Front government in particular, the problematic combination of parliamentary democracy and inter-national emergency became a matter for urgent debate. Félix Gouin, representative for the Socialist deputies in the Chamber, posed the ques-tion in unequivocal terms during the parliamentary discussion of Blum's proposals for full powers on 6 April 1938. Regretfully, he explained that economic liberalism was too weak to resolve the financial problems of the moment, and parliamentary democracy too constraining. The gov-ernment required 16 billions francs for national defence as well as a reliable increase in industrial productivity, and such demands could not be met within the existing system of government, taxation, and indus-trial relations. Gouin's suggestion that sacrifices be demanded from the 'affluent classes' must have led to suspicions of socialist statism, but the primacy of the state over social classes and of the common good over individual rights was scarcely in question, as even Blum's opponents were ready to acknowledge. Thus while the former premier Pierre-Étienne Flandin doubted Léon Blum's chances for success with a new government based on the Popular Front, he did not dispute the submission of production to the national interest. The future Finance Minister and premier Paul Reynaud likewise insisted that 'the country is above the regime', and that the salvation of the former should take precedence. Even the Socialist Alphonse Tellier, while recognizing the rival needs of state and workers, identified the salvation of the peo-ple as the most pressing concern, which now meant acting for their good without consulting them. 'The moment has come,' he admitted, 'to remind ourselves that our role is not to follow the people, but to guide them.' To applause from left, right, and centre, he then asserted that it would be an abuse of the 'popular will' to pander to the people's superficial and transitory demands while neglecting their lasting security. The people would never pardon the faults they had caused their leaders to commit.[17]

When Daladier became premier with an overwhelming vote of confidence, the themes that would be characteristic of his regime were thus already defined. In response to the dangers of the international situation, the needs of people as workers, crowd, or electorate were to be subordinated to the needs of the nation. The situation of emergency justified strong leadership, possibly without parliament, as successive demands for full powers suggested. Although Daladier was not always popular (*L'Humanité* accused him of creating an atmosphere of 'terror', *Le Populaire* criticized his alleged alienation of the 'masses', and Blum in particular deplored his excessive repression of parliament), his chosen representation of the people was not a sudden volte-face. His emphasis on national union and leadership gave voice to a new 'community of thought' that was already developing around these themes.

A similar conclusion may be drawn from an analysis of Daladier's social and foreign policy. On 21 August 1938, Daladier justified his new social policies with a radio broadcast urging the French to 'return to work', emphasizing the dangers of the international situation and the consequent need for rearmament. To safeguard national defence, he explained, the 40-hour week would need to be extended, and any industrial unrest swiftly repressed. Daladier expected forthright opposition, and there was indeed some vocal hostility to his proposals. Shortly after the speech, the Ministers of Work and of Public Works Paul Ramadier and Ludovic-Oscar Frossard resigned, complaining that they had not been consulted. The harsh implementation of extended working hours in autumn 1938 (a set of confidential instructions from the CGPF enjoined employers to fire leaders—even all strikers—in cases of serious unrest)[18] provoked angry reactions from CGT members and leaders. 'Every possible consequence must be discussed, even the possibility of a revolutionary strike,' asserted one regional leader to an assembly of unions from the north of France in November, describing Daladier as a dictator inimical to the working class.[19] Similarly, a union at Cercy-la-Tour in the Nièvre issued a three-page programme to the CGT which called for the imposition of the popular will as in 1936, inciting workers to take control of production and the CGT to take control of national government.[20]

Despite this resentment, however, the ensuing conflict was not dominated by rhetorical opposition between the people (or the working classes) and the nation. The battle over the 40-hour week was not a battle for or against the Popular Front and its reforms:[21] by August 1938 the necessity of sacrificing the 40-hour week was already widely recog nized. Although the number of unemployed was now in decline, the index of production had failed to rise, and the contrast with flourishing production in Germany was only too keenly felt. Even Blum had asked for the extension of the 40-hour week in his second demand for full powers, while other Socialists—such as Georges Boris—were prepared to support the shorter working week if it received international endorsement.[22] Both during and after the 30 November strike, CGT leaders were at pains to emphasize the compatibility of working-class demands with national defence. Although the strike was directed against the decree laws and the recent policy of Daladier, contended the CGT leader Léon Jouhaux, the CGT recognized the necessities of the moment and would contribute fully to economic recovery. Indeed, he found it inconceivable that the workers should act against the nation since they themselves were a vital member of the 'national body'.[23] Even the former CGTU militant Julien Racamond underlined the importance of national defence, which could only be achieved through the united action of rural and urban workers with both government and democracy.[24]

The importance of national defence and the willingness of the workers (sometimes described as the people) to work towards this end likewise characterized the retrospective depiction of the strikes. Daladier pre-empted the strikers, who were unable to disseminate their account of the strike until the following day, by broadcasting on the evening of 30 November itself, emphasizing that the strike had, through its very failure, indicated the workers' resolution to co-operate more readily with the government than with the trade-union militants. He also suggested that their decision had been taken out of respect for national security.[25] In the right-wing press, the failure of the strike was similarly attributed to the patriotic sentiments of French workers. 'Yesterday, the people of France reaffirmed by their behaviour that they intend to work in peace and quiet,' concluded *Action Française*,[26] while Jacques Doriot explained that the PPF had even occupied a factory in Toulouse to enable the workers to continue with their work, noting with satisfaction that 'the working class has said "no" to the adventurers from Moscow.'[27] Meanwhile, Colonel de la Rocque attested that 'trade unionism remains one of the essential elements of French renewal,' and insisted that the workers would continue to print *Le Petit Journal* despite the obstructive action of the Communists. 'The people, who form the majority of the PSF, will not lend their support to Moscow's attempted control of a French newspaper,' he concluded. 'And it is the people who will have the final word.'[28]

In foreign policy, Daladier's pursuit of an agreement with Hitler in Munich at the end of September 1938 similarly responded to a 'community of thought' on the defence of the nation, as the majority of the French approved the preservation of peace at the cost of appeasement. This community of thought was, however, only partial, for the Munich agreement also divided the French along new lines, undermining divisions between left and right as former right-wing nationalists began to support appeasement, and former internationalists and pacifists demanded more aggressive action against fascism.[29] Thus the Fédération Républicaine preferred to preserve the existing social order rather than to risk war for France's national glory,[30] while even notoriously pacifist primary school teachers acknowledged the necessity for a more bellicose defence of their views.[31] Divisions within parties other than the PCF were also marked. The Socialists were deeply divided, and while many Radicals were willing to sacrifice Czechoslovakia for peace, a notable few, including Édouard Herriot and Jules Jeanneney (President of the Senate), continued to protest.

Daladier, a man of the people?

Founding his government on explicit principles of national union and defence, Daladier also developed an image of himself as a man of the people and as a leader in direct contact with the French. While not unprecedented, this was nonetheless distinct from the images developed by Blum and Chautemps, and a step further from an emphasis on the people as crowd, masses, workers, or electorate towards an emphasis on the people as the nation. In his rhetoric, Daladier presented himself as a strong national leader in close partnership with the French people, spurring them on to sacrifice in the name of the nation. Behind the facade of strong personal authority, he was pragmatic, even pessimistic, about France's future and capabilities.

When Daladier emphasized his popular origins in the speech of 12 April that secured such a powerful vote of confidence, he was not exaggerating for effect. Born on 18 June 1884, he came from a peasant and artisan family which ran a bakery in Carpentras (Provence). A series of scholarships paid for his education, through which he progressed from the Lycée Ampère to the University of Lyons, and then to Paris, where he passed the challenging *agrégation* examination to become a teacher of history in 1909. Returning to the south to take up a position at a school in Nîmes, he became renowned for his inspiring lessons on the Revolution of 1848 and on the history of the early Third Republic. In 1912 Daladier was elected mayor of Carpentras, in the First World War he fought bravely, was decorated three times and promoted to the rank of lieutenant, and as a deputy after the war he was proud to serve in politics as one of a generation of veteran soldiers. Described as the 'Bull of Vaucluse' for his forceful interventions and solid, glowering appearance, Daladier cultivated a Napoleonic stance, with one hand in his jacket. Some said he was visibly of peasant origin; others that he combined the appearances of a man of thought and a man of action. Certainly he had a formidable capacity for hard work and self-discipline, for which he was highly respected by his colleagues. As a rising star in the post-war Radical Party, he favoured closeness with the Socialists while Herriot preferred to compromise with the right, and he helped to prepare the left-wing coalition that triumphed in the elections of 1924. Nonetheless he was always more interested in pragmatic than ideological politics, committed above all to the preservation of the strong Republic for which his father and grandfather had fought. During the Radicals' periods in power he was closely involved in government, whether as Minister for the Colonies, War, or Public Works. 1934 was a challenging year: he had recently lost his wife Madeleine to tuberculosis, and in the aftermath of the riot on 6 February he lost his own confidence and that of his colleagues. Yet he remained central to republican government, becoming Minister for War once again in May 1936, and preparing France for rearmament. In 1938–39 he was to pursue this goal even more vocally.

'Millions of Frenchmen demand a courageous leader,' wrote Gaston Jèze in November 1938, 'economical with words and energetic in action: a leader who says what needs to be done and who does it without concern for noisy politicking; someone who will raise the country out of the quagmire into which it has sunk.'[32] It was a role that Daladier was certainly determined to fulfil. In his radio broadcasts he communicated directly with the French, justifying the rule by decree law that sidelined parliamentary debate, and using his increasingly tight control of communications to forestall or undermine criticism of his policies. He proved adept at choosing the appropriate register for his audience (lapsing into local idioms when addressing the people of Provence), and his broadcasts had a considerable impact, both in France and elsewhere.[33] National security remained paramount in these speeches, but beneath this obligation that symbolically united him with his people, he sought to present himself as both benevolent and decisive: in close contact with the people while not prepared to accede to their every demand. When he defined 'what France wants' to his radio audience on 29 March 1939, he emphasized this composite self-image.

Head of the government, responsible for French politics, it is as a man that I wish to address myself to the French, and, beyond the frontiers of my country, to all those in the world with loyal and generous hearts. There is a language that has no need of translation in order to be universally understood: the language of the heart.[34]

In this direct, outspoken style of public address, Daladier implicitly presented his listeners as a people capable of understanding the urgency and complexity of national demands, and yet willing to leave matters of state to political leaders. If it had become expedient to submit particular interests to the 'notion of public safety', he claimed that the French would accept this necessity with 'virile resolution', secure in the knowledge that the French fatherland did not make unjust or irrational demands on its people.[35] National sentiments—'love of peace, respect for honour, complete devotion to the fatherland'—were the bond uniting the French with the leader of the government, and that also transcended them both.[36] Although Daladier adopted a paternalistic stance, he did not necessarily present himself as worthy of homage: rather, he endeavoured to appear as a determined but dutiful servant of Republic and nation, and it was a similar obedience that he expected from the people. Together, he proclaimed, they would work for the triumph of 'wisdom and reason'.[37]

Such rhetoric certainly corresponded to the image of leadership that, according to Jèze, the French people were so anxiously seeking. Daladier's solid appearance, taciturn nature, and ability to speak forcefully and directly when required seemed on the surface to suit him to the role of a resolute national leader. Yet he was not a man to be taken at face value, and the frankness that he liked to attribute to his popular origins could also lead him to bitter appraisals of France's international position. While capable of decisive discourse and action, Daladier remained at heart a hesitant man, tormented by the choices with which France was confronted, and by his pessimistic (and perhaps realistic) assessment of French military potential. When he dissuaded Blum from intervening in the Spanish Civil War it was because he doubted France's ability to stand alone; and when General Vuillemin informed him at the end of

August 1938 that Germany was producing 12 times as many aeroplanes as France, this served only to confirm his existing suspicions. Daladier had no illusions at Munich: his meeting with Hitler merely convinced him of latter's intention to dominate Europe, and he was ashamed at the compromise which seemed, in the light of France's weakness, the only possible option. As he returned to France, he was deeply apprehensive of the crowd's response: their cheers when he descended from the plane both surprised and dismayed him. That evening, he remarked to his young son Jean: 'As for war, don't worry, you'll fight in it. And it will continue much longer than you'd like.'[38] Daladier was committed to preparing France and the French for war (much as he detested the reality of warfare after his own personal experience in the trenches), yet he often doubted how far this could be achieved. On the surface, Daladier's leadership was marked by a confident closeness with the people, a paternalistic desire to guide and strengthen. Behind the mask, the pragmatism of his popular origins drew him to quite different conclusions.

The crowd: From actors to spectators

Daladier's rhetoric and policies conveyed a determination to prioritize national union and defence, and to represent the people through strong, individual leadership while repressing other putative expressions of the popular will. Reactions to his policies, though not always positive, suggested a general consensus on the primacy of national interest over partisan demands, and an increasing (though not universal) tendency to conceive of the people as the national community, displacing previous emphases on the crowd, electorate, or workers. This conclusion also emerges from a consideration of street politics in 1937–39. It remained problematic (for both practical and ideological reasons) to portray the crowd as the people, and political rivalry focused increasingly on the commemoration of national symbols, notably Joan of Arc. Meanwhile, the large-scale official commemorations on 11 November 1938 and 14 July 1939 concentrated the focus on the nation and also furthered the transformation of the crowd from actors to spectators. As in Daladier's speeches, however, the celebration of national unity and grandeur masked ongoing divisions, as well as uncertainty about France's future.

As the previous chapter suggested, the changing dynamics of power in 1937 and the often violent nature of street politics significantly challenged the representation of the crowd as the people. Difficulty in securing official permission for demonstrations and mass meetings limited their consequent potential, and the meetings that took place in defiance of official prohibition were frequently disorderly. The increasing disunity of the Popular Front made the street more likely to foster antagonism than unity, while bitter strikes and protests led to a strong shift in emphasis in political rhetoric from the workers to the middle classes and peasantry.

Similar problems persisted after the Clichy riot in the organization and representation of the people in the street. In response to the riot the Prefect of Paris outlawed all demonstrations in the Parisian region, seeking to bring an end to the counter-demonstrations that were becoming the habitual reaction to the meetings of the PSF and PPF.[39] This meant that large-scale mass assemblies and spectacles were possible only within existing and well-established commemorations. Furthermore, the collapse of the first Popular Front government made it difficult for the parties within the alliance to find common ground for their appeals to the people. The CGT demonstrated against the rising cost of living while Communists demonstrated against the policy of non-intervention in Spain; Communists and Socialists demonstrated in separate processions, while the Radicals refused to participate at all. Where local sections of the PCF and SFIO did succeed in organizing common meetings, this was often in commemoration of the Commune, where references to 'the union of the French people' were counterbalanced by a renewed emphasis on the revolutionary potential of the proletariat.[40] Attendance at all demonstrations was on the decline, also undermining the portrayal of the crowd as the people.

On the left, the result of these accumulated difficulties was a widening gulf between dwindling numbers in the street and the images projected of such occasions by left-wing leaders. Established celebrations such as 1 May or 14 July attracted lower levels of support in 1937–38, and, largely retrospective in character, were difficult to present as expressions of the popular will. The celebration of 1 May 1937 was, for example, noticeably lacking in common themes: Socialists celebrated the occasion as the first to receive official government support; Communists proclaimed their solidarity with Spanish Republicans; and the CGT emphasized the social achievements of the previous year. Despite the traditional association of 1 May with proletarian militancy, there was little interest in describing a powerful and independent people. Léon Jouhaux's speech reduced the people to a purely supportive role, explaining that the 'revolutionary romanticism' of the past was no longer appropriate, and that the working class should rather aim to support the government during the difficult implementation of the 'pause'.[41] Celebrations of 14 July 1937 likewise commemorated the

Popular Front movement and government rather than revolution, recollecting the popular grandeur of 14 July in 1935 and 1936 rather than referring to 1789. In an attempt to provide some cohesion, the Coordinating committee of the Popular Front had compiled a series of Popular Front slogans for the occasion: the application of the Popular Front programme, fidelity to the oath of 14 July 1935, and support for republican Spain.[42] But the demonstration was a pale reflection of the occasions that it recalled. 100,000 participants gathered in the Place de la Nation (compared with the estimated million that attended in 1936), and listened to speeches by party militants that lasted little over an hour, and the principal party leaders were noticeably absent. Gaston Allemane represented the SFIO, Jacques Duclos the PCF, and the Radical Pierre Cot read out a speech in which Chautemps promised 'the French people' to remain faithful to the Popular Front programme. Subsequently, Jacques Duclos and Paul Vaillant-Couturier described the celebration as exemplifying the ever-increasing confidence of the people in the Popular Front, but their very urgency suggested the strength of opinion to the contrary.[43] Charles Maurras was, for one, only too keen to point out that the Communist-dominated Popular Front had retreated to its former, partisan status. 'The republican and democratic symbolism to which it lays claim has become the affair of a party,' he said, 'not of the people, nor of the country as a whole.'[44]

While celebrations attracted dwindling numbers, protests fared likewise. The demonstrations organized after the collapse of Popular Front governments in June 1937 and April 1938 did not attract the desired support, and suggested that the people in the street were no longer capable of providing political direction. 150,000 attended the demonstration in June 1937, and 200,000 marched from the Place de la Bastille to the Place de la Nation on 10 April 1938, but the disappointment in partisan accounts was thinly veiled.[45] Moreover, Socialists and Communists formed separate groups for the speeches in the Place de la Nation on 10 April, and there seemed to be little common focus in the slogans shouted by supporters. Tension between the Popular Front's leaders and supporters was also evident in the responses of the crowd during mass meetings. On 26 March 1938, during a fresh outbreak of strikes, Léon Jouhaux was shouted down at a mass CGT meeting in the Buffalo Stadium: a show of independent popular will that met with short shrift in *Le Populaire*.[46] By 14 July 1938, even *L'Humanité* was downplaying the significance of the left-wing demonstrations, making no mention of the numbers present and including only a small photograph of the occasion.[47] 'The re-emergence of national peril has prompted Paris to return to national and military celebrations of 14 July,' wrote Charles Maurras, who no longer denigrated the monopoly of the occasion by the unruly hordes of the left.[48] *L'Émancipation nationale* described this as the last demonstration of the Popular Front, an alliance superseded by a national union that was no longer based on the dynamics of opposition between left and right.[49]

On the right, the difficulty of organizing demonstrations and the shift away from the street as a place of political impetus likewise prompted a general decline in images of the crowd as the people. Public and private meetings proposed by the PSF and the PPF were often banned by the authorities, leading to unauthorized and violent interchanges between militants of these parties and those of the Popular Front.[50] Police reports on the activity of the PSF in 1938 recorded frequent complaints from Parisians about private—and extremely noisy—PSF meetings at local level.[51] Both parties were in potential danger, for when Doriot handed in his resignation as a deputy in response to his enforced resignation as mayor, La Rocque was facing charges for the reconstitution of a dissolved league. In December 1937, Doriot was reinstated as mayor but La Rocque was formally accused of reconstituting the league of the Croix de Feu, a decision confirmed on 17 June 1938. In the event, Daladier made the conciliatory gesture of reducing the fines imposed and allowing the PSF to continue, but the possibility of official prohibition remained.[52] Doriot used his comparatively greater freedom to organize meetings in favour of nationalist Spain, and *L'Émancipation nationale*, not yet the victim of the crisis of confidence that was to deprive Doriot of many of his theorists, became increasingly favourable towards fascism. 'Die as democrats or survive as fascists,' wrote Pierre Drieu la Rochelle, with unknowing irony in the light of his own destiny.[53]

One occasion, however, represented an opportunity to find political impetus in the street and a continuation of the rivalry between the Popular Front and its right-wing opponents. This was the commemoration of Joan of Arc, now as fervently acclaimed by the Communists as she was by *Action Française*. In 1937 the authorities banned the traditional procession of the right with the intention of preventing disorder, and insisted that the official military homage to the statue in the Place des Pyramides should be followed only by small delegations or individual marks of respect between 10 a.m. and 1 p.m. Léon Daudet took this as an indication of Léon Blum's personal dislike of Joan of Arc on the grounds of her ethnicity and virginity—he had not forgotten Blum's once notorious apology for free unions in *Du Mariage*—and Cardinal Verdier of Paris complained that the official ban might prompt angry reprisals.[54] On 9 May the police succeeded in excluding additional sup-porters from participation in the official celebrations, but the authorized delegations nonetheless included as many of these supporters as possi-ble. *Action Française* described the crowd as 'an immense people' whose harmonious singing of *La Marseillaise* suggested the hand of an unseen conductor.[55] The delegations—and the processions elsewhere in the country—were similarly portrayed as examples of unity across classes and among opponents of the Popular Front. In particular, a demonstra-tion in Toulouse had assembled members of the PSF, the PPF, Action Française, and the Parti Républicain National et Social. Any lack of har-mony was, in contrast, blamed on Blum's obstructive decision to restrict this display of national fervour.

Meanwhile, *L'Humanité* was seeking to rival its inveterate enemies in its own claims to the saint. Approving the celebrations in Orléans, and describing with equal appreciation the official ceremony presided over by Daladier and Marx Dormoy and the orderly Catholic procession, *L'Humanité* portrayed the demonstrations of the right-wing parties as a noisy and discourteous disturbance of 'national respect and religious faith'.[56] This somewhat surprising criticism was in line with the claims to Joan of Arc as both national and popular that were being made by the Communists from 1936 onwards, which ironically brought them closer to the PPF than to the Socialists. For while the Socialist authorities had sought to limit the celebrations, the PPF described the aptness of com-memorating both Joan of Arc and the Mur des Fédérés. Not only was it important to celebrate both the national and also the social, wrote Paul Marion, but the Communards were themselves great examples of national fervour, to whom the Communists—'foreign agents'—should lay no claim.[57]

In 1938, the celebration of Joan of Arc was a focus for enthusiasm from left to right. The official state commemoration took place on 8 May, but in the preceding week the première of Léon Chancerel's *Mission de Jeanne d'Arc* was held in front of the Basilica at Domrémy, and a torch lit the previous day was carried in relay from Rheims to Paris, and finally to Rouen, where it was cast into the Seine. A candle was also lit from the torch to burn before Joan's statue in Rouen Cathedral until the follow-ing year.[58] The official ceremony was attended by Daladier (who offered a substantial donation for a statue of the saint at Tours),[59] and was commemorated in photographs in *L'Humanité*, which loudly acclaimed Joan of Arc as a 'popular heroine'.[60] Although *Le Populaire* dismissed the Parisian celebration as 'an overly conspicuous effort to appear "sponta-neous" and "popular", '.[61] it naturally won the enthusiasm of the right, appreciative of this opportunity to take to the street. Right-wing processions included a number of parties and organizations from the Liberty Front, among them Doriot's factory delegations, as well as the Action Française associations that were still legal. La Rocque, on trial and in any case increasingly distanced from the rest of the right, was not present, but his former ally Joseph Pozzo di Borgo processed with other former members of the Croix de Feu, and the PSF was also well represented. *Action Française* described the enthusiastic crowd as the largest ever to attend the celebration of Joan of Arc,[62] and the PSF's *Petit Journal* identified Joan of Arc as the first to 'impose [in France] the meaning and reality of the fatherland.'[63]

It was no accident that the commemoration of this national icon should become a centre of controversy between left and right, and that national street parades should displace the previous centrality of the mass meeting and the more spontaneous demonstration. Not only was this a reaction against the disorder and division associated with demonstrations, but these patriotic occasions seemed more likely to achieve the sense of reconciliation and transitory unanimity that had previously been sought elsewhere. Demonstrations and associations of the right already emphasized popular unity under strong leadership, and fraternity in memory of the First World War. Now the 'patriotic turn' of the left and the national tone of street politics under Daladier made this focus of reconciliation widely popular, if not quite unanimous. Partisan divisions remained strong ('Joan of Arc belongs to the PSF,' remarked *Le Petit Journal* possessively), but certain national images and icons were nonetheless widely acclaimed.

This 'community of thought' around the nation was also evident in the national celebrations and commemorations organized by Daladier's government in 1938–39, notably the visit of the British sovereign in July 1938, the commemoration of the twentieth anniversary of the armistice in November 1938, and the one hundred and fiftieth anniversary of the French Revolution in July 1939. Both the arrival of the British sovereign and the commemoration of the Armistice provided Daladier's government with the opportunity to exalt military sacrifice and victory in the First World War while also suggesting the contemporary strength of the French army and alliances. The official visit of George VI and Queen Elizabeth from 19 July 1938 to 22 July was celebrated not only in the street but also in the press, with closely comparable reactions across the political spectrum. 'A free people prepares to celebrate the sovereigns of another free people,' wrote Léon Blum in *Le Populaire*, seeing in the Parisian welcome of the British King and Queen the acclamation of the British nation as well as of their royal family. The people of Paris were similarly described as representing France as a whole. Given Hitler's escalating ambitions, the visit was clearly seen to reflect the two democracies' commitment to peace in Europe.[64] *La Lumière* depicted the occasion as the symbolic meeting and union of two peoples, and emphasized the common defence of peace and liberty.[65] Colonel de la Rocque was of the same opinion. 'Franco-British solidarity is the cornerstone of European peace,' he contended, and in the month of July *Le Petit Journal* featured a series of articles by the popular historian, essayist, and novelist André Maurois—'How best to understand the English'—which aimed to enlighten the French on the nature and functioning of British customs and institutions.[66]

Challenges to peace—and divided reactions to the Munich agreement—also determined reactions to commemoration of 11 November. This was particularly spectacular in 1938 (Figure 21). As well as the ceremony on 11 November itself, when troops processed to the Arc de Triomphe before the President of the Republic and a large number

Figure 21 The commemoration of the Armistice in November 1938 at La Pierre d'Haudroy, *L'Illustration*, 12 November 1938, © *L'Illustration* (Courtesy of *L'Illustration*).

of veteran soldiers and representatives of France's colonies and allies, there were also a number of further rituals. On 10 November, 117 torches had been brought to Paris from all points of the provinces and the Empire, and on the evening of 11 November these were solemnly lit from the torch burning above the tomb of the Unknown Soldier before being returned to their places of origin. The following afternoon, torches were lit by young athletes who then ran in relay to war cemeteries across the country. On the same day, Albert Lebrun and Daladier addressed a veteran's banquet: Lebrun spoke briefly and particularly praised the participation of colonial soldiers in the Parisian celebrations, while Daladier discoursed at length on the rights and primacy of the fatherland. Emphasizing that he too was a veteran of the First World War, he called upon his listeners to defend peace with 'virile resolution', and distinguished such defence from an ideological, pacifist desire to avoid war. This robust defence of peace necessitated the acknowledgement of certain truths—the first of which was 'that the service of the country should take precedence over the service of other interests, whatever they may be.' To considerable applause, Daladier identified common submission to the demands of the fatherland as the certain path towards fraternity, and established a clear moral distinction between those sensible to such a call, and those remaining resolutely defiant. He admitted that such demands were challenging, but made no apology for his government's appeal for hard work as national service: such frank and uncompromising language was the language of the trenches, which he hoped that 'no-one has forgotten.'[67]

Despite considerable opposition to Daladier's policies, the official commemoration of 11 November was widely applauded. *L'Ère nouvelle* praised the 'truly exemplary discipline' of the Parisian crowds, noting also that they were increased by provincial and colonial visitors and offered a truly national aspect.[68] *Le Petit Journal* described the particular grandeur of the ceremonies with approval, seeing this as a reassuring vision of peaceful unity after the recent Munich crisis.

> In the autumn sun that illuminated the triumphal avenue yesterday morning, one felt that the people, crowded near the Arc de Triomphe and along the Champs-Élysées, came not only to render the Unknown Soldier the pious homage that is his due, but also to seek reassurance, and the possibility of reconciliation.[69]

Similarly, Paul Marion described the ceremonies as symbolizing the PPF's hope that French regeneration would spring from collaboration with those who had experienced the First World War. 'It is from the understanding between the veteran generation and the post-war generations that the necessary French renewal must surely come,' he wrote.[70] The SFIO and PCF, whatever their internal divisions, likewise sought in the image of the crowd on the Champs-Élysées the symbol of a people united in defence of the nation and in solidarity with the veterans of the First World War. That the War was still referred to in *Le Populaire* as a 'great massacre' did not prevent the celebration of unity between the people and the veterans: 'Yesterday especially, the people of Paris were truly themselves, and on their own territory, on the Champs-Élysées. The Unknown Soldier was reunited with his brothers, in order and dignity.'[71] *L'Humanité* emphasized this same solidarity, while criticizing the 'Munichois' for their threat to international peace and national security.[72]

The culmination of the lavish public spectacles of the Daladier regime was the commemoration of the hundred and fiftieth anniversary of the Revolution in 1939. Reactions to the celebrations and their symbolic significance were twofold. On the one hand, the concept of celebrating 1789 provoked highly divergent responses; on the other, the image of an ordered people acclaiming the unity and strength of the French provinces, Empire, and army was greeted with widespread approval as an image of national reconciliation.

It might appear inappropriate that Daladier and his government, who were after all so anxious to secure national reconciliation, should choose to invest such effort and funding into the commemoration of 1789. The Revolution was a highly divisive subject, and its commemoration provoked 'civil wars of the mind' as historians of left and right elaborated their conflicting interpretations.[73] With the approach of the festivities there were certainly some extremely vocal criticisms. Many deputies (including members of the PSF) were outraged that so much public money was to be spent on celebration when the future of France was at stake.[74] La Tradition Nationale, an organization linked to Action Française, argued that 60 million francs would be better spent on charitable work, and that there was a deeply troubling similarity between the violence and division of the revolutionary period and the current unstable situation.[75] Léon Daudet, editor of *Action Française*, offered his reflections on the Revolution by publishing a new history of the period: *Deux Idoles sanguinaires: la Révolution et son fils Bonaparte*. Exalting the courage of the Vendéens and condemning the bloodthirsty injustice of the revolutionaries, Daudet's account was intended to reveal the failings of successive apologists for the Revolution—Jules Michelet and Edgar Quinet, Alphonse Aulard and Albert Mathiez—and was based, as he announced defiantly to *L'Humanité*, on irrefutable evidence.[76] Action Française also called for subscriptions to continue the work of counter-revolution. Even less extreme critics of the Revolution were nonetheless equivocal about its celebration at a time when political consensus appeared to be so fragile. On 6 March 1939 Daladier received a fervent letter from an anonymous veteran of the First World War enjoining him not to celebrate 14 July 1789, since 11 November was the only truly national commemoration.

> Prime Minister—you recall the unforgettable Fraternity, the Equality before the dangers of the front when defending French Liberty (which is also the liberty of the world). Is it not possible that this image, distant now and yet still living in your memory, can move your heart?[77]

There were, no doubt, many reasons why Daladier paid little heed to such criticisms. One of them may well have been that although 1939 was strictly speaking the hundred and fiftieth anniversary of 1789, it was very rare that there was any mention of 14 July 1789 in the official celebrations. 'Particular facts, singularly odious, have been forgotten,' observed *Le Temps* on 11 July 1939, 'in favour of remembering the symbolic.' Indeed, the committee of the Ministries of Fine Art and Education planning the commemoration made this conciliatory aspiration abundantly clear in their report of March 1939. The object of the celebration was a 'veritable mobilization of republican France', designed to unite all who respected the ideals on which the Republic had been founded (whatever their current political allegiance). The events of the Revolution deemed suitable for celebration were chosen from the period between the opening of the Estates General in May 1789 and the battle of Valmy in 1792. There was to be no mention either of the execution of the king or of the Terror. 14 July 1790 was accorded pride of place, but attention was also directed to the renunciation of privilege on 4 August 1789, to the Declaration of the Rights of Man and the Citizen, and to the defence of the fatherland by Girondins and Montagnards. Equally significantly, there was little mention of specific revolutionary heroes: the committee had chosen to focus instead on 'the innumerable, anonymous crowd of modest people, those people who, through suffering and bloodshed, secured the foundations of a new world.' The people, then, were to have their role in this commemoration: not the guiding role of the crowd of 14 July 1789, but the supportive and sacrificial role of a people dedicated to the building of the Republic or to the defence of their country. Their role in 1939 was to be twofold. At a local level they were encouraged to unite with teachers, archivists, and historians in the rediscovery of the Revolution and of its impact on their particular department, and to take part in local ceremonies. On a national level they were to be incorporated as spectators into the official displays of military strength and national unity, and treated to the customary music and dance of 14 July celebrations.[78]

Under the direction of the committee for the commemoration of the anniversary of the Revolution (presided over by Édouard Herriot and supported by Jean Zay, Minister for Education),[79] a number of these projects began to take shape. Although some of the planned celebrations—notably the celebration of the victory at Valmy and the commemoration of the intellectual impact of the Revolution, which had been proposed for November 1939—had obviously to be cancelled, the state had earlier on provided financial support for the development of local initiatives, such as exhibitions of documents and artefacts, and the planting of local 'liberty trees'.[80] The Musée Carnavalet in Paris assembled a collection of paintings from the revolutionary period, including Jacques-Louis David's *Le Triomphe du Peuple français*,[81] while the Orangerie was used for a special exhibition of drawings and prints from the collection of Edmond de Rothschild, received with considerable acclaim.[82] Popular images and artefacts were also being assembled on a grander scale in the new Musée des Arts et Traditions Populaires. On 22 June 1939, the President of the Republic entrusted the Ministry of Education with establishing a national commission for the study of popular arts and traditions, intended to encourage popular crafts, and the propagation of a wider interest in music, dance, and festivals of popular origin.[83] This novel initiative sought to research and preserve rural trades and customs, but as well as prefiguring the policies of Vichy it also emerged from the interest in regional customs and festivals in the fêtes and demonstrations of the Popular Front period.[84] In that the project aimed not merely to preserve existing traditions but also to incorporate them into films and radio broadcasts, it built on the popularization of culture endorsed by the Popular Front.

The commemorative ceremonies of 1939 were designed to encompass the entire French people. Local ceremonies in the French provinces were echoed in celebrations across the Empire,[85] and amnesty was extended on the one hand to La Rocque, and on the other to workers dismissed for their involvement in the strikes of 30 November. The two most grandiose national events—the festival of the tricolour on 13 July and the processions of the following day—lavishly evoked national unity and military splendour in a broadly republican framework, even if they failed to attract the vast multitudes of spectators for which they were intended.

The festival of the tricolour took place outside the Hôtel de Ville, and was attended by the President of the Republic, several diplomats, numerous military officials, and representatives of Togo, Madagascar, Indochina, and Morocco. Édouard Herriot, President of the Chamber of Deputies and also of the Committee for the Commemoration of the Revolution, praised the tricolour as a symbol of unity and reconciliation, declaring that 'we must not divide the history of our people—who have always retained the purity and ardour of their patriotism, despite their errors and divisions.'[86] The tricolour, he insisted, had both identified the French in war and provided the focus for unity in time of danger: now was the time to ensure that it was also a focus for peace. As Herriot concluded his speech, a large tricolour was raised while 21 guns were fired in the Jardin des Tuileries. Five thousand schoolchildren, divided into three groups across the square, waved blue, white, and red silk handkerchiefs, forming a vivid and living tricolour in front of the President's platform. The musicians of the army and air force played *La Marseillaise*, and the children parted ranks to allow a procession of soldiers bearing flags to this central platform. Each flag was inscribed with the name of a French military victory. The quasi-military formation of the children, and their integration into such a spectacle, suggested only too poignantly how their youth and energy might potentially be deployed. That the tricolour was a sign of times to come seemed to be the implicit message of the ceremony, and, as Herriot made clear, 'the people will remain faithful to their flag.'[87]

A similar role was designated for the people at the military procession, and during the Festival of national unity on the afternoon of 14 July. The military procession was notable in that British soldiers marched next to their French counterparts for the first time, greeted by a profusion of tricolours and Union flags. Indeed, the short documentary film made to record the occasion paid especial attention to this initiative, intended as a conscious expression of the willingness of France's allies to join with France in the defence of liberty.[88] The afternoon ceremony was organized in explicit remembrance of the Fête de la Fédération, and for this reason took place largely on the Champ de Mars where the original Festival had been held in 1790, with the President of the Republic and representatives of the French Empire watching from the Palais de Chaillot and the Trocadéro. Appeals were made to the people of Paris to attend the occasion, and large areas equipped with loudspeakers were set aside for the general public—although the crowds attending were in the end far smaller than had been envisaged. It was not in any case the people attending who were the principal actors in the spectacle, but the carefully organized delegations whose role it was to represent the strength and unity of the national community. A group of schoolchildren dressed in white stood at the foot of the terrace of the Palais de Chaillot, which was decorated with tricolours and with a copy of *La Marseillaise* (a sculpture produced by the nineteenth-century artist François Rude for one of the panels of the Arc de Triomphe). Meanwhile, the military delegations (as in the festival of the tricolour) included regiments from Algeria, Tunisia, Senegal, Morocco, and Indochina.[89]

The ambitious goals of the celebration were made clear in speeches by both Daladier and Lebrun. Daladier paid tribute to the Revolution by describing Jacobinism as the ancestor of contemporary French patriotism, and also identified the Fête de la Fédération as a point of reference for the unity of the French Empire. He praised the revolutionary transformation of people into citizens, and citizens into soldiers, commemorating in particular the integration of regional federations into a national army. Such an army both exemplified national unity and secured the defence of the nation against foreign invasion. The defence of Paris against invasion and counter-revolution had a clearly contemporary resonance, and it was at this point that Daladier's speech moved from the revolutionary period to the current celebrations of July 1939. 'This love of the fatherland,' he said, 'is surely the same as that beating in the hearts of the French as they watched the proud soldiers of our magnificent armies processing from the Place de l'Étoile to the Place de la Concorde.'[90] Reinforcing this message of national unity, Albert Lebrun then gave a speech that was broadcast across the French Empire, concluding with the broadcasting of replies from workers and officials in metropolitan France and in the colonies. This liturgy of communion of the French people and nation concluded the ceremony, which was followed by exhibitions of regional dance, fireworks, and then the traditional popular balls.

The commemorations offered a twofold image of the people: the ordered crowd in the street and the united national community. It was the nation that took centre stage, exemplified in the gathering on the Champ de Mars that clearly commemorated the Fête de la Fédération of 1790 rather than the violent popular politics of 14 July 1789. Not only was this an image of the nation united and reconciled with itself, it was also an image of a nation prepared for defence and sacrifice. Military discipline, youthful energy, and past heroism for the sake of national grandeur were all deliberately on display, designed to impress the French themselves as much as their neighbours and allies.

Differences over the contemporary significance of 14 July 1789 remained profound, but the official commemorations of the Revolution (which paid little attention to this date at all) won a broad acceptance. Naturally, Radical newspapers praised the discipline and splendour of the military displays. *La Lumière* praised this evident determination to defend liberty against the contemporary resurgence of despotism, and followed Daladier's example by associating 14 July 1790 with the foundation of the French Nation; *L'Ère nouvelle* described 14 July 1939 as a celebration of 'French union, resolution, and strength', and of Franco-British co-operation.[91] The honouring of the tricolour was particularly praised, and seen to efface the more recent reverence for the red flag, while the patriotism of 1939 was taken as proof that 'liberty is not defended or maintained by demonstrations, shouts, placards, and electoral posters saluted with raised fists'. The patriotic celebrations of 1939 revealed instead 'the true and noble face of France: resolute, heroic, and pacific.'[92]

Similarly positive responses could be found from right to left (other than among dissident left-wing groups and the PCF, which organized its own rival demonstrations). *Action Française* described the military procession as the most grandiose and well attended since the victory celebrations of the Armistice, and was, unusually, even disposed to be positive about the British flags displayed to welcome France's allies to Paris. Daladier's reference to revolutionary Jacobinism was treated with contempt, but Lebrun's radio broadcast to the Empire was approved.[93] Colonel de la Rocque's attitude towards the Revolution was more multi-faceted. Far from being the *Coblenzard* described by his enemies, he argued that even the counter-revolutionary writer Joseph de Maistre would have fought for the Committee of Public Safety rather than against it, for to oppose the Committee would have been to oppose France itself. Moreover, he insisted, 'we should not close our eyes to the popular heroism that, in response to the Jacobins' appeal, saved the fatherland.' While regretting the violence of the revolutionary period and its legacy of disunity and inadequate leadership, he was nonetheless drawn to the Revolution as a time of individual and national grandeur,[94] echoing Alexis de Tocqueville's attraction to this 'time of immortal memory'.[95] He therefore approved of the official commemorations of the Revolution in 1939 as a display of (and incentive to) patriotism. 'The whole of France communed in the same fervour, the same certainty,' he asserted, while calling once again for national leadership.

> Our people turn towards those in power. They expect to be guided with political clarity, with a fierce independence rigorously maintained and imposed on foreign powers, whoever they may be. [This is] the supreme opportunity to ensure peace, and the supreme guarantee of being a precious ally, a formidable enemy, a certain conqueror.[96]

The PPF's response to the commemorations was similarly to exalt the national grandeur of the Revolution and to perceive in the ceremonies of 13–14 July the image of a powerful army and a united Empire, the triumphant expression of the strength of the French race. *L'Émancipation nationale* described France's revolutionary past as a 'noble and exalted destiny: which people can boast of having known its equal?'[97] In the SFIO, even Léon Blum saw in the Revolution and in its commemoration of 1939 a synthesis of people and nation. Blum observed that 'for the French people of today, republican faith and revolutionary passion are inseparable from the idea of the nation (...) did not the very notion of the nation emerge from the revolutionary tumult?'[98]

In the end, the PCF was the most strident critic of the official ceremonies, partly because of its distance from the regime, partly because the Communists had organized their own procession from the Bastille de la Nation and had devoted almost as much effort to the commemoration of the revolution as had Daladier's government itself. As early as June 1938, Communist deputies in the Chamber had offered their own proposals for the coming festivities, notably for the creation of a permanent museum—which they themselves realized in Montreuil—and for the commemoration of the Fête de la Fédération with the participation of the army, very similar to what was eventually organized in July 1939.[99] Nonetheless, Daladier's adoption of a commemoration prefigured by the PCF did not meet with a positive response. 'There is an army in France,' contended *L'Humanité* on 16 July 1939, 'and it is the army of the people, who know what they want'. While the festival of national unity was described without enthusiasm—'an attractive spectacle, perhaps, but scarcely appreciated by the ordinary soldiers'[100] the exhibition of regional dance was more favourably received (similar provincial dances had taken place during a recent meeting of the PCF on 26 June). The main focus remained the PCF's separate demonstration at the Bastille, intended to signify continuing support for the Popular

Front while also contesting Daladier's images of national and republican unity.

> From the Place de la Bastille to the Place de la Nation, on the historic route through the Faubourg Saint-Antoine, there were communists, socialists, democrats, trade unionists, Jews, Catholics, Protestants, free-thinkers, men and women, young and old; all fraternally united, testifying to the profound unity and invincible strength of republican France in the face of external and internal fascism.[101]

When Daladier broadcast to the French people to describe their unity within the nation and to emphasize the primacy of national over individual interest, he appealed to a 'community of thought' uniting many groups and parties in France—even those that did not support him personally. As independent political actors, the people had become problematic in theory and practice, with bitter strikes, disorderly demonstrations, and official control of the streets undermining the portrayal of partisan crowds as a single, united people. In street politics, the main emphasis was now on the nation: Communists vied with the PSF and PPF to claim Joan of Arc, while the Daladier government supervised the lavish commemorations on 11 November 1938 and 14 July 1939. The symbolic unity of France around the sacrifice of war, the discipline of its army, and the energy of its young people fitted neatly with Daladier's emphasis on national defence, while also building on the legacy of the mass meetings of the Popular Front. Under Daladier, the image of the people in the street was transformed from one of actors to one of spectators, obedient under national leadership; while the portrayal of the people as community moved away from the visible crowd to the imagined community of the nation.

Beneath the fervour for national unity and defence, and the widespread approval of the grandiose commemorations of 1938–39, divisions and uncertainty clearly remained. Daladier, for all his apparent forcefulness and authoritarian rule, remained hesitant and doubtful about France's future. The same could be said for many political groups and parties, and for the French people themselves. 'If the Frenchman is particularly conscious of the nation as the essential bond between French people, and as the determining factor of his personality,' the right-wing author Thierry Maulnier had once observed, 'then this is because the French have scarcely any other link between them, any shared community other than France.'[102] Recognizing that the nation was an essential common bond could be a strength, but it could also be a weakness. What did the national allegiance supposedly binding the French people really signify? Was it more patriotic to negotiate with Germany and protect French territory from attack, or to safeguard honour by opposing a national enemy? Was it more patriotic to defend an ailing democracy, or to vote full powers for the renewal of the French political system? Daladier had made nationalism a form of civic religion, even proclaiming the right of the nation to demand the supreme sacrifice from its members. But it was perilously unclear for which purpose this sacrifice should be made.

Conclusion

'With imagination and willpower one can remodel the world,' wrote the political journalist and theatre critic Gabriel Boissy in 1936, as he reflected on the relationship between the French people and their leaders.[1] His dual assumption that a fundamental transformation of this relationship was both desirable and possible was widely shared by his contemporaries. Throughout the 1930s, political leaders, militants, journalists, playwrights, and film directors battled to represent the masses as the people, endeavouring to define the role that the people should play as political actors and as a reconciled community. Imagining the people was one challenge, translating this image into reality was quite another. The pursuit of the people, whether as the crowd, workers, strikers, or electorate offered both perils and possibilities. Where was the true voice of the people? How could a sense of community or unanimity be created and sustained? What if the people failed to conform to their allotted role?

This book has explored the pursuit of the people in the highly charged atmosphere of 1934–39, revealing tensions and convergences in political culture, and suggesting that this decade was not so much a time of stalemate as a time of creativity and experimentation. Drawing on the contemporary press, as well as on government, police, trade union, theatre, and film archives, the book has sought to understand the 1930s on its own terms: to see beneath the rhetorical battles of left and right to some of the shared hopes and fears of an anxious generation.

The first conclusion is that, contrary to the impression that has often emerged from previous research, the pursuit of the people was at the heart of an ongoing political contest. The representation of the people was not the exclusive domain of the Popular Front, nor was the Popular Front's image of the people as powerful or immutable as has sometimes appeared. Building on recent research into the political imagery of the Popular Front,[2] this book emphasizes that the image of the people as independent, victorious, and rational was—although widely accepted by the left—nonetheless constructed to counter internal divisions and external challenges. The 'new incarnation of the people turned sovereign, marching towards a future of which they are consciously masters'[3] rested on extremely fragile foundations, despite its eventual centrality to collective (left-wing) memory of the *Front popu.* Paradoxically, the survival of this image depended not on the people behaving as independent political actors, but rather on their conforming to the expectations of the Popular Front leaders. The challenge of popular disorder and violence in 1937–38 led to a disintegration of this image that has not previously been charted, with leaders of the SFIO and the CGT placing a new emphasis on the relationship between the people and their leaders. The Popular Front's image of the people was, moreover, consistently challenged by the leagues, press, and new parties of the right, which also proposed their own images of the people as political actors, emphasizing the corruptibility of the crowd and the popular need for leadership.

Critical portrayals of Popular Front supporters and demonstrations should not, however, be equated with contempt for the people. Rather, the leagues and parties that opposed the Popular Front were actively searching for their own solutions to the 'problem of the masses.' Some historians have denied that the extreme right developed an idea of the people in the street, or that its mass gatherings were characterised by the cultural innovation and conviviality of the left. Yet the police reports, film, and press articles on which this book is based suggest a different picture. Not only did the leagues and parties refer to the crowd as the people, but they also employed cultural and technological innovation to reach out to and organize them, as the films of Action Française and the Croix de Feu/Parti Social Français reveal. From 1934 onwards, mass meetings and demonstrations by the Popular Front and its adversaries developed into a deliberate battle for the public space: rival spectacles of numerical strength and popular fervour, often on the same day and sometimes even in the same area of Paris. Such mass events were not, of course, without their risks—and a persistent challenge to images of the people on both left and right was the fact that crowds, workers, or strikers did not necessarily act as their leaders intended.

The second conclusion of this book is that the pursuit of the people reveals important areas of convergence as well as contest in the political culture of the 1930s. Jean Le Cour Grandmaison's 'partial community of thought' between the French was grounded in very real developments, even if—as he himself admitted—the realization of this community was constantly frustrated by entrenched antipathies within an often inflexible political system. While the ideological traditions underpinning images of the people on left, right, and centre were sharply divergent, there were significant parallels in the organization and portrayal of the people as political actors, and in their imagination as a reconciled community. In the ongoing search to define and represent the 'voice of the people', there was a general (although not all-encompassing) shift from the angry crowd in the street in 1934 to the organized masses, workers, and electorate of 1936, a shift that emerged as movements on both left and right began to seek reform within the existing Republic rather than against it, and to address the cultural as well as the political aspirations of their supporters. The growing problem of street violence and the practical difficulties of organizing strikes and demonstrations in the face of increasingly repressive legislation then led to an important change in focus from the visible crowd to the imagined community, from the workers to the middle classes, and from the clamour of the crowd to the voice of the leader. Meanwhile, theatre and film were also seeking to depict a united, popular community in the face of tension and division. By 1939 there was a strong common focus on the primacy of the national community over the individual, and on the importance of a direct relationship between the leader and the people.

Throughout this period, the left remained faithful (at least in part) to the image of a militant working people and a rational crowd, while the right (and the Radicals) remained suspicious of the dangerous potential of crowd action, and preferred to emphasize discipline and authority. But it was not the case that the left identified themselves only with an independent, rational, working people, while the right focused only on order and leadership. In 1934 both described the crowd in the street as the voice of the people; in 1936 both claimed to represent the workers and called for social reforms; and in 1938 both asserted the importance of national union and defence. The pursuit of the people thus involved left and right in an evolving, interdependent relationship, rather than in a more straightforward case of consecutive action and reaction.

The imagination of the people as a reconciled community is a particularly interesting example of boundary crossings between left and right. The importance of ideological borrowings in this particular period can be attributed in part to the 'patriotic turn' of the left in 1935, and to the evolving social aspirations of the right. For while the leagues and parties of the right developed their claims to the workers, thus trespassing on

the traditional territory of the left, the Popular Front explicitly appropriated national celebrations such as the commemoration of the Armistice
and the military parade of 14 July within its own political rituals. In
the rhetorical battle that developed in close relation to street politics,
the Popular Front and its adversaries sought to imagine a reconciled
community that would transcend social and geographical divisions and
draw the French into a single people, while simultaneously excluding
and ridiculing 'foreign' influences, whether capitalist or Communist. In
part, this was a search for a sense of belonging to compensate for the
instability and anonymity of the age of the masses—a search that was
by no means restricted to politics. Indeed by exploring reflections on
the relationship between the individual and the collective not only in
Popular Front propaganda, plays, and films but also in the rhetoric of
its political adversaries and in contemporary Catholic theatre, this book
suggests that the Popular Front's search for reconciliation in the people
was symptomatic of a wider development. The cultural innovations of
the Popular Front must be seen alongside the films of Action Française
and the Croix de Feu, the plays of Léon Chancerel and the Jeunesse
Ouvrière Chrétienne. They must be identified with a deeper concern
with rebuilding community, expressed by the Parti Social Français in its
search for 'a collective soul that was believed to have disappeared',[4] or
by the Jewish journalist Bertrand de Jouvenel in his aim to realize the
'spiritual reformation of France'[5] through the publications of the PPF.

In the shared characteristics of these reconciled communities it is possible to discern elements of a common reaction to the 'problem of the
masses' in an industrialized world: a reaction to antagonism and alienation, and to what Jean-Richard Bloch had described as the gulf between
technological and human progress. The 1930s cannot be reduced to a
struggle between a reactionary right and a modernizing left, for there
were political groups across the spectrum that employed the latest tech-
nology and communications to present reassuring images of traditional
communities. Colonel de la Rocque addressed motorized meetings on
the importance of the peasantry; Jean-Richard Bloch created a mass
spectacle in a sports stadium that celebrated a utopian rural community in which industrialized workers could become artisans. In 1935,
the CGT theatre critic Georges Altman described with enthusiasm the
performance of medieval mystery plays outside Notre-Dame,[6] and in
1936 the PCF was equally impressed by festivals of folk dancing, and
included delegates in regional costume in its celebration of electoral
victory.[7] Such examples clearly demonstrate that the ideological ambiguities identified by Roderick Kedward in his study of Vichy France and

the Resistance had an important pre-history in the 1930s.[8] The contest to claim rural France is a particularly clear example.

Left-wing enthusiasm for ideas more frequently associated with the right has been described by some historians as 'puzzling'.[9] Herman Lebovics, for example, castigates the spread of 'essentialist' thought from right to left, and attributes it to a 'conservative political project that took in good people',[10] considering this development to have played 'a major deleterious role in French thought and cultural practice.'[11] Yet it seems unlikely that CGT and Communist commentators were pre-disposed to adopting right-wing modes of thought *per se*, and, situated in a context in which the right was also borrowing from the left, this emergence of a 'partial community of thought' suggests a necessary ide-ological evolution in a time of crisis, rather than a political conspiracy. (This is not to deny, however, that men such as Charles Maurras were unashamedly delighted when the Communist electoral manifesto of 1936 consisted almost entirely of right-wing principles of order, family, nation, and property.)[12]

The third conclusion of this book is that this period was a time of political creativity and fluidity: an observation that has often been made with regard to 'nonconformist' groups,[13] but that deserves to be more generally applied. Indeed, this was a characteristic on which contem-poraries on both left and right remarked. Jean Touchard once observed, quoting the interwar philosopher Alain (Émile Chartier), that anyone who described the opposition between left and right as outmoded was certainly not a man of the left.[14] Yet there were people across the polit-ical spectrum who recognized that the traditional definitions of left and right could not fully explain the political struggles and evolution of the 1930s. Jean-Richard Bloch noted the inability to describe new phenomenon with existing vocabulary,[15] and the 'obscure fraternity of condition' that linked him, and others on the left, with those who joined right-wing leagues.[16] Charles Vallin of the PSF likewise recognized that the division into right and left was both real and unreal.

> A great number of our compatriots still speak and think as right- or left-wingers. What does this mean? Often a touching and almost tangible fidelity to a youthful passion; a sudden burst of enthusiasm, generosity, or anger; an obstinate allegiance to a party or to a man who has known how to deserve esteem or simple gratitude. Often also it is a refusal: one is left-wing 'against' the priest, the army offi-cer, the local notable. And likewise on the right. But now I hear men of left and right protesting together.[17]

Vallin recognized that left and right possessed their own 'mystiques': progress, justice, and human rights on the left; order, tradition, and patriotism on the right. But now the right castigated capitalism, and the left adopted patriotic attitudes; their appeals to the people became curiously similar. And like political movements and parties across Europe, the French left and right took advantage of the streets to create their own political theatre, attempting to stage reconciliation through their organization and depiction of the masses. As Georges Altman commented in July 1935, 'with summer coming and the month of July, both official and popular organizations see the streets and squares of Paris and in the provinces as a potential "theatre": more vibrant and vast than those with which we are familiar.'[18] For practical reasons, this book has focused principally on Paris: the confrontation of left and right in the provinces offers rich possibilities for further research.

If this 'partial community of thought' was so powerful, why did it remain unrealized? Léon Blum suggested an explanation when, on 8 April 1938, he accused the Senate of rejecting his appeal for full powers on the grounds of personal antipathy. Any other leader, he claimed, could demand the same powers and be granted them—and Édouard Daladier was shortly to prove him correct. Paradoxically, the shared ideological currents and concerns between right and left did not lead to any diminution of political antagonism in the 1930s, even if they may partially explain the initial support for Vichy's National Revolution in 1940. Men and institutions were often less malleable than ideas and practices. Colonel de la Rocque might adopt an explicit concern for republican legality, but for the left he remained the man of 6 February 1934, indelibly associated with ominous references to 'H-Hour' and with the potential for a fascist coup. And no doubt they were right to be sceptical of his sudden public conversion to republicanism, for had La Rocque attained power he would certainly have sought to transform the democratic parliamentary Republic along more authoritarian lines. Similarly, the right was cynical of the PCF's dramatic conversion to patriotic rhetoric, refusing to believe that the Stalinist Maurice Thorez and his followers could have French interests at heart. Following the Nazi-Soviet pact of 1939, the sudden exchange of patriotic rhetoric for a renewed emphasis on 'revolutionary defeatism' by a number of PCF leaders proved that at least some of the right's suspicions had been correct. The left—especially the Communists—remained in the minds of the right indelibly associated with revolution, and Blum's very genuine commitment to the national interest in his Popular Front governments could never overcome latent and overt suspicions that a Socialist Jew could not fully represent the French. It required the breakdown of the Republic in the wake of wartime defeat in 1940 for some of the common concerns to converge, creating an initially widespread support for Marshal Pétain as national leader. But these were certainly not the most favourable conditions for a genuine and lasting consensus on the reform of France in the interests of the people. Jean Le Cour Grandmaison was certainly right to identify a 'partial community of thought' beneath the vocal hostility of political adversaries in the 1930s. But when he predicted its final fulfilment on 'the day, perhaps closer than we realize, when the iron law of events definitively shatters the worm-eaten [parliamentary] benches that separate us', he was perhaps unduly optimistic.[19]

Notes

Introduction: The People on Stage, 1934–39

1. See Archives de la Préfecture de Police (hereafter APP), Ba 1863.
2. Jean Le Cour Grandmaison, deputy and vice-president of the Fédération Nationale Catholique, speaking to the Chamber of Deputies. *Le Journal officiel: débats parlementaires, Chambre des Députés*, 7 June 1936.
3. Jacques Dupâquier et al., *Histoire de la population française* (Paris: PUF, 1988), 4, *De 1914 à nos jours*, p. 3. See also Richard Tomlinson, 'The disappearance of France, 1896–1940: French politics and the birth-rate', *Historical Journal* 28 (1985), pp. 405–15. On immigration, see Daniel Gordon, 'The back door of the nation state: Expulsions of foreigners and continuity in twentieth-century France', *Past and Present* 186 (2005), pp. 210–32.
4. Serge Berstein, *La France des années trente* (Paris: Armand Colin, 2001), p. 11.
5. Henri Noguères, *La Vie quotidienne en France au temps du Front populaire, 1935–38* (Paris: Hachette, 1977), p. 107.
6. Gérard Noiriel, *Workers in French Society in the Nineteenth and Twentieth Centuries* (Oxford: Berg, 1990), p. 116. French manufacturers were, however, generally slower than their British or American counterparts to convert to mass production. See Herrick Chapman, *State Capitalism and Working-Class Radicalism in the French Aircraft Industry* (Berkeley, Los Angeles, Oxford: University of California Press, 1991).
7. Noiriel, *Workers in French Society*, p. 117.
8. Noiriel, *Workers in French Society*, p. 134.
9. Robert Frost, 'Machine liberation: Inventing housewives and home appliances in interwar France', *French Historical Studies* 18 (1993), p. 113.
10. Jean-Richard Bloch, *Naissance d'une culture: quatrièmes essais pour mieux comprendre mon temps* (Paris: Éditions Rieder, 1936), p. 158; Simone Weil, *L'Enracinement: prélude à une déclaration des devoirs envers l'être humain* (Paris: Gallimard, 1949), p. 45. On Weil, see David McLellan, *Simone Weil: Utopian Pessimist* (London: Macmillan, 1989).
11. Andrée Jouve, 'Notes sur l'Amérique', *Europe, revue mensuelle*, 15 October 1924.
12. On fears prompted by the 'new woman', see Julian Jackson, *France: The Dark Years, 1940–1944* (Oxford: OUP, 2001), pp. 33–35; and Mary Louise Roberts, *Civilisation Without Sexes: Reconstructing Gender in Postwar France, 1917–1927* (Chicago: University of Chicago Press, 1994).
13. Tony Syme, 'La France aux Français: Displacing the foreign worker during the 1930s Depression', *Oxford Economics Department Paper* 54 (2000), p. 5.
14. Noiriel, *Workers in French Society*, p. 133.
15. Noguères, *La Vie quotidienne*, p. 100. See also Noiriel, *Workers in French Society*, p. 133; and Gordon, 'The back door of the nation state'.
16. Noiriel, *Workers in French Society*, p. 132.
17. Romy Golan, *Modernity and Nostalgia. French Art and Politics Between the Wars* (New Haven and London: Yale University Press, 1995), p. 23.

18. Shanny Peer, *France on Display: Peasants, Provincials, and Folklore in the 1937 Paris World's Fair* (New York: State University of New York Press, 1998).
19. *Guide à l'Exposition Internationale de 1937*, p. 4. Archives de la CGT, Montreuil (hereafter ACGT), Box 23.
20. Jackson, *The Dark Years*, p. 29. On the widespread popularity of Pagnol's cinematic celebrations of the countryside, see Brett Bowles, 'Politicizing Pagnol: Rural France, film and ideology under the Popular Front', *French History* 19 (2005), pp. 112–42.
21. Noguères, *La Vie quotidienne*, p. 111.
22. Berstein, *La France des années 30*, p. 36.
23. See Julian Jackson, *The Politics of Depression in France, 1932–36* (Cambridge: CUP, 1985).
24. Paul Reynaud, *Mémoires*, Vol. 1, *Venu de ma Montagne* (Paris: Flammarion, 1960), p. 405.
25. Ironically, this had been itself a devaluation, stabilizing the franc at only 20 per cent of its pre-war value. On reactions to devaluation, see Benjamin Martin, *France in 1938* (Louisiana: Louisiana State University Press, 2005), p. 25.
26. Noiriel, *Workers in French Society*, p. 160.
27. Noguères, *La Vie quotidienne*, p. 99.
28. Gilles Le Béguec, *L'Entrée au Palais-Bourbon: les filières privilégiées d'accès à la fonction parlementaire, 1919–39* (Unpublished thesis, Université de Paris-Nanterre, 1989).
29. Charles Maurras, *La Contre-Révolution spontanée* (Paris: H. Lardanchet, 1943), pp. 49–55.
30. Bruno Goyet, ' "Entre le Louvre et la Bastille": The topology, sociology, and mythology of Paris in the works of Charles Maurras', in Jessica Wardhaugh (ed.), *Paris and the Right in the Twentieth Century* (Newcastle: CSP, 2007), pp. 148–68. See also Bruno Goyet, *Charles Maurras* (Paris: Presses de la FNSP, 2000).
31. 'P.P. février 1909', Archives Nationales, Paris (hereafter AN), F7 12864.
32. Michel Dreyfus, *Histoire de la CGT: Cent ans de syndicalisme en France* (Paris: Éditions Complexe, 1995), p. 45.
33. Georges Duhamel, 'Anniversaire', *Europe, revue mensuelle*, 15 July 1924.
34. Tony Judt, *The Burden of Responsibility: Blum, Camus, Aron and the French Twentieth Century* (London and Chicago: University of Chicago Press, 1998), p. 53. On Blum and the divisions within the SFIO, see also Helmut Gruber, 'Léon Blum, French Socialism and the Popular Front: A Case of Internal Contradictions' (New York: Cornell University, Western Societies Programme Occasional Paper no. 17, 1986).
35. Peter Larmour, *The French Radical Party in the 1930s* (Stanford: Stanford University Press, 1960), p. 9. See also Serge Berstein, *Histoire du Parti Radical* (Paris: Presses de la FNSP, 1981), 2, *La Crise du radicalisme*.
36. Elisabeth du Réau, *Édouard Daladier, 1884–1970* (Paris: Fayard, 1993), p. 10.
37. Du Réau, *Daladier*, p. 16.
38. Jackson, *The Dark Years*, pp. 55–7. On Tardieu, see François Monnet, *Refaire la République: André Tardieu, une dérive réactionnaire, 1876–1945* (Paris: Fayard, 1993).
39. Kevin Passmore, 'Catholicism and nationalism: The Fédération Républicaine, 1927–1939'; David Curtis, 'True and false modernity: Catholicism and communist Marxism in 1930s France', in Kay Chadwick (ed.), *Catholicism, Politics*

and Society (Liverpool: Liverpool University Press, 2000). On the Catholic intellectual renewal, see Frédéric Gugelot, *La Conversion des intellectuels au catholicisme en France, 1885–1935* (Paris: CNRS, 1998); Philippe Chenaux, *Entre Maurras et Maritain: une génération intellectuelle catholique, 1920–1930* (Paris: Cerf, 1999), and Stephen Schloesser, *Jazz Age Catholicism: Mystic Modernism in Postwar Paris, 1919–1933* (Toronto, Buffalo, London: University of Toronto Press, 2005).

40. The Ligue des Droits de l'Homme was still an important presence in the 1930s. Its president, the Hungarian-born Jew Victor Basch, was also to preside over the Rassemblement Populaire, an umbrella organization that co-ordinated the forces of the left during the Popular Front.

41. On the development of the leagues, see, for example, Michel Winock, *Nationalism, Anti-Semitism and Fascism in France* (Stanford: Stanford University Press, 1998); Brian Jenkins (ed.), *France in the Era of Fascism: Essays on the French Authoritarian Right* (Oxford: Berghahn Books, 2005); and Robert Soucy, *French Fascism: The Second Wave 1933–39* (New Haven and London: Yale University Press, 1995).

42. The activity of these early cells was closely documented by the police. See, for example, AN F7 13098. On the growth of the PCF in the 1930s, see Annie Kriegel, *Le Pain et les roses: jalons pour une histoire des socialismes* (Paris: PUF, 1968).

43. Pierre Drieu la Rochelle, *Le Jeune Européen* (Paris: Plon, 1927), p. 191.

44. Henri Daniel-Rops cites many key works by this group of intellectuals in the bibliography to his book *Le Monde sans âme* (Paris: Plon, 1932).

45. Jackie Clarke, 'Imagined productive communities: Industrial rationalization and cultural crisis in 1930s France', *Modern and Contemporary France* 8 (2000), pp. 345–57. On the intellectual significance of these nonconformists, see Jean Touchard, 'L'Esprit des années trente: une tentative de renouvellement de la pensée politique française', in Guy Michaud (ed.), *Tendances politiques dans la vie française depuis 1789* (Paris: Hachette, 1960), pp. 89–120, and Olivier Dard, *Le Rendez-vous manqué des relèves des années 30* (Paris: PUF, 2002).

46. Henri Daniel-Rops described it as 'an adulterated form of the universal'. *Le Monde sans âme*, p. 145.

47. M. Champetier de Ribes, leader of the centrist Parti Démocrate Populaire, at a meeting on 16 December 1936. 'P.P. 17 décembre 1936', APP, Ba 1975.

48. See, for example, the documentary *Ceux qui se souviennent: tout va très bien 1936–39*, produced by Hubert Knapp for TF1 in 1980 (Bibliothèque Nationale de France, Paris, hereafter BN), as well as Denis et Rémi Lefebvre, *Mémoires du Front populaire* (Paris: OURS, 1997). Dudley Andrew and Steven Ungar likewise celebrate the Popular Front as an expression of 'social solidarity and the possibility of democratic attainment of humane values' in their recent study: *Popular Front Paris and the Poetics of Culture* (Cambridge, MA and London: The Belknap Press of Harvard University Press, 2005), p. 1.

49. See, for example, Robert Capa, *Front populaire* (Paris: Agence Magnum, 1936–39); Willy Ronis, *Premiers congés payés et loisirs divers* (Paris: Agence Rapho, 1933–70); and Willy Ronis, *Défilés, grèves, et manifestations avant 1938* (Paris: Agence Rapho, 1934–38).

50. Jean-Paul Rioux (ed.), *Le Front populaire* (Paris: Tallendier, 2006), p. 10.

51. Antoine Prost, *Autour du Front populaire: aspects du mouvement social au XXe siècle* (Paris: Seuil, 2006), p. 70.

52. Daniel Grason, René Mouriaux, and Patrick Pochet (eds), *Éclats du Front populaire* (Paris: Éditions Syllepse, 2006), p. 13.

53. Jules Moch, a fervent supporter of Léon Blum, insisted on the non-revolutionary nature of the workers in 1936 in *Le Front populaire, grande espérance* (Paris: Perrin, 1971); later Socialist politicians such as the premier Michel Rocard similarly stressed the non-threatening aspect of the Popular Front 'people', for example in the documentary *Mémoire d'un Peuple*, produced by Claude Santelli in 1991 (BN). Communist accounts have often emphasized the Party's independence from Moscow and its primary importance in the construction of a united front policy. See, for example, J.-F. Gelly, 'À la Recherche de l'unité organique: la démarche du Parti Communiste 1934–38', *Mouvement Social* 121 (1982), pp. 97–116. Accounts by dissident left-wingers of the period have preferred to emphasize the revolutionary possibilities of the Popular Front—for example, Louis Bodin and Jean Touchard, *Front Populaire 1936* (Paris: Armand Colin, 1961, 1985), and Daniel Guérin, *Front populaire, révolution manquée: témoignage militant* (Paris: Maspero, 1970).

54. The point was stressed by Pierre Mauroy, First Secretary of the Socialist Party, in a documentary made on the paid holidays in 2000. *Les Congés payés, 1936*, produced by Philippe Kohly in 2000 (BN).

55. Danielle Tartakowsky, *Le Front populaire: la vie est à nous* (Paris: Gallimard, 1996); Danielle Tartakowsky, *Les Manifestations de rue en France, 1918–68* (Paris: Publications de la Sorbonne, 1997); Danielle Tartakowsky and Michel Margairaz, *'L'Avenir nous appartient': histoire du Front populaire* (Paris: Larousse, 2006); and Pascal Ory, *La Belle Illusion: culture et politique sous le signe du Front populaire* (Paris: Plon, 1994). The breaking down of boundaries between culture and the people is also an important theme in Julian Jackson's history of the Popular Front: *The Popular Front in France: Defending Democracy 1934–38* (Cambridge: CUP, 1988).

56. Simon Dell, *The Image of the Popular Front. The Masses and the Media in Interwar France* (Basingstoke: Palgrave Macmillan, 2007).

57. René Rémond, *La Droite en France, de 1815 à nos jours* (1954); *Les Droites en France* (Paris: Aubier-Montaigne, 1982).

58. Zeev Sternhell, *Maurice Barrès et le nationalisme français* (Paris: Armand Colin, 1972), *La Droite révolutionnaire: les origines françaises du fascisme, 1885–1914* (Paris: Fayard, [1978] 2000), *Ni Droite, ni gauche: l'idéologie fasciste en France* (Paris: Seuil, [1983] 2000); Soucy, *French Fascism*.

59. See, in particular, Soucy, *French Fascism*; Jacques Nobécourt, *Le Colonel de la Rocque, 1885–1946, ou les pièges du nationalisme chrétien* (Paris: Fayard, 1996); William Irvine, 'Fascism in France and the strange case of the Croix de Feu', *Journal of Modern History* 63 (1991), 271–95; Kevin Passmore, *From Liberalism to Fascism: The Right in a French Province* (Cambridge: CUP, [1997] 2002); Kevin Passmore, 'The Republic in crisis: Politics 1914–45', in James McMillan (ed.), *Modern France, 1880–2002* (Oxford: Oxford University Press, 2003), pp. 39–73; and Sean Kennedy, *Reconciling France against Democracy: The Croix de Feu and the Parti Social Français 1927–1945* (Montreal, London: McGill-Queen's University Press, 2007).

60. Irvine, 'Fascism in France'; and Soucy, *French Fascism*.

61. Michel Winock, *Nationalism, Anti-Semitism and Fascism in France* (Stanford: Stanford University Press, 1998).

62. Kennedy describes his work as an endeavour 'to locate the CDF and the PSF on the spectrum of interwar European politics, but without becoming preoccupied with categorization.' *Reconciling France against Democracy*, p. 10. On this recent move away from the fascism debate, see also Laurent Kestel, 'L'engagement de Bertrand de Jouvenel au PPF, 1936–38: intellectuel de parti et entrepreneur politique', *French Historical Studies* 30 (2007), pp. 105–25.

63. Kevin Passmore's excellent study of the Croix de Feu around Lyons (*From Liberalism to Fascism*) emphasizes its populism, but his concern is not to study its organization of meetings and demonstrations, or the portrayal of the people in a theatrical sense. Christophe Prochasson has written on 'the extreme right at ground level', but with reference to theory rather than practice; and Michel Dobry has analysed the right in February 1934, but without discussing the question of representation or the image of the people in the street. Christophe Prochasson, 'Elusive fascism: Reflections on the extreme right at the end of the nineteenth century', in Edward Arnold (ed.), *The Development of the Radical Right in France from Boulanger to Le Pen* (Basingstoke: Macmillan, 2000), pp. 69–79; and Michel Dobry, 'February 1934 and the discovery of French society's allergy to the "Fascist Revolution" ', in Jenkins (ed.), *France in the Era of Fascism*, pp. 129–51.

64. Roderick Kedward and Roger Austin (eds), *Vichy France and the Resistance: Culture and Ideology* (London: Croom Helm, 1985), p. 6.

65. There is an increasing conviction that the struggles of the 1930s cannot be fully comprehended within the framework of a battle between an urban, modernist left and a reactionary, fascist right. This is, in part, a reaction against the teleological view of French history that described the yearning for a more organic, rural society in the interwar and wartime period as an unfortunate detour on the supposedly linear path to post-war consumerism and liberal democracy. For examples of this new trend, see Jackie Clarke, 'Imagined productive communities: Industrial rationalization and cultural crisis in 1930s France', *Modern and Contemporary France* 8 (2000), pp. 345–57; Jackie Clarke, 'France, America and the Metanarrative of Modernisation: From postwar social science to the new culturalism', *Contemporary French and Francophone Studies* 8 (2004), pp. 365–77; and Bowles, 'Politicizing Pagnol'.

66. Jean-Richard Bloch, interviewed for *Les Nouvelles Littéraires* on 28 March 1931.

67. *Je suis partout*, 13 June 1936.

68. This interpretation of the term relates closely to recent research on political culture encompassing forms of activity (such as the demonstration) as well as forms of language and symbolism (such as speeches and images). Historical studies of political culture in the 1980s often marked their rejection of social history by focusing strongly on language—for instance, Keith Baker (ed.), *The French Revolution and the Creation of Modern Political Culture* (Oxford: Pergamon Press, 1987). In contrast, more recent works have employed the same term to signify a return to the dynamics of power relations and thus to political activity, organization, and coercion. See, for example, David Andress, *Massacre at the Champ de Mars: Popular Dissent and Political Culture during the French Revolution* (Woodbridge: Boydell Press, 2000), p. 3. See also Orlando Figes and Boris Kolonitskii, *Interpreting the Russian Revolution: The Language and Symbols of 1917* (New Haven and London: Yale University Press, 1999). 'Language' is understood by Figes and Kolonitskii in a very broad sense, including dress, body language, parades, and demonstrations.

1   From the Crowd in the Street to the Voice of the People: February 1934

1. *La Voix du Peuple*, February 1934, p. 132.
2. The events of February 1934 are essential to any history of the Popular Front, yet the question of representing the crowd as the people has received little attention. Most studies focus on internal divisions between left and right and on the emergence of anti-fascist unity. See, for example, Berstein, *La France des années trente*, pp. 103–5 and Jackson, *The Popular Front*, pp. 28–30.
3. Le Béguec, *L'Entrée au Palais-Bourbon*, p. 39.
4. Monnet, *Refaire la République*, p. 309.
5. Le Béguec, *L'Entrée au Palais-Bourbon*, p. 46.
6. Eugen Weber, *Action Française* (Paris: Fayard, 1985), p. 355. See also Martin, *France in 1938*, p. 32.
7. On the 'elusive' people, see Pierre Rosanvallon, *Le Peuple introuvable: histoire de la représentation démocratique en France* (Paris: Éditions Gallimard, 1998). Rosanvallon devotes little specific attention to the 1930s, other than to the trade unions of this period.
8. Jean Guéhenno, *Ce que je crois* (Paris: Grasset, 1964), p. 113.
9. Guéhenno, *Ce que je crois*, p. 21.
10. Jean Guéhenno, *Jeunesse de la France* (Paris: Grasset, 1936), p. 105.
11. Michelet, cited by Jean Guéhenno in *L'Évangile éternel: étude sur Michelet* (Paris: Grasset, 1927), p. 128.
12. 'Most intellectuals speak of mass-man only in so far as they are afraid of becoming him.' Jean Guéhenno, *Journal d'une "Révolution"* (Paris: Grasset, 1937), p. 32.
13. André Malraux believed that the Popular Front represented for many socialist intellectuals 'the revenge of Michelet over Marx'. Malraux, introduction to Jean Guéhenno and Romain Rolland, *L'Indépendance de l'esprit. Correspondance entre Jean Guéhenno et Romain Rolland, 1919–44* (Paris: Albin Michel, 1975), p. 9.
14. Nathanael Greene, *Crisis and Decline: The French Socialist Party in the Popular Front Era* (New York: Cornell University Press, 1969), p. 13.
15. 'My refusal of violence will be categorical. Violence is counter-revolutionary. The Revolution is not that dream of blood, terror, and death after which, according to some, and by who knows what miracle, we must discover paradise.' Guéhenno, *Journal d'une "Révolution"*, p. 208.
16. Marceau Pivert, *Révolution d'abord!* (Paris: Nouveau Prométhée, 1936).
17. Greene, *Crisis and Decline*, p. 278.
18. Judt, *The Burden of Responsibility*, p. 53; and Greene, *Crisis and Decline*, p. 4.
19. Daniel Brower, *The New Jacobins: The French Communist Party and the Popular Front* (New York: Cornell University Press, 1968), p. 233.
20. (AN).
21. This group has received very little attention to date. Pascal Ory refers to its monthly publication, *La Scène ouvrière*, in his *La Belle Illusion*, but makes no mention of the files in the police archives, which have been hitherto neglected.
22. *La Scène ouvrière: organe mensuel de la Fédération du Théâtre Ouvrier de France*, February 1931.

23. 'Juin 1932, rapport', Archives de la Préfecture de Police, Paris (hereafter APP), Ba 2032.
24. *La Scène ouvrière*, February 1931.
25. *La Scène ouvrière*, March 1931.
26. *La Scène ouvrière*, June 1931.
27. Michel Dreyfus, *Histoire de la CGT: cent ans de syndicalisme en France* (Paris: Éditions Complexe, 1995), p. 150.
28. 'XXIe Congrès National de la CGT, Paris, 15 au 18 septembre: rapports et documents', *La Voix du Peuple*, October 1931, p. 7.
29. Benoît Frachon, *S'Unir entre Travailleurs: Discours prononcé par Frachon devant le Comité Confédéral Nationale de la CGTU des 4–5–6–7 octobre 1934* (CGTU, 1934).
30. *La CGTU et les Paysans: discours de Racamond, secrétaire de la CGTU, au CCN de mars 1934, précédé d'une étude sur les paysans travailleurs, de Marius Vazeilles, secrétaire de la Fédération des Paysans Travailleurs de la Corrèze* (CGTU, 1934), p. 8.
31. 'Après la marche de la faim: bulletin pour tous les comités de chômeurs et les organisations membres des comités de soutien, 25 janvier 1934', Archives de la CGT, Montreuil (hereafter ACGT), Box 23: Marche de la Paix, 1933.
32. On the Radicals in this period, see Serge Berstein, *Histoire du Parti Radical* (2 vols., Paris: Presses de la FNSP, 1981), 2, *La Crise du Radicalisme*.
33. 'Commission sur la Réforme de l'État présenté au Congrès du Parti Radical et Radical-Socialiste, le 26 octobre 1934', AN, F7 13192.
34. *Le Courrier d'Alsace*, 1 July 1935, AN, F7 13305.
35. Georges Bonnet, *Le Parti Radical et les problèmes du temps présent* (Paris, 1936), p. 8.
36. 'It is this [individualism] which reveals the gulf separating the Radical Party from the Socialist Party, and which links it to the other so-called moderate parties.' 'P.P. 13 octobre 1926', AN, F7 13191.
37. Maurice Sarraut, speaking to the Radical Congress in Bordeaux in October 1926. *L'Œuvre*, 18 October 1926.
38. *Le Journal officiel*, 7 February 1934.
39. Cesare Lombroso, *L'Homme criminel* (Paris: Félix Alcan, 1895), 1, p. 148.
40. Hippolyte Taine, *Les Origines de la France contemporaine* (Paris: Hachette, 1902), 1, p. 84.
41. Gustave Le Bon, *La Psychologie des foules* (1895) (Paris: PUF, 1998), p. 12.
42. Taine, *Origines de la France*, 2, p. 282.
43. Taine, *Origines de la France*, 2, p. 275.
44. Le Bon, *La Psychologie*, p. 37.
45. Gustave Le Bon, *The French Revolution and the Psychology of Revolution* (1913) (London and New Brunswick: Transaction books, 1980), p. 70; and Taine, *Origines de la France*, 2, p. 282.
46. Le Bon, *La Psychologie*, p. 2.
47. Le Bon, *La Psychologie*, p. 4.
48. Georges Sorel, *La Décomposition du Marxisme* (Paris: Marcel Rivière, 1926), p. 11. On Sorel's importance for the left, see Madeleine Rebérioux, 'La place de Georges Sorel dans le socialisme au tournant du siècle', Jacques Julliard and Schlomo Sand (eds), *Georges Sorel en son temps* (Paris: Seuil, 1995), p. 38.

49. Georges Sorel, *Réflexions sur la violence* (1910) (Paris: Seuil, 1990), p. 79.
50. Jack Roth, *The Cult of Violence: Sorel and the Sorelians* (London and Stanford: University of California Press, 1980), p. 244.
51. Their early history has been recounted in detail by their leader Maurice Pujo in *Les Camelots du Roi* (Paris: Flammarion, 1933).
52. Christopher Forth describes them as exemplifying a new culture of force in the early twentieth century. Forth, *The Dreyfus Affair and the Crisis of French Manhood* (London and Baltimore: Johns Hopkins University Press, 2003), pp. 203–4.
53. See Jessica Wardhaugh, 'Un Rire nouveau: Action Française and the Art of Political Satire', *French History* 22 (2008), pp. 79–94.
54. 'P.P. 16 novembre 1932: Réunion de rentrée des Camelots du Roi et Commissaires d'Action Française', APP, Ba 1874.
55. Léon Daudet, *Paris vécu* (Paris: Gallimard, 1969), p. 27.
56. 'P.P. 16 novembre 1932', APP, Ba 1874.
57. Charles Maurras, *La Contre-Révolution spontanée* (Paris: H. Lardanchet, 1943), p. 26.
58. 'Personifying the *pays réel*, the street had won a complete victory.' *La Contre-Révolution*, p. 189. See *Action Française*, 13 February 1934 for Charles Maurras's exposition of the distinction between the *pays légal* and the *pays réel*.
59. Maurras, *La Contre-Révolution*, p. 99.
60. Maurras, *La Contre-Révolution*, p. 20.
61. Steven Wilson, 'Action Française in French Intellectual Life', *The Historical Journal* 12 (1969), pp. 328–50.
62. Some even condemned the prevalence of rival 'doctrines' as one of the evils of the time. See the interview with Colonel de la Rocque in *Paris-Midi*, 29 March 1934.
63. See Kennedy, *Reconciling France against Democracy*.
64. Philippe Machefer, 'Les Croix de Feu', *L'Information Historique* 34–35 (1972–73), p. 29.
65. 'Tracts et documents du mouvement des Croix de Feu et du Parti Social Français dirigés par le Colonel de la Rocque 1934–39' (BN).
66. Nobécourt, *Le Colonel de la Rocque*, p. 11; and Kennedy, *Reconciling France against Democracy*, pp. 26–30.
67. '17 février 1934', APP, Ba 1941.
68. Georges Cormont, 'Au-dessus des clans: enfin l'union se réalise', *Journal de la Solidarité Française, mouvement national et social*, 25 August 1934, APP, Ba 1960.
69. 'P.P. 13 juillet 1935', APP, Ba 1907.
70. His enigmatic character has been commented on by his son and by his biographer. Du Réau, *Édouard Daladier*, p. 12.
71. See *Le Journal officiel*, 7 February 1934.
72. Kennedy, *Reconciling France against Democracy*, pp. 45–6.
73. Du Réau, *Édouard Daladier*, p. 126.
74. *L'Ami du Peuple*, 15 March 1934.
75. *Action Française*, 7 February 1934.
76. *Action Française*, 7 February 1934.

77. *Action Française*, 10 February 1934.
78. *Action Française*, 7 February 1934.
79. *Je suis partout*, 10 February 1934. Gaxotte's mention of the 'bloody week' (semaine sanglante) was a reference to the 'semaine sanglante' following the repression of the Paris Commune, during which an estimated 20,000 died.
80. *Je suis partout*, 10 February 1934.
81. *Je suis partout*, 10 February 1934.
82. *Action Française*, 13 February 1934.
83. Louis Mouilleseaux, 'Le Gouvernement de demain', *Journal de la Solidarité Française*, 25 August 1934 (APP, Ba 1960).
84. *Je suis partout*, 10 February 1934.
85. *Action Française*, 7 February 1934. In fact, Action Française was better known than the Communists for its attacks on the 'statuemania' of the Third Republic. See Neil McWilliam, 'Conflicting manifestations: Parisian commemoration of Joan of Arc and Étienne Dolet in the early Third Republic', *French Historical Studies* 27 (2004), pp. 381–419; and Wardhaugh, 'Un Rire nouveau', p. 90.
86. *Je suis partout*, 10 February 1934.
87. *Je suis partout*, 10 February 1934.
88. *Action Française*, 13 February 1934.
89. La Rocque, *Les Annales politiques et littéraires*, 2 March 1934.
90. *L'Ère nouvelle*, 7 February 1934.
91. *La Lumière*, 10 February 1934.
92. *La Lumière*, 17 February 1934; *L'Ère nouvelle*, 13 February 1934.
93. *L'Humanité*, 6 February 1934; *La Vie Ouvrière*, 26 January 1934.
94. *Le Populaire*, 7 February 1934.
95. *L'Humanité*, 7 February 1934. Communist participation in the riot of 6 February was later denied. See Jacques Duclos, introduction to Jacques Chambaz, *Le Front Populaire, pour le pain, la liberté et la paix* (Paris: Éditions Sociales, 1961), p. 33.
96. *Le Populaire*, 9 February 1934. The reference was to Marcel Pagnol's recent play *Topaze*, in which the eponymous upright schoolmaster advances in life by abandoning his maxims entirely.
97. *L'Humanité*, 13 February 1934.
98. *Le Populaire*, 13 February 1934.
99. *L'Humanité*, 18 February 1934.
100. *L'Humanité*, 13 February 1934. The Communists blamed the government for the injuries and deaths resulting from encounters with the police.
101. *Le Populaire*, 10 February 1934.
102. *Le Travailleur Parisien*, 138–40 (January–March 1934), ACGT, Box 22.
103. *L'Humanité*, 18 February 1934.
104. *L'Humanité*, 14 February 1934.
105. *L'Humanité*, 14 February 1934.
106. *L'Humanité*, 13 February 1934.
107. *L'Humanité*, 17 February 1934.
108. *Le Populaire*, 13 February 1934.
109. *Le Populaire*, 10 February 1934.
110. *Le Populaire*, 6 February 1934.

111. *Le Populaire*, 13 February 1934.
112. *Le Travailleur Parisien*, 138–140 (January–March 1934).
113. *Le Populaire*, 7 February 1934.
114. Paul Vaillant Couturier in *L'Humanité*, 19 February 1934.
115. *L'Humanité*, 13 February 1934.
116. *L'Humanité*, 18 February 1934.
117. 'Lettre au Président du Conseil', ACGT 22, Dossier 2, 'février 1934'. Eugène Frot was Minister of the Interior at the time of the February riots.
118. *Le Flambeau*, 6 February 1936.
119. *L'Ami du Peuple*, 28 April 1934.
120. 'P.P. 7 mai 1935: réunion privée organisée par la Solidarité Française le 6 mai', APP, Ba 1960.
121. Jean-Richard Bloch, 'Commentaire: le 12 février', *Europe, revue mensuelle* 15 March 1934.
122. Emmanuel Berl, 'Jeune France', *Marianne*, 14 February 1934.
123. Bloch, 'Commentaire'.
124. Pierre Favre (ed.), *La Manifestation* (Paris: Presses de la FNSP, 1990); Tartakowsky, *Les Manifestations de rue*; and Alain Corbin et al., *Les Usages politiques des fêtes aux XIX–XX siècles* (Paris: Publications de la Sorbonne, 1994).
125. Berl, 'Jeune France'.
126. Jean-Richard Bloch, *Carnaval est mort: premiers essais pour mieux comprendre mon temps* (Paris: Éditions de la NRF, 1920), p. 121.
127. *Le Journal officiel*, 16 February 1934.
128. Monnet, *Refaire la République*, pp. 311–12.
129. *Le Journal officiel*, 16 February 1934.
130. *Le Journal officiel*, 16 February 1934, 20 February 1934, and 23 February 1934.
131. *Le Journal officiel*, 20 February 1934.

2 A Double Mobilization Against the Established Disorder, 1934–36

1. 'Paris, le 13 juillet, voie TSF', AN, F7 13305. The interview also appeared in *Action Française* on 13 July 1935.
2. The phrase was coined by the philosopher Emmanuel Mounier. Michel Barlow, *Le Socialisme d'Emmanuel Mounier* (Toulouse: Privat, 1971), p. 38.
3. Antoine Prost's recent synthesis of his work on social movements in this period moves directly from the foreshadowing of the Popular Front in February 1934 to the strikes of spring 1936, and does not discuss the popular organizations or aspirations of the right. The 'double mobilisation' of 1934–36 is likewise difficult to locate in Robert Soucy's detailed and thematic study of right-wing organizations in this period. Prost, *Autour du Front populaire*, p. 70. Soucy, *French Fascism*.
4. Philippe Burrin's article on the contagion of political symbolism during the Popular Front offers an analysis of rhetorical and ritual borrowings, but contrasts the French left with the (German) fascist right, rather than considering its French rivals. Philippe Burrin, 'Poings levés et bras tendus: la

contagion des symboles au temps du Front populaire', *Vingitème siècle* 11 (1986), pp. 7–20.

5. See, for example, Ruth Ben-Ghiat, *Fascist Modernities: Italy, 1922–1945* (Berkeley and London: University of California Press, 2001); Günter Berghaus (ed.), *Fascism and Theatre: Comparative Studies on the Aesthetics and Politics of Performance* (Oxford: Berghahn, 1996); and Eric Hobsbawm, writing in the foreword to Dawn Ades (ed.), *Art and Power: Europe under the Dictators 1930–45* (London: Thames and Hudson, 1995).

6. 'La Semaine radicale', *L'Ère nouvelle*, 25 May 1936. On the important influence of Communist and Socialist municipal authorities on local political culture, see Margairaz and Tartakowsky, '*L'Avenir nous appartient*', p. 61.

7. See, for example, John Santore, 'The Comintern's United Front initiative of May 1934: French or Soviet inspiration?' *Canadian Journal of Modern History* 16 (1987), pp. 405–21.

8. The peasants were an increasingly important target for Communist propaganda. See Marcel Cachin's article in *L'Humanité*, 3 September 1934.

9. *Le Travailleur Parisien*, 140 (March 1934), ACGT, Carton 23.

10. Susan Whitney, 'Embracing the status quo: French Communists, young women and the Popular Front', *Journal of Social History* 30 (1996), p. 29.

11. Jean-Pierre Bernard, *Le Parti Communiste Français et la question littéraire 1921–39* (Grenoble: Presses Universitaires de Grenoble, 1972), p. 150.

12. Nicole Racine and Michel Trebitsch, 'Dossier: la revue *Europe*', *Lendemains*, 86–7 (1997), pp. 93–107; Régis Antoine, *La Littérature pacifiste et internationaliste française 1915–35* (Paris: L'Harmattan, 2002); Géraldi Leroy and Anne Roche, *Les Écrivains et le Front populaire* (Paris: Presses de la FNSP, 1986); and Anne Roche and Christian Tarting, *Des Années trente: groupes et ruptures* (Paris: Éditions du CNRS, 1985).

13. Quoted by Serge Wolikow, *Le Front Populaire en France* (Paris: Éditions Complexe, 1996), p. 198.

14. This manifesto was reprinted in full in *Europe, revue mensuelle* on 15 April 1934. For an overview of the CVIA's activity in this period, see Nicole Racine-Furland, 'Le Comité de Vigilance des Intellectuels Antifascistes 1934–39: anti-fascisme et pacifisme', *Mouvement Social* 101 (1977), pp. 88–114; and Jean-Paul Gautier, 'L'Antifascisme en France dans les années 1930', in Grason et al. (eds), *Éclats du Front populaire*, pp. 151–60.

15. Racine-Furland, 'Le CVIA', p. 89.

16. Jean-François Gelly, 'À la recherche de l'unité organique: la démarche du Parti communiste français, 1934–38', *Mouvement Social* 121 (1982), p. 101.

17. Ory, *La Belle Illusion*, p. 103.

18. Jacques Kergoat, *La France du Front populaire* (Paris: Éditions de la Découverte, 1986), p. 368. The Mur des Fédérés in the Père-Lachaise cemetery in Paris marks the place where the Communards were executed in 1871.

19. Both films are conserved at the Bibliothèque Nationale.

20. E. Cerquant in *L'Humanité*, 31 January 1936.

21. 'P.P. 2 février 1935', APP, Ba 1960.

22. 'Mouvement des Croix de Feu', APP, Ba 1973.

23. 'P.P. 6 décembre 1935', APP, Ba 1960.

24. Kennedy, *Reconciling France Against Democracy*, p. 89.

25. 'P.P. 9 novembre 1935', APP, Ba 1960.

26. *Le Courrier d'Alsace*, 1 July 1935, AN, F7 13305.
27. 'P.P. 31 octobre 1935', APP, Ba 1960.
28. 'Sommaire du Francisme', APP, Ba 1907.
29. '1934, Correspondance et rapports d'ensemble', APP, Ba 1960.
30. *Le Bulletin officiel*, 6 July 1934, p. 2502, APP, Ba 1901.
31. *Le Populaire*, 15 July 1935. In October 1935, the police noted that Colonel de la Rocque had indeed rented a substantial townhouse from the Comtesse de Mortemart at 3, Avenue George V in Paris for the use of his Croix de Feu and Briscards. 'P.P. 19 octobre 1935', APP, Ba 1901.
32. *Le Flambeau*, 6 February 1936.
33. La Rocque in *Le Flambeau*, 1 January 1935.
34. 'P.P. février 1936', APP, Ba 1893.
35. The 'dispos' were established in 1931 by Maurice Genay. 'Rapport de Police, avril 1936', APP, Ba 1973.
36. 'Rapport sur le mouvement des Croix de Feu', APP, Ba 1973.
37. Parliamentary debate, *Le Bulletin officiel*, 6 July 1934. The Croix de Feu also received financial support from a number of electricity, transport, and steel companies.
38. *Le Flambeau*, 26 May 1935 and 6 June 1935.
39. The role of women within the Croix de Feu has been studied by Cheryl Koos and Danielle Sarnoff, although they focus more on rhetoric than on activity. Koos and Sarnoff, 'France', in Kevin Passmore (ed.), *Women, Gender and Fascism in Europe, 1918–45* (Manchester: Manchester University Press, 2003), pp. 168–89.
40. 'P.P. 2 juin 1936', APP, Ba 1901.
41. 'P.P. 10 juillet 1935', APP, Ba 1901.
42. 'P.P. 9 décembre 1935', APP, Ba 1902.
43. Reproduced in full in Madeleine Rebérioux, 'Théâtre d'agitation: le Groupe Octobre', in *Mouvement Social*, 91 (1975), pp. 112–19.
44. *La Lumière*, 23 February 1935.
45. *Le Flambeau*, 9 March 1935.
46. 'P.P. 8 mars 1936', APP, Ba 1901.
47. M. Kieffer, speaking at the Centre Social Français in March 1936, 'P.P. 1 mars 1936', APP, Ba 1901.
48. 'Rapport sur le mouvement des Croix de Feu', APP, Ba 1973.
49. 'Rapport sur le mouvement des Croix de Feu', APP, Ba 1973.
50. Danielle Tartakowsky suggests in particular that the festivals of the right lacked the cultural innovation of the PCF and of the Popular Front more broadly. 'Les Fêtes de la droite populaire', Alain Corbin, Noëlle Gérôme, and Danielle Tartakowksy (eds), *Les Usages politiques des fêtes*, p. 314.
51. Tartakowksy, *Les Manifestations*, p. 412.
52. Charles Vallin recalled the making of the Croix de Feu films in *L'Activité du Parti Social Français* (Paris: PSF, 1937), p. 26.
53. 'P.P. 8 décembre 1935', APP, Ba 1902.
54. 'P.P. 10 février 1936', APP, Ba 1902.
55. Jean-Paul Llausu in *Le Flambeau*, 4 January 1936.
56. Kergoat, *La France du Front populaire*, p. 370.
57. For the theatrical activity of the Camelots du Roi, see Bibliothèque Nationale, Arts du Spectacle (hereafter ASP), Rt 3794, Théâtre d'Action française. See also Wardhaugh, 'Un Rire Nouveau'.

58. 'P.P. 4 avril 1935', APP, Ba 1893.
59. 'Spectacle de l'Œillet blanc, le 9 juin 1932', ASP, Rt 3794.
60. 'P.P. 9 mars 1931', APP, Ba 1901.
61. 'P.P. 9 janvier 1936', APP, Ba 1902.
62. 'Les Chants francistes no.3: le chant des travailleurs', APP, Ba 1907.
63. 'P.P. 17 août 1936', APP, Ba 1902.
64. Wolikow, *Le Front Populaire en France*, p. 197.
65. George Henry, *Le Drapeau tricolore, les Croix de Feu* (Paris: Jouve, 1935); and Gérard Jaussaud, *Aurores Croix de Feu* (Caen: SIBN, 1936).
66. The poems referred to here are 'L'Anniversaire', 'Impuissance', and 'Feu de camp' respectively.
67. Kennedy, *Reconciling France against Democracy*, p. 63.
68. Jeannine Verdès-Leroux, 'The intellectual extreme right in the thirties', in Edward Arnold (ed.), *The Development of the Radical Right in France* (Basingstoke: Macmillan, 2000), pp. 119–32.
69. The dramatic and literary criticism of Action Française journalists has been studied by Paul Renard in *L'Action française et la vie littéraire, 1931–44* (Lille: Presses Universitaires du Septentrion, 2003).
70. Christian Delporte, *Intellectuels et Politique* (Paris: Casterman, 1995), p. 50.
71. Tartakowsky, *Les Manifestations*, p. 308.
72. For further details, see Jessica Wardhaugh, 'Fighting for the streets of Paris during the Popular Front, 1934–38', in Jessica Wardhaugh (ed.), *Paris and the Right in the Twentieth Century* (Newcastle: Cambridge Scholars' Publishing, 2007), pp. 43–63.
73. Tartakowsky, *Les Manifestations*, p. 350.
74. The Latin Quarter was, however, generally seen as a stronghold of the right, and left-wing demonstrators in this area were often insulted or attacked by bands of student members of Action Française.
75. *Le Bulletin officiel*, 6 July 1934, p. 2503.
76. 'Lettre du Président du Conseil, Ministre de l'Intérieur, à M. le Préfet de Police, 28 janvier 1935, au sujet d'une réunion Croix de Feu au Havre', APP, Ba 1901.
77. 'Juillet 1929', AN, F7 13119.
78. *La Lumière*, 16 November 1935. On rival conceptions of nation in the 1930s, see Jessica Wardhaugh, 'Fighting for the unknown soldier: The contested territory of the French nation, 1934–38', *Modern and Contemporary France* 15 (May 2007), pp. 185–201.
79. *La Fête de Jeanne d'Arc, 1935*, Centre National de la Cinématographie, Bois D'Arcy (hereafter CNC).
80. *L'Humanité*, 21 May 1935.
81. *L'Humanité*, 21 May 1935.
82. *Le Populaire*, 20 May 1935.
83. 'Dans la coulisse du parlement', APP, Ba 1861.
84. 'Lettre du Ministre de l'Intérieur à MM. les Préfcts, 17 juin 1935', AN, F7 13305.
85. *L'Œuvre*, 13 July 1935.
86. 'Dans la coulisse du Parlement', APP, Ba 1861.
87. 'P.P. 12 juillet 1935', APP, Ba 1861.
88. *Front mondial*, 28 June 1935.

89. 'P.P. 13 juillet 1935', AN, F7 13305.
90. 'P.P. 28 juin 1935', AN, F7 13305.
91. *Le Populaire*, 11 July 1935.
92. *Dépêche Algérienne*, Algiers, 1 July 1935.
93. Jackson, *The Popular Front*, p. 41.
94. 'P.P. 5 juin 1935', AN, F7 13305.
95. *Front mondial*, July 1935.
96. Georges Lefranc, *Les Gauches en France 1789-1972* (Paris: Payot, 1973), p. 217.
97. Dell, *The Image of the Popular Front*, p. 60.
98. Abbé Sieyès, *Qu'est-ce que le Tiers État?* (Paris, 1789).
99. See Chapter 1.
100. 'P.P. 13 juillet 1935', AN, F7 13305.
101. 'P.P. 14 juillet 1935', AN, F7 13305.
102. *Le Populaire*, 15 July 1935.
103. *Le Populaire*, 15 July 1935.
104. The Fête de la Fédération took place on 14 July 1790 on the Champ de Mars, a year after the storming of the Bastille. It was a grand assembly of delegates from across France, chosen from regional sections of the National Guard. Mass was celebrated by Talleyrand, Bishop of Autun, and oaths to the new constitution (not implemented until 1791) were sworn by Lafayette, captain of the National Guard in Paris, by Louis XVI, and by his family. When the Third Republic instituted 14 July as a national holiday, this was to commemorate 1790 rather than 1789.
105. 'P.P. 12 juillet 1935', APP, Ba 1860.
106. Coincidentally, the funeral of Alfred Dreyfus was held on the afternoon of 14 July 1935 in the Montparnasse cemetery.
107. 'P.P. 14 juillet 1935', AN, F7 13305.
108. 'P.P. 14 juillet 1935', AN, F7 13305.
109. Jacques Duclos, introduction to Chambaz, *Le Front populaire*. This was increasingly characteristic of the PCF, as Daniel Brower demonstrates in *The New Jacobins: The French Communist Party and the Popular Front* (New York: Cornell University Press, 1968).
110. 'P.P. 14 juillet 1935', AN, F7 13305.
111. 'P.P. 14 juillet 1935', APP, Ba 1860.
112. 'P.P. 14 juillet 1935', APP, Ba 1860.
113. André Wurmser, 'Les temps heureux', *Cahiers du Communisme*, 9 (1966), p. 189.
114. *Le Peuple*, 15 July 1935.
115. *La Lumière*, 15 July 1935.
116. 'P.P. 6 juillet 1935', AN, F7 13305.
117. 'P.P. 1 juillet 1935', AN, F7 13305.
118. *L'Ami du Peuple*, 6 July 1935.
119. *L'Ami du Peuple*, 10 July 1935.
120. *Action Française*, 6 July 1935.
121. *Je suis partout*, 13 July 1935.
122. *Action Française*, 28 July 1935.
123. *Action Française*, 9 July 1935.
124. *Je suis partout*, 13 July 1935.

125. *Action Française*, 10 July 1935.
126. *Le Flambeau*, 11 May 1935.
127. 'P.P. 20 juin 1935', APP, Ba 1893.
128. Tartakowsky, *Les Manifestations*, p. 342.
129. 'P.P. 6 juillet 1935', AN, F7 13305.
130. 'P.P. 28 juin 1935', AN, F7 13305.
131. 'P.P. 25 juin 1935', AN, F7 13241.
132. 'P.P. 13 juillet 1935', AN, F7 13305.
133. 'P.P. 13 juillet 1935', AN, F7 13305.
134. *Le Flambeau*, 20 July 1935.
135. *Le Flambeau*, 20 July 1935.
136. *L'Ami du Peuple*, 14 July 1935.
137. 'Deuxième séance du 13 février', *Journal officiel*, 14 February 1936.
138. *L'Humanité*, 17 February 1936.
139. 'P.P. 17 février 1936', APP, Ba 1862.
140. *À bas Sarraut!* (tract produced by the Groupes d'Action Révolutionnaire), APP, Ba 1862.
141. 'Circulaire, 16 février 1936', APP, Ba 1862.
142. *Le Populaire*, 17 February 1936.
143. *Le Populaire*, 17 February 1936.
144. *La Lumière*, 22 February 1936.
145. 'Le mouvement des Croix de Feu', APP, Ba 1973.
146. See the speech by Georges Cousin on 21 February in *Le Journal officiel*, 22 February 1936.
147. *Le Journal officiel*, 22 February 1936.
148. The Communist Arthur Ramette attacked Philippe Henriot, a defender of the leagues, on 21 February.

3 'His Majesty the People'? Elections, Strikes, and the Perils of Victory in 1936

1. René Belin in *Le Peuple*, 12 June 1936.
2. See Chapter 1.
3. Jean Chiappe was the Prefect of Police in Paris between 1927 and 1934; he was then elected President of the Municipal Council of Paris in 1935 and deputy in 1936.
4. *Le Populaire*, 10 May 1936. Similar images appeared in other Popular Front newspapers. *La Lumière* pictured a giant 'man of the people' standing on an undersized capitalist, watched by an approving Marianne (2 May 1936).
5. Capa, *Front Populaire*; Ronis, *Premiers Congés payés et loisirs divers* and *Défilés, grèves, et manifestations avant 1938*.
6. *Léon Blum before his judges at the Supreme Court of Riom, 11 and 12 March 1942* (London: Routledge, 1942), p. 98.
7. *L'Humanité*, 30 May 1936.
8. *La Révolution prolétarienne*, 10 June 1936. Weil, an intellectual with anarchist sympathies, had worked in a factory in 1934–35.
9. Antoine Prost, for example, describes the strikes as a mythical experience, while Jacques Girault emphasizes their restoration of working-class pride.

Prost, *Autour du Front populaire*, p. 97, and Girault, *Au-devant du Bonheur: les Français et le Front populaire* (Paris: CIDE, 2006), p. 105. For similar assessments, see Jackson, *The Popular Front in France* (1988); Tartakowsky, *Le Front populaire* (1996); Berstein, *La France des années 30* (2001); and Margairaz and Tartakowsky, *'L'Avenir nous appartient'* (2006).

10. Berstein, *La France des années 30*, pp. 114–15.
11. Dell, as a Gramscian art historian, argues that the Popular Front's image of a classless people was challenged by the more militant images in the Communist magazine *Regards* and in the (former) CGTU newspaper *La Vie ouvrière*, leading the Popular Front to over-emphasize the festival character of the strikes. Dell, *The Image of the Popular Front*, Chapter Three, pp. 92–127. See also Simon Dell: 'Festival and revolution: the Popular Front in France and the press coverage of the strikes of 1936', *Art History* 23 (2000) pp. 599–621.
12. 'Chiffres donnés à M. le Directeur du Cabinet de M. le Ministre de l'Intérieur, 7 juillet 1936', APP, Ba 1874.
13. The English version, *Léon Blum Before His Judges at the Supreme Court of Riom*, was prefaced by Clement Attlee, who described Léon Blum's speeches as a dramatic defence of socialism and democracy.
14. *Léon Blum Before His Judges*, p. 52.
15. *Léon Blum Before His Judges*, p. 135.
16. Dell, for example, underlines the right's sceptical reception of the Popular Front's image of the people as a 'façade concealing revolution'. Dell, *The Image of the Popular Front*, p. 117.
17. On 11 and 18 April 1936, *La Documentation catholique* reproduced the manifestos of the following groups and parties presenting or endorsing candidates for the elections, thus facilitating their comparison: Parti Communiste Français, Parti Démocrate Populaire, Parti Néo-Socialiste de France, Alliance Démocratique, Royalistes d'Action Française, Parti Socialiste, Union Républicaine du Sénat, Parti National Populaire, Alliance Nationale pour l'Accroissement de la Population Française, Comité d'Entente des Grandes Associations pour l'Union Nationale, Croix de Feu, Fédération Nationale Catholique, Front Laïque, Front National, Front Paysan, Jeune-République, Ligue de l'Éducation Française, Ligue Maritime et Coloniale, Mouvement Fédéraliste, Union Nationale des Combattants, Confédération Nationale des Anciens Combattants, Comité de Salut Économique.
18. There is a copy of the film at the Bibliothèque Nationale.
19. *En avant pour une France libre, forte, heureuse! Manifeste du VIIIe Congrès du Parti Communiste* (Villerbanne: PCF, 1936).
20. This has been emphasized by Susan Whitney, who notes that Communist policy towards women and the family related very closely to that proposed by the Family Code of 29 July 1939. 'Embracing the status quo', pp. 25-53. The broader consensus on the depopulation crisis has been widely evoked, for example by Paul Dutton in *Origins of the French Welfare State: The Struggle for Social Reform in France, 1914-1947* (Cambridge: Cambridge University Press, 2002), p. 138.
21. 'Manifestation organisée par le comité de coordination d'Issy-les-Moulineaux à l'occasion de l'inauguration d'une plaque commémorative de la Commune, le 10 mai 1936', AN, F7 13983.
22. 'P.P. 30 avril 1936', AN, F7 13983.

23. *Action Française*, 23 April 1936.

24. The programmes of both leagues and parties were published in *La Documentation catholique* on 11 and 18 April 1936.
25. Colonel de la Rocque, *Elections législatives de 1936: Manifeste Croix de Feu – Pour le peuple, par le peuple* (n.p., 1936), p. 4.
26. *Pour le peuple, par le peuple*, p. 8.
27. Paul Christophe, *1936, les catholiques et le Front populaire* (Paris: Éditions Ouvrières, 1989), p. 12.
28. The Fédération Nationale Catholique noted with some alarm that by the time of the elections in 1936, the ideas of the left had already made substantial progress among Catholic groups in Paris, particularly among students and professors at the Institut Catholique. 'P.P. 15 mai 1936', APP, Ba 1953.
29. J. Mora, *M. Ducos et la gratuité: servir ou asservir le peuple?* (Paris, n.d.), p. 5 (APP, Ba 1905).
30. Jean Le Cour Grandmaison, *Catholiques et Communistes: la main tendue* (n.p., n.d.), p. 6 (APP, Ba 1905). Le Cour Grandmaison observed that similar debates had taken place between Catholics and the left in the early twentieth century, following in the wake of Leo XIII's demand for a 'just wage' in the encyclical *Rerum Novarum*.
31. See, for example, *La Jeunesse Ouvrière*. Gaëtan Bernoville, a regular correspondent in the Fédération Nationale Catholique's newspaper *France catholique*, voiced such fears in his pamphlet *La Farce de la main tendue: du Frente Popular au Front populaire* (Paris: Grasset, 1937), and noted that, despite Maurice Thorez's conciliatory words, violent antipathy continued unabated between working-class Communists and Catholics in France (p. 91).
32. *Journal officiel*, 8 June 1936.
33. *Journal officiel*, 8 June 1936.
34. *Le Peuple*, 5 May 1936.
35. 'P.P. 30 mai 1936' and 'P.P. 31 mai 1936', AN, F7 13983.
36. 'P.P. 25 mai 1936: au sujet de la manifestation au Mur des Fédérés', AN, F7 13983.
37. *Le Peuple*, 25 May 1936 and *Le Populaire*, 25 May 1936.
38. *Le Populaire*, 25 May 1936.
39. *Le Peuple*, 25 May 1936.
40. 'P.P. 14 mai 1936', AN, F7 13983.
41. *L'Ère nouvelle*, 25 May 1936.
42. 'P.P. 25 mai 1936', AN, F7 13983.
43. Du Réau, *Édouard Daladier*, p. 170.
44. 'P.P. 5 juin 1936', APP, Ba 1874.
45. *Action Française*, 1 June 1936.
46. *Action Française*, 25 May 1936.
47. *Le Temps*, 25 May 1936.
48. See *Le Flambeau*, 16 May 1936, and *Action Française*, 11 May 1936.
49. *Le Flambeau*, 16 May 1936.
50. Jackson, *The Popular Front*, p. 85.
51. 'P.P. 4 juin 1936', APP, Ba 1874 and 'P.P. 5 juin 1936', APP, Ba 1874.
52. 'P.P. 5 juin 1936', APP, Ba 1874.
53. 'P.P. 5 juin 1936', APP, Ba 1874.

54. 'P.P. 13 juin 1936', APP, Ba 1874.
55. *La Lumière*, 6 June 1936.
56. *L'Ère nouvelle*, 5 June 1936.
57. *L'Ère nouvelle*, 13 May 1936.
58. *Le Populaire*, 6 June 1936.
59. *Le Peuple*, 12 June 1936.
60. *Le Peuple*, special edition of 1 May 1936, ACGT, Box 22.
61. *La Vie ouvrière*, 5 June 1936.
62. *L'Humanité*, 28 May 1936.
63. *L'Expérience Blum: un an du Front populaire* (Paris: Éditions du Sagittaire, 1937), p. 31.
64. Tartakowsky, *Les Manifestation*, p. 399.
65. *Grèves d'occupation* (CGT, 1936) (BN).
66. *Le Populaire*, 29 May 1936.
67. *Le Populaire*, 8 June 1936.
68. See, for example, Prost, *Autour du Front populaire*, p. 92.
69. 'A.S. des associations de défense économique', APP, Ba 1874.
70. J. Kolbloom, *La Revanche des patrons: le patronat face au Front populaire* (Paris: Flammarion, 1986), p. 349.
71. 'P.P. 8 juin 1936', APP, Ba 1874.
72. 'P.P. 14 mai 1936', AN, F7 13983. The projects were curtailed by the dissolution of the league in June 1936.
73. 'P.P. 2 juin 1936', APP, Ba 1901.
74. Christophe, *Les Catholiques*, p. 108.
75. *Le Flambeau*, numéro hors série, 4 June 1936.
76. *Je suis partout*, 4 July 1936.
77. 'P.P. 9 juin 1936: réunion organisée par le PNP, salons de l'Hôtel du Louvre, Place du Palais Royal, le 8 juin', APP, Ba 1941.
78. 'P.P. 8 juin 1936', APP, Ba 1874.
79. *Le Peuple*, 18 June 1936.
80. 'P.P. 18 juin 1936', APP, Ba 1901.
81. 'The French bourgeois will awaken; shaken out of his passivity, he will act differently from the Russian bourgeois of 1917. He will show of what regeneration he is capable, shoulder to shoulder with his rural, peasant brothers.' *Le Flambeau*, 13 June 1936.
82. *Je suis partout*, 13 June 1936.
83. *Je suis partout*, 13 June 1936.
84. *Action Française*, 28 May 1936.
85. *Le Flambeau*, 18 July 1936.
86. *Action Française*, 1 June 1936.
87. Dell's *The Image of the Popular Front* can also be situated in this tradition.
88. Daniel Guérin, *Front populaire, révolution manquée: témoignage militant* (Paris: Maspero, 1970).
89. Jacques Danos and Marcel Gibelin, *June '36: Class struggle and the Popular Front in France* (London: Bookmarks, 1986), p. 236.
90. Jacques Kergoat, *Marceau Pivert, socialiste de gauche* (Paris: Éditions Ouvrières, 1994), p. 100.
91. Marceau Pivert, *La Révolution avant la guerre* (Paris: Nouveau Prométhée, 1936), p. 13.

92. Jean Zyromski, *Sur le Chemin de l'unité* (Paris: Nouveau Prométhée, 1936), p. 50.

92. Jean Zyromski, *Sur le Chemin de l'unité* (Paris: Nouveau Prométhée, 1936), p. 50.
93. 'P.P. 23 mai 1936: transmission d'une brochure éditée par les Jeunesses Socialistes Révolutionnaires', AN, F7 13983.
94. 'P.P. mai 1936: au sujet des Groupes d'Action Révolutionnaire', APP, Ba 1939.
95. 'P.P. mai 1936', APP, Ba 1939.
96. 'P.P. 5 juillet 1936', APP, Ba 1874.
97. 'P.P. mai 1936', APP, Ba 1939.
98. Kergoat, *Marceau Pivert*, p. 107.
99. Pivert, *La Révolution avant la guerre*, p. 19.

4 The Challenge from the Right: The Parti Social Français and the Parti Populaire Français

1. 'P.P. 5 juillet 1936', APP, Ba 1874.
2. In January 1936 Charles Maurras published an article in *Action Française* in which he implied that kitchen knives should be used against national enemies. After the attack on Léon Blum on 13 February by dissidents from Action Française, this article was interpreted as an incitement to murder, leading to Maurras' arrest and imprisonment.
3. 'P.P. 5 juillet 1936', APP, Ba 1874.
4. Ory, *La Belle Illusion*, p. 797 and Girault, *Au-devant du Bonheur*, p. 127.
5. On their activities, see Siân Reynolds, 'Women and the Popular Front in France: The case of the three women ministers', *French History* 8 (1994), pp. 196–224.
6. On the image of sovereignty, see Tartakowsky, *Les Manifestations*, p. 398, and on the more combative image of the Spanish republicans, see Dell, *The Image of the Popular Front*, p. 147.
7. On the PPF, see Jean-Paul Brunet, *Jacques Doriot: du communisme au fascisme* (Paris: Éditions Balland, 1986); Dieter Wolf, *Doriot: du communisme à la collaboration* (Paris: Fayard, 1969); Gilbert Allardyce, 'Jacques Doriot et l'esprit fasciste en France', *Revue d'Histoire de la Deuxième Guerre Mondiale* 97 (1975), pp. 33–41; and Laurent Kestel, 'The emergence of anti-semitism within the PPF: Party intellectuals, peripheral leaders and national figures', *French History* 19 (2005), pp. 364–84. On the PSF, see Nobécourt, *Le Colonel de la Rocque*, Irvine; 'Fascism in France'; and Soucy, *French Fascism*. Kennedy's *Reconciling France Against Democracy* explicitly moves away from the question of political classification.
8. 'P.P. 30 mai 1936: XXXIIIème congrès national du Parti Socialiste SFIO, Gymnase Huyghens (XIVe) les 30, 31 mai, 1 et 2 juin (1ère journée, séance du matin)', AN, F7 13983.
9. 'A.S. des comités locaux du Front Populaire, 14 mai 1936', AN, F7 13983.
10. *L'Humanité*, 15 June 1936.
11. 'Correspondance, 6 juin 1936: A.S. de la manifestation du 14 juin', APP, Ba 1862.
12. 'Manifestation populaire organisée par le PC au Vélodrome Buffalo, le 14 juin', APP, Ba 1862. The ambiguity of Communist discourse was echoed in concurrent attacks on those wearing tricolour symbols, a matter heatedly discussed in parliament. *Le Journal officiel*, 1 July 1936.

13. *Le Populaire*, 15 July 1936.
14. 'Programme des fêtes du 14 juillet 1936: pain, paix, liberté', APP, F60 475.
15. 'Note du sous-secrétaire d'État de l'Organisation des Loisirs et des Sports à M. le Ministre de l'Éducation Nationale', AN, F60 475.
16. 'Le Président du Conseil à M. le Ministre des Postes, Télégraphes et Téléphones, 10 juillet 1936', AN, F60 475.
17. *L'Œuvre*, 15 July 1936.
18. 'P.P. 24 juillet 1936', APP, Ba 1862.
19. 'Programme des fêtes du 14 juillet 1936: pain, paix, liberté', APP, F60 475.
20. *La Vie ouvrière*, 24 July 1936.
21. *L'Œuvre*, 15 July 1936.
22. *L'Œuvre*, 15 July 1936.
23. *Le Populaire*, 15 July 1936.
24. *Le Populaire*, 15 July 1936.
25. 'Revendications du Rassemblement Populaire: revendications politiques', APP, Ba 1862.
26. 'A.S. d'un projet d'utilisation de la "Radio" par un gouvernement de Front populaire, 15 mai 1936', AN, F7 13983.
27. Georges and Émilie Lefranc, *La CGT et l'éducation ouvrière en France* (Genève: Bureau International du Travail, 1938), p. 8.
28. 'P.P. 2 mai 1936: A.S. du papillon édité par les JEUNES', AN, F7 13983.
29. *Journal officiel*, 1 July 1936.
30. 'P.P. 27 février 1936', APP, Ba 1941.
31. 'P.P. 14 juillet 1936', APP, Ba 1862.
32. Charles Vallin, *Le Parti Social Français* (Paris: CEDA, 1938), p. 11.
33. 'Déclaration, Parti Social Français', APP, Ba 1952.
34. 'P.P. le 12 juillet 1936: réunion du PSF, Salle Wagram, le 12 juillet', APP, Ba 1952.
35. Paul Chopine, *Le Colonel de la Rocque veut-il la guerre civile?* (Paris: Bureau d'Éditions, 1937), p. 4.
36. Only those who had been awarded the Légion d'Honneur or the Croix de Guerre were initially eligible to join the Croix de Feu, whereas membership of the Briscards was dependent on service in the front line. 'Les Croix de Feu et Briscards, extrait des statuts', BN, LB57 16185.
37. 'P.P. 12 juillet 1936: réunion du PSF', APP, Ba 1952.
38. *Le Flambeau*, 18 July 1936.
39. 'P.P. 12 juillet 1936: réunion du PSF', APP, Ba 1952.
40. *Le Flambeau*, 11 July 1936.
41. 'P.P. 9 juillet 1936', APP Ba 1902.
42. Charles Vallin, *L'Activité du Parti Social Français* (Paris: PSF, 1937), p. 27.
43. Vallin, *L'Activité du PSF*, p. 36.
44. *Réunion du PSF à Lille*, CNC.
45. This was the figure given by *Le Flambeau* on 12 July. According to the police, there were only 5500 people present. 'P.P. 12 juillet 1936: réunion du PSF, Salle Wagram', APP, Ba 1952.
46. *Le Flambeau*, 18 July 1936.
47. Wolf, *Doriot* and Brunet, *Jacques Doriot*. Paul Jankowski has studied the Marseilles branch of the PPF in *Communism and Collaboration: Simon Sabiani and Politics in Marseille 1919–44* (New York and London: Yale University

Press, 1989), charting the evolution of the movement from a political clan to a fascist party, and finally to a motley collection of opportunists and criminals.

48. See Laurent Kestel, 'L'engagement de Bertrand de Jouvenel au PPF,1936–38: Intellectuel de parti et entrepreneur politique', *French Historical Studies* 30 (2007), pp. 105–25.

49. Pierre Drieu la Rochelle, *Socialisme fasciste* (Paris. Gallimard, 1934).

50. Jacques Doriot, *La France ne sera pas un pays d'esclaves* (Paris: Les Œuvres Françaises, 1936), p. 80. Certainly his popular, working-class origins were as genuine as those of his Communist rival Maurice Thorez, the son of a grocer from a mining village in the Nord who had worked only intermittently and whose life was principally characterized by his work for the PCF.

51. Simon Sabiani, *La Colère du Peuple* (Paris: Les Œuvres Françaises, 1936), p. 25.

52. Kestel, 'L'engagement de Bertrand de Jouvenel', p. 106.

53. 'Bulletin du VIe arrondissement du PPF', APP, Ba 1945.

54. Doriot, *La France ne sera pas un pays d'esclaves*, p. 97.

55. Jacques Doriot, *La France avec nous* (Paris: Flammarion, 1937), p. 116.

56. Sabiani, *La Colère du Peuple*, p. 25.

57. Doriot, *La France ne sera pas un pays d'esclaves*, p. 128.

58. Doriot, *La France ne sera pas un pays d'esclaves*, p. 12.

59. Doriot, *La France ne sera pas un pays d'esclaves*, p. 130.

60. *L'Émancipation nationale*, 13 February 1937.

61. *L'Émancipation nationale*, 1 August 1936.

62. There are also occasional photographs in which the crowd greets Doriot or other PPF leaders with a raised fist.

63. Jacques Doriot, *La France avec nous*, p. 124.

64. *Le Populaire*, 30 June 1936.

65. *L'Humanité*, 30 June 1936.

66. *L'Humanité*, 12 July 1936.

67. Jean-Paul Brunet, *Saint-Denis, la Ville rouge: socialisme et communisme en banlieue ouvrière, 1890–1939* (Paris: Hachette, 1980), pp. 404–7.

68. Jean Guéhenno, *Jeunesse de la France* (Paris: Grasset, 1936), p. 58.

69. Guéhenno, *Jeunesse de la France*, p. 72.

70. PCF, *En avant pour une France libre, forte, heureuse!* (1936).

71. *La Victoire*, 7 July 1936. Maurice Barrès (1862–1923) was a nationalist writer who held particular reverence for the nation as 'the earth and the dead' (*la terre et les morts*).

72. *Bulletin Mensuel du Mouvement Croix de Feu du XVIIe arrondissement*, 1 May 1936, APP, Ba 1901.

73. For example, *Le Mouvement Croix de Feu au secours de l'agriculture française* (n.d.), APP, Ba 1901.

74. 'P.P. 9 juin 1936 (réunion organisée par le PNP) salons de l'Hôtel du Louvre, Place du Palais Royal, le 8 juin', APP, Ba 1941.

75. *Le Jour*, 1 July 1936.

76. *L'Humanité*, 15 July 1936.

77. *La Vie est à nous* (1936) (Bibliothèque Nationale).

78. 'P.P. 30 mai 1936: A.S. de la propagande parmi les paysans', APP, F7 13983.

79. 'Lettre de Christide Walleau au secrétaire de la CGT, 11 avril 1936', ACGT, Box 22.

80. Danielle Tartakowsky, 'Le cinéma militant des années trente: source pour l'histoire du Front populaire', *Les Cahiers de la Cinémathèque* 71 (2000), p. 32.
81. 'P.P. 7 mai 1936', AN, F7 13983.
82. Regionalism was also to be celebrated in the International Exhibition of the following year. See Peer, *France on Display*.
83. *Le Populaire*, 15 July 1936.
84. *L'Œuvre*, 15 July 1936.
85. *Le Journal officiel*, 7 June 1936.
86. *Le Peuple*, 8 June 1936.
87. *L'Émancipation nationale*, numéro spécial, 4 July 1936.
88. *L'Émancipation nationale*, 13 February 1937.
89. *Le Mouvement Croix de Feu au secours de l'agriculture française.*
90. Colonel de la Rocque, *Le Paysan sauvera la France avec le PSF* (Paris: PSF, 1937), p. 18.
91. Doriot, *La France ne sera pas un pays d'esclaves*, p. 124.
92. Doriot, *Refaire la France* (Paris: Grasset, 1938), p. 101.
93. Revier, 'Discours de Revier au premier Congrès National du PPF à Saint-Denis, les 9–10–11 novembre 1936', *Pour que la paysan français vive!* (Saint-Denis: PPF, 1936).
94. *L'Humanité*, 15 July 1936.
95. *Le Flambeau*, 1 January 1935 and 22 June 1935.
96. Charles Vallin, 'Rapport présenté au Congrès National du PSF, Lyon, novembre 1937', *L'Activité du PSF*, p. 7.
97. *Manifeste du Parti Populaire Français*, APP, Ba 1946.
98. Kennedy, *Reconciling France Against Democracy*, p. 153.
99. 'P.P. 14 juin 1936', APP, Ba 1901.
100. See Gordon, 'The back door of the nation state'.
101. PCF, *En avant pour une France libre, forte, heureuse!*
102. *L'Humanité*, 2 July 1936.
103. Maurice Thorez, 'Union de la Nation Française' (1936) in Thorez, *Une Politique de grandeur française* (Paris: Éditions Sociales, 1945), p. 73.
104. 'P.P. 17 juin 1936: réunion organisée par la huitième section des Croix de Feu', APP, Ba 1901.
105. Doriot, *La France ne sera pas un pays d'esclaves*, p. 120.
106. *Le Flambeau*, 18 July 1936.
107. 'P.P. 2 octobre 1936', APP, Ba 1899.
108. 'P.P. 31 octobre 1936' APP, Ba 1738.
109. 'Lettre du Ministre de l'Intérieur, Direction Générale de la Sûreté Nationale, à MM. les Préfets, le 8 octobre 1936', APP, Ba 1738.
110. *Le Populaire*, 2 October 1936.
111. 'Correspondance, le 3 octobre 1936', APP Ba 1863.
112. 'Correspondance, le 3 octobre 1936', APP, Ba 1863.
113. 'P.P. 4 octobre 1936', APP, Ba 1863.
114. 'Manifestation organisée par le Parti Communiste au Parc des Princes, 4 octobre 1936', APP, Ba 1863.
115. 'Manifestation organisée par le Parti Communiste', APP, Ba 1863.
116. 'P.P. 4 octobre 1936', APP, Ba 1863.
117. 'P.P. 4 octobre 1936', APP, Ba 1863.
118. *Le Journal*, 5 October 1936.
119. *Le Flambeau*, 10 October 1936.
120. *Le Matin*, 6 October 1936.

5   Building the Ideal City in Popular Culture, 1936–37

1. *Esprit*, 1 November 1937.
2. Vsevolod Meyerhold (1874–1940) had directed symbolist plays and opera in the early twentieth century, and became a Communist and a leading avant-garde director in 1917. His experimental theatre was not popular with Stalin, and he was executed in prison in 1940.
3. 'Lettre de Jacques Copeau à Jean-Richard Bloch, le 5 juillet 1937', 'Correspondance Jean-Richard Bloch–Jacques Copeau', *Revue d'Histoire du Théâtre* 44 (1992), p. 286.
4. Jean-Richard Bloch, 'Naissance d'une cité', in *Toulon et autres pièces* (Paris: Gallimard, 1948), Introduction, p. 199.
5. Ory, *La Belle Illusion*.
6. Tartakowsky, *Le Front populaire* and Jackson, *The Popular Front*, Chapter 4.
7. Tartakowsky, *Le Front populaire*, p. 110.
8. Ory, *La Belle Illusion*, p. 338.
9. *Le Populaire*, 4 October 1936.
10. 'P.P. 11 juillet 1936', APP, Ba 1952.
11. *L'Émancipation nationale*, 14 November 1936.
12. This lists the titles and authors of most plays performed in France, together with the date and place of the first performance.
13. *Le Peuple*, 22 January 1936.
14. Léon Chancerel, *Récitations chorales: Chant de la route, Cantique de la bonne mort, Le Roi Renaud* (Paris: CERD, 1936) (unpaginated).
15. Georges Altman, *Le Peuple*, 22 January 1936.
16. *La Voix du peuple*, 162 (March 1934).
17. *Je suis partout*, 10 October 1936.
18. Léon Lemonnier, *Le Populisme* (Paris: La Renaissance du Livre, 1931), p. 199.
19. *Je suis partout*, 4 July 1936.
20. *L'Émancipation nationale*, 25 July 1936.
21. *L'Émancipation nationale*, 15 August 1936.
22. *La Voix du peuple*, March 1934.
23. See, for example, Gabriel Boissy 'Paraphrases sur le plein air', *Le Feu* 101 (September 1913); idem, 'Les Spectacles de plein air et le peuple,' (1907) (ASP, Rf 81108) and idem, 'La Préservation du Théâtre Antique d'Orange', *Mercure de France*, 1 June 1906 (ASP, 8 Rt 11760).
24. *Le Flambeau*, 15 December 1936.
25. Jean-Richard Bloch, *Le Destin du Théâtre* (Paris: Gallimard, 1930), p. 155.
26. *Comœdia*, 14 July 1936.
27. *Le Peuple*, 9 May 1938.
28. *Le Petit Journal*, 15 July 1938.
29. Ory, *La Belle Illusion*, p. 260.
30. Ory, *La Belle Illusion*, p. 251.
31. Ory, *La Belle Illusion*, p. 251.
32. Ory, *La Belle Illusion*, p. 234.
33. André-Jean Tudesq, 'L'Utilisation gouvernementale de la radio', in René Rémond and Janine Bourdin (eds), *Édouard Daladier, chef de gouvernement* (Paris: Presses de la FNSP, 1977), p. 255.
34. *Radio-Liberté*, 24 September 1937.

35. *Radio-Liberté*, 5 February 1937.
36. *Radio-Liberté*, 14 May 1937.
37. *Radio-Liberté*, 18 December 1936.
38. *Le Travailleur du Film*, 22 December 1936, Archives Départementales de la Seine-Saint-Denis (hereafter ADS), 65J 69.
39. *Le Peuple*, 13 September 1936.
40. The Cinéma du Peuple was founded in 1913 by a group of anarchists, anarcho-syndicalists, freemasons, and socialists, and aimed to portray workers at work while combating the perceived dangers of alcoholism, clericalism, and nationalism. Tangui Perron, 'Vie, mort et renouveau du cinéma politique', *L'Homme et la Société: revue internationale de recherches et de synthèses en sciences sociales* 127–128 (1998), pp. 7–14. See also Tangui Perron, 'Le Cinéma ouvrier, un cinéma militant', *Cahiers de la cinémathèque* 71 (2000), pp. 9–13.
41. Girault, *Au-devant du Bonheur*, p. 132.
42. 'Pour l'éducation de la classe ouvrière', a special supplement to *Le Peuple* on 1 May 1938.
43. Roberto Escobar and Vittorio Giacci, *Il Cinema del Fronte popolare: Francia 1934–37* (Milan: Edizioni il formichiere, 1980), p. 218.
44. Pascal Ory, *Théâtre citoyen: du théâtre du peuple au théâtre du soleil* (Avignon: Association Jean Vilar, 1985), p. 45.
45. Georges Pitoëff and his wife, the actress Ludmilla, had emigrated from Russia to France after the First World War and staged over 200 plays in Paris. *Le Peuple*, 19 May 1936.
46. Ory, *La Belle Illusion*, p. 375.
47. Léon Chancerel, 'Le Théâtre à l'Exposition', *Études: Revue catholique d'intérêt général*, ASP, Rt 4442, p. 227.
48. Chancerel, 'Le Théâtre à l'Exposition', p. 236.
49. *Guide à l'Exposition, Brochure réalisée par l'Union Départementale de la Seine*, ACGT, Box 23, p. 8.
50. Jean Renoir, *My Life and My Films* (London: Collins, 1974), p. 127.
51. 'Lettre du Président de l'Union des Artistes à M. Cebron, Paris, le 16 mars 1937', in 'Dossier *La Marseillaise*, 1937', ADS, 175J 187.
52. Elizabeth Strebel, 'Jean Renoir and the Popular Front', in K. R. M. Short (ed.), *Feature Films as History* (London: Croom Helm, 1981), pp. 176–93.
53. Danielle Tartakowsky, 'Le cinéma militant des années trente: source pour l'histoire du Front populaire', *Cahiers de la Cinémathèque* 71 (2000), pp. 19–22.
54. Boris Peskine, *Sur les Routes d'acier* (1938) (BN).
55. Tartakowsky, 'Le Cinéma militant des années trente', p. 23; and Margairaz and Tartakowsky, *L'Avenir nous appartient*, p. 172.
56. Pottecher's initiatives and legacy are described by Frédéric Pottecher in his *Histoire du Théâtre du Peuple* (n.p., 1981) as well as in Maurice Pottecher's own work *Le Théâtre du Peuple: renaissance et destinée du théâtre populaire* (Paris: Paul Ollendorf, 1899).
57. Pottecher, *Le Théâtre du Peuple*, p. 42.
58. Romain Rolland, *Le Théâtre du Peuple: essai d'esthétique d'un théâtre nouveau* (Paris: Albin Michel, 1903, 1913), p. 3.
59. Rolland, *Le Théâtre du Peuple*, Preface to the first edition, xii.

60. Romain Rolland, *Théâtre de la Révolution: le Quatorze Juillet* (Paris: Albin Michel, 1926), 1901 Preface, p. 3.
61. Henri Ghéon in *La Nouvelle Revue Française*, 1 November 1911, p. 504; Jean-Richard Bloch, 'Le Théâtre du Peuple, critique d'une utopie', published in *L'Effort* on 1 June 1910 and reprinted in Bloch, *Destin du Théâtre*, p. 37.
62. *L'Excelsior*, 11 July 1936.
63. *La Revue*, 15 April 1902, ASP, Rf 71 145.
64. Rolland, *Le Quatorze Juillet*, p. 68.
65. Rolland, *Le Quatorze Juillet*, p. 36.
66. Rolland, *Le Quatorze Juillet*, p. 80.
67. Rolland, *Le Quatorze Juillet*, p. 83.
68. Rolland, *Le Quatorze Juillet*, p. 50.
69. Rolland, *Le Quatorze Juillet*, p. 53.
70. Rolland, *Le Quatorze Juillet*, 1901 Preface.
71. Rolland, *Le Quatorze Juillet*, p. 140.
72. Jacques Chabannes, *Paris à vingt ans* (Paris: Éditions France-Empire, 1974), p. 277.
73. Bloch, 'Le Théâtre du Peuple, critique d'une utopie', p. 36.
74. *Comœdia*, 14 July 1936.
75. *La République*, 18 July 1936.
76. Charles-Henry, writing in *L'Ère Nouvelle* on 4 August 1936.
77. *Le Petit Bleu*, 17 July 1936.
78. *La Revue de Paris*, 1 August 1936.
79. Chabannes, *Paris à vingt ans*, p. 284.
80. Léon Ruth, writing in *Le Populaire*, 3 May 1937.
81. Chabannes, *Paris à vingt ans*, p. 285.
82. Chabannes, *Paris à vingt ans*, p. 285.
83. Ory, *La Belle Illusion*, pp. 406–8.
84. Bloch, 'Naissance d'une cité', p. 297.
85. The stagehands were introduced to the audience as meriting the same respect as the actors.
86. *Les Nouvelles Littéraires*, 28 March 1931.
87. Bloch, *Naissance d'une culture*, p. 158.
88. Bloch, *Naissance d'une culture*, p. 150.
89. Bloch, 'Naissance d'une cité', p. 269.
90. Bloch, 'Naissance d'une cité', p. 270.
91. Bloch, 'Le Théâtre du Peuple, critique d'une utopie', p. 37.
92. Bloch, *Destin du Théâtre*, pp. 136–7.
93. *Les Nouvelles Littéraires*, 28 March 1931.
94. Bloch, *Naissance d'une culture*, p. 22.
95. 'Lettre à Jacques Chevalier, le 20 septembre 1932', Emmanuel Mounier, *Œuvres Complètes* (Paris: Seuil, 1961), 4, p. 503.
96. Emile Mersch, *Le Corps Mystique du Christ: études de théologie historique* (Paris: Desclée, de Brouwer et Cie, 1936), p. 190.
97. Mersch, *Le Corps Mystique*, Introduction, xvii.
98. Lebreton, Preface to Mersch, *Le Corps Mystique*, xv.
99. 'P.P. 10 juin 1938: Réunion organisée par les Catholiques, Salle Soulange-Bodin, 16, rue Vercingétorix, Paris (14e) le 9 Juin 1938', APP, Ba 1953.
100. Marie-Dominique Chénu, *Dimension nouvelle de la chrétienté* (Paris: Cerf, 1937), p. 10.

101. Chénu, *Dimension nouvelle*, p. 9.
102. *La Documentation catholique* 851, 31 July 1937.
103. John Hellman, *Emmanuel Mounier and the New Catholic Left in France 1930–50* (London: Croom Helm, 1981), p. 49.
104. Jacqueline Levaillant, 'Henri Ghéon, genèse d'une esthétique théâtrale', *Revue d'Histoire du Théâtre* 50 (1998), p. 66.
105. Jacques Maritain, *Les Nouvelles Littéraires*, 19 July 1924, ASP, Rf 60 491.
106. Henri Ghéon, *Les Nouvelles Littéraires*, 22 August 1925, ASP, Rf 60 491.
107. Levaillant, 'Henri Ghéon', p. 66.
108. Léon Chancerel, writing in the programme for *La Compassion de Notre Dame*, performed at the Salle Pleyel on 7–8 April 1933. ASP, Rt 4438.
109. 'Les Comédiens Routiers', ASP, Rt 4423.
110. P. Werrie, writing in *Vingtième Siècle* on the performance of *La Compassion de Notre Dame*. ASP, Rt 4438.
111. Chancerel in the programme for *La Compassion de Notre Dame*.
112. Léon Chancerel, *Répertoire des comédiens routiers: Chant de la route, Cantique de la bonne mort, Le Roi Renaud, Nocturne* (Paris: CERD, 1936).
113. Léon Chancerel, 'Avertissement', *Un Trésor est caché dedans: action chorale en trois parties, en marge du 'Laboureur et ses enfants' de La Fontaine* (Paris: La Hutte, 1939), p. 4.
114. 'Chancerel et l'Exposition', ASP, Rt 4442.
115. Michel Launay, 'La JOC dans son premier développement', Pierre Pierrard, Michel Launay and Rolande Trempé, *La JOC: regards d'historiens* (Paris: Éditions Ouvrières, 1984), p. 42. On the development of the movement, see also the detailed study by the former JOC chaplain, Jean-Pierre Coco, collaborating with Joseph Debès in *1937, L'Élan Jociste: le dixième anniversaire de la JOC, Paris, juillet 1937* (Paris: Éditions Ouvrières, 1989). There are also some lyrical portraits of the movement's founders by Henri Tonnet, *Au Berceau de la Jeunesse Ouvrière Chrétienne* (Brussels: L'auteur, 1961) and idem, *Fernand Tonnet: Président-Fondateur de la JOC 1894–1945* (Brussels: Librairie Saint-Luc, 1947).
116. *L'Équipe ouvrière féminine*, January 1935.
117. *L'Appel de la JOC* (Paris: Éditions Jocistes, 1938), p. 27.
118. For a detailed comparison of the JOC spectacle and Jean-Richard Bloch's *Naissance d'une cité*, see Jessica Irons, 'Staging reconciliation: popular theatre and political utopia in France in 1937', *Contemporary European History* 14 (2005), pp. 279–94.
119. Jean Rodhain, *Dixième anniversaire de la JOC Française: la fête nocturne du samedi soir 17 juillet 1937 en la veille du congrès jociste—'La Joie du travail', 'Le Sens du travail'* (Paris: Librairie de la Jeunesse Ouvrière, 1937), p. 9.
120. *Dixième anniversaire*, p. 15.
121. *Dixième Anniversaire*, p. 3.
122. *Dixième Anniversaire*, p. 2.
123. *Dixième Anniversaire*, p. 2.
124. Henri Lesieur, writing in *Radio-Liberté* on 24 September 1937.

6 In Search of the Middle Classes: The Tragedy at Clichy and its Consequences

1. 'Vers la Tunisie, à bord du Général-Lépine, 4 avril 1937', Mounier, *Œuvres* 4, p. 603.
2. Jackson, *The Popular Front in France*, p. 169.

3. The evolution of the Popular Front's image of a rational, triumphant people in the colder climate of the 'exercise of power' is a largely untold story. Certainly the causes of the gradual disintegration of the Popular Front have been much debated, but the representation of the people after the summer of 1936 has been largely unexplored. Many histories of the Popular Front conclude with the summer of 1936, thus preserving its myth intact, such as Jacques Chambaz and Claude Willard, *Le Front populaire: pour la pain, la liberté et la paix* (Paris: Éditions Sociales, 1961) and Rossel, *Eté 1936* (1976). Similarly, Grason's *Éclats du Front populaire* (2006) includes photographs of the strikes of summer 1936 under the rubric 'Jours inoubliables à Nanterre', but does not represent the later strikes. Tartakowsky's *Le Front populaire* (1996) devotes little attention to the decline of the movement; Tartakowsky and Margairaz's, *L'Avenir nous appartient* (2006) makes a brief reference to Clichy, but not to the representation of the crowd.

4. 'P.P. 11 septembre 1936', APP, Ba 1874.

5. Arthur Mitzman, 'The French working class and the Blum government, 1936–37', *International Review of Social History* 9 (1964), p. 378.

6. 'P.P. 20 novembre 1936, A.S. des ouvriers bouchers aux Halles centrales', APP, Ba 1874.

7. 'P.P. 2 décembre 1936', APP, Ba 1874.

8. 'Lettre de M. Janvier au Ministre de l'Intérieur, le 18 décembre 1936', APP, Ba 1874.

9. *Le Populaire*, 30 December 1936.

10. *L'Humanité*, 30 December 1936.

11. 'P.P. 8 octobre 1936: perquisition chez de la Rocque', AN, F7 14817.

12. 'P.P. décembre 1936', AN, F7 14817.

13. 'Communication téléphonique, le 17 décembre 1936', AN, F7 14817.

14. 'Incidents survenus à Martigues à la suite d'une réunion du PSF', AN, F7 14817.

15. *L'Humanité*, 22 November 1936.

16. *Le Temps*, 25 November 1936.

17. *Le Populaire*, 22 February 1937.

18. Tartakowsky, *Les Manifestations* and Sandrine Lachaumette, 'Masses, foules, peuple vus dans la presse *L'Illustration* et *Regards*', in Noëlle Gérôme (ed.), *Archives sensibles: images et objets du monde industriel et ouvrier* (Paris: Éditions de l'ÉNS-Cachan, 1995), pp. 84–97.

19. On the tension between the Popular Front's protection of order and defence of republican liberty, see Simon Kitson, 'The Police and the Clichy Massacre, March 1937', in Richard Bessel and Clive Emsley (eds), *Patterns of Provocation: Police and Public Disorder* (Oxford: Berghahn, 2000), pp. 29–41.

20. 'P.P. 17 mars 1937', APP, Ba 1865.

21. 'Rapport d'Imbert', AN, F7 13985.

22. Some of the police accounts alleged that there was shooting on both sides, although this was a subject for heated debate after the event.

23. Alexander Werth, 'L'Ombre de Clichy', APP, Ba 1865.

24. 'P.P. 17 mars 1937', APP, Ba 1865.

25. 'Grèves à l'Exposition', APP, Ba 1874 and 'A.S. des incidents de Clichy et de leurs conséquences, 19 mars 1937', APP, Ba 1865.

26. 'Grève générale du 18 mars 1937', APP, Ba 1874.
27. 'P.P. 18 mars 1937', APP, Ba 1866.
28. *Le Populaire*, 17 March 1937.
29. *L'Humanité*, 17 March 1937.
30. *L'Humanité*, 20 March 1937.
31. *La Lumière*, 20 March 1937.
32. *Action Française*, 18 March 1937.
33. *Le Temps*, 20 March 1937.
34. Declaration and comments by the CGPF, published in *Le Jour*, 19 March 1937.
35. *L'Émancipation nationale*, 20 March 1937.
36. *L'Émancipation nationale*, 20 March 1937.
37. *Action Française*, 18 March 1937.
38. *L'Émancipation nationale*, 20 March 1937.
39. 'P.P. 18 mars 1937', APP, Ba 1865.
40. 'P.P. 20 mars 1937', APP, Ba 1865.
41. *Action Française*, 18 March 1937.
42. *Le Journal officiel*, 24 March 1937.
43. Antoine Prost, 'Le Climat social', in Rémond and Bourdin (eds), *Daladier, chef de gouvernement*, p. 100.
44. Dutton, *Origins of the French Welfare State*, p. 161.
45. André Tardieu, *Alerte aux Français* (Paris: Flammarion, 1936), p. 5.
46. *L'Expérience Blum: un an de Front populaire* (Paris: Éditions du Sagittaire, 1937), p. 32.
47. Klaus-Peter Sick's theoretical study of the development of the 'middle classes' as a political concept from the eighteenth to the twentieth century notes their particular importance in the discussion and strategies of left and right in this period. See Klaus-Peter Sick, 'La notion des classes moyennes: notion sociologique ou slogan politique?' *Vingtième Siècle* 37 (1993), p. 28.
48. *Le Flambeau*, 20 March 1937.
49. J.L. Chastanet, *La République des crabes: six mois du Front populaire* (Paris: Éditions Alsatia, 1936), p. 12.
50. *Le Flambeau*, 1 May 1937.
51. *L'Émancipation nationale*, 13 March 1937.
52. *L'Émancipation nationale*, 20 March 1937.
53. *L'Émancipation nationale*, 13 March 1937.
54. Patrick Fridenson, 'Le patronat français', in René Rémond and Janine Bourdin (eds), *La France et les Français* (Paris: Presses de la FNSP, 1978), pp. 150–1. See also 'P.P. 28 mai 1937', APP, Ba 2002.
55. 'P.P. 19 mars 1937', APP, Ba 1865.
56. 'P.P. 18 juillet 1937', APP Ba 1952. See also the embittered testimony of the ex-Croix de Feu member Paul Chopine, *Le Colonel de la Rocque veut-il la guerre civile?* (Paris: Bureau d'éditions, 1937), pp. 20–1.
57. 'P.P. 18 mars 1937', APP, Ba 1865.
58. Doriot, *Refaire la France*, p. 8.
59. Maurice Thorez, *Un an de Front populaire* (Paris: Imprimerie Centrale du Croissant, 1938), p. 15.
60. Doriot, *La France avec nous!* p. 121.
61. Brunet, *Jacques Doriot*, p. 246.

62. 'P.P. 2 juin 1937', APP, Ba 2002.
63. 'P.P. 15 juin 1937', APP, Ba 2002.
64. *La Lumière*, 27 February 1937.
65. *La Lumière*, 9 January 1937.
66. Albert Milhaud, 'Le Vent tourne', *L'Ère nouvelle*, 13 March 1937.
67. *Le Courrier d'Alsace*, 1 July 1935, AN, F7 13305.
68. *L'Ère nouvelle*, 13 March 1937.
69. 'Rapport, 18 novembre 1930', APP, Ba 1915.
70. 'P.P. 29 février 1933: A.S. du Parti Républicain Social Agraire', APP, Ba 1915.
71. 'P.P. 14 février 1937', APP, Ba 1915.
72. 'Anarchie et Personalisme' was published in *Esprit* in April 1937 and subsequently reprinted in *Œuvres* (Paris: Seuil, 1961), 1, pp. 653–725.

7 The Call of the Nation, 1937–39

1. One of his listeners, Edward A. Jones, recalled this experience in 'Royalism in French Politics', *Phylon* 8 (1947), pp. 58–9.
2. Gaston Jèze, 'Les Conditions du rétablissement de la prospérité économique', *L'Ère nouvelle*, 11 February 1938.
3. *Journal officiel*, 13 April 1938.
4. Girault, *Au-devant du Bonheur*, p. 163
5. Bourdé, *La Défaite du Front populaire*, p. 289. See also Rossel, *Été 36*.
6. Janine Bourdin, 'Introduction', in Rémond and Bourdin (eds), *La France et les Français en 1938–39*, p. 16.
7. Studies identifying a consensus around national union and defence under Daladier do not always recognize that this emerged from a community of thought developing in preceding years. See, for example, the essays in Rémond and Bourdin (eds), *Édouard Daladier*.
8. *Le Populaire*, 1 January 1937.
9. *Journal officiel*, 24 March 1937.
10. *Journal officiel*, 14 January 1938.
11. *L'Ère nouvelle*, 21 March 1938.
12. *Le Populaire*, 13 March 1938.
13. *Le Populaire*, 14 March 1938.
14. See, for example, *L'Émancipation nationale*, 19 March 1938 and Philippe Thibaud in *Le Flambeau de Franche-Comté*, 30 March 1938.
15. Michael Torigian, 'The End of the Popular Front: The Paris metal strike of spring 1938', *French History* 13 (1999), pp. 464–91.
16. *Journal officiel* (Senate), 9 April 1938.
17. *Journal officiel*, 7 April 1938. Tellier was quoting Premier Waldeck-Rousseau at this point.
18. 'Instructions confidentielles de la CGPF' (s.d.) ACGT, Box 25.
19. 'Procès verbal de la réunion du 23 novembre 1938 entre les responsables des unions locales, les militants des régions et sections fédérales, et quelques membres du bureau de l'Union Départementale', ACGT, Box 25.
20. *Programme à soumettre aux délégués de la CGT du Congrès de Nantes 1938* (Syndicat de Cercy-la-Tour, Nièvre) (n.d.) ACGT, Box 25.
21. Daladier's biographer Elisabeth du Réau also recognizes that interpretations of this social conflict need to be revised. See du Réau, *Édouard Daladier*,

p. 229. Likewise, Herrick Chapman notes that CGT militants did not attempt to undermine rationalization between 1936 and 1940, and that trade-union spokesmen called for a more efficient use of manpower and material. Chapman, *State Capitalism*, p. 178.

22. Du Réau, *Édouard Daladier*, p. 232.
23. 'Lettre des techniciens agents de maîtrise et employés de la métallurgie CGT aux sections d'entreprises, Lyon, 23 novembre 1938', ACGT, Carton 25. See also *Le Peuple*, 20 November 1938.
24. Jean Bruhat, 'La CGT', in Rémond et al., *La France et les Français*, p. 182.
25. 'M. Daladier commente l'échec de la grève (texte de l'allocution prononcée ce soir à la TSF)', *L'Ère nouvelle*, 1 December 1938.
26. *Action Française*, 1 December 1938.
27. *L'Émancipation nationale*, 2 December 1938.
28. *Le Petit Journal*, 1 December 1938.
29. See, for example, Norman Ingram, *The Politics of Dissent: Pacifism in France, 1919–39* (Oxford: Clarendon Press, 1991), p. 116.
30. William Irvine, *French Conservatism in Crisis: The Republican Federation of France in the 1930s* (Baton Rouge and London: Louisiana State University Press, 1979), p. 197.
31. Mona Siegel, *The Moral Disarmament of France: Education, Pacifism and Patriotism 1914–40* (Cambridge: Cambridge University Press, 2004), p. 4.
32. Gaston Jèze, 'Le Salut du régime', *L'Ère nouvelle*, 10 November 1938.
33. Du Réau, *Édouard Daladier*, p. 319.
34. Édouard Daladier, *Ce que veut la France* (Paris: Fasquelle, 1939), p. 7.
35. Daladier, *Ce que veut la France*, p. 11.
36. 'Discours de Daladier, le 25 août 1939', *Discours d'Édouard Daladier* (BN, audio recording).
37. *Discours d'Édouard Daladier*.
38. Du Réau, *Édouard Daladier*, p. 285.
39. Tartakowsky, *Les Manifestations*, p. 426.
40. For example, during the commemorations of the Commune in Issy-les-Moulineaux in May 1937 and in Stains in June. 'P.P. 3 mai 1937' and 'P.P. 3 juin 1937', APP, Ba 2038.
41. 'Allocation Jouhaux, 1 mai 1937', ACGT, Box 22.
42. 'P.P. 14 juillet 1937: au sujet de la manifestation organisée par le Comité National du Rassemblement Populaire', APP, Ba 1867.
43. Jacques Duclos in *Retour au programme! Lutte contre les trusts! Parti unique de la classe ouvrière! Union du Front populaire! Rapport prononcé à la réunion du Comité Central du 22 juillet 1937 par Jacques Duclos* (Paris: Éditions du Comité Populaire de Propagande, 1938), p. 11; see also the article by Paul Vaillant-Couturier in *L'Humanité*, 15 July 1937.
44. *Action Française*, 15 July 1937.
45. *Le Populaire*, 11 April 1938.
46. *Le Populaire*, 28 March 1938.
47. *L'Humanité*, 15 July 1938.
48. *Action Française*, 15 July 1938.
49. *L'Émancipation nationale*, 16 July 1938.
50. For example at Clermont Ferrand and Martigues, where there were confrontations between PSF members and the CGT and PCF respectively. AN, F7 14817.

51. 'Parti Social Français: correspondance et rapports, 1938', APP, Ba 1952.
52. 'Lettre du Ministre de l'Intérieur à MM. les Commissaires Régionaux et MM. les Préfets, 6 avril 1945', APP, Ba 1952.
53. *L'Émancipation nationale*, 28 October 1938. Drieu la Rochelle hoped in vain for a great Franco-German entente during the German Occupation of 1940–44, and committed suicide in March 1945.
54. *Action Française*, 8 May 1937.
55. *Action Française*, 10 May 1937.
56. *L'Humanité*, 10 May 1937.
57. *L'Émancipation nationale*, 5 June 1937.
58. Léon Chancerel and Raoul Serène, *La Mission de Jeanne d'Arc* (Paris: La Hutte, 1938).
59. 'Lettre du comité des fêtes de Jeanne d'Arc à Tours à M. Daladier, le 29 août 1938', AN, F60 475.
60. *L'Humanité*, 9 May 1938.
61. *Le Populaire*, 9 May 1938.
62. *Action Française*, 9 May 1938.
63. *Le Petit Journal*, 9 May 1938.
64. *Le Populaire*, 19 July 1938.
65. *La Lumière*, 22 July 1938.
66. *Le Petit Journal*, 19 July 1938.
67. 'Discours d'Édouard Daladier au banquet des anciens combattants, le 12 novembre 1938', *Discours d'Édouard Daladier*.
68. *L'Ère nouvelle*, 12 November 1938.
69. *Le Petit Journal*, 12 November 1938.
70. *L'Émancipation nationale*, 11 November 1938.
71. *Le Populaire*, 12 November 1938.
72. *L'Humanité*, 12 November 1938.
73. Joan Tumblety explores how the events of summer 1939 were employed by the extreme right 'as an opportunity to deconstruct the national myths that were engendered by generations of secular and republicanised education in French primary school, and to offer instead a critique of French history that situated 1789 at the birth of a decadent modernity.' Joan Tumblety, ' "Civil wars of the mind": the commemoration of the 1789 revolution in the Parisian press of the radical right, 1939', *European History Quarterly* 30 (2000), pp. 389–429, here p. 391.
74. Pascal Ory, 'La Commémoration révolutionnaire', Rémond and Bourdin (eds), *La France et les Français*, p. 122.
75. 'P.P. 29 avril 1939', APP, Ba 1895.
76. *Action Française*, 4 July 1939.
77. 'Supplique à M. le Président du Conseil', AN, F60 475.
78. 'Rapport fait au nom de la Commission de l'Enseignement et des Beaux-Arts chargée d'examiner le projet de loi ayant pour objet la célébration, par une commémoration nationale, du cent cinquantième anniversaire de la Révolution française', APP, F60 475 .
79. Édouard Herriot was himself an historian of the French Revolution, and the author of *Lyon n'est plus* (Paris, 1940).
80. 'Le Ministre de l'Education Nationale à MM. les Préfets: commémoration du cent cinquantenaire de la Révolution Française', AN, F60 475.

81. 'Arrêté: travaux d'art, musées, expositions (12 juin 1939)', AN, F21 4766.
82. *Le Petit Journal*, 23 June 1939.
83. *Journal officiel*, 22 June 1939.
84. For a reflection on this continuity, see Herman Lebovics, *True France: The Wars over Cultural Identity, 1900–45* (Ithaca and London: Cornell University Press, 1992), p. 161 and also Peer, *France on Display*.
85. 'Lettre de G. Pertuis à M. le Ministre de l'Intérieur (Service de l'Afrique du Nord)', AN, F60 475.
86. *Le Temps*, 14–15 July 1939.
87. *Le Temps*, 14–15 July 1939.
88. Marianne Benteli, Daniel Jay, and Jean-Pierre Jeancolas, 'Le cinéma français: thèmes et public', in Rémond and Bourdin (eds), *La France et les Français*, p. 40.
89. *Le Temps*, 11 July 1939.
90. 'Discours d'Édouard Daladier à l'occasion du cent cinquantième anniversaire de la Révolution française, Paris, Palais Chaillot, le 14 juillet 1789', *Discours d'Édouard Daladier*.
91. *La Lumière*, 14 July 1939.
92. *L'Ère nouvelle*, 13 July 1939.
93. *Action Française*, 15 July 1939.
94. *Le Petit Journal*, 14 July 1939.
95. Alexis de Tocqueville, *L'Ancien Régime et la Révolution* (1856) (Paris: Gallimard, 1967), p. 317.
96. *Le Petit Journal*, 15 July 1939.
97. *L'Émancipation nationale*, 14 July 1939.
98. *Le Populaire*, 15 July 1939.
99. 'Note pour M. le Directeur des Beaux-Arts, 8 juin 1938', AN, F21 4766.
100. *L'Humanité*, 15 July 1939.
101. *L'Humanité*, 14 July 1939.
102. Thierry Maulnier, *La Crise est dans l'homme* (Paris: A. Redier, 1932), p. 69.

Conclusion

1. *Comœdia*, 8 March 1936.
2. Dell, *The Image of the Popular Front*.
3. Tartakowsky, *Le Front populaire*, p. 110.
4. *Le Petit Journal*, 14 July 1938.
5. *L'Émancipation nationale*, 14 November 1936
6. *Le Peuple*, 17 July 1935.
7. 'P.P. 7 mai 1936', AN, F7 13983.
8. Roderick Kedward and Roger Austin (eds), *Vichy France and the Resistance: Culture and Ideology* (London: Croom Helm, 1985), p. 6.
9. Herman Lebovics, *True France: The Wars over Cultural Identity* (Ithaca and London: Cornell University Press, 1992), p. 157.
10. Lebovics, *True France*, p. 189
11. Lebovics, *True France*, p. xvi.
12. *Action Française*, 23 April 1936.
13. Jean Touchard, 'L'esprit des années 30: une tentative de renouvellement de la pensée politique française', in Guy Michaud (ed.), *Tendances politiques*

dans la vie Française depuis 1789 (Paris: Hachette 1960), pp. 89–120; Olivier Dard, *Le Rendez-vous manquée des relèves des années 30* (Paris: PUF, 2002).

14. Jean Touchard, *La Gauche en France depuis 1900* (Paris: Seuil, 1977), p. 16.
15. *Les Nouvelles Littéraires*, 28 March 1931.
16. Bloch, *Naissance d'une culture*, p. 48.
17. Vallin, *Le PSF*, pp. 8–9.
18. *Le Peuple*, 17 July 1935.
19. *Journal officiel*, 7 June 1936.

Bibliography

Anonymous works are listed alphabetically by title.

Primary sources

Manuscript and archival sources
Archives Nationales de France, Paris

F7 12863	Action Française.
F7 12864	Camelots du Roi.
F7 12948	Groupements politiques.
F7 13080	Activité du Parti Socialiste.
F7 13098	Organisation des cellules communistes.
F7 13119	Notes sur le Parti Communiste.
F7 13131	Notes sur le Parti Communiste, 1933.
F7 13134	Notes sur le Parti Communiste, 1934.
F7 13138	Fêtes Champêtres Communistes.
F7 13191	Parti Radical.
F7 13192	Parti Radical.
F7 13193	Parti Radical.
F7 13241	Croix de Feu.
F7 13305	Journée du 14 juillet 1935.
F7 13306	Fêtes de Jeanne d'Arc, 1930–39.
F7 13951	Camelots du Roi.
F7 13983	Documentation Politique, 1936.
F7 13985	Rapport Imbert sur les événements de Clichy.
F7 14614	Action Catholique, Jeunesse Ouvrière Chrétienne.
F7 14817	Parti Social Français, Parti Populaire Français, 1936–38.
F7 14782	Action Française.
F7 14786	Anarchisme en 1937.
F7 14792	Parti Communiste Français.
F21 4766	Commémoration de la 150e anniversaire de la Révolution Française.
F60 645	Fêtes, 1935–40.
F60 570	Radiodiffusion, 1937–40.

Archives de la Préfecture de Police, Paris

Ba 1738	Congrégations, groupements religieux, 1889–1944.
Ba 1735	Congrégations, attitudes politiques, 1875–1951.
Ba 1893	Action Française.
Ba 1894	Ligues d'Action Française, Camelots du Roi, 1924–37.
Ba 1895	Action Française.
Ba 1860	Manifestations, 1934.

Ba 1861	Manifestations, 1935.
Ba 1862	Manifestations, 1936.
Ba 1863	Manifestation organisée par le PCF, octobre 1936.
Ba 1864	Manifestations d'hiver 1936.
Ba 1865	16 mars 1937.
Ba 1866	Manifestation et bagarre de Clichy.
Ba 1867	Manifestations, 1937.
Ba 1870	Grèves, 1929–36.
Ba 1871	Grèves.
Ba 1872	Grèves.
Ba 1874	Grèves de 1936: diverses affaires contentieuses.
Ba 1899	Anarchistes.
Ba 1901	Croix de Feu et Briscards.
Ba 1902	Croix de Feu et Briscards.
Ba 1905	Fédération Nationale Catholique, rapports et tracts, 1922–43.
Ba 1907	Le Francisme.
Ba 1915	Mouvements fascistes et antifascistes, 1922–35.
Ba 1941	Parti Nationale Populaire, rapports, 1936.
Ba 1939	Groupe d'action révolutionnaire, Que Faire? 1936–38.
Ba 1942	Jeunesses Patriotes, 1925–36.
Ba 1945	Parti Populaire Français, comptes rendus, 1931–38.
Ba 1946	Parti Populaire Français, correspondance, rapports, 1938–39.
Ba 1951	Parti Républicain et Social.
Ba 1952	Parti Social Français, correspondance, 1936–40.
Ba 1953	Parti Catholique, 1918–40.
Ba 1960	La Solidarité Française, 1934–35.
Ba 1966	Syndicats et groupements professionnels.
Ba 1973	Briscards et Croix de Feu, les fils des Croix de Feu.
Ba 1975	Partis, ligues, mouvements politiques.
Ba 2002	Front de la Liberté.
Ba 2005	Francisque Gay.
Ba 2019	Jacques Maritain.
Ba 2021	Ortega y Gasset.
Ba 2024	Parti Néo-Socialiste de France.
Ba 2032	Théâtre Ouvrier (Parti Communiste), fondé le 23 janvier 1931.
Ba 2037	Jean Zyromski.
Ba 2038	Commémorations de la Commune, 1880–1944.
Ba 2042	Marcel Bucard, Marcel Déat.
DB 645	Colonel de la Rocque.

Archives Départementales de la Seine-Saint-Denis, Bobigny

65J 52	Syndicats CGT du Spectacle.
65J 69	Correspondance, 1934.
65J 70	Correspondance, 1935.
175J 187	Syndicat Français des Artistes Interprètes, 1917–97.

Bibliothèque Nationale de France, Paris

Films

CGT, *Grèves d'occupation* (1936).

Clair, René, *À Nous la liberté* (1931).

Durandeau, Yves, *Un Goût de bonheur: l'essor culturel en 1936* (1977).

Duvivier, Julien, *La Belle Équipe* (1936).

Knapp, Hubert, *Ceux qui se souviennent: tout va bien, 1936–39* (1980).

Kohly, Philippe, *Les Congés payés, 1936* (2000).

Peskine, Boris, *Sur les Routes d'acier* (1938).

Prévert, Pierre, *L'Affaire est dans le sac* (1932).

Renoir, Jean, *Le Crime de Monsieur Lange* (1936).

——, *La Grande Illusion* (1937).

——, *La Marseillaise* (1937).

——, *La Vie est à nous* (1936).

Santelli, Claude, *La Mémoire d'un Peuple* (1991).

Audio recordings

Front Populaire 1936–66: trentième anniversaire (BN SDCR 001351).

Discours d'hommes politiques du parti socialiste (BN SDCR 001347).

Discours de membres des partis communiste et socialiste français, 1936–46 (BN SDCR 001344).

Léon Blum 1872–1950: discours politiques (BN SDCR 001345).

Discours d'Édouard Daladier (BN SDCR 1338).

Photographs

Capa, Robert, *Front populaire* (Paris: Magnum, 1936–39).

Ronis, Willy, *Premiers Congés payés et loisirs divers* (Paris: Agence Rapho, 1933–70).

——, *Défilés, grèves, et manifestations avant 1938* (Paris: Agence Rapho, 1934–38).

——, *Métiers divers* (Paris: Agence Rapho, 1936–59).

——, *Paris, scènes de rue et intérieurs* (Paris: Agence Rapho, 1934–83).

Unpublished documents

Tracts et documents du mouvement des Croix de Feu et du Parti Social Français dirigés par le Colonel de la Rocque, 1934–39.

Elections législatives de 1936: Manifeste Croix de Feu 'Pour le peuple, par le peuple'.

Parti Républicain Radical et Radical-Socialiste, Tracts politiques, 1928–39.

Tracts politiques du Parti Populaire Français, 1932–38.

Bibliothèque Nationale de France, Département des Arts du Spectacle

Rf 52690   Recueil d'articles de presse sur Jean-Richard Bloch.

Rf 69491   Articles sur Henri Ghéon.

Rf 81108   Gabriel Boissy.

Rt 71145   Articles sur *Le 14 Juillet*.

Rt 4423   Comédiens Routiers.

Rt 4424   Comédiens Routiers.

Rt 4438   Léon Chancerel, *La Compassion de Notre-Dame.*
Rt 4442   Léon Chancerel, 'Le Théâtre et l'Exposition', *Études* (20 October
             1937), 227–41.
8Rt 11760   Gabriel Boissy.

Catalogue de la Société des Auteurs et Compositeurs Dramatiques.

Bibliothèque Historique de la Ville de Paris

Bellon, Denise, *Métiers à Paris: 17 photographies* (N.A. Album, 4o 249: 17–32).
——, *Exposition internationale des arts et techniques dans la vie moderne. Paris mai–nov. 1937: 48 photographies* (N.A. Album, 4o 249).
Doisneau, Robert, *Parisiens au travail: 80 photographies* (N.A. Album 4o 70: 2, 3).
Foucault, Marc, *Il faut bien gagner sa croûte: 7 photographies 1926–38* (N.A. Album, 4o 250: 1–7).
——, *Scènes Parisiennes, 26 photographies, 1934–65* (N.A. Album, 4o 250: 24–49).
Jahan, Pierre, *Fête, 14 juillet. Spectateurs du bal du 14 juillet à leur balcon ou à leur fenêtre, dans un immeuble de la rue Boissière, 1935* (N.A. Divers IX, 68).
——, *Le bassin inférieur d'une fontaine de la place de la Concorde et les panneaux représentant divers emblèmes à l'occasion de l'exposition universelle de 1937: vue prise vers la statue de la ville de Strasbourg* (N.A. Album, Fol. 7–28).
Rand, H., *La vie à Paris entre 1930 et 1937. Page de couverture d'une revue illustrant l'exposition internationale à Paris en 1937: 'Un Regard sur Paris'* (N.A. Album, 4o 262: 20).
Ronis, Willy, *À travers Paris: 158 photographies 1934–81* (N.A. Album 4o 149).

Centre National de la Cinématographie, Bois d'Arcy

Les Croix de Feu se déplacent . . . Paris–Reims, avril 1935.
Les Dispos de la 18ᵉ Croix de Feu à Reims, le 14 avril 1935.
La Messe des morts de la guerre et des maréchaux, organisée par les Croix de Feu à Notre Dame le 12 mai 1935.
La Fête de Jeanne d'Arc, 1935.
Les Croix de Feu commémorent l'armistice, 1935.
La réunion 'Croix de Feu' d'Amiens, 1935.
Activité de section Croix de Feu en, 1935.
80.000 Croix de Feu se rassemblent rue Royale le 10 mai 1936 pour la fête de Jeanne d'Arc (1936).
Réunion du PSF en plein air à Lille.
Réunion du PSF en Seine et Marne, 1937.
La section PSF de Montrouge, 1938.
Des Croix de Feu au PSF, 1938.
Un Meeting du PSF en plein air, 1938.
Congrès régional du PSF à Boyelles, 1938.
Paris, 14 mai 1939: Parti Social Français.
Une Journée au village de la Rochefoucault.
14 Juillet 1940 à Champeix (Puy de Dôme).
Un beau dimanche, 1941.
Vente de charité à Versailles, 1945.
Défilé du 11 novembre 1945.

Matches de foot organisés par la SPES de 1945 à 1948.
Les Obsèques de la Rocque à St Clément, 1946.
Pèlerinage sur la tombe du colonel de la Rocque, 1947.
Congrès de la Réconciliation à Vic-sur-Cère c. 1950.

Institut d'Histoire Sociale de la Confédération Générale du Travail, Montreuil

Boxes 22, 23, 25.
Brochures de la CGTU.
La Voix du Peuple.

Newspapers and periodicals

Action Française.
L'Ami du Peuple.
Les Annales politiques et littéraires.
Candide.
Comœdia.
La Documentation catholique.
L'Émancipation nationale.
L'Équipe ouvrière.
L'Équipe ouvrière féminine.
L'Ère nouvelle.
Europe, revue mensuelle.
Le Flambeau.
Le Flambeau de Franche-Comté.
Le Flambeau d'Indochine.
France-monde catholique.
Gringoire.
L'Humanité.
L'Illustration.
Le Jour.
Le Journal officiel. Débats parlementaires.
Le Journal de la Solidarité Française.
Je suis partout.
Jeunesse ouvrière.
Jeunesse ouvrière chrétienne.
La Lumière.
La Lutte ouvrière.
Marianne.
La Nouvelle revue française.
L'Œuvre.
L'Ouvrier libre.
Paris-midi.
Le Peuple.
Le Petit Journal.
Le Populaire.
La Scène ouvrière.
Le Temps.
Le Travailleur du film.

Le Travailleur parisien.
La Vie ouvrière.
La Voix du Peuple.
Vu.
Le Journal.
Radio-liberté.
Vendredi.

Books

[Anonymous], *L'Expérience Blum: un an de Front populaire* (n.p., 1937).
Angel, Pierre, *Essais sur Georges Sorel: vers un idéalisme constructif* (Paris: M. Rivière, 1936).
Armand, Émile, *Les Ouvriers, Les syndicats et les anarchistes* (Orléans: Éditions de l'En-Dehors, 1930).
Baudrillart, Alfred, *Au Grand mal des vrais remèdes: opera tenebrarum, arma lucis* (Paris: Société Générale d'Imprimerie, 1935).
——, *Et vous aussi, soyez prêts!* (Paris: Firmin-Didot et Cie., 1936).
Bedel, Maurice, *Bengali* (Paris: Œuvres Françaises, 1937).
Benda, Julien, *La Trahison des clercs* (Paris: Grasset, 1928).
Berdiaeff, Nicholas, *Le Nouveau Moyen Âge* (Paris: Plon, 1927).
Bernoville, Gaëtan, *La Farce de la main tendue: du Frente popular au Front populaire* (Paris: Grasset, 1937).
Besnard, Pierre, *Les Syndicats Ouvriers et la Révolution Sociale* (Gentilly: Éditions de la CGT, 1930).
Bloch, Jean-Richard, *Carnaval est Mort: premiers essais pour mieux comprendre mon temps* (Paris: Éditions de la NRF, 1920).
——, *Destin du Théâtre* (Paris: Gallimard, 1930).
——, *Naissance d'une culture: quatrièmes essais pour mieux comprendre mon temps* (Paris: Rieder, 1936).
——, *Toulon et autres pièces* (Paris: Gallimard, 1948).
Bloch, Jean-Richard and Jacques Copeau, 'Correspondance, Jean-Richard Bloch—Jacques Copeau', *Revue d'histoire du théâtre*, 41 (1992), 121–88.
Blum, Léon, *Léon Blum before his judges at the Supreme Court of Riom, 11 and 12 March 1942* (London: Routledge, 1942).
——, *L'Œuvre, 1914–28* (Paris: Albin Michel, 1971).
Bonnet, Georges, *Le Parti Radical devant les problèmes du temps présent* (Paris: E. Desfossés, 1936).
Bourgin, Hubert, *De Jaurès à Léon Blum* (Paris: Armand Colin, 1938).
Briefs, Goetz, *Le Prolétariat industriel* (préfacé de Jacques Maritain) (Paris: Desclée de Brouwer et Cie., 1926).
Chancerel, Léon, *La Compassion de Notre Dame: célébration par personnages des mystères joyeux, douloureux et glorieux* (Paris: La Hutte, 1933).
——, *Récitations chorales: Chant de la route, Cantique de la bonne mort, Le Roi Renaud, Nocturne* (Paris: CERD, 1936).
——, *Huit récitations chorales: deux complaintes de Cornouaille* (Paris: La Hutte, 1936).
——, *Un Trésor est caché dedans: action chorale en trois parties, en marge du 'Laboureur et ses enfants' de la Fontaine* (Paris: La Hutte, 1939).

—— and Raoul Serène, *La Mission de Jeanne d'Arc* (Paris: La Hutte, 1938).

Chastanet, J. L., *La République des crabes: six mois du Front populaire* (Paris: Alsatia, 1936).

Chénu, Marie-Dominique, *Dimension nouvelle de la chrétienté* (Paris: Éditions du cerf, 1937).

Chopine, Paul, *Le Colonel de la Rocque veut-il la guerre civile?* (Paris: Bureau d'éditions du PSF, 1937).

Claudel, Paul, *Positions et propositions* (Paris: Gallimard, 1928).

Confédération Général du Travail, *Qu'est-ce que le Fascisme?* (Paris: Confédération Général du Travail, n.d.).

Confédération Général du Travail Unitaire, *'S'Unir entre travailleurs': Discours prononcés par Frachon devant le Comité Confédéral Nationale de la CGTU des 4–5–6–7 Octobre 1934* (Paris: Confédération Général du Travail Unitaire, 1934).

Daladier, Édouard, *Ce que veut la France* (Paris: Fasquelle, 1939).

Daniel-Rops, Henri, *Le Monde sans âme* (Paris: Plon, 1932).

Déat, Marcel, *Le Front populaire au tournant* (Paris: La Concorde, 1937).

——, *Mémoires politiques* (Paris: Denoël, 1989).

Doriot, Jacques, *La France ne sera pas un pays d'esclaves* (Paris: Œuvres françaises, 1936).

——, *La France avec nous* (Paris: Flammarion, 1937).

——, *Le Front de la Liberté face au communisme* (Paris: Flammarion, 1937).

——, *Toutes les preuves: c'est Moscou qui paie* (Paris: Flammarion, 1937).

——, *Refaire la France* (Paris: Grasset, 1938).

Drieu La Rochelle, Pierre, *Socialisme fasciste* (Paris: Gallimard, 1934).

——, *Le Jeune Européen* (Paris: Plon, 1927).

Duclos, Jacques, *'Retour au programme! Lutte contre les trusts! Parti unique de la classe ouvrière! Union du Front populaire!': Rapport prononcé à la réunion du comité central du 22 juillet 1937 par Jacques Duclos* (Paris: Éditions du Comité Populaire de Propagande, 1938).

——, *'Vive la Commune de Paris!': discours prononcé par Jacques Duclos le 23 mars 1939 à la Mutualité* (Paris: Imprimerie Centrale du Croissant, 1939).

Duclos, Jacques, et al., *Pas de blocus contre l'Espagne républicaine!* (Paris: Comité Mondial contre la Guerre et le Fascisme, 1936).

Frachon, Benoît and Gaston Monmousseau, *'Pour une CGT unique! Pour l'action de masse!': Discours prononcés à la Conférence Nationale du Parti Communiste, Ivry, 23–26 Juin 1934* (Paris: Publications révolutionnaires, 1934).

Gibaudan, René, *Les Idées sociales de Taine* (Paris: Éditions Argo, 1928).

Gouttenoire de Toury, Fernand, *Le Front populaire ruiné par ses chefs* (Paris: Fernand Sorlot, 1939).

Guéhenno, Jean, *L'Évangile éternel: étude sur Michelet* (Paris: Grasset, 1927).

——, *Jeunesse de la France* (Paris: Grasset, 1936).

——, *Journal d'une 'Révolution'* (Paris: Grasset, 1939).

——, *Ce que je crois* (Paris: Grasset, 1964).

Guéhenno, Jean and Romain Rolland, *'L'Indépendance de l'esprit': correspondance entre Jean Guéhenno et Romain Rolland, 1919–44* (Paris: Albin Michel, 1975).

Herriot, E., et al., *Marc Sangnier: Témoignages rassemblés par les soins de l'office de publicité générale et de la librairie Bloud et Gay* (Paris: Bloud et Gay, 1950).

Henry, George, *Le Drapeau tricolore* (Paris: Jouve, 1935).

Jaussaud, Gérard, *Aurores Croix de Feu* (Caen: SIBN, 1936).

Jeunesse Ouvrière Chrétienne, *L'Appel de la JOC* (Paris: Éditions Jocistes, 1938).

La Rocque, François de, *Service public* (Paris: Grasset, 1934).

——, *Le Complot socialo-communiste: l'insurrection armée dans l'unité d'action* (Paris: Grasset, 1935).

——, *Pourquoi j'ai adhéré au PSF* (Paris: SEDA, n.d.).

——, *Le Paysan sauvera la France, avec le PSF* (Paris: PSF, 1937).

Le Bon, Gustave, *La Psychologie des foules* (1895) (Paris: PUF, 1998).

——, *The French Revolution and the Theory of Revolution* (London and New Brunswick: Transaction books, 1980).

Lefebvre, Denis et Rémi Lefebvre, *Mémoires du Front populaire* (Paris: Éditions Bruno Leprince/Office Universitaire de Recherche Socialiste, 1997).

Lefebvre, Georges, 'Les Foules révolutionnaires', *Les Annales historiques de la Révolution française*, 11 (1934), 1–26.

——, *Quatre-vingt-neuf* (Paris: Maison du Livre Français, 1939).

Lefranc, Georges, *Cours d'histoire du mouvement ouvrier* (Paris: Institut supérieur ouvrier, Confédération Général du Travail, 1935).

——, *Le Syndicalisme en France* (Paris: PUF, 1953).

——, *Histoire du Front populaire* (Paris: Payot, 1965, 1974).

——, *Juin '36: L'explosion sociale du Front populaire* (Paris: Julliard, 1966).

——, *Les Gauches en France 1789–1972* (Paris: Payot, 1973).

Lefranc, Georges and Émilie Lefranc, *La CGT et l'éducation ouvrière en France* (Genève: Bureau International du Travail, 1938).

Lemonnier, Léon, *Le Populisme* (Paris: La Renaissance du Livre, 1931).

Lombroso, Cesare, *Les Applications de l'anthropologie criminelle* (Paris: Félix Alcan, 1892).

——, *L'Homme criminel* (Paris: Félix Alcan, 1895).

Malherbe, Henry, *La Rocque: un chef, des actes, des idées* (Paris: Plon, 1934).

Maulnier, Thierry, *La Crise est dans l'homme* (Paris: A. Redier, 1932).

Maurras, Charles, *La Démocratie religieuse (Le dilemme de Marc Sangnier, la politique religieuse, l'Action française et la religion catholique)* (Paris: Nouvelles Éditions Latines, 1921).

——, *La Contre-révolution spontanée* (Paris: H. Lardanchet, 1943).

Mersch, Emile, *Le Corps mystique du Christ: études de théologie historique* (Paris: Desclée de Brouwer et Cie., 1936).

Millet, Raymond, *Doriot et ses Compagnons* (Paris: Plon, 1937).

Monmousseau, Gaston, *Un Épisode de la lutte de classe en France: la grève à Vienne. Manifestation du 13 Mars 1932* (Paris: Petite Bibliothèque de l'Internationale Syndicale Rouge, 1932).

Mora, J., *M. Ducos et la gratuité: servir ou asservir le peuple?* (Paris, n.d.).

Mounier, Emmanuel, *Œuvres*, Vol. 1, *1931–39* (Paris: Seuil, 1961).

——, *Œuvres*, Vol. 4, *Recueils posthumes, correspondance* (Paris: Seuil, 1961).

——, *Mounier et sa génération: lettres, carnets et inédits* (Saint-Maur: Éditions Parole et Silence, 2000).

Mouvement des Croix de Feu, *Le Mouvement des Croix de Feu et l'ordre social* (Paris: Bureau d'Éditions, 1935).

Parti Communiste Français, *'En avant pour une France libre, forte, heureuse!': Manifeste du VIIIe Congrès du Parti Communiste* (Villerbanne, 1936).

Parti Social Français, *Le Parti Social Français et la semaine de 40 heures* (n.p., Imprimerie spéciale du Parti Social Français, n.d.).

Piatnitski, O., *Les questions vitales du mouvement syndicale révolutionnaire international* (Paris: Confédération Général du Travail Unitaire, Bureau d'éditions, 1931)

Pivert, Marceau, *Révolution d'abord!* (Paris: Nouveau Prométhée, 1936).

——, *Tendre la Main aux catholiques? Réponses et réflexions d'un socialiste* (Paris: Éditions du Parti Socialiste, 1937).

Pottecher, Maurice, *Le Théâtre du Peuple: Renaissance et destinée du théâtre* (Paris: Paul Ollendorf, 1899).

de Préval, A., *In Memoriam: conférence faite le 6 octobre 1946* (n.p., Imprimerie des Tournelles, 26, rue des Tournelles, n.d.)

Pujo, Maurice, *Comment La Rocque a trahi* (Paris: Fernard Sorlot, 1937).

——, *Les Camelots du Roi* (Paris: Flammarion, 1933).

Racamond, Julien and Marius Vazielles, *'La CGTU et les Paysans': Discours de Racamond, secrétaire de la CGTU, au CCN de mars 1934, précédé d'une étude sur les paysans travailleurs, de Marius Vazeilles, secrétaire de la Fédération des Paysans Travailleurs de la Corrèze* (Paris: Confédération Général du Travail Unitaire, Bureau d'éditions, 1934).

Reiman, Paul, *Premier mai 1934* (Paris: Confédération Général du Travail Unitaire, Bureau d'éditions, 1934).

Renoir, Jean, *My Life and My Films* (London: Collins, 1974).

Revier, *Pour que le paysan français vive!* (Paris: PPF, 1936).

Reynaud, Paul, *Mémoires*, Vol 1., *Venu de ma Montagne* (Paris: Flammarion, 1960).

Rist, Charles, *Une Saison gâtée* (Paris: Fayard, 1973).

Rodhain, Jean, *Dixième anniversaire de la JOC Française* (Paris: Librairie de la Jeunesse Ouvrière, 1937).

Rolland, Romain, *Le Théâtre du Peuple: essai d'esthétique d'un théâtre nouveau* (Paris: Albin Michel, 1913).

——, *Le Théâtre de la Révolution* (Paris: Albin Michel, 1926).

Sabiani, Simon, *La Colère du Peuple* (Paris: Œuvres Françaises, 1936).

Schumacher, Louis, *Deux Mois en Russie: un monde nouveau* (Paris: Confédération Général du Travail Unitaire, Bureau d'éditions, 1928).

Sorel, Georges, *L'Avenir socialiste des syndicats* (Paris: Libraire de l'Art Social, 1898).

——, *Réflexions sur la violence* (1910) (Paris: Scuil, 1990).

——, *La Décomposition du Marxisme* (Paris: Marcel Rivière, 1926).

Taine, Hippolyte, *Les Origines de la France contemporaine* (Paris: Hachette, 1902).

Tardieu, André, *Alerte aux Français* (Paris: Flammarion, 1936).

Thorez, Maurice, *France Today and the People's Front* (London: Victor Gollancz, 1936).

——, 'Toujours unir!', *l'Humanité*, 27 July 1937, supplement.

——, *'La France de la Révolution 1788–1938': Discours prononcé à Grenoble, le 17 juillet 1938, à l'occasion du Cent cinquantenaire des États provinciaux du Dauphiné*, in *La Brochure Populaire*, mensuel 2e année, 17 (July 1938) (Paris: Imprimerie Centrale du Croissant, 1938).

——, *Un an du Front populaire. L'Unité ouvrière': Rapport présenté par Maurice Thorez à l'assemblée des militants de la Région Parisienne le 9 juin 1937 à la Mutualité. Intervention de Jacques Duclos* (Paris: Imprimerie Centrale du Croissant, 1938).

——, 'One hundred and fiftieth anniversary', in William Zak (ed.), *Essays on the French Revolution* (London: Lawrence and Wishart, 1945).

——, *Une Politique de grandeur française* (Paris: Éditions Sociales, 1945).

Tonnet, Henri, *Fernand Tonnet: Président-Fondateur de la JOC 1894–1945* (Brussels: Librairie Saint-Luc, 1947).

——, *Au Berceau de la Jeunesse Ouvrière Chrétienne* (Chez l'auteur, 23a, Avenue Broustin, Brussels IX, 1961).

Vallin, Charles, *Le Parti Social Français* (Paris: Imprimerie du PSF, 1937).

——, *L'Activité du PSF* (Paris: SEDA, 1938).

Weil, Simone, *L'Enracinement: prélude à une déclaration des devoirs envers l'être humain* (Paris: Gallimard, 1949).

Zyromski, Jean, *Sur le Chemin de l'unité* (Paris: Nouveau Prométhée, 1936).

Secondary sources

Ades, Dawn (ed.), *Art and Power. Europe under the Dictators 1930–45* (London: Thames and Hudson, 1995).

Alexander, Martin and Helen Graham (eds), *French and Spanish Popular Fronts: Comparative Perspectives* (Cambridge: CUP, 1989).

Allardyce, Gilbert, 'Doriot et l'esprit fasciste en France', *Revue d'histoire de la Deuxième Guerre Mondiale*, 97 (1975), 31–44.

Amadieu, Jean-François, *Les Syndicats en miettes* (Paris: Seuil, 1999).

Anderson, Benedict, *Imagined Communities: Reflections on the Origins and Spread of Nationalism* (London: Verso, 1983).

Andress, David, *Massacre at the Champ de Mars: Popular Dissent and Political Culture during the French Revolution* (Woodbridge: Boydell Press, 2000).

Andreu, Pierre, et al., *Drieu la Rochelle: témoignages et documents* (Paris: Sept couleurs, 1958).

Andrew, Dudley and Steven Ungar, *Popular Front Paris and the Poetics of Culture* (Cambridge, MA and London: The Belknap Press of Harvard University Press, 2005).

Antoine, Régis, *La Littérature pacifiste et internationaliste française, 1915–35* (Paris: L'Harmattan, 2002).

Aron, Raymond, *The Opium of the Intellectuals* (London: Secker and Warburg, 1957).

Arnold, Edward, *The Development of the Radical Right in France: From Boulanger to Le Pen* (Basingstoke: Macmillan, 2000).

Asholt, Wolfgang, 'Le Destin de Jean-Richard Bloch au théâtre', *Revue d'histoire du théâtre*, 44 (1992), 199–220.

Atkin, Nicholas and Frank Tallett, *The Right in France, 1789–1997* (London, NY: Taurus, 1998).

Aubert, Michelle, 'Le Cinéma ouvrier: la collection de films du PCF', *Cahiers de la Cinémathèque*, 71 (2000), 25–7.

Aulard, F. Alphonse, *Taine: Historien de la Révolution française* (Paris: Armand Colin, 1907).

Aumont, Bernard, 'La Chasse aux papillons à Paris en 1935', *Vingtième Siècle*, 11(1986), 21–39.

Badie, Bernard, 'Les Grèves du Front Populaire aux usines Renault', *Mouvement Social*, 81 (1972), 69–109.

Baker, Keith, 'Politics and opinion under the old regime: some reflections', in Jeremy Popkin (ed.), *Press and Politics in Pre-Revolutionary France* (London: University of California Press, 1987), 207–46.

——, 'Representations', in Keith Baker (ed.), *The French Revolution and the Creation of Modern Political Culture* (Oxford: Pergamon Press, 1987), 469–92.

Bakhtin, Mikhail, *Rabelais and his World* (London: MIT Press, 1968).

Barlow, Michel, *Le Socialisme d'Emmanuel Mounier* (Toulouse: Édouard Privat, 1971).

Barrault, Jean-Louis, *Souvenirs pour demain* (Paris: Seuil, 1972).

Barrows, Susanna, *Distorting Mirrors: Visions of the Crowd in Late Nineteenth-Century France* (London: Yale University Press, 1981).

Barthes, Roland, *Œuvres Complètes* (Paris: Seuil, 1993).

——, 'Théâtre et collectivité', *ibid.*, 1, 387–8.

——, 'Pour une définition du théâtre populaire', *ibid.*, 1, 430–1.

——, 'Espoirs du théâtre populaire', *ibid.*, 1, 529–31.

——, 'Le théâtre est toujours engagé', *ibid.*, 1, 545–6.

Battaglia, Valérie, 'Romain Rolland et le théâtre de la Révolution', *Revue d'histoire du théâtre*, 41 (1989), 178–95.

Bazin, André, *Jean Renoir* (Paris: Éditions Gérard Lebovici, 1989).

Bedeneau, Mireille, 'Copeau et Antoine: un même idéal', *Revue d'histoire du théâtre*, 50 (1998), 45–52.

Bellanger, Claude, Jacques Godechot, Pierre Guiral, and Fernand Terrou (eds), *Histoire Générale de la Presse Française* (Paris: PUF, 1972).

Ben-Ghiat, Ruth, *Fascist Modernities: Italy 1922–45* (Berkeley and London: University of California Press, 2001).

Berghaus, Günter (ed.), *Fascism and Theatre: Comparative Studies on the Aesthetics and Politics of Performance* (Oxford: Berghahn, 1996).

Bernard, Jean-Pierre, *Le Parti Communiste Français et la Question Littéraire, 1921–39* (Grenoble: Presses Universitaires de Grenoble, 1972).

Berstein, Serge, *Histoire du Parti Radical*, Vol. 2, *La Crise du radicalisme* (Paris: Presses de la FNSP, 1981).

——, *La France des années trente* (Paris: Armand Colin, 2001).

Bertheuil, Bruno, 'De l'Image souvenir à l'imaginaire social: quand les cheminots filment leur grève', *L'Homme et la société*, 127–8 (1998), 15–17.

Blinkhorn, Martin (ed.), *Fascists and Conservatives: The Radical Right and the Establishment in Twentieth Century Europe* (London: Unwin Hyman, 1990).

Bodin, Louis, *Les Intellectuels existent-ils?* (Paris: Bayard, 1997).

—— and Jean Touchard, *Front Populaire 1936* (Paris: Armand Colin, 1961, 1985).

Bonardi, Christine and Nicolas Roussiau, *Les Représentations sociales* (Paris: Dunod, 1999).

Bonitzer, Pascal, Jean-Louis Comolli, Serge Daney, Jean Narboni, and Jean-Pierre Oudart, '*La Vie est à nous*, film militant', *Cahiers du cinéma*, 218 (1970), 44–51.

Bourdé, Guy, 'La grève du 30 novembre 1938', *Mouvement Social*, 55 (1966), 87–93.

——, *La Défaite du Front Populaire* (Paris: Maspero, 1977).

Bourdieu, Pierre, et al., *Photography: A Middle-Brow Art* (Cambridge: Polity Press, 1990).

Bourdieu, Pierre, Alain Darbel, and Dominique Schnapper, *The Love of Art: European Art Museums and their Public* (Cambridge: Polity Press, 1991).

Bowles, Brett, 'Politicizing Pagnol: Rural France, film and ideology under the Popular Front', *French History*, 19 (2005), 112–42.

Braud, Philippe (ed.), *La Violence politique dans les démocraties européennes* (Paris: L'Harmattan, 1993).

Brèteque, François de la, 'Cinéma ouvrier, histoire / histoire du cinéma', *Cahiers de la Cinémathèque*, 71 (2000), 73–5.

Brooks, Charles William, 'Jean Renoir's "The Rules of the Game"', *French Historical Studies*, 7 (1972), 264–83.

Broué, Pierre and Nicole Dorcy, 'Critiques de gauche et opposition révolutionnaire 1936–38', *Mouvement Social*, 54 (1966), 91–133.

Brower, Daniel, *The New Jacobins: The French Communist Party and the Popular Front* (New York: Cornell University Press, 1968).

Brunet, Jean-Paul, 'Le PPF de Doriot, 1936–39', *Revue française de science politique*, 33 (1983), 255–80.

——, *Jacques Doriot: du communisme au fascisme* (Paris: Balland, 1986).

——, *Saint-Denis, la ville rouge: socialisme et communisme en banlieue ouvrière 1890–1939* (Paris: Hachette, 1980).

Burger-Roussenac, Annie, '1932: l'Année incertaine: deux politiques Communistes de rassemblement des intellectuels et de lutte contre la guerre: l'AEAR et le mouvement d'Amsterdam', *Communisme*, 32–4 (1993), 129–46.

Burke, Peter, 'Bakhtin for historians', *Social History*, 13 (1988), 85–90.

—— (ed.), *New Perspectives on Historical Writing* (Oxford: Polity Press, 1991).

Burrin, Philippe, 'Poings levés et bras tendus: la contagion des symboles au temps du Front populaire', *Vingtième Siècle*, 11 (1986), 7–20.

——, *La Dérive fasciste: Doriot, Déat, Bergery, 1933–45* (Paris: Seuil, 1986, 2003).

Cadé, Michel, 'L'Écran gréviste: la repré sentation des ouvriers de la Belle Époque dans le cinéma français', *Les Cahiers de la cinémathèque*, 62 (1995), 67–79.

——, *L'écran bleu: la représentation des ouvriers dans le cinéma français* (Perpignan: Presses Universitaires de Perpignan, 2000).

Caute, David, *Communism and the French Intellectuals* (London: André Deutsch, 1964).

Chabannes, Jacques, *Paris à vingt ans* (Paris: Éditions France-Empire, 1974).

Chadwick, Kay (ed.), *Catholicism, Politics and Society in Twentieth-Century France* (Liverpool: Liverpool University Press, 2000).

Chambaz, Jacques and Claude Willard, *Le Front Populaire: pour le pain, la liberté et la paix* (Paris: Éditions Sociales, 1961).

Chapman, Herrick, *State Capitalism and Working-Class Radicalism in the French Aircraft Industry* (Berkeley, Los Angeles, Oxford: University of California Press, 1991).

Charpentier, Jacques and René Kaës, *La Culture Populaire en France* (Paris: Éditions Ouvrières, 1962).

Chavardès, Maurice, *Le 6 Février 1934: la république en danger* (Paris: Calmann-Lévy, 1966).

Chenaux, Philippe, *Entre Maurras et Maritain: une génération intellectuelle catholique, 1920–1930* (Paris: Cerf, 1999).

Chevalier, Louis, *Classes laborieuses et classes dangereuses à Paris pendant la première moitié du dix-neuvième siècle* (Paris: Plon, 1958).

Christophe, Paul, *1936: Les Catholiques et le Front populaire* (Paris: Éditions Ouvrières, 1989).

Clark, Timothy, *Image of the People: Gustave Courbet and the 1848 Revolution* (London: Thames and Hudson, 1973).

——, *The Absolute Bourgeois: Artists and Politics in France 1848–51* (London: Thames and Hudson, 1973, 1999).

Clarke, Jackie, 'Imagined productive communities: industrial rationalisation and cultural crisis in 1930s France', *Modern and Contemporary France*, 8 (2000), 345–57.

——, 'France, America and the Metanarrative of Modernisation: from postwar social science to the new culturalism', in *Contemporary French and Francophone Studies*, 8 (2004), 365–77.

Clouet, Stéphane, *De la Renovation à l'utopie socialiste: Révolution Constructive, un groupe d'intellectuels socialistes des années trente* (Nancy: Presses Universitaires de Nancy, 1991).

Coco, Jean-Pierre and Joseph Debès, *1937, l'élan jociste: le dixième anniversaire de la JOC, Paris, juillet 1937* (Paris: Éditions Ouvrières, 1989).

Cohen, Évelyne, *Paris dans l'imaginaire nationale de l'entre-deux guerres* (Paris: Publications de la Sorbonne, 1999).

Collinet, Michel, *L'Ouvrier français: esprit du syndicalisme* (Paris: Éditions Ouvrières, 1951).

Colton, Joel, *Léon Blum, Humanist in Politics* (Cambridge: MIT Press, 1974).

Conway, Martin, *Collaboration in Belgium: Léon Degrelle and the Rexist Movement, 1940–44* (London: Yale University Press, 1993).

——, *Catholic Politics in Europe, 1918–45* (London: Routledge, 1997).

—— and Tom Buchanan (eds), *Political Catholicism in Europe, 1918–45* (Oxford: OUP, 1996).

Corbin, Alain, Noëlle Gérôme, and Danielle Tartakowsky (eds), *Les Usages politiques des fêtes aux dix-neuvième et vingtième siècles* (Paris: Publications de la Sorbonne, 1994).

Courtade, François, *Les Malédictions du cinéma français* (Paris: Éditions Alain Moreau, 1978).

Dard, Olivier, *Le Rendez-vous manqué des relèves des années 30* (Paris: PUF, 2002).

Davies, Peter, *The Extreme Right in France, 1789 to the present* (London: Routledge, 2002).

Dell, Simon, *The Image of the Popular Front: The Masses and the Media in Interwar France* (Basingstoke: Palgrave Macmillan, 2007).

——, 'Festival and revolution: the Popular Front in France and the press coverage of the strikes of 1936', *Art History*, 23 (2000), 599–621.

Delporte, Christophe, *Intellectuels et Politique* (Paris: Casterman, 1995).

Desvages, Hubert, '*La Marseillaise* et 1788: deux images de la Révolution française vue par le Parti Communiste', in Michel Vovelle (ed.), *Les Images de la Révolution française* (Paris: Publications de la Sorbonne, 1988), 379–88.

Dreyfus, Michel, *Histoire de la CGT: Cent ans de Syndicalisme en France* (Paris: Éditions Complexe, 1995).

Dullin, Charles, *Ce sont les Dieux qu'il nous faut* (Paris: Gallimard, 1969).

Dumazedier, Joffre, *Vers une Civilisation du loisir?* (Paris: Seuil, 1962).

Dupâquier, Jacques, et al., *Histoire de la population française* (Paris: Presses Universitaires de France, 1988), Vol. 4, *De 1914 à nos jours*.

Dutton, Paul, *Origins of the French Welfare State: The Struggle for Social Reform in France, 1914–47* (Cambridge: CUP, 2002).

Escobar, Roberto and Vittorio Giacci, *Il cinema del Fronte Popolare: Francia, 1934–37* (Milan: Edizioni il formichiere, 1980).

Estier, Claude, *La Gauche hebdomadaire* (Paris: Armand Colin, 1962).

Falasca-Zamponi, Simonetta,*Fascist Spectacle: The Aesthetics of Power in Mussolini's Italy* (Berkeley and London: University of California Press, 1997).

Favre, Pierre (ed.), *La Manifestation* (Paris: Presses de la FNSP, 1990).

Fentress, James and Chris Wickham, *Social Memory* (Oxford: Blackwell, 1992).

Fer, Bryony, David Batchelor, and Paul Wood, *Realism, Rationalism, Surrealism: Art between the Wars* (London: Yale University Press in association with the Open University, 1993).

Figes, Orlando and Boris Kolonitskii, *Interpreting the Russian Revolution: The Language and Symbols of 1917* (New Haven and London: Yale University Press, 1999).

Fisher, David, 'The origins of the French popular theatre', *Journal of Contemporary History*, 12 (1977), 461–97.

Flower, John, *Writers and Politics in Modern France 1909–61* (London: Hodder and Stoughton, 1977).

Flower, John and Philippa Broadbent, 'The intellectual and his role in France between the wars', *Journal of European Studies*, 8 (1978), 246–57.

Fofi, Goffredo, 'The cinema of the Popular Front in France', *Screen*, 13 (1972–3), 5–57.

Formisano, Ronald, 'The concept of political culture', *Journal of Interdisciplinary History*, 31 (2001), 393–426.

Fourcault, Annie, *Banlieue Rouge 1920–60: années Thorez, années Gabin—archétype du populaire, banc d'essai des modernités* (Paris: Éditions Autrement, 1992).

Fremontier, Jacques, *La Vie en bleu: voyage en culture ouvrière* (Paris: Fayard, 1980).

Friedland, David, *Political Actors: Representative Bodies and Theatricality in the Age of the French Revolution* (London and New York: Cornell University Press, 2002).

Fritz, Gérard, *L'Idée du peuple en France du XVII au XIX siècle* (Strasbourg: Presses Universitaires de Strasbourg, 1988).

Fritzsche, Peter, 'Did Weimar fail?', *Journal of Modern History*, 68 (1996), 629–56.

Frost, Robert, 'Machine liberation: inventing housewives and home appliances in interwar France', *French Historical Studies*, 18 (1993), 109–30.

Gauteur, Claude, *Jean Renoir: la double méprise,1925–39* (Paris: Les Éditeurs Français réunis, 1980).

Gelly, Jean-François, 'À la recherche de l'unité organique: la démarche du Parti communiste français, 1934–38', *Mouvement Social*, 121 (1982), 97–116.

Gérôme, Noëlle, *Archives sensibles: images et objets du monde industriel et ouvrier* (Paris: Éditions de l'ÉNS-Cachan, 1995).

Gibelin, Jacques and Marcel Danos, *June '36: Class struggle and the Popular Front in France* (London: Bookmarks, 1986).

Gildea, Robert, *The Past in French History* (New Haven and London: Yale University Press, 1994).

——, *Marianne in Chains: In Search of the German Occupation, 1940–45* (London: Pan Macmillan, 2002).

Girault, Jacques, *Au-devant du Bonheur. Les Français et le Front populaire* (Paris: CIDE, 2006).

Golan, Romy, *Modernity and Nostalgia. French Art and Politics between the Wars* (New Haven and London: Yale University Press, 1995).

Gordon, Bertram, *Collaborationism in France during the Second World War* (London and New York: Cornell University Press, 1980).

Gordon, Daniel A., 'The back door of the nation state: expulsions of foreigners and continuity in twentieth-century France', *Past and Present*, 186 (2005), 210–32.

Graham, Helen, 'Spain 1936. Resistance and revolution: the flaws in the Front', in Tim Kirk and Anthony McElligott (eds), *Opposing Fascism* (Cambridge: CUP, 1999), 63–80.

Grason, Daniel, René Mouriaux, and Patrick Pochet (eds), *Éclats du Front populaire* (Paris: Éditions Syllepse, 2006).

de Grazia, Victoria, *The Culture of Consent: Mass Organisation of Leisure in Fascist Italy* (Cambridge: CUP, 1981).

Greene, Nathanael, *Crisis and Decline: The French Socialist Party in the Popular Front Era* (New York: Cornell University Press, 1969).

Griffin, Roger, *Fascism* (Oxford: OUP, 1995).

Gruber, Helmut, *Léon Blum, French Socialism and the Popular Front: A Case of Internal Contradictions* (New York: Cornell University, Western Societies Programme Occasional Paper no.17, 1986).

Guérin, Daniel, *Front populaire, révolution manquée: témoignage militant* (Paris: Maspero, 1970).

Guerrieri, Sandro, 'L'affaiblissement du Parlement français dans la dernière législature de la Troisième République, 1936–1940', *Parliaments, Estates and Representation/Parlements, États et Représentation*, 23 (2003), 195–207.

Gugelot, Frédéric, *La Conversion des intellectuels au catholicisme en France, 1885–1935* (Paris: CNRS, 1998).

Guillaume-Grimaud, Geneviève, *Le Cinéma du Front populaire* (Paris: L'Herminier, 1986).

Harr, Karl, *The Genesis and Effect of the Popular Front in France* (Lanham: University of America Press, 1987).

Haslam, Jonathan, 'The Comintern and the origins of the Popular Front, 1934–35', *The Historical Journal*, 22 (1979), 673–91.

Hazareesingh, Sudhir, *Intellectuals and the French Communist Party: Disillusion and Decline* (Oxford: Clarendon, 1991).

Hellman, John, 'French left Catholics and communism in the 1930s', *Church History*, 45 (1976), 507–23.

——, *Emmanuel Mounier and the New Catholic Left in France, 1930–50* (London and Toronto: University of Toronto Press, 1981).

Hobsbawm, Eric, *Age of Extremes: The Short Twentieth Century* (London: Abacus, 1995).

Hughes, Stuart, *The Obstructed Path: French Social Thought, 1930–60* (1968) (New Brunswick, NJ: Transaction Publishers, 2002).

Ingram, Norman, *The Politics of Dissent: Pacifism in France, 1919–39* (Oxford: Clarendon Press, 1991).

Ionascu, Michel, 'Le Cinéma des cheminots ou l'introuvable parole ouvrière', *Cahiers de la cinémathèque*, 71 (2000), 41–6.

Irons, Jessica, 'Staging reconciliation: popular theatre and political utopia in France in 1937', *Contemporary European History*, 14 (2005), 279–94.

Irvine, William, *French Conservatism in Crisis: The Republican Federation of France in the 1930s* (Baton Rouge and London: University of Louisiana Press, 1979).

——, 'Fascism in France and the strange case of the Croix de Feu', *Journal of Modern History*, 63 (1991), 271–95.

Jackson, Julian, *France: The Dark Years 1940–44* (Oxford: OUP, 2001).

——, *The Popular Front in France: Defending Democracy 1934–38* (Cambridge: CUP, 1988).

——, *The Politics of Depression in France, 1932–36* (Cambridge: CUP, 1985).

——, *The Fall of France* (Oxford. OUP, 2003).

Jankowski, Paul, *Communism and Collaboration: Simon Sabiani and Politics in Marseille, 1919–44* (London: Yale University Press, 1989).

Jenkins, Brian (ed.), *Nationalism in France: Class and Nation since 1789* (London: Routledge, 1990).

——, *France in the Era of Fascism: Essays on the French Authoritarian Right* (Oxford: Berghahn, 2005).

Johnson, Douglas, 'Léon Blum and the Popular Front', *History*, 55 (1970), 199–206.

—— and Madeleine Johnson, *The Age of Illusion: Art and Politics in France, 1918–40* (London: Thames and Hudson, 1987).

Judt, Tony, 'Une historiographie pas comme les autres: the French Communists and their history', *European History Review*, 12 (1982), 445–78.

——, *The Burden of Responsibility: Blum, Camus, Aron and the French Twentieth Century* (London and Chicago: University of Chicago Press, 1998).

Julliard, Jacques, *Fernand Pelloutier et les origines du syndicalisme d'action directe* (Paris: Seuil, 1971).

——, *Autonomie Ouvrière: études sur le syndicalisme d'action directe* (Paris: Seuil, 1988).

—— and Shlomo Sand (eds), *Georges Sorel en son temps* (Paris: Seuil, 1985).

Kedward, Harry Roderick, *Resistance in Vichy France: A Study of Ideas and Motivation in the Southern Zone, 1940–42* (Oxford: OUP, 1978).

Kedward, Harry Roderick and Roger Austin (eds), *Vichy France and the Resistance: Culture and Ideology* (London: Croom Helm, 1985).

Kennedy, Sean, *Reconciling France against Democracy: The Croix de Feu and the Parti Social Français, 1927–1945* (Montreal, London: McGill-Queen's University Press, 2007).

Kergoat, Jacques, *La France du Front populaire* (Paris: Éditions de la Découverte, 1986).

——, *Marceau Pivert, socialiste de gauche* (Paris: Éditions Ouvrières, 1994).

Kestel, Laurent, 'L'engagement de Bertrand de Jouvenel au PPF, 1936–38: Intellectuel de parti et entrepreneur politique', *French Historical Studies*, 30 (2007), 105–25.

——, 'The emergence of anti-Semitism within the PPF: party intellectuals, peripheral leaders and national figures', *French History*, 19 (2005), 364–84.

Kirk, Tim and Anthony McElligot (eds), *Opposing Fascism: Community, Authority and Resistance in Europe* (Cambridge: CUP, 1999).

Kitson, Simon, 'The police and the Clichy massacre, March 1937', in Richard Bessel and Clive Emsley (eds), *Patterns of Provocation: Police and Public Disorder* (Oxford: Berghahn, 2000), 29–41.

Kolboom, J., *La Revanche des patrons: le patronat français face au Front populaire* (Paris: Flammarion, 1986).

Kriegel, Annie, 'Notes sur l'idéologie dans le Parti Communiste', *Contrepoint*, 3 (1971), 95–104.

——, *Le Pain et les roses: jalons pour une histoire du socialisme* (Paris: PUF, 1968).

Kvapil, Joseph, *Romain Rolland et les amis d'Europe* (Statni Pedagogicke: Nakladatelstvi Praha, 1971).

Labica, Georges (ed.), *Les Nouveaux espaces politiques* (Paris: L'Harmattan, 1995).

Lachaumette, Sandrine, 'Masses, foules, peuple vus dans la presse *L'Illustration* et *Regards*', in Noëlle Gérôme (ed.), *Archives sensibles; images et objets du monde industriel et ouvrier* (Paris: Publications de la Sorbonne, 1995), 84–97.

Lagny, Michèle 'Documentation et commandité: conséquences pour le cinéma ouvrier', *Cahiers de la cinémathèque*, 71 (2000), 35–40.

Larmour, Peter, *The French Radical Party in the 1930s* (Stanford: Stanford University Press, 1960).

Larnal, Oscar, 'Alternatives to the Third Republic among Catholic leftists in the 1930s', *Historical Reflections*, 5 (1978), 177–95.

Lazitch, Branko, 'Pour les cinquante ans du PCF', *Contrepoint*, 3 (1971), 87–94.

Le Béguec, Gilles, *L'Entrée au Palais-Bourbon: les filières privilégiées d'accès à la fonction parlementaire, 1919–39* (Unpublished thesis, Université de Paris-Nanterre, 1989).

Lebovics, Herman, *True France: The Wars over Cultural Identity* (Ithaca and London: Cornell University Press, 1992).

Le Crom, Jean-Pierre, *Syndicats, nous voilà! Vichy et le corporatisme* (Paris: Éditions Ouvrières, 1995).

Le Gallou, Jean-Yves, 'Le Vrai Bilan du Front populaire', *Contrepoint*, 52–3 (1986), 15–18.

Lemarchand, Ginette, 'Juin '36 à Caen', *Mouvement Social*, 55 (1966), 75–85.

Leroy, Géraldi and Anne Roche, *Les Écrivains et le Front populaire* (Paris: Presses de la FNSP, 1986).

Levaillant, Jacqueline, 'Henri Ghéon, genèse d'une esthétique théâtrale', *Revue d'histoire du théâtre*, 50 (1998), 57–68.

Lloyd, Christopher and Peter Whyte (eds), *La Culture populaire en France* (Durham: Durham Modern Language Series, 1997).

Machefer, Philippe, 'Les Croix de Feu', *L'Information historique*, 34–5 (1972–73), 28–34.

——, 'Le Parti Social Français', *L'Information historique*, 34–5 (1972–73), 74–81.

——, *Ligues et fascisme en France* (Paris: PUF, 1974).

Maigret, Eric (ed.), *Histoire économique de la France au vingtième siècle* (Paris: Documentation Française, 1992).

Maitron, Jean, *Paul Delesalle, un anar de la Belle Époque* (Paris: Fayard, 1985).

Maitron, Jean and Claude Pennetier (eds), *Dictionnaire biographique du mouvement ouvrier français* (Paris: Éditions Ouvrières, 1988).

Marchais, Georges, *Les Intellectuels, la culture et la révolution* (Paris: Éditions Sociales, 1980).

Marchand, Bernard, *Paris: histoire d'une ville XIXe–XXe siècle* (Paris: Seuil, 1993).

Margairaz, Michel, *L'État, les finances et l'économie: histoire d'une conversion, 1932–52* (Paris: Comité pour l'Histoire Économique et Financière, 1991).

Martin, Benjamin, *France in 1938* (Louisiana: Louisiana State University Press, 2005).

Martin, John, *The Golden Age of French Cinema, 1929–39* (London: Columbus Books, 1987).

Mazower, Mark, *Dark Continent: Europe's Twentieth Century* (London: Penguin, 1999).

McLellan, David, *Simone Weil: Utopian Pessimist* (London: Macmillan, 1989).

McMillan, James, *Twentieth-Century France* (London: Arnold, 1992).

—— (ed.), *Modern France, 1880–2002* (Oxford: OUP, 2003).

McWilliam, Neil, *Dreams of Happiness: Social Art and the French Left* (Princeton: Princeton University Press, 1993).

——, 'Conflicting manifestations: Parisian commemoration of Joan of Arc and Étienne Dolet in the early Third Republic', *French Historical Studies*, 27 (2004), 381–419.

Miller, Paul, *From Revolutionaries to Citizens: Antimilitarism in France, 1870–1914* (Durham North Carolina and London: Duke University Press, 2002).

Mitzman, Arthur, 'The French working class and the Blum government, 1936–37', *International Review of Social History*, 9 (1964), 369–89.

Moch, Jules, *Le Front populaire: grande espérance* (Paris: Perrin, 1971).

Moliner, Pascal (ed.), *La Dynamique des représentations sociales* (Grenoble: Presses Universitaires de Grenoble, 2001).

Monnet, François, *Refaire la République: André Tardieu, une dérive réactionnaire 1876–1945* (Paris: Fayard, 1993).

Moreau, Roland, *Marc Sangnier et nos chrétiens sociaux, 1887–1987* (Bordeaux: Bègles, 1987).

Moscovici, Serge and Gerard Duveen (eds), *Social Representations: Explorations in Social Psychology* (Cambridge: Polity Press, 2000).

Mosse, George L., *The Nationalisation of the Masses: Political Symbolism and Mass Movements in Germany from the Napoleonic Wars through the Third Reich* (London and New York: Cornell University Press, 1975).

——, *Masses and Man: Nationalist and Fascist Perceptions of Reality* (New York: Howard Fertig, 1980).

Mousseigne, Alan, *Pablo Picasso: le quatorze juillet* (Milan: Skira, 1998).

Neoclaus, Mark, *Fascism* (Oxford: OUP, 1997).

Nicolet, Claude, *L'Idée républicaine en France, 1789–1924* (Paris: Gallimard, 1982).

Nivet, Philippe and Yvan Combeau, *Histoire politique de Paris au XXe siècle: une histoire locale et nationale* (Paris: PUF, 2000).

Nobécourt, Jacques, *Le Colonel de Rocque, 1885–1946, ou les pièges du nationalisme chrétien* (Paris: Fayard, 1996).

Noguères, Henri, *La Vie quotidienne en France au temps du Front populaire, 1935–38* (Paris: Hachette, 1977).

Noiriel, Gérard, *Workers in French Society in the Nineteenth and Twentieth Centuries* (Oxford: Berg, 1990).

Ory, Pascal, 'De Ciné-Liberté à *La Marseillaise*: espoir et limites d'un cinéma libre', *Mouvement Social*, 91 (1975), 153–75.

——, *Théâtre Citoyen: du Théâtre du Peuple au Théâtre du Soleil* (Avignon: Association Jean Vilar, 1985).

——, *Une Nation pour mémoire: 1889, 1939, 1989, trois jubilées révolutionnaires* (Paris: Presses de la FNSP, 1992).

——, *La Belle Illusion: culture et politique sous le signe du Front populaire* (Paris: Plon, 1994).

Passmore, Kevin, *From Liberalism to Fascism: The Right in a French Province* (Cambridge: CUP, [1997] 2002).

——, 'The Republic in crisis: politics, 1914–45', in James McMillan (ed.), *Modern France 1880–2002* (Oxford: OUP, 2003), 39–73.

—— (ed.), *Women, Gender and Fascism in Europe, 1919–45* (Manchester: Manchester University Press, 2003).

——, 'The construction of crisis in interwar France', in Brian Jenkins (ed.), *France in the Era of Fascism: Essays on the French Authoritarian Right* (Oxford: Berghahn, 2005), 151–99.

Paxton, Robert, *Vichy France: Old Guard, New Order* (1972) (New York: Columbia University Press, 2001).

Peer, Shanny, *France on Display: Peasants, Provincials, and Folklore in the 1937 Paris World's Fair* (New York: State University of New York Press, 1998).

Perron, Tangui, 'Histoire, cinéma, CGT et peu de banlieue', in Jacques Girault (ed.), *Ouvriers en banlieue* (Paris: Éditions de l'Atelier, 1998), 369–78.

——, 'Vie, mort et renouveau du cinéma politique', *Homme et la société: revue internationale de recherches et de synthèses en sciences sociales*, 127–8 (1998), 7–14.

——, 'Le Cinéma ouvrier: un cinéma militant', *Cahiers de la cinémathèque*, 71 (2000), 9–13.

Petitfils, Jean-Christian, *La Droite en France de 1789 à nos jours* (Paris: PUF, 1994).

Phocas, Paul, *Gide et Guéhenno polémiquent* (Rennes: PUF, 1987).

Pickering, William S. (ed.), *Durkheim and Representations* (London: Routledge, 2000).

Pierrard, Pierre, Michel Launay, and Roland Trempé, *La JOC: regards d'historiens* (Paris: Éditions Ouvrières, 1984).

Pottecher, Frédéric, *Histoire du Théâtre du Peuple* (n.p., 1981).

Poulle, François, *Renoir 1938: ou Jean Renoir pour rien? Enquête sur un cinéaste* (Paris: Éditions du Cerf, 1969).

Preston, Paul, *A Concise History of the Spanish Civil War* (London: Fontana, 1996).

—— (ed.), *Revolution and War in Spain, 1931–39* (London and New York: Routledge, 1993).

Prost, Antoine, 'Les Manifestations du 12 février 1934 en province', *Mouvement Social*, 54 (1966), 6–27.

——, *Autour du Front populaire: aspects du mouvement social au XXe siècle* (Paris: Seuil, 2006).

Racine-Furland, Nicole, 'Le Comité de Vigilance des Intellectuels Anti-fascistes 1934–39: anti-fascisme et pacifisme', *Mouvement Social*, 101 (1977), 88–114.

——, 'La Revue Europe et le pacifisme des années vingt', in Maurice Vaïsse (ed.), *Le Pacifisme en Europe des années 1920 aux années 1950* (Brussels: Bruylant, 1993), 51–69.

—— and Michel Trebitsch, 'Dossier: la revue *Europe*', *Lendemains* (Berlin), 86–7 (1997), 93–107.

Rauch, William, *Politics and Belief in Contemporary France: Emmanuel Mounier and Christian Democracy 1932–50* (The Hague: Martius Nijhoff, 1972).

——, 'La Revue Europe et l'Allemagne, 1929–1936', in Hans Manfred Bock, Reinhart Mayer-Kalkus, and Michel Trebitsch (eds), *Entre Locarno et Vichy: les relations culturelles franco–allemandes dans les années 1930* (Paris: Éditions du CNRS, 1993), 631–38.

Rearick, Charles, 'Paris Revisited', *French Historical Studies*, 27 (2004), 1–8.

Réau, Elisabeth du, *Édouard Daladier, 1884–1970* (Paris: Fayard, 1993).

Rebérioux, Madeleine, 'Culture et militantisme', *Mouvement Social*, 91 (1975), 3–12.

——, 'Théâtre d'agitation: le groupe *Octobre*', *Mouvement Social*, 91 (1975), 109–19.

Régine, Robin, *Masses et culture de masse dans les années trente* (Paris: Éditions Ouvrières, 1991).

Rémond, René, *Les Droites en France* (Paris: Aubier-Montaigne, 1982).

Rémond, René and Janine Bourdin (eds), *Édouard Daladier, chef de gouvernement* (Paris: Presses de la FNSP, 1977).

Rémond, René and Janine Bourdin (eds), *La France et les Français en 1938–39* (Paris: Presses de la FNSP, 1978).

Rémond, René, et al., 'Léon Blum, chef de gouvernement 1936–37', *Cahiers de la Fondation Nationale des Sciences Politiques*, 155 (Paris: Armand Calin, 1976).

Reynaud, Jean-Daniel, *Les Syndicats en France* (Paris: Armand Colin, 1963).

Reynolds, Siân, 'Women, men and the 1936 strikes in France', in Martin S. Alexander and Helen Graham (eds), *The French and Spanish Popular Fronts: Comparative Perspectives* (Cambridge: CUP, 1989).

——, 'Women and the Popular Front in France: the case of the three women ministers', *French History*, 8 (1994), 196–224.

Ridley, Frederick, *Revolutionary Syndicalism in France: The Direct Action of its Time* (Cambridge: CUP, 1970).

Rioux, Jean-Pierre, *Révolutionnaires du Front populaire: choix de documents* (Paris: Union Générale d'Éditions, 1973).

——, *Le Front populaire* (Paris: Tallendier, 2006).

Robert, Jean-Louis and Danielle Tartakowsky, *Paris le Peuple* (Paris: Publications de la Sorbonne, 1999).

Rosanvallon, Pierre, *Le Peuple introuvable: histoire de la représentation démocratique en France* (Paris: Gallimard, 1998).

Ross Dickinson, Edward, 'Biopolitics, fascism, democracy: some reflections on our discourse about "modernity"', *Central European History*, 37 (2003), 1–48.

Rossel, André, *Été 1936: 100 jours du Front Populaire* (Paris: Éditions de la Courtille, 1976).

Roth, Jacques, *The Cult of Violence: Sorel and the Sorelians* (London and Stanford: University of California Press, 1980).

Russell, Bertrand, *Le Monde qui pourrait être: socialisme, anarchisme et anarcho-syndicalisme* (Paris: Éditions Denoël, 1973).

Santore, John, 'The Comintern's United Front initiative of May 1934: French or Soviet inspiration?', *Canadian Journal of History*, 16 (1981), 405–21.

Schloesser, Stephen, *Jazz Age Catholicism: Mystic Modernism in Postwar Paris, 1919–1933* (Toronto, Buffalo, London: University of Toronto Press, 2005).

Schnapp, Jeffrey, *Staging Fascism: 18BL and the Theatre of Masses for Masses* (Stanford: University of California Press, 1996).

Sick, Klaus-Peter, 'La Notion des classes moyennes: notion sociologique ou slogan politique?', *Vingtième Siècle*, 37 (1993), 13–33.

Siedmann, Michael, 'The birth of the weekend and the revolts against work: the workers of the Paris region during the Popular Front, 1936–38', *French Historical Studies*, 12 (1981), 249–76.

Siegel, Mona, *The Moral Disarmament of France: Education, Pacifism and Patriotism, 1914–40* (Cambridge: CUP, 2004).

Smith, Michael Stephen, *The Emergence of Modern Business Enterprise in France, 1800–1930* (Cambridge, MA and London: Harvard University Press, 2006).

Soucy, Robert, *French Fascism: The Second Wave, 1933–39* (New Haven and London: Yale University Press, 1995).

Stearns, Peter, *Revolutionary Syndicalism and French Labour: A Cause without Rebels* (New Brunswick: Rutgers University Press, 1971).

Sternhell, Zeev, *Ni Droite, ni Gauche: l'Idéologie fasciste en France* (Paris: Seuil, 1983).

——, *Maurice Barrès et le nationalisme français* (Paris: Armand Colin, 1972).

——, *La Droite révolutionnaire: les origines françaises du fascisme, 1885–1914* (Paris: Fayard, [1978] 2000).

Storey, John (ed.), *Cultural Theory and Popular Culture* (New York: Harvester Wheatsheaf, 1994).

Strebel, Elizabeth, 'French social cinema and the Popular Front', *Journal of Contemporary History*, 12 (1977), 499–519.

——, 'Jean Renoir and the Popular Front', in K. R. M. Short (ed.), *Feature Films as History* (London: Croom Helm, 1981), 176–93.

Strinati, Dominic, *An Introduction to the Theories of Popular Culture* (London and New York: Routledge, 1995).

Syme, Tony, 'La France aux Français: Displacing the foreign worker during the 1930s Depression', *Oxford Economics Department Paper* no. 54 (December 2000).

Tartakowsky, Danielle, 'Manifestations ouvrières et théories de la violence 1919–1934', in Philippe Braud (ed.), *La Violence politique dans les démocraties européennes* (Paris: L'Harmattan, 1993).

——, 'Les Fêtes de la droite populaire', in Alain Corbin, Noëlle Gérôme, and Danielle Tartakowksy (eds), *Les Usages politiques des fêtes aux XIX–XX siècles* (Paris: Publications de la Sorbonne, 1994), 305–16.

——, *Le Front populaire: la vie est à nous* (Paris: Gallimard, 1996).

——, *Les Manifestations de rue en France, 1918–68* (Paris: Publications de la Sorbonne, 1997).

——, 'Le Cinéma militant des années 30: source pour l'histoire du Front populaire', *Cahiers de la Cinémathèque*, 71 (2000), 15–24.

——, 'La Construction sociale de l'espace politique: les usages politiques de la Place de la Concorde des années 1880 à nos jours', *French Historical Studies*, 27 (2004), 145–75.

—— and Michel Margairaz, *L'Avenir nous appartient: histoire du Front populaire* (Paris: Larousse, 2006).

Timms, Edward and Peter Collier, *Visions and Blueprints: Avant-Garde Culture and Radical Politics in early Twentieth-Century Europe* (Manchester: Manchester University Press, 1988).

Tomlinson, Richard, 'The disappearance of France 1896–1940: French politics and the birth rate', *The Historical Journal*, 28 (1985), 405–15.

Torigian, Michael, 'The end of the Popular Front: The Paris metal strike of spring 1938', *French History*, 13 (1999), 464–91.

Touchard, Jean, 'L'Esprit des années trente: une tentative de renouvellement de la pensée politique française', in Guy Michaud (ed.), *Tendances politiques dans la vie française depuis 1789* (Paris: Hachette, 1960), 89–120.

——, *La Gauche en France depuis 1900* (Paris: Seuil, 1977).

Traugot, Mark, *The French Worker: Autobiographies from the Early Industrial Era* (London and Stanford: University of California Press, 1993).

Trebitsch, Michel, 'Paris "capitale culturelle" de l'Europe centrale?', *Vingtième Siècle*, 47 (1995), 201–5.

——, 'Les Revues européennes de l'entre-deux-guerres', *Vingtième Siècle*, 44 (numéro spécial: *La Culture politique*) (1994), 135–8.

Truesdell, Matthew, *Spectacular Politics: Louis-Napoléon Bonaparte and the Fête Impériale, 1849–70* (Oxford: OUP, 1997).

Tumblety, Joan, ' "Civil wars of the mind": The commemoration of the 1789 revolution in the Parisian press of the radical right, 1939', *European History Quarterly*, 2000 (30), 389–429.

Verdès-Leroux, Jeannine, 'The intellectual extreme right in the thirties', in Edward Arnold (ed.), *The Development of the Radical Right in France* (Basingstoke: Palgrave Macmillan, 2000), 119–32.

Wallis, Mick, 'The Popular Front pageant: its emergence and decline', *New Theatre Quarterly*, 41 (1995), 17–32.

Wardhaugh, Jessica (née Irons), 'Fighting for the unknown soldier: The contested territory of the French nation, 1934–38', *Modern and Contemporary France*, 15 (2007), 185–201.

—— (ed.), *Paris and the Right in the Twentieth Century* (Newcastle: Cambridge Scholars' Publishing, 2007).

——, 'Between parliament and the people: The problem of representation in France, 1934–39', *Parliaments, Estates and Representation/Parlements, États, et Représentation*, 27 (2007), 207–26.

——, 'Popular theatre and revolutionary identity: Anarchist and communist culture in Paris, 1900–34', in Roger Spalding and Alyson Brown (eds), *Entertainment, Leisure and Identities* (Newcastle: Cambridge Scholars' Publishing, 2007), 96–111.

——, 'Un Rire Nouveau: Action Française and the art of political satire', *French History*, 22 (2008), 74–93.

Weber, Eugen, *Action Française* (Paris: Fayard, 1985).

——, 'Nationalism socialism and national-socialism in France', *French Historical Studies*, 2 (1962), 273–307.

——, *Varieties of Fascism* (London: Van Nostrand, 1964).

——, *The Hollow Years: France in the 1930s* (London: Sinclair Stevenson, 1995).

Welch, David, *Propaganda and the German Cinema 1933–45* (Oxford: Clarendon, 1983).

Whitney, Susan, 'Embracing the status quo: French communists, young women and the Popular Front', *Journal of Social History*, 30 (1996), 25–53.

Williams, Alan, *Republic of Images: A History of French Film-Making* (London and Harvard: Harvard University Press, 1992).

Williams, Raymond, *The Long Revolution* (London: Hogarth Press, 1961, 1992).

Wilson, Steven, 'Action Française in French intellectual life', *The Historical Journal*, 12 (1969), 328–350.

Winock, Michel, 'Les Intellectuels français et l'esprit de Munich', in Anne Roche and Christian Tarting (eds), *Des Années trente: groupes et ruptures* (Paris: Éditions du CNRS, 1985), 147–56.

——, *Nationalism, Anti-Semitism and Fascism in France* (Stanford: Stanford University Press, 1998).

Wolf, Dieter, *Doriot: du communisme à la collaboration* (Paris: Fayard, 1969).

Wolikow, Serge, *Le Front populaire en France* (Paris: Éditions Complexe, 1996).

Wurmser, André, 'Les Temps heureux', *Cahiers du communisme*, 9 (1966), 169–96.

Index

Page numbers in **bold** refer to figures